THE ATLANTIC MIGRATION

LONDON : HUMPHREY MILFORD

OXFORD UNIVERSITY PRESS

THE EMIGRANT'S FAREWELL: THE LORD BE WITH YOU!

THE EMIGRANTS' RETURN: THE LORD BE PRAISED!

The Winner of the 1940 Pulitzer Prize

Marcus Lee Hansen

The Atlantic Migration
1607 - 1860

A History of the Continuing Settlement of the United States

Edited with a Foreword by

Arthur M. Schlesinger

Simon Publications

2001

Copyright © 1940 by Harvard College

First published in 1940 by Harvard University Press

Reprint 2001 by Simon Publications

Library of Congress Card Number: 400006920

ISBN: 1-931313-29-6

Distributed by Ingram Book Company

Printed by Lightning Source Inc., La Vergne, TN

Published by Simon Publications, Safety Harbor, FL

The process of settlement and naturalization, together with the freedom of our institutions, and the fertility of our soil, have invited the denizens of the world, wherever assembled, or dispersed, to come among us and become fellow-citizens. And from every degree of latitude and of longitude, and from every isle and continent, under the whole heaven, the flood of emigration has poured in upon the United States. . . . There has been nothing like it in appearance since the encampments of the Roman empire, or the tents of the crusaders.

Democratic Review, June, 1852, page 566.

CONTENTS

ILLUSTRATIONS

(With Notes by the Editor)

This lithograph, owned by Kennedy & Company, New York
City, was drawn by James Fagan, printed by Day & Son, lithog-
raphers to the Queen, and published by Ackermann & Company
in London on February 24, 1853. Contrast this tearful scene
with the companion piece, "The Emigrants' Return."

This lithograph was drawn by Nathaniel Bliss Stocker, printed
by the Leighton Brothers, and published by Ackermann & Company, London, on May 21, 1853. It is owned by Kennedy &
Company, New York City. A comparison with "The Emigrant's
Farewell" will show that the family is now much older and has
an additional member. Their clothing and the amount of their
luggage indicate that they have found the land of promise also
the land of performance.

From *Harper's New Monthly Magazine*, IX, 861 (November,
1854). The artist is Richardson Cox. This picture was also used
as an advertising poster by Enoch Train & Company of Boston,
the wording on the broadsides being altered to refer to its own
vessels. For a reproduction of the picture so changed, see *Some
Merchants and Sea Captains* (State Street Trust Company,
Boston, 1918), 46.

This poster advertises the services of the shipping line established in 1842 by Enoch Train of Boston; the names of the
company's twenty-four vessels appear. They are said to make an
average run between Liverpool and Boston in seventeen days.
Other information follows. "Provisions supplied passengers in
conformity with the laws of Great Britain and the United
States." "The most extensive arrangements having been made
with the Worcester and Western Rail Road Corporations (by
which Passengers will be protected from numerous frauds hith-

erto practised by the 'Runners'), Train & Co. are now prepared
to furnish Emigrants with Through Tickets by the above
Packets, Steamers and Railroads, from the principal Ports of
Great Britain, Germany, France, and all the large Cities of the
Continent . . ." to points in the United States and Canada as
far inland as New Orleans, Iowa City and Hamilton. The vessel
pictured on the poster is the clipper ship *Staffordshire*, one of
Donald McKay's creations. Launched in 1851, she is described
by *Gleason's Pictorial Drawing-Room Companion*, I, 275 (August 20, 1851), as "the largest, and designed to sail the fastest,
of all Atlantic sailing vessels." For a time, Train & Company did
a business of $1,000,000 a year in sending immigrant remittances
to Europe.

Both sketches are from the *Illustrated London News*, XVIII, 386
(May 10, 1851). The upper one is entitled "Irish Emigrants
Leaving Home. — The Priest's Blessing"; the lower, "Emigrants
Arrival at Cork. — A Scene on the Quay." As the signs indicate,
from Cork the traveler could take passage for Quebec, Boston,
New York or New Orleans.

Both sketches are from the *Illustrated London News*, XVII, 20,
17 (July 6, 1850). The upper one, entitled "The Departure,"
portrays a scene at Waterloo Dock in Liverpool. "As the ship
is towed out," says the accompanying article, "hats are raised,
handkerchiefs are waved, and a long-continued shout of farewell is raised . . . ." This same picture is reproduced, without
credit, in *Frank Leslie's Illustrated Newspaper*, I, 77 (January 12,
1856). The second sketch is entitled "Scene between Decks."
Note the crowded, gloomy quarters and the lack of ventilation.

The upper sketch, entitled "Emigrant-Landing in New York"
and drawn by W. J. Hennessy, is from *Harper's Weekly*, II,
405 (June 26, 1858). The lower sketch is the centerpiece of a
double-page set of illustrations, collectively captioned "Newly-Arrived Emigrants at Castle Garden," in the same magazine,
IX, 552–553 (September 2, 1865). The artist is A. R. Waud.
With the conversion of the famous Castle Garden into a receiving station for immigrants in 1855, the federal government
greatly smoothed the way for European newcomers.

From the *Illustrated London News*, XIII, 380 (December 16, 1848). The accompanying article quotes the *Tipperary Vindicator* as saying: "Whole districts are cleared. Not a roof-tree is to be seen where the happy cottage of the labourer or the snug homestead of the farmer at no distant day cheered the landscape."

This map, showing the local origins of German emigration at the period of its flood tide, is based on a variety of sources. For Baden, figures are available only from 1850: *Beiträge zur Statistik der inneren Verwaltung des Grossherzogthums Baden*, V (1857), 34–35. For Bavaria, see *Beiträge zur Statistik des Königreichs Bayern*, III (1854), 322–323; VIII (1859), 240–241. The Brunswick figures are the totals for the years 1847–1855: *Hübners Jahrbuch für Volkswirtschaft und Statistik*, VI, pt. ii (1860), 283. In the case of Hanover, figures are available only for the provinces of Hanover, Lüneburg and Osnabrück: *Zur Statistik des Königreichs Hannover*, IX, pp. xvi–xvii. For Hesse, see *Beiträge zur Statistik des Grossherzogthums Hessen*, III (1864), 53; for Oldenburg, *Statistische Nachrichten über das Grossherzogthum Oldenburg*, IX (1867), 164; for Prussia, *Zeitschrift des Königlichen preussischen statistischen Bureaus*, I (1861), 56–82. The only available figures for Saxony appear in E. v. Philippovich, *Auswanderung und Auswanderungspolitik in Deutschland (Schriften des Vereins für Sozialpolitik*, LII, Leipzig, 1892), 290, 386; they begin with 1851. The statistics for Württemberg are taken from the *Württembergische Jahrbücher*, *1853*, pt. ii, 118–119; *1854*, pt. i, 50; *1855*, pt. i, 51.

EDITOR'S FOREWORD

IN THE SWIRL OF EVENTS following the first World War probably few persons realized that the year 1924 marked a great divide in American history. Congress then passed a law providing that, after a preparatory period, the number of European immigrants annually admitted to the United States should be restricted to one hundred and fifty thousand and that these should be so apportioned among the various countries as not to alter the existing composition of the American people. Both provisions of the statute involved a radical break with historic practice. From earliest colonial days to the close of the World War newcomers of white stock had been welcomed regardless either of their number or of the lands from which they came. In some years more than a million had entered the country. The melting pot, whose workings Hector St. John Crèvecœur had approvingly described as early as 1782, had been left to simmer or seethe as it willed.

The new system went into effect in 1929. Since then, what was once a flood of immigration has become no more than a trickle. The lines of Emma Lazarus inscribed on the base of the Statue of Liberty apply to a past that seems gone beyond recall:

> Give me your tired, your poor,
> Your huddled masses yearning to breathe free,
> The wretched refuse of your teeming shore,
> Send these, the homeless, tempest-tossed, to me . . . .

For a variety of reasons the United States decided to preserve that balance of foreign strains in the population which the accidents of history had produced. Though the term was not fashionable when the action was taken, the law of 1924 involved "national planning" of far-reaching import both for America and for the rest of the world.

It is not surprising that this changed aspect of affairs should have an effect on scholarly studies of immigration. In earlier years the subject engaged the energies principally of economists and sociologists eager to describe and evaluate the impact of the arriving hordes on American society. They regarded immigration as a social problem rather than as a social process, and they often wrote for the purpose of influencing governmental policy. Today the subject is exciting the increasing attention of professional historians. More clearly than ever before, they are able to survey the phenomenon at a focal distance and appraise its results with judicial detachment. Even when they confine their inquiries to a single nationality, as most of them do, they seldom succumb to the temptation which led some earlier writers to magnify the importance of one group at the expense of other elements of the population.

Professor Hansen's volume deals with the great transatlantic migration of white peoples, first to the thirteen colonies, and then to the early Republic down to the eve of the Civil War. It is the latter movement which he emphasizes. Unlike most historians of immigration, he takes his stand in Europe rather than in America. Leaving other scholars to tell the story of the newcomers after they reached the United States, he opens to view what has hitherto been largely a *terra incognita*. He describes the various conditions in the Old World which made people dissatisfied with their lot: the changes in agriculture and landholding, the rise of industrialism, natural disasters, political oppression, religious discrimination, the high-pressure activities of emigrant agents. He explains why the vision of America as a Land of Promise sometimes burned brightly and sometimes dimly, quickening or retarding the oversea movement. He shows how improvements in land transportation made the ports of embarkation more accessible to peasants in the European hinterland and how more modern conditions of ocean travel increased their willingness to undertake the American adventure. He tells how people who were down and out contrived to finance the journey and sheds new light on the sporadic experiments in collective settlement.

These various strands the author weaves into a coherent pattern of Old-World emigration, tracing their interaction and assessing the results. Though concerned primarily with migration to the United States, he discusses alternative proposals and enterprises that impinged on it — the organized efforts to colonize peasants in the thinly settled districts of Poland and south Russia, the outflow of British subjects to Canada, the emigrant undertakings in Algeria, Australia, Central America and Brazil. It will come as a surprise to many that there was a time when Latin America held a greater fascination for the European common man than did the United States.

As the story grows under the author's pen, no reader can fail to perceive its epic character. Less familiar than the advance of the pioneers into the American West, the long-continuous migration across the ocean forms the necessary background for that movement. To the courage and determination of these humble folk from Europe historians ascribe some of the finest traits of the national character. Americans who cannot boast of ancestors who came over in the *Mayflower* may take pride in forebears who with equal fortitude and self-sacrifice, but with less attention from historians, braved the Atlantic at later times.

Professor Hansen never forgets that he is writing about flesh-and-blood human beings. His pages afford constant glimpses of their hopes, follies, achievements and failures. One sees the mysterious Madame Krüdener distributing food to the hungry, and exciting the peasants of Switzerland with a desire for change; the brightly clad German families encamped in the gardens of the Louvre while waiting to sell their horses and resume their journey by boat to Le Havre; the Irish cottiers harried by hunger and abandoning their infirm and dying along the roadside; the throngs of persons clamoring for passage in the Dutch ports; the huddled voyagers on the emigrant vessels frightened by the ravages of ship fever. In remote German villages the people learn of America from reading President Jackson's messages in their newspapers. In Ireland the temporary return of an emigrant with money in his pocket occasions a flurry of fresh departures. Everywhere letters from friends and relatives in the United States vie with the inexpensive guidebooks in arousing interest in the far land. Such incidents, garnered by patient research, enliven a narrative which in less skillful hands might have consisted largely of dry statistical generalizations.

In the course of gathering his materials the author spent a total of nearly four years abroad, chiefly in the British Isles, Germany, France, Switzerland, the Netherlands and the Scandinavian countries. Professor Hansen's untimely death on May 11, 1938, while Professor of History at the University of Illinois, removed from the historical profession an able scholar at the full flood of his productive career. The present volume, though complete in itself, was planned as the first of a trilogy. As nearly as can be learned, he proposed in the second volume to treat the period from 1860 to 1882. Without neglecting the European causes for emigration, he expected to stress the remarkable Americanizing effect of the Civil War on the nationalities already settled in the country. In this influence he saw the principal reason why the United States was able to avoid the creation of powerful racial and national minorities such as have plagued many European countries. The third volume would have focused on the growing immigration from central and southern Europe and would have carried the story within reach of the present. It is certain that these later volumes would have been marked by the same freshness of approach and wealth of illustration that characterize his earlier treatment.

At the time of his death Professor Hansen had brought the manuscript of the present work to the point of a final literary revision. This task has fallen to my hands, and I have tried to execute it with scrupulous regard for the author's conception of his theme. His organization of the material and his interpretations and conclusions remain unchanged. From her extensive knowledge of his notebooks Miss Esther McKenzie rendered valuable service in completing the footnote citations. These have been collected at the end of the book, since they will interest only historical scholars who wish to ascertain the sources of the author's information. Mr. C. Frederick Hansen accorded me many courtesies, and Mr. Theodore L. Agnew, Jr., also put me in his debt. Miss Elizabeth F. Hoxie prepared the manuscript for the press and compiled the index.

ARTHUR M. SCHLESINGER

THE ATLANTIC MIGRATION

I

THE WESTWARD IMPULSE

EARLY IN THE NINETEENTH CENTURY when the peace of 1815 was preparing the way for the greatest migration in the history of mankind a newspaper commentator expressed his amazement at the caravans of peasants hopefully and apparently light-heartedly setting off for the New World. "Emigration," he declared, "is a form of suicide because it separates a person from all that life gives except the material wants of simple animal existence." [1] This theme formed the recurrent refrain of every writer who felt it a duty to warn would-be emigrants against a hasty decision to exchange the known for the unknown. There was companionship in the fields and work for youth, protection in the invisible presence of fathers and forefathers resting in the village cemetery, inspiration in the spire of the parish church. The community of one's childhood was a little world of family and friends with whom joys and sorrows might be shared, and whose familiar association made the future secure. Was it wise to surrender these advantages for the uncertain prospect of acquiring more acres and a larger house in a distant land?

But sentiment was not the only tie binding the villager to his native soil. Often he was ignorant of what lay beyond the market town where twice a year he bought and sold. There he saw new faces, heard strange dialects, and traded with men whose customs and behavior he regarded with suspicion. To come back to the familiar ways of his townsfolk was a relief. To be sure, a few of the villagers had traveled farther afield. The goldsmith who had been to Italy and the wheelwright who had been to Switzerland told stories of their wanderings which revealed a surprising world where clothing, food, language and even religion were of another sort. And if this was Europe, what might not America be — that vague mystery of continent and islands which lay somewhere beyond the broad Atlantic? But with most people, "Remain in the land and prosper therein" was not merely a scriptural admonition; it was common sense distilled from experience and strengthened by every hesitating contact with the unknown lands across the sea.

These two deterrent influences, sentiment and ignorance, found an ally in the difficulties that attended transportation. "To take the pilgrim's staff in hand" remained the stereotyped expression long after railroads and steamboats had become the handmaids of emigration; but it harked back to the time when the emigrant depended entirely upon his own energy and resources. He carried his possessions in a pack upon his back because he lacked other means of transport. Viewed at every parish boundary as a suspect, he was questioned as to actions and motives; his pass was scrutinized; he was watched at the inn and on the road until a new set of parish inquisitors took him in hand. When he entered a city, the guardsman at the gate searched his pack for wares that the guilds had prohibited; and at every national frontier officers collected a toll on his simple belongings. For weeks, perhaps for months, he lodged in a port, asking every chance sailor he met whether any ship in the harbor were bound for America, and pleading with the captain for a berth in the officers' cabin or, at least, for a place as an unpaid member of the crew.

The time spent in the port entailed days and nights of vigilance. Long before Shanghai gave it a name, the kidnaping of able-bodied young men into service on vessels bound for distant seas was practised wherever ships and sailors gathered. Merchants and trading companies with overseas possessions recruited soldiers of fortune for their private armies from among the persons who loitered about the docks; mercenaries were hired for wars with interlopers and campaigns against rebellious natives. Whaling expeditions offered excitement and a liberal share to each of the hands if the catch were good. The wait was long and the temptation and danger great; and many an impatient youth, who aspired to own a plantation in the New World, found himself at last a trader in the South Seas, or a tattooed wanderer sailing before the mast.

Many of these men had only with difficulty secured the official permission necessary for legal departure; those who avoided the formality were fugitives from the moment they left home. For the state had a claim upon them — not only to their military service but to their physical presence. Population was wealth, an investment that would not be allowed to betake itself at will beyond the possibilities of some counterbalancing return. No longer, it is true, was the individual a slave, the possession of some king or noble; but he was the property of the state which might cede him to another or banish him into exile, although it recognized on his part no right of expatriation — the right to depart at will and transfer allegiance to another sovereignty. Even when permission to leave was given, it was not a free grant. A percentage of all property was retained to compensate the state for its loss, and the individual obtained his liberty only by payment of this price.

To secure this privilege, however, proved simple compared with the difficulties of freeing himself from the meshes of the commune. Besides belonging to the body politic, every person was also a member of the body economic. For the country dweller the one was far-off, distant; the other, a daily presence. The emigration of the nineteenth century was predominantly rural, and in the organization of agricultural life the peasant and the village artisan were firmly entwined. Not until these bonds became loosened did the individuals acquire that mobility which was fundamental to a numerous migration.

The disappearance of serfdom, however, did not automatically endow the individual with independence of action. He was still a member of the commune which determined his immediate relations of life. Its officers decided when the fields should be planted and which strips should be assigned to each individual. They regulated the use of the common lands of pasture and forest. They determined the share of communal burdens that each should carry. No artisan could set himself up in trade until consent had been granted, and then his prices and methods were established by the inexorable law of local custom, as interpreted by the chosen few. Nor could a young man marry without similar permission. In like fashion, the duties that the commune owed to the province and state were apportioned among the inhabitants. The tyranny of the commune became finally one of the strongest incentives to emigration and, at the same time, constituted one of the greatest obstacles to ready departure.

Such was the commune of the later Middle Ages, a form of regimentation that gradually moderated as changes in government withdrew some privileges and as the passage of time caused others to fall into disuse. Few generalizations hold true of all western Europe. National law and local law evolved new theories regarding the status of the individual with respect to the realm and to his neighbors. Every country experienced a special evolution, and almost every province developed particular circumstances. One fact, however, is indisputable: throughout the whole of northern and western Europe a steady growth occurred in the mobility of the people. In the places where this was greatest, emigration first took place.

In Great Britain the economic revolution of the sixteenth

century broke up the long-established forms of rural society. After England destroyed the clan in Ireland with its primitive control over the fate of men and flocks, Englishmen and Irishmen found themselves free to go where they would within the possessions of the Crown. Only the Elizabethan poor law with its hindrances to removal put a check upon permanent migration. The Scotch Highlander waited longer to secure this right because in his instance clan and lord retained their power until the rebellions of the eighteenth century crushed not only the lords but the system over which they ruled. Holland also early abolished all restrictions. A commercial empire which had to be adequately manned broke down the selfish claims of the parish and province, and the Dutchman could farm or trade wherever his capital or inclination led him.

In the neighboring countries, however, progress proved less rapid, and the rights were not so early obtained. France's incessant involvement in wars made her man power too valuable for a generous policy of voluntary migration. She even placed so many restrictions upon the dispatch of colonists to New France that settlement was retarded; and the colony itself, intent on retaining its sparse inhabitants, inflicted the death penalty on deserters from its soil. Not until the French Revolution did the choice of emigration win recognition as a natural right; and even this recognition remained but a philosophical principle during the ensuing generation of wars when the nation had need of all her sons.

Each of the host of states and principalities that made up the medieval German Empire possessed its own code concerning the emigration of its subjects. The eastward trend which had gone on over several centuries gave the population a fluidity hardly in keeping with the strict regulations which theoretically governed all comings and goings. Permission to depart was accorded with a regularity that almost nullified the restrictions. But in the eighteenth century, mercantilism, with its doctrine that the most thickly settled state is the richest, brought a sharp reaction. No longer were the emissaries of sovereigns allowed to lead bands of settlers afar to till the moors and forests of the east; and only such elements as the authorities were glad to speed on their way — religious sectarians especially — were granted the license to depart. In the Scandinavian countries the laws resembled those in Germany, but the presence of the sea with its opportunity for employment to sailors opened a way of escape for all who itched for distant adventure. Here, as in Germany, emigration as a universal right awaited the nineteenth century.

Though the thirteen American colonies owed their growth and prosperity largely to the recurrent additions of population from Europe, the century from 1815 to 1914 marked the most significant period in the foreign peopling of the United States. The years from the fall of Napoleon to the outbreak of the World War spanned exactly one hundred seasons of migration in which a great flood of humanity rolled westward across the Atlantic and swept over the waiting continent. To that flood every nation, every province, almost every neighborhood, contributed its stream. Beginning in Ireland and the valley of the Rhine, the fever of emigration extended toward the north and east, gripping the English midlands, the Scandinavian countries and the north of Germany, spread southward through the Baltic provinces, Poland and Austria into Italy and, before it finally ran its course, afflicted the Balkans and the Near East. Only France and Spain proved immune so far as the United States was concerned. It is clear that the cause of so vast an exodus was wider than race or nationality and deeper than legislation or politics. It was not the mania of a single generation, nor of ideas that prevailed for a mere decade or two. The cause was as universal as the movement itself.

Quite as marked as its universality was the periodicity of the movement. It advanced in a series of waves, each greater than the preceding. After a period of flow there followed an interval during which the current hesitated or seemed to reverse itself, only to be followed by a sudden rush of even greater volume. For an understanding of the underlying factors the ebb is no less important than the flow. The source of each gives the significant clue to a solution of the puzzling problem of cause.

Three distinct stages of migration marked the nineteenth century. The first, of special interest for the present volume, began in the 1830's and continued until 1860, reaching its crest in the years 1847–1854. To this exodus the adjective "Celtic" may properly be applied. The emigrants came from Ireland, the Highlands of Scotland and the mountains of Wales — regions where the language and blood were predominantly Celtic and where the land system grew directly out of the agrarian customs of the early tribes. Though many came also from the upper Rhine Valley of Germany and the adjoining districts, these newcomers may in a sense also be regarded as Celtic, for the first peoples to cultivate their hills and valleys had been Celts and, when the conquering German tribes occupied the villages and fields, they took over the divisions and the customs which in primitive times formed such an important feature of the agricultural routine. As elsewhere, the centuries had wrought changes; but the transformed rural economy had more in common with the prevailing system in Ireland than it did with the conditions in the purely German lands to the east. The Belgian and Dutch farmers who sought America also had inherited an economic organization descended from the Celts, and even the Norwegian pioneers of the time came from the districts along the coast to which the Celts had clung long after being expelled from the Continent as a whole.

The next great period of migration covered the decades between 1860 and 1890. Now Englishmen predominated numerically — yeoman farmers and their sons, and agricultural laborers — but the biggest Scandinavian emigration of all time took place within these years, and Germany was represented by Prussians and Saxons, and Austria by Bohemians. As before, the diverse national groups possessed a common denominator, and again that denominator was the system by which land was held. Its origin was Germanic, for the emigrants came from regions where the early Teutonic tribes had fixed the customs that governed agricultural practice and land succession. These Germanic regions stand out on the map with distinct prominence: England from north of the Thames to the Scotch Highlands, Germany east of the Elbe, Austria west of the mountain range that divides its territories, the plains of Denmark and southern Sweden, and the interior valleys of Norway. This exodus was Teutonic in blood, in institutions, and in the basis of its language, forming the most homogeneous of all the migrations to America.

In the third period, that from 1890 to 1914, two distinct geographic regions mingled their diverse currents in the New World. One was Mediterranean in origin, the other Slavic. The latter possessed the same unifying element of land as had the Celtic and Germanic newcomers. Finns, Latvians, Lithuanians, Poles, Karelians and Ukrainians — most of them were subjects of the Russian Empire and all of them enjoyed a common agricultural inheritance. But the Mediterranean peoples present a more complex spectacle, one impossible to simplify. Too many civilizations and cultures had flourished one after the other, too many populations had been swept away by wars and pestilence, to leave intact and distinct the original agrarian unity that may once have existed in Italy and Greece and the countries of the Near East. Commerce and politics remained as binding threads.

The magnitude of this century-long movement, involving the transplantation of thirty-five million people, becomes even more impressive when viewed at the moments of greatest intensity. In the first of the three periods fully half of the migrants arrived in America between 1847 and 1854; in the second, the decade from 1880 to 1890 accounted for a similar percentage; in the third, the years 1909 to 1914 brought an equal proportion. More than seventeen millions crossed the sea in the space of these twenty-five years! This horde of human beings overshadows all other population movements in peace or war. The barbarian invasions of the late Roman Empire and the transportation of American troops in the World War fade into numerical insignificance.

But along with the characteristic of size, attention should be given to the individual aspect and the unofficial nature of the movement in which these multifarious peoples participated. Mankind had moved before this time — as conquering tribes, as organized bands of settlers, as companies of traders. In such migrations the individual had been a cog in a mechanism greater than himself. A section of an established society, detached from its environment, was transferred to the edge of a wilderness or to the midst of a strange and perhaps hostile people. The adventurers brought with them the institutions to which they had been accustomed, and a trained group among them was charged with the sole duty of preserving and developing those institutions, no matter how alien they were to the new surroundings.

But the European of 1815 or 1914 left the Old World and settled in the New usually as an individual. A human atom wrenched itself from an old society and attached itself to a new. In his unfamiliar home he felt no conscious mission or urge to reproduce any but the most personal features of the life to which he was habituated. No patriotic considerations prompted him to remove to America; and whether the culture of his native country was forever restricted within its existing limits or spread to the ends of the earth did not concern him. To be sure, he brought with him the germs of institutions — a preference for the forms of association, worship and pleasure to which he had been accustomed. This sometimes meant that, if he were thrown with fellow immigrants upon his arrival and if the environment were not definitely hostile, they would reproduce a part of the homeland and found a "colony." But in time the chemistry of the new scene dissolved even such Old-World attachments.

With this mass exodus of individuals, governments had little or nothing to do, apart from legislative efforts early in the nineteenth century to ameliorate the sufferings of passengers who sought the cheapest mode of conveyance. Such attempts, inspired by humanitarian motives, sought merely to improve the conditions of transportation, leaving the transported to go when and where they wished. Not until the last years of the century did any European country adopt a policy of emigration or the United States a policy of immigration, and then the legislation came too late to change appreciably the nature of the movement. Though this outflow of people altered many of the fundamental relationships of the modern world, no nation interfered to direct it along a course profitable to itself.

This migration does not constitute an isolated story. It touches the stream of human history at many points. It forms part of the agrarian development which revolutionized the European countryside. It is related to the hygienic progress that doubled the population in the course of three generations. It helped to bring about a new era in Atlantic transportation by furnishing merchant vessels with one of their most reliable wares. Not least important was its contribution to the westward movement in the United States.

From the standpoint of the Old World this mass movement was emigration. As has been indicated, it was related to a fundamental reorganization of rural economy in every country that was affected. But from the standpoint of the United States the phenomenon was immigration and, as such, it involved a very different type of problem. How could the millions of aliens be amalgamated into the American population and welded into the American economic structure? This problem has received little attention because of the all-dominating presence of the frontier and the abundance of land called "free." Open spaces were awaiting, and open spaces received them. But this simple conception ignores what was known to every writer of emigrant guides — and carefully concealed by every land agent of the time — that pioneering was a highly specialized occupation successfully carried out only by men trained in a hundred practical methods that two centuries of expansion had taught the American settler.

The westward movement was not the simple process that it seems to be in the annals of pioneer history. The theme of those pages is: one man against the wilderness, his equipment being fortitude, resourcefulness and patience. To a soldier in the front-line trenches the conflict is primarily a hand-to-hand encounter with the enemy; but the historian must recall the complex and ever shifting lines that served as the base upon which every advance, great or small, rested. Behind the fringe of the frontier, roads, canals and railways were woven into a network of communication that supported squatter and homesteader. In the wake of the settlers came capital; the migration of gold is an essential part of every chapter of the advance. Battalions of labor were necessary to transform the gold into instruments of service, and regiments of replacement had to fill in the lands which the restless pioneer evacuated.

The European immigrant was not a frontiersman. By neither experience nor instinct was he equipped to battle with forest or prairie. He could not handle that deadly tool, the American ax; he was unskilled in building the log cabin or the sod hut. Moreover, some were incapacitated by ague, others struck down by the summer's sun, while every season of the year brought its pests of insects and fowls. Other conditions were equally difficult to cope with. Every European system of agriculture failed in the rich and luxuriant virgin soil. Lonesome weeks, far from the sight of all humanity, clouded the optimism that alone could make monotony bearable. Day by day, in spite of ceaseless toil, the woods grew thicker and the plains became wider, until the newcomer, seized with despair, confessed defeat by deserting to the city slum or the laborers' camp. No attempt to found a colony of foreigners on the edge of the wilderness ever succeeded, and this fact was so well-known that many a newly arrived immigrant, eager to conquer a home from Nature, discarded his romantic plans to follow the advice of wiser heads.

Yet this was exactly the environment in which the native Westerner could thrive. Neighbors, far from being a necessity, were regarded as a nuisance, and a few visits a year to the trading post provided all the social intercourse he craved. His nomadic instincts have become legendary: a distant thread of smoke, signifying the presence of another civilized being, was enough to send him on his way. After putting out his fire and whistling to his dog, his preparations were complete, and with ax, gun and hoe he ventured forth to a new existence.

Legend, however, must be tempered with fact. Undoubtedly such persons did exist, but they did not typify the much larger and more substantial class of the backwoods families. These latter cut the trail, built the first habitation, cleaned out the spring, cleared and fenced a few acres. The river and the forest yielded fish and game, and the settlers were as dependent on the bounty of the wilderness as on the harvest of the cultivated field. With that life and its surroundings they were content. Then why did they move on to new surroundings? The reason is simple. The thread of smoke meant not only a new neighbor; more acutely, it signified another competitor whose gun would hasten the destruction of the fast-disappearing game. And so the family gathered their equipment together and departed, bound for the next valley where they could continue the life they knew; and when they left, the farm and its rude improvements were sold to another type of occupant.

It is at this stage that the immigrant makes his appearance. The purchaser was a Yankee or New Yorker, a German, Englishman or Norwegian. At each phase of the economic development of nineteenth-century America there existed a technique of immigration, a standardized procedure by which the newcomer shifted from place to place, from job to job, until he was shaken into that niche for which he was fitted by inclination, resources or necessity. Before the Civil War the process usually culminated in the transformation of the European into an independent, landowning American farmer. This was achieved in one of two ways. If he possessed more than enough capital to keep him during the preliminary arrangements and the voyage, the path was direct and easy. Backed by several hundred dollars — a thousand was ideal — he bought the semi-improved farm, supported himself until he learned the rudiments of the new agricultural life and gradually extended his cultivated area until it sufficed for all his wants.

But most of the immigrants had exhausted their funds

when they stood on the American shore. Their labor gave life to the capital of others. The great hinterland swallowed them up as they scattered to communities in need of ready arms and strong backs. A few, skilled in trades, found employment as mechanics or as factory workers; masons and carpenters were welcomed in every booming village. The majority took pick and shovel and dug canals and graded railroads — tasks which they despised but which usually headed them toward the West and their eventual homes. This experience involved a survival of the fittest. The mortality was high, but at the end of two or three seasons their capital accumulated and the coveted land could be bought.

A thousand variations of this process appear. In increasing proportion the alien newcomers obtained work as "hired hands" upon the more prosperous farms. If the immigrating unit were a family, it often divided, the wife and children going out into "service" until their combined earnings reunited them in a home of their own. As foreign settlements increased in area, they attracted immigrants of their own nationality, took care of them in their need and, in the course of time, sent them out into the less cordial world. In all these experiences, on the public works and throughout the countryside, immigrants served an apprenticeship that groomed them for a place in the growing society of America.

The periodicity evident in the flow of migration over the Atlantic is reflected in the wavelike motion with which population crossed the continent to the Pacific. Among the few generalizations that can be made regarding immigration from Europe is that the periods of greatest volume corresponded with the eras of liveliest industrial activity in the United States.[2] With a regularity which, however, does not exhibit perfect coördination, the westward movement was strongest at times of industrial depression. If these two circumstances are put together they illuminate the relationship between the two movements. Good business demanded labor, and Europe provided an abundant source of supply; but when the canals, railroads, factories and warehouses had been built to a point exceeding profitable returns, business came to a standstill and the workmen were discharged. Equipped with their savings, they continued the broken journey to the West, where they bought up the lands of those who had preceded them. This fluctuating inflow of Europeans and their subsequent dispersion over the continent furnish the main chapters in the history of American immigration.

Viewed from a different angle, the migration to America was one aspect of the growth and spread of the population of Atlantic Europe. The exodus was so directly the outcome of the unprecedented population increase of the nineteenth century that its background would not be complete without some consideration of the broader features of that development during the preceding centuries.[3] When the peace and prosperity of the Roman Empire gave way to the confusion of the barbarian invasions, the number of inhabitants was perhaps halved. By the thirteenth century, awakening trade and the stabilization of government had restored the earlier total and gave promise of attaining new heights. Then came the wars and plagues of the fourteenth and fifteenth centuries. Again the number was halved, and in the year 1500 western Europe probably contained no more people than a millennium before. During the next hundred years Nature began patiently to restore the loss, and shortly after 1600 this had been accomplished. Great Britain and France thereafter enjoyed a progressive growth; but Germany and the north suffered another setback from the devastation of the Thirty Years' War, while the Italian peninsula stagnated because of the decline of Mediterranean commerce. The powers of recuperation, however, were now stronger and, except in Italy

where malaria had fastened itself upon the coastal plains, a
new era began with the dawn of the eighteenth century.

In the absence of official censuses in any of the countries
at the opening of the new century, the extent of this increase
can only be surmised, but it seems safe to say that the population doubled between 1700 and 1800. One indication of
the phenomenal advance is the interest which governments
displayed in the connection between their economic policies
and population growth. "Political arithmetic" struggled to
become a science; and to provide data for their calculations,
the bureaucrats of one nation after the other undertook at
definite intervals a census which would cover all its territory
and use a uniform system of classification. Not until the last
third of the century did the practice become general, but the
rate of increase there indicated, if projected back to 1700,
provides the basis for the above estimate — an opinion
strengthened by the corroborating information contributed
by gleanings from local church records and statistics of trade.

The reasons for this growth are shrouded in no mystery.
For more than a thousand years population had shown its
vitality; again and again it gave promise of filling the lands
with human beings only to have disease and wars wipe out
the gains. The eighteenth century was happily free from
serious plagues; and until the last decade its battles were
fought by professional soldiers, many of them in distant parts
of the colonial world. The practice of medicine became less
an occult art and evolved the first principles of the science of
healing. No longer were the majority of infants and children
doomed to death, for their ailments were looked upon as
something other than a divine visitation which it would be
sacrilege to oppose. The same enlightened spirit widened the
use of inoculation, with the result that the scourge of small-
pox, which in many villages took an annual toll of lives, was
confined to ever narrowing bounds, and its virulence was

moderated so that death was not almost inevitably the sequence.

It is difficult to demonstrate to what extent this increase in population grew out of the policies fostered by the prevailing doctrine of mercantilism. The tenets of mercantilism on the point were clear and direct. People were wealth, and a nation in order to prosper must encourage their multiplication, entice settlers and artisans from other lands, and prohibit the departure of its own subjects. In its most exaggerated form the doctrine appeared in the statement of the Prussian Minister Johannes von Justi: "No nation can have too many inhabitants." [4] Various measures were adopted by Continental states to fill their cradles to overflowing. Laws restricting marriage to those whose worldly goods indicated their ability to support a family were moderated. The terms of military service were liberalized in answer to the criticism that, like the monasteries of the Middle Ages, armies absorbed too many potential fathers. Though the suggestion made by a patriotic clergyman that polygamy be legalized was not followed, many curious laws and decrees indicate the intensity of the desire to swell the census rolls.

These policies may have had little or no direct effect, but the changes the mercantilists introduced into agriculture facilitated the extension of cultivated fields and hence greatly increased the food supply for the poor. Authority to divide the common lands was generally granted, thereby converting to arable fields extensive wastes that had formerly pastured a few sheep and cattle. On many royal domains steps were taken to break up the vicious agricultural communism and to transform the workers into peasant proprietors whose self-interest might lead to better methods of farming. Kings and nobles took pride in ruling over model estates where rotation of crops sustained fertility from season to season and restored life to worn-out fields.

In the eighteenth century a humble root achieved a popularity that was to bring security and then tragedy. What rice was to China, the potato became to the poor of western Europe. When first brought to a village it was received with contempt or suspicion. A local philanthropist — often the parish minister — stood sponsor, and his efforts were rewarded by a grudging acceptance which finally turned into a chorus of praise. The virtues of the potato were soon obvious: the abundant yield from even the most paltry bit put into the ground, the ease of cultivation in which women and children could effectively handle the hoe, the relative freedom from insect enemies, the few precautions necessary for winter storage, the score of satisfying dishes which it provided for the most untutored housewife. The potato patch flourishing beside every cottage banished from the fireside the age-old fear of hunger. Not until the eighteenth century had gone and the next had come was the conquest complete, but without the potato the population figures of 1800 would not have exhibited their gratifying sums.

The rise of population was reflected in nearly every aspect of life. The last quarter of the century proved a busy time. The overgrown fields of remote ancestors were early reclaimed. Cultivation now crept up the hillsides, and the steeper slopes were terraced. Meandering rivers were confined to narrow beds, and rich bottom lands put under the plow. On the northern plains the heaths were cleared, and the moors were drained. Dykes pushed back the North Sea, from the peninsula of Danish Jutland to the entrance of the English Channel. In Sweden and Norway the period was known as the age of the "great uprooting" because of the devastation wrought in the mountain forests. From north to south, villages grew into market towns and market towns into cities as communities gained additional inhabitants who came to trade and enjoy the advantages of urban life. Many of the older sections developed a thriving household industry in spinning and weaving to supply the newer regions with the linens and woolens which they had neither skill nor equipment to prepare.

By such methods the bulk of the increased population was accommodated, but intermigration also played a part. To cross the Elbe River in search of lands in the German "Colonial East" had long been a practice in the valley of the Rhine, and people from the Low Countries had occasionally been called in to settle and improve the marshes of the north. Now a persistent and effective propaganda, carried on by Frederick the Great, populated broad stretches of his eastern provinces, and Catherine of Russia planted Swiss and Germans along the plains of the lower Volga. Spain also caught the idea of mercantilism and attempted to recover some of her lost prosperity by establishing German farmers and artisans in the midst of her great sheep ranches. These ventures were accompanied by disappointments and bitter complaints, and from each of them stragglers wandered back to their native villages. The idea of emigration, however, was gradually finding lodgment in the popular mind, horizons were being widened, and even the Atlantic was ceasing to be regarded as a barrier. But this early transatlantic migration is reserved for later and more complete discussion.

The cumulative nature of population growth impressed everyone who observed the increase in the first half of the eighteenth century; and the prospect of its continuation at the same rate gratified those who measured national wealth by the census returns. What might not a few generations more of parenthood accomplish! But this same prospect was already producing another sort of reaction among some whose acquaintance with conditions was based on a first-hand knowledge of the social consequences. Chancellors and cameralists might rejoice in what the impersonal figures revealed, but men who went from household to household and saw the ever narrowing fields could not banish a feeling of anxiety. It is no mere coincidence that village clergymen figured among the writers who in the latter part of the century questioned the unmixed blessings of unrestricted generation.

Robert Malthus has loomed so large in economic literature that his opinions have obscured those expressed earlier by persons who did not condense their conclusions into a mathematical formula. Each was moved to write out of his own experience and observations, and the spontaneous appearance of such warnings in almost every language of western Europe indicates that the problem was not entirely imaginary. Mirabeau the Elder, the "friend of the people," described the congestion of his own province in France. Justus Moser who spent a lifetime among the peasants of north Germany wrote caustically of the "patriotic fantasies" of impractical statesmen who would burden the land with more beings than it could support. A Danish clergyman, Otto Litken, labored to reconcile the divine command to multiply and replenish with the poverty that he saw about him, and ended by expressing his belief that, although conditions were rapidly becoming worse, still an all-knowing Nature would intervene before they got too bad. When the Swedish Academy in 1769 offered a prize for a discussion of the reasons why so many young men took service in the merchant vessels of other nations and what should be done about it, another clergyman, Anders Chydenius, boldly wrote an essay on the theme that there were too many people in Sweden and that the number should not be allowed to increase.

That others, especially local officials, were advancing toward the same opinion may be deduced from their more conservative attitude concerning matters of administration within their control. When possible they restored the hindrances in the way of marriage. The adoption of new ordinances regarding settlement indicates the closer attention now given to paupers and the responsibility for their support. A further impetus in the same direction resulted from the famine which in 1770 visited many parts of the Continent. A series of poor crops of wheat and rye caused a shortage which a generation or two before would have culminated in one of the greatest calamities of all time. It was the potato which saved the situation, and from that date no peasant hesitated to plant it in his garden or welcome it to his table. But many authorities with a prophetic foresight realized that this new dependence might prepare the way for an even greater disaster, and their precautions were accordingly the stricter. Old regulations compelling every commune to keep a magazine filled with grain were revived, and the future was thereafter viewed with more assurance.

These measures were adopted principally in the German kingdoms and principalities. The population history of Great Britain is so closely interwoven with its industrial and imperial expansion that the worries of its agricultural areas had relatively little effect on legislation. France also pursued a course of her own. The French Revolution may, in many respects, be regarded as the breakdown of an economic system that was thoroughly saturated with people whom it could not support. Arthur Young's pages offer evidence to support this view; the *cahiers* sent up to the central government constantly repeated the question, "What are we to do with our sons when land and industry are monopolized by our local tyrants?"; and the members of the Convention who held that a war and a little bloodletting might not be bad for the nation touched on a theme that was to determine many of the fundamental conditions out of which the migration of the next century was to arise.

With the opening of the wars of the French Revolution questions of immediate concern dimmed such fears. In all the countries affected the armies needed man power and food. Every patriot was thankful for the abundance of young men which his country had accumulated, and every acre that was cleared yielded a marketable harvest. The feverish prosperity of the time colored the judgment of critical observers. Again a new era of agricultural expansion was inaugurated; each of the nations was encouraged to self-sufficiency; behind artificial barriers cities swarmed with new manufacturers, and lands that Nature had predestined to lie in waste were put under cultivation.

To Great Britain, Germany and the neutral north, war meant not so much the destruction of lives as the foundation of new families and the stimulation of nearly every line of economic activity. Far different was the situation of France. One army after the other was called up from the villages, sent off to the front, and annihilated on the fields of battle. The peasantry was bled white, and in the last campaigns of Napoleon sixteen-year-old boys filled in the places left vacant by their fathers. From this drain upon her man power France did not recover. During the next century dread of over-population was never to trouble the minds of her rulers, and they were never to witness a multitude of their citizens departing into willing expatriation. But in the neighboring countries conditions were created the consequences of which found no other solution. Fortunately for their social peace a new world was at hand to receive them.

II

THE PEOPLING OF THE COLONIES

T HE TWELVE HUNDRED MILES of coast line stretching northward from Spanish Florida was not the scene of the first British ventures in colonization. Experience elsewhere had already established the practices to be followed. Lawyers of the Crown were skilled in drawing up charters; merchants knew how to promote the sale of company shares; and in every port of the south and west of England courageous adventurers stood ready to embark on any enterprise offering a prospect of excitement and a little gold. As yet, however, no policy had been devised to secure for remote plantations a population of British subjects fitted to reduce the wilderness to cultivation.

The earlier companies organized to trade in the Levant and the European north had evolved many features later adopted by colonizing groups, but these companies had not concerned themselves greatly with matters of personnel. The sailors, commercial agents and officials who had carried on the foreign establishments had depended upon the natives of the country for the ordinary necessities of life. The first attempts made in North America assumed the possibility of using the same system, but it soon became evident that the Indians would not "be contented to serve those that shall with gentleness and humanitie goe about to allure them," as Hakluyt had promised.[1] Moreover, the migrants had only a scanty surplus of corn and meat and on this store no reliance could be placed. Since it was impracticable to transport all supplies from the British Isles, the nature of these new outposts had to be broadened. Successful trade must involve settlement, and settlement could not be left to chance. The transportation of colonists became a vital part of every project of Western planting.

In this indirect way the problem of migration arose. Its solution depended on the judgment and needs of each individual company. When in the course of time the colony as a political body succeeded to the rights of the colony as a trading corporation, it also inherited the privilege of determining its own policy of immigration. Consequently there never was, in the old British Empire, a consistent imperial program of settlement. When the thirteen continental colonies declared their independence, their white inhabitants numbered approximately two and a half millions.[2] Though they were all referred to as "colonials," neither they nor their ancestors had a homogeneous origin. They included prudent heads of families, prisoners transported for major crimes and minor offenses, stray adventurers, military deserters, trading-company servants and bond laborers of a half-dozen different categories. Along with these there were religious sectarians who, individually or in groups, had sought a refuge. In addition, the population embraced the human residue of two rival empires that had disappeared — New Netherland and New Sweden. The history of their coming is a record of confusion that easily loses coherence in the mass of details. But out of the maze there gradually emerges a clear-cut type which was not the product of law or policy but the creation of experience — the individual who could be spared in Europe, who was needed in America: the standard immigrant of the nineteenth century.

If the Virginia and New England settlements had been started fifty years earlier, it is possible that national interest would have injected some semblance of unity into the peopling of the New World. Elizabethan England was troubled by the multitude of its inhabitants. The country

roads and city streets were filled with "sturdy vagabonds."
The poor had multiplied beyond any relief that private
charity could extend. How was the nation to find a vent
for its hungry unemployed? In answer to this question, some
sought to arouse their fellow countrymen to the importance
of undertakings across the sea. Let those whom old England
could not support be the nucleus of a new England in
America, and both old and new would draw strength from the
presence of the other.

But by 1600 the emergency had passed, and colonization
as a remedy had fallen into disrepute. The transition from
arable to pasture, from the raising of grain to the production
of wool, was complete, and the dislocation of population
occasioned by these changes had subsided. The Elizabethan
poor law had provided the parishes with a social stabilizer
which received credit for all the improvement that the times
revealed. Moreover, schemes for the settlement of Ireland,
loudly advertised as cures for overpopulation, had aroused
considerable popular resentment. Thousands of families,
it is true, had been established in the north and west of that
island, but the Irish were hostile, and England was too close
at hand. Hundreds of the settlers were massacred by their
embittered neighbors, and hundreds fled back to the poverty
and safety of their native parishes with stories of hardships
that dampened enthusiasm for similar ventures. Only the
Scots seemed to thrive. For the next century Ulster was a
colony of Scotland, serving as a training school for a race of
pioneers who were to perform hardier exploits beyond the
Atlantic.

The Virginia plantation of 1607 began in an atmosphere
still strongly tinged with the old spirit of romance. Every
petty Indian chief was described as an emperor, and every
squalid village as a city. But the organizers, realizing that
these cities had no riches to loot, believed that whatever

wealth Virginia was to yield must come from the forests and
the subsurface wealth. Therefore, along with the soldiers on
the first expedition, were sent artisans and miners. The terms
were hard, and there was no press of people seeking passage.
Even under the royal charter of 1609, seven years of service,
ruled by military discipline, were required before a settler
could receive a grant of land, the possibilities of which were,
of course, entirely unknown.[3] Captain John Smith, years
later, recorded that it cost "many a forgotten pound to hire
men to go." [4] The disasters of the first expeditions need not
be recounted. Within a few years everyone was disillusioned.
No gold mines had been discovered, no passage to the Pacific
had been traced. The expense of obtaining naval stores from
the pine forests devoured all profit, and the Indians did not
provide the market for English woolens anticipated by many
of the merchant adventurers who had invested in the enterprise. All the original objects of the company had failed.[5]

But in both London and Virginia were men who would not
admit failure. If the territory could not be exploited it could
be developed, and a recognition of the true nature of the
country's resources created an entirely new situation as re-
gards the plan of peopling. The régime of John Smith had
begun, and his communications emphasized the need of carpenters, smiths, masons, husbandmen and "diggers up" of
trees and roots.[6] The bands sent out in 1609 suffered shipwreck and fever, and less than half reached their destination,
but even the gloom engendered by such experiences did not
discourage the leaders. They clung to the land and the people
they possessed, and saw to it that deserters when captured
were shot, hanged or broken on the wheel.[7] Fortunately by
1616 the survivors among the first comers had served their
terms of service, and with the acquisition of their own land
a new spirit became apparent.[8] Most of them, however, still
considered themselves exiles and dreamed of the time when

they could return to England with the profits of their labor.[9] The authorities, no longer possessing any legal claim to their presence, adopted measures more subtle than hanging or breaking on the wheel. They began the introduction of ship-loads of maidens, "whereby the Planters minds may be the faster tyed to Virginia by the bonds of Wyves and children," and thus completed the process of transforming the trading post into a settlement.[10]

Private property and family life influenced the attitude of individuals, but it was tobacco that gave the principal impulse to the extension of settlement. Virginia had discovered a staple richer than gold, with the result that the desire to migrate thither was now one rather to be regulated than fostered.[11] In order to replenish the company's treasury, the policy of "particular plantations" was adopted in 1616–1617: a definite tract of land was granted to organized groups of Englishmen who agreed to settle servants within these "hundreds" at their own expense. Within four years, fifty such patents had been issued, each providing for the transportation of from one hundred to four hundred men.[12] The company itself continued to assist migrants as its means allowed, some for settlement on lands which the company still held, others for the use of the "old planters" who, greatly needing helpers, had no other means of securing them in England. In order to aid the latter, a broadside issued in 1620 promised anyone who would transport a person before 1625 a grant of fifty acres on a "first division" and fifty more on a second.[13]

This last method, known as the head-right system, became the standard technique of immigration into seventeenth-century Virginia. With the dissolution of the Virginia Company in 1625, all these methods lost their sanction; but that of head rights, having demonstrated its value, was immediately reëstablished. Every planter, great or small, who met the conditions, was rewarded for his efforts by a grant of that

which the colony had in abundance but which lacked value
until people had been settled upon it. No longer was immigration financed from the Old World; that obligation had
been assumed by the New.

During the next fifteen years the influx of colonists continued at a gratifying rate. They came not only from England
and Ireland, but also from Bermuda which was beginning to
show signs of overpopulation. Enterprising captains filled
their ships with penniless passengers, carried them to the
Virginia rivers, and there sold them to planters for the cost
of transportation. The planters then filed claim for additional
tracts of fifty acres and set about growing still more tobacco.
As long as the market could buy all that was raised, the process
continued with unabated vigor. Not until the civil war in
England brought economic depression in its train did the
first great wave of immigration subside.

So successful was the head-right policy that in the middle
of the 1630's, when the settlement of Maryland was begun,
it was promptly adopted. In addition to his religious motive,
Lord Baltimore desired the profits his colony might yield
and, in order to secure an income independent of the fluctuations of the tobacco market, he subjected every acre in
private possession to an annual quitrent, small in itself but
aggregating a comfortable fortune. Then with the zeal and
industry that every American land jobber henceforth was to
exhibit he began to dispose of his princely estate. A few personal friends were given land grants without any stipulation
as to the importation of servants; but these "manors" formed
a small part of the total. Ordinary settlers received a hundred
acres each and could get more only by financing the immigration of others.[14] In order to meet the demands of the "tobacco
boom," Englishmen, Irishmen and Welshmen were awarded
grants for the passage of themselves and their companions;
and from Virginia the desertion of bond servants proved so

great as to arouse widespread complaint and protest.[15] By 1640 the shores of Maryland had lost their wilderness appearance and boasted of a thriving commerce and prosperous people.

While the Southern colonies were evolving a policy of immigration, developments in the North were likewise determining the future trend. The Council for New England was not misled by dreams of gold: it sought fish and furs. Until 1620 the few employees who may have wintered along the coast were such temporary residents that their huts cannot be described as settlements. Even when the Pilgrim Fathers disembarked on the shores of Massachusetts Bay and were granted a patent to the land they had occupied, the Council was not encouraged to seek more groups of the same nature. It continued half-heartedly to establish fishing and trading stations until finally in 1628, when in the depths of financial depression, it ceded its choicest territory to the Massachusetts Bay Company which had no doubt as to what it wanted to do.

Now followed the "great migration" of the Puritans. The company had no trouble in finding congregational groups willing to go, and the groups had no trouble in recruiting members. A rage of emigration swept through the eastern and midland counties of England, arousing in the authorities an apprehension which was to be shared by many other local officials of Europe during the next two and a half centuries. The popular interest anticipated most of the features appearing in later periods. The ballad, "Summons to New England," was sung on the streets; a "great giddiness" to depart prevailed; "incredible numbers" sold their lands; and debtors attempted to get away under the pretext of religion.[16] When John Winthrop, Jr., in 1635 passed through Ireland, Scotland and the north of England, he found that the contagion had spread also to these parts; everywhere he stopped, eager inquirers sought him out.[17] In these circumstances the fathers of the colony needed no advertising campaign, and they were so pleased with those who came that in 1633 and 1634 they proclaimed days of thanksgiving for the harvests and for the ships that had brought "persons of spetial use and quality." [18]

The magistrates knew the quality of the arrivals because they scrutinized each individual with painstaking care. From the very beginning their policy was to select from among those who appeared, and this exclusive attitude of New England remained a tradition throughout almost three centuries of immigration. The official records of Massachusetts reveal the basis for this tradition. Some arrivals were sent back to England "as persons unmeete to inhabit here," and the governor was authorized to put on a month's probation anyone he thought not fit "to sit down among us without some trial of them." As the incoming current swelled, bringing in those of less property and weaker orthodoxy, a stricter law forbade a person or town to entertain a stranger longer than three weeks except with special permission.[19] In Rhode Island, both Providence and Portsmouth decreed that only such newcomers should be allowed to remain as were accepted as freemen or inhabitants by a vote of the town.[20] New Haven appointed a committee of townsmen to sit in judgment upon all strangers, and undesirables were not only denied grants of land, but might be "whipped and sent out of the plantation." [21]

Political troubles at home increased the life-giving stream to New England. Every year brought a market to its doors — shiploads of families, well-provided with pounds and shillings, who had to be fed and housed until they learned something about pioneering. Even Virginia found it profitable to send wheat and corn to the Northern settlements. But by 1640 the influx came to an end. The brighter prospects at home, in the words of Winthrop, "caused all men to stay in England in expectation of a new world." [22] The first American crisis

and depression resulted. Money grew scarce, debts went un-
paid, lands and cattle fell to a fourth or a half of their former
value. Disappointed settlers sold their farms and dispersed,
some to England, some to the West Indies, but most to the
"far West" of the day — Long Island and the settlements of
the Dutch.[23] During the succeeding years, when politics in
the home country bred civil strife, discontent and misery
again caused many Englishmen to seek an untroubled refuge
beyond the Atlantic, but the stories of the intolerance of
New England, everywhere prevalent, caused them to favor a
place where clericalism (from which they also suffered in
England) did not dominate all the affairs of life.

Virginia and Maryland reaped the benefit of this decision.
They did not feel the pressure of the times as acutely as
New England because their prosperity stemmed from the
sale of tobacco. For about a decade the two colonies remained
loyal to the Crown, and on their isolated plantations many
refugees found peace from England's confusion. Were they
"Cavaliers"? One of the fondest traditions of American
genealogy cherishes the view that families of noble blood
flocked to Virginia to become the ancestors of the *ante-bellum*
aristocracy. Critical research has shorn most of them of their
coats-of-arms and left them what they actually were: merchants, farmers and country gentlemen.[24] Their numbers
were considerable. Between 1642 and 1664 the population
of Virginia rose from ten thousand to thirty-eight thousand,
of which not more than half could have been due to natural
increase.[25] The warrants that have been preserved show a
rapid taking up of land in this period; [26] and the Virginia
articles of capitulation in 1651 provided that all who had
served the king and taken refuge in the colony were to be
"free from all dangers and punishments whatever." [27]

Added to those who came voluntarily were those who were
sent. How early the practice of dumping undesirables on

the colonies began is lost in the uncertainty that enshrouds the identity of most of the early immigrants. In 1617 and 1618 the Privy Council authorized the transportation of prisoners to Virginia, but how many came is unknown.[28] Captain John Smith records laconically, "some did chuse to be hanged ere they would go thither, and were." [29] In 1620 children and vagrants were gathered up under the apprenticeship statute of Elizabeth and shipped off.[30] Even some of the maidens, whose romantic mission it was to ameliorate life for the settlers, were "impressed" in small parishes.[31] But for the next thirty years no further mention of such forced migration appears. Then in 1651 the Council of State ordered that the Scots taken at the Battle of Worcester should be deported to America. Two years later a hundred Irish Tories were sent to Virginia, and in 1654 certain other prisoners hostile to the Commonwealth were shipped to the colonies.[32] The device of sending military prisoners was soon extended to rid the country of other classes whose rapid multiplication was adding to the social unrest. On various occasions from 1653 to 1656, the authorities were directed to apprehend vagrants, rogues, paupers, idle persons and those who were "lewd and dangerous" and to treat with merchants for their passage overseas.[33]

The reception accorded these exiles varied with their character and the current demand for labor.[34] The Scotch soldiers were welcomed even in New England where, as many family histories reveal, they not only worked at humble employments, but became husbands of Puritan daughters. At about the same time, however, appeared another group of whom no one had a good opinion. In 1655 they reached Massachusetts Bay, "a cursed set of heretickes lately risen up in the world"; [35] and the General Court ordered that those persons known as Quakers should be sent back whence they came — many to Barbados. When they reappeared the next year, a new law levied a fine of one hundred pounds upon any shipmaster who carried them. Further regulations proved necessary when they undertook to enter overland. The loss of ears proving ineffective, the Quaker intruders were banished on pain of death. Because some of them "presumptorily" remained or returned to the jurisdiction, two of the most persistent were executed.[36] Virginia also felt it necessary to take action, the records listing many measures which, had they been applied in the North, would have been attributed to "Puritan intolerance." Quakers were ordered to depart; they were whipped and fined; and in June, 1658, a "general persecution" was directed.[37] Only in Rhode Island were they safe. Their zeal for martyrdom is suggested by the statement of the Rhode Island officials in 1658 "that they begin to loath this place, for that they are not opposed by the civill authority." [38]

The twenty years during which the colonists were left very largely to their own devices did not affect their immigration policy apart from the strengthening of New England exclusiveness. The Restoration in 1660 began an era in which the Crown sought to strengthen its control over the Empire, but no governmental program of overseas settlement was undertaken. The new Stuarts were as poor as the old, with the result that they preferred, for the time at least, to leave to their subjects all enterprises involving investment. The confused population history between 1660 and 1690 can be clarified by considering it from three points of view: first, the continued growth of the colonial areas already planted; second, the nature of the population acquired by the conquest of New Netherland in 1664; third, the settlement of new colonies.

New England made little effort to increase its inhabitants. Winthrop told a correspondent that laboring men, artisans and their children could find good employment and named a sea captain in London who from his knowledge of the country could give all the necessary information.[39] But the Bay Colony authorities showed little eagerness, and in 1680 Governor Bradstreet reported from Boston that few settlers had arrived in several years. He added that since the Massachusetts coast was entirely appropriated the trend was towards the south, and he warned that the interior country could be subdued only by seasoned and trained native residents.[40] At about the same time Connecticut declared that the immigrants into the colony from Great Britain did not number more than one or two a year.[41] In 1684 an Irishman was in Boston looking for a place for a hundred families, but the records do not indicate any official encouragement.[42] All the evidence confirms the opinion of an English merchant who described the New Englanders in 1689 as "a very home-bred people" and "exceeding wedded to their own way." [43]

Nevertheless there occurred a gradual infiltration of individuals whose coming was so unobtrusive that few New Englanders were aware of it. Desertion from vessels in the harbors was a common practice. The drain from the merchant marine and navy during the wars between the English and the Dutch reached dangerous proportions, and the refusal of the local authorities to restore the fugitives upon demand was one of the aggravating policies that the British government chalked up against the Bay Colony.[44] Just as ineffectual were the attempts to stop the leakage from the large fishing fleet which every year set out from the western ports of England for the Newfoundland Banks. Once the season's catch was secured, the captains willingly left behind members of the crew whose services were no longer needed, and these men readily found opportunities to ship with the colonial fishermen to Maine and Cape Ann. Though the Council for Foreign Plantations required every skipper to bring back to Britain as many men as he had taken out, he could always plead that the missing seamen were deserters who had escaped into the woods.[45] The loss was permanent, a governor reported, because they "marry in New England and make it their home." [46]

As earlier, Virginia and Maryland received arrivals of all descriptions. Like the Commonwealth, the Restoration régime continued to deport vagabonds and criminals to America. Virginia was the reluctant recipient of most of these undesirables, and the Crown refused to respect any local law or decree aiming to exclude them.[47] Almost as objectionable from the colonial point of view were the children and youths spirited away by professional abductors. Such persons, however, were probably fewer than the complaints suggest, since many who had agreed to sell their services in return for transportation considered it advantageous, when opportunity arose, to claim that they had been forcibly carried off.[48]

The comparative ease with which both these classes were absorbed indicates the lively demand for labor in the tobacco colonies. The head-right system was employed with such vigor that a specialized type of merchant captain arose who brought shiploads of servants to the river landings where he negotiated with the planters for their disposal. After the planter paid the passage and arranged the terms of service, he applied for the head warrants to which he was entitled. Very often, however, it was labor more than land that he desired, in which case the merchant would accept the warrants in payment of the passage, and either take over the land himself as an investment or dispose of the warrants at a higher price to others.[49] A cumbersome system at best, it resulted in many abuses and frauds. Yet it did provide these colonies with the cheap labor they needed. All parties concerned hoped for an imperial regulation of the trade, together with a clarification of the British statutes which occasionally punished merchants for offenses they had innocently committed.[50] But apart from local provincial laws no labor code was forthcoming.

When the Dutch Governor of New Netherland capitulated in 1664, he handed over to the British Empire not only the valuable soil between the Hudson and the Delaware, but also several thousand inhabitants whose descendants were to be both numerous and influential. Like its English prototypes, the Dutch West India Company had been obliged to formulate a population policy. It did not, however, provide a means by which the company servants or soldiers might become independent landowners; after they served their time a return to Holland was the normal sequence. In order to develop its agricultural resources and protect its frontier, the company devised the patroon system. This plan worked satisfactorily; but since it did not encourage a large influx of Hollanders, the growth in numbers owed more to the often illegal intrusions of New Englanders who settled in Long Island and many of the short, fertile valleys east of the Hudson. In like fashion, the thriving commercial city of New Amsterdam drew to itself Yankee traders together with merchants from every island in the West Indies and from most of the Atlantic ports of Europe.

Diversity of population rather than numbers distinguished this annexation. New Netherland had already absorbed New Sweden and, although probably no more than five hundred Swedes and Finns were involved, their pioneering had prepared the way for the unprecedented migration soon to follow the founding of Penn's commonwealth. Frenchmen were also present in the colony. Some of them had drifted down from Canada to enjoy a freer atmosphere, others had come up from the Caribbean as the commercial connection with the islands grew closer. A congregation of Portuguese Jews, a community of Spanish traders, a group of Scotch interlopers who made the town the base of their expeditions, a sprinkling of Norwegians and Danes formerly in the Dutch service, and occasional Bohemians, Poles, Germans and Italians (the residue of Stuyvesant's disbanded army) added to the ethnic variety. Besides, many Negro slaves belonged to the households of the prosperous, and free blacks and mulattoes already formed a special class. The eighteen languages spoken in New Amsterdam remain the best early illustration of its cosmopolitan character.[51]

Proprietary governments usually encouraged rapid colonization; but when New Netherland was bestowed upon the Duke of York, he chose to pursue a different course. All those directly concerned with the administration of the province realized the desirability of overawing the alien and often unfriendly inhabitants by fostering the settlement of loyal subjects. Some even urged the expulsion or scattering of the Dutch and the break-up of the patroonships.[52] The Duke of York, however, following the example of his royal brother, made gifts of millions of acres to his supporters and friends to pay off his debts. Almost without exception the recipients considered their new possessions as investments which would increase in value with the improvements they hoped their neighbors would make. In the circumstances not only was effective assistance lacking, but independent settlers found it almost impossible to purchase the lands they wanted. Accordingly, the growth of population was slow, resulting largely from the natural increase in the older settlements and in the city of New York.

In the lands east of the Delaware the story was otherwise. Here Lords Berkeley and Carteret set up the provinces of East and West Jersey which in time passed into the hands of others, many of them Quakers. The new proprietors, while interested in the persecuted members of their sect, sought an immediate financial return as well. The region was widely advertised and, in both old and New England, companies, not unlike those which had founded Boston and New Haven, undertook the development of the most promising locations. From the settlements made at Trenton, Newark and Amboy population spread rapidly into the adjacent territory.[53] English Quakers who were inclined to emigrate naturally preferred these provinces; some Scots who dreamed of a colony of their own also made a beginning on the Raritan; [54] while the inflow from New York was so large that the governor of that province found it a useful argument against those who wanted to break up the large estates lying unoccupied along the Hudson.[55]

The newer colonies founded in the period of the Restoration were also confided to proprietors. Of these the great domain of Carolina was the first. After the example of Virginia and Maryland, the head-right system was adopted; but John Locke's cumbersome scheme of government doomed the servants to a lifetime as subservient "leetmen," and thereby eliminated the expectation of achieving personal independence after an apprenticeship of forced labor. As a result, the proprietors met great difficulty in recruiting migrants. Turning to Ireland, they discovered from their agents there that emigration was something that seemed "new and foreign" to the people and "they are loth to leave the smoke of their cabins." [56] Moreover employment existed for all at home. Consequently the first expeditions were manned by persons who, to judge by the official accounts, were nothing but lazy scoundrels.[57]

Only after the Carolina government had been modified did the colony succeed in securing bands of Scots and Quakers as settlers.[58] By this time, however, the proprietors had discovered a source of population closer at hand; and these seasoned pioneers were so obviously superior that plans for importing Europeans were temporarily put aside. A revolutionary transformation was taking place in the British West Indies and, like all economic overturns, it unsettled the people and made them eager for a new start in life.

No history of colonial population is complete which does not recognize the many connections that bound mainland and islands together. In a sense, each formed a way station for migration to the other. Disappointed settlers on the continent moved south to the Caribbean; in larger numbers, traders and planters who failed to prosper in the tropics crossed over to the mainland. These islands enjoyed an early prosperity that excited the envy of the other colonies. It was not difficult to secure capital or labor for their exploitation. Investors soon grew rich and servants quickly achieved economic independence.[59] Through the importation of Irish pork and grain a commercial exchange was established which facilitated the immigration of Irishmen; a Jesuit who visited St. Christopher in 1643 estimated their number at twenty thousand.[60] During war periods the population of the islands increased even more rapidly. Royalists and gentry found a safe refuge there, and prisoners taken in battle were shipped there from England with such regularity that the expression, "to Barbados a man," was used for this type of punishment." [61]

Since the prosperity of war time had made possible the support of all these people, peace necessitated some readjustment. This process was the more difficult because Barbados had meanwhile begun the culture of sugar cane. So profitable did it prove that every acre which could be so planted was put to use. The new crop involved different methods of agriculture, a different system of landholding and a different organization of labor. Small farms were thrown together into large plantations and slaves took the place of white servants. The Negroes, numbering sixty-four hundred in 1643, totaled over fifty thousand in 1666, and for nearly every one who came, an Englishman, Scotchman or Irishman had to depart.[62] Some went to Jamaica, though its uncertain future discouraged most. Others found a welcome in the Dutch and French islands, a migration which the English authorities sought to hinder. Every year the condition of the small landowner grew more hopeless.

Such was the situation when the Carolina proprietors began their search for people. The Barbadians, following the progress of events, made known their active interest. But it was not until the other experiments had failed that the proprietors sent a vessel to Barbados and a proclamation announced the terms on which lands were available. As a result, the vessel was kept busy transporting to Carolina not only small farmers, but also men whose capital and experience made them doubly welcome. Year after year the process continued until Barbados, having developed into one vast slave-cultivated sugar plantation, had caused Carolina to be stocked with hardy settlers whose prickly individualism proved a disturbing influence in the early years of its history.[63]

The Crown made one further magnificent gift, that to William Penn. When Penn began his colonization in 1681, he had a considerable fund of experience on which to draw. A shrewd businessman, he required quitrents as a source of income, but the eagerness of Quakers and others to remove to Pennsylvania made it unnecessary to adopt the head-right system. Lands were granted to settlers according to their needs. The migration of a few thousand Friends was less noteworthy than the fact that they came from other countries as well as from England. This event foreshadowed the new phase of population development into which the colonies were entering. Among the first arrivals were Quakers from Ireland and Wales and Mennonites from the valley of the upper Rhine. Their successful pioneering served as the opening wedge for multitudes of their fellow countrymen.[64]

Pennsylvania profited greatly from the French-English hostilities which began in 1689. Lying in a comparatively sheltered position, it attracted settlers living on the exposed frontiers of neighboring colonies. Many such persons fled from the Albany region of New York where the French menace was particularly threatening. The authorities in New York found it difficult to secure recruits for their forces, as most of those who could be spared from agriculture had hastened to neighboring provinces. Virginia and Maryland reported that their young men, too, had gone to Pennsylvania. The pacifist nature of the Quaker government may also have proved a magnet, but lack of military enthusiasm was not the only reason. The war had interrupted commercial connections with England, tobacco remained unsold, servants and sons were unemployed. Little wonder that the reputation which the Pennsylvania lands had acquired acted as a lure, so great, in fact, that privates in the British army sent to America deserted to the Quaker communities, and Maryland was obliged to maintain a patrol along its western border to apprehend deserters from the fleet in Baltimore.[65]

Pennsylvania's success in attracting propertied Europeans and landless Americans was an important factor leading to the change in policies of settlement which began in the late seventeenth century. The period between 1689 and 1713, embracing two wars, disturbed the commercial development of the colonies, turned their attention increasingly from the sea to the land, and prompted a redistribution of population which helped to fill in unoccupied areas and establish a base for a new frontier advance. Thereafter the population needs were different, and methods formerly necessary and effective yielded to policies better suited to the times.

The usefulness of the head-right system had already been outlived. When a planter paid for the transportation of servants, he was more interested in their labor than in the lands to which they brought him a claim. The lands now available were remote from his cultivated estates and difficult of access, and their ownership entailed a greater payment of quitrents. When the market for tobacco was active, he willingly bore the cost of passage if slave labor was not available. In such cases, the claims to land were sometimes forgotten or, more often, disposed of recklessly to merchants and officials who carried on a lucrative trade in their further sale.[66] Although this traffic was legal, it defeated the end for which the system had originally been created, that of fostering the speedy development of lands and resources. The land jobbers held on to the acquired warrants as an investment for the future, or demanded prices that were likely to be beyond the reach of servants who had worked out their time, sailors who wanted to leave the sea, or farmers who had come up from the Caribbean.

When Maryland and Virginia after investigating conditions learned of the haphazard way in which warrants were issued and the many fraudulent claims that were entered, they abolished head rights, substituting therefor a system of cash sale.[67] This action separated land policy from labor policy. The situation of labor was henceforth conditioned principally by the institution of slavery, which had taken possession of the tobacco areas and was now bringing in the first large influx of Negroes, and by the redemptioner system, which became the characteristic mode of individual white immigration.

The redemptioner system was nothing but that of head rights, shorn of the bonus of land to the planter. The character of the immigrants was the same, the captains and merchants engaged in the trade were the same, the terms of service were the same. The only difference lay in the fact that now the one who paid for the transportation received for his outlay merely a claim upon the labor of the bound redemptioner. When the term of service ended, the latter was free to become a paid laborer, or to purchase lands if he had accumulated sufficient funds.

Each of the colonies, however, still possessed an unrealized fortune in the vast stretches of wilderness country. Many reasons rendered the speedy occupation of these areas desirable. Settlement provided the best frontier protection; it constituted an effective argument in the confused boundary disputes; it tapped the lucrative fur trade. Since a slow occupation by freed servants and farmers' sons might involve a loss of existing advantages, early in the eighteenth century all the colonial governments experimented with schemes of frontier group settlement, granting special privileges in land and taxation and often defraying the costs of transportation and temporary support. But to enroll native colonists in such ventures was hardly possible; and since England was no longer considered overpopulated, organized plans to secure settlers there met with disfavor. Consequently the efforts turned to other countries, making the encouragement of non-English subjects a distinctive feature of the new immigration policy.

Hitherto foreigners, including even Scots, Welsh and Irish, had generally been unwelcome. The Virginia Company had made use of aliens skilled in trades — Dutch, French, Italians, Germans, Poles — even a "John Martin, the Persian," appears in the early records.[68] But when a group of Walloons in 1621 petitioned to enter the colony, the request was granted on condition that they should not exceed three hundred and that they conform to the Church of England.[69] Not until 1649 did Maryland allow any but English and Irish to hold land, and these were denied any political rights until 1674.[70] Typical of the exclusive spirit of the time are the terms of the grant made to Sir Robert Heath in 1630 when he planned the first colony of Carolina. No aliens were to be allowed except by special permission, and many certificates regarding religion and good conduct were demanded.[71] Toward the close of the century, with the increasing number of Irish immigrants, Maryland suspended for a time their further importation as servants; and in 1690 the Council of Virginia decreed that no more than twenty Irishmen were "to be sold on any one river." [72]

The history of the French Huguenot migration well illustrates the attitude of the seventeenth century. Between 1660 and 1690 groups of them were allowed to settle in every colony from Massachusetts to South Carolina. It was believed they would introduce the cultivation of the vine and the manufacture of silk, and their Protestantism removed one of the principal prejudices against foreigners. Yet only in South Carolina, where the Huguenots chiefly settled and an early arrival placed them on the same economic footing as the English, did they find fortune and peace. Elsewhere suspicion and even violence greeted them, while prohibitions against their participation in trade worked a severe handicap.[73] During the war the ill will intensified, and probably contributed to the rapid amalgamation which soon destroyed most of the characteristics of the Gallic stock.

While the British colonists were turning their war-time patriotism against the French in their midst, another large group of Continental immigrants made their appearance. The history of the Palatines had been not unlike that of the Huguenots. When the land of these German Protestants was ravaged by the armies of Louis XIV, many of the refugees fled to England which at the time stood forth as the protector of Protestants. Although Queen Anne welcomed them politely, their presence in London proved a problem for which the ministers of state could find no local solution. But the ministry recalled the complaints of the Governor of New York that the lands of the province were being deserted by settlers and its resources lying undeveloped. In America, moreover, the Germans would at least be out of the way. So in 1708–1709 naval vessels carried to New York several thousand Palatines who were placed in camps along the Hudson and ordered to cut down trees and prepare stores for the Queen's navy.[74]

The misfortunes and wanderings of these pioneers constitute the heroic chapter characteristic of the beginning of any national migration. Their trail led from the Hudson to the Mohawk and from the Mohawk over the hills and down the Susquehanna to the Pennsylvania frontier.[75] At each pause in the migration a substantial residue remained, and served as a nucleus to which future comers would be attached. Those who continued on to Pennsylvania joined their praises of the new Canaan with those of the Mennonites who had preceded them. Henceforth family and community ties might draw some Germans to New York, but the vast bulk found in Pennsylvania their Promised Land.

The Peace of Utrecht in 1713 inaugurated a generation of European peace which enabled the colonies of all the powers to prosper. The English Parliament gave new encouragements to industry and trade, with fertilizing effects on both sides of the Atlantic. A commercial empire took shape which created exclusive markets for the surplus products of each colonial section. New England fish went to the Mediterranean and the Caribbean, plantation tobacco filled the pipes of Great Britain, and the fertile valleys of the Hudson, the Delaware, the Shenandoah and the Potomac fed the sugar producers of the West Indies. Since the New England households were full of sons, and Negro slaves supplied the labor needs of the plantation provinces, it was to the middle region that the main current of immigration turned.

This immigration, for the most part, followed the forms already established. The redemptioner trade now assumed a regularized aspect, with recruiting agents assembling gangs

of young men in the European ports and the colonial legis-
latures fixing the conditions of the indentureship.[76] The
planting of frontier group settlements continued to be made
under the supervision of individual colonies, immediate
needs and circumstances determining the fate of each. To
list these ventures would add nothing to a survey of the development of policy. The significance of the period between
1713 and 1742 from this point of view rests on a consideration
of the extent to which each nationality contributed to the
incoming tide.

Not many Englishmen came. Religious oppression was no
longer a spur to migration, and industrial expansion at home
absorbed whatever hands agriculture could not employ.
There were, however, some merchants, agents and factors
sent to the colonies by London houses engaged in the importation of American products. An occasional manufacturer
set up a workshop. The Society for the Propagation of the
Gospel sent over personnel to conduct its churches and
schools. Professional men seeking a more promising field
for their talents brought law and science to the cities.
Younger sons of the rural gentry, impelled by necessity or
adventure, transplanted branches of old families and laid
the foundations of new fortunes. This influx, being composed of Englishmen, attracted little attention; but continuing from year to year, it added strength to the original
colonial stock.

After the Act of Union in 1708 the Scots proceeded to
make the most of the empire which they felt they had acquired. The Scotch merchant, customs officer, clergyman
and schoolmaster were familiar figures in the eighteenth-
century colonial world. These emigrants were Lowlanders
who had already absorbed much of the life to the south.
The Highlanders, living their own independent existence,
showed no interest in emigration until the repression fol-

lowing the ill-fated rising of 1715 caused a group of the pardoned rebels to seek a retreat in the Carolina mountains. Their number was not great nor was their colonizing success noteworthy.[77] Nonetheless, adjustment to a new environment did not prove difficult; in the Indian trade, and as frontier scouts and professional backwoodsmen, they earned some of the renown that tradition has lavished upon others.

Not unlike these two varieties of Scotchmen was the traditional backwoodsman who called himself an Irishman, though most of his blood was Scotch. For a century these Scots had dwelt in north Ireland where they had farmed their acres, woven the Empire's linen and reared large families. Then, in 1716–1717, crop failures and the first fear of cotton competition initiated an exodus from Ulster which took the form of organized companies in which clergymen were active. The ecclesiastical connection of many of these men with New England divines caused the Massachusetts and New Hampshire authorities to temper their feelings toward "foreigners" and to establish a half-dozen congregations in townships to which they were given title.[78] The common folk, however, did not share the official cordiality. As individuals the Ulstermen received a resentful welcome, even to the extent of the burning of their Presbyterian meetinghouse in Worcester.[79]

A far different fate befell other congregations which at the same time had been induced to try the Quaker commonwealth. As a result, the influx of Ulstermen into Pennsylvania soon surpassed that of any other nationality. The peculiar land relationships existing in the north of Ireland caused a periodical "falling in of leases," and whenever this occurred an extensive exodus of families took place, endowing the migratory movement with its wavelike character. The redemptioner system, acting continuously, also carried off a stream of young men, the process being facilitated by the export trade in flaxseed from Philadelphia and Newcastle, Delaware, to Belfast and Londonderry. Maryland and New Jersey offered the same advantages as Pennsylvania. In consequence, these colonies became the seat of a new Ulster whence in time sons and grandsons started off for the valley of Virginia and the Carolina back country.[80]

The term "Irishman" was used so generally by contemporaries to describe an Ulsterman that it is difficult to distinguish those who were of Catholic Irish lineage. Shipping records reveal an increasing number of colonial vessels sailing to the southern ports of the island, but after unloading their fish, timber and stores, most of these boats cleared for the West Indies to secure a return cargo. Though with them perhaps went a south Irish youth to act as tutor or overseer on the insular plantations, only a few of these continued on to the American mainland. The Newfoundland fisheries also caused stray individuals to reach the coast of Maine and the interior of northern New England. But in the first half of the eighteenth century, the Catholic Irishman was a comparative rarity in the continental colonies.

In somewhat similar fashion, the adjective "German" — or, more often, "Dutch" — was applied to two racial elements, one from Germany and the other from Switzerland. Group migration characterized this inflow because the governments concerned, eager to end the sectarian controversies raging in southern Germany and Switzerland, relaxed their stringent emigration restrictions. Between 1720 and 1740 several of these dissenting congregations transferred bodily to the Pennsylvania, Virginia, Carolina and Georgia frontiers, in some instances with the help of imperial funds and colonial subsidies. Thus the Moravians, Schwenckfelders, Inspirationalists and Mennonites found their way to America. Through their willingness to bear hardships, and the competence of their leaders, they overcame the difficulties of pioneering, and their success strengthened the appeal of the American colonies for their countrymen.

As with the Ulstermen, the redemptioner system played a part. In the case of the Germans and Swiss, this business fell into the hands of Dutch merchants and shipping brokers whose attention had first been directed to its possibilities by the contracts for passage made with congregations. Very soon the traffic acquired an ill repute, due largely to the distance separating Amsterdam and Rotterdam from the communities where the passengers were secured. Advertisement and solicitation proved necessary — tasks performed by traveling agents, called "Newlanders," whose fabulous stories of America entered into the local folklore. Their efforts kept the current moving in spite of the repeated warnings of officials and realists.

The war breaking out between England and Spain in 1739 inaugurated another generation of conflict, though not until 1742, when France was involved, did the commerce of the colonies with northern Europe suffer real inconvenience. Then the migration of settlers came to an end and, except for the interlude of peace from 1749 to 1753, did not resume until the final defeat of France in the Seven Years' War led to the greatest of all colonial migrations. This war, like its predecessor, marks both the beginning and the end of an era, and produced changes in population policy to conform with the new needs. During the heat of the conflict foreigners lost favor in the colonies, notably the Germans whose strange language and customs and whose indifference to the outcome of the war excited patriotic reprisals. The danger of colonies within colonies became apparent, with the result that henceforth public aid to immigration in the form of funds or lands ceased.

The redemptioner system, on the other hand, entered its period of greatest usefulness. After the sharp economic readjustment following the peace of 1763 times turned prosperous again. The expansion of commerce, shipbuilding, agriculture, lumbering, transportation and manufacturing required additional man power. The response was immediate. Workers crowded the Atlantic ships, eager to bind themselves to temporary servitude for the rewards that would ensue.[81] At the same time, propertied families were lured overseas by the prospects of real-estate bargains in the lands being opened to the west. During the years 1770–1773, when the political difficulties with the mother country slumbered, this movement was especially brisk. Among the Englishmen whose rejection of conciliation led to the break in 1775 were those who saw in the rapid mounting of the colonial population a threat to imperial security and who believed that, unless firmness should now be shown, the child would soon be too strong for parental discipline. The year 1776 brought the Declaration of Independence; and until the British disaster at Yorktown in 1781, the unsettled conditions discouraged further immigration.

III

THE FIRST AMERICANIZATION

EVEN BEFORE the preliminary peace treaty of 1782 had
been signed, in fact before the last battle had been
fought, the broken ties of Atlantic commercial life
were beginning to reknit. Though trade between Great
Britain and her rebelling colonies was still illegal, Irishmen
who since 1775 had themselves been smoldering with revolt
willingly violated decrees so easy to evade, and Scotchmen,
anticipating the upswing of business certain to follow the
final peace, hastened to plant themselves and their wares
beyond the Atlantic. Trading vessels off the northern coasts
of Scotland and Ireland smuggled men and goods aboard;
and when they had escaped the patrols and the privateers of
the Atlantic, the passengers connived with American officials
to allow them on shore in spite of local legislation. Travelers
from the Continent were less fortunate because the British
fleet effectively guarded the channel routes.

As in the prewar years, these emigrants of 1781 and 1782
consisted of farmers, traders and redemptioners. It was the
economic incentive rather than an interest in the fledgling
nation that spurred them on. But when the peace of 1783
was formally announced, a wave of enthusiasm for the new
republic spread through England, causing many a yeoman
family to migrate to Kentucky, Vermont, New York or Pennsylvania. The other British peoples also caught the spirit;
and in 1784 and 1785 a movement, comparable in size to
that of 1770–1773, was under way.

The migrants had assumed that patriots who had defended
the rights of man would welcome the oppressed of the old

country; but they learned differently. Lands and privileges won by blood and treasure were not to be shared too freely with belated colonists from overseas. Other factors helped to bring about a sharp decline of immigration about 1786. The Northwest land ordinance adopted in 1785 gave little promise of a generous policy; [1] Indian hostilities threatened the frontier from Lake Erie to the mouth of the Ohio; financial distress and bankruptcies attended the unsold importations of European goods; and Parliament, aroused by the loss of man power that the migration portended, prohibited the recruiting and transportation of redemptioners. [2]

One racial element from the Continent added to the ethnic variety of the new republic as a direct legacy of the war itself. [3] During the course of the struggle the British government had employed nearly thirty thousand mercenaries, mostly from Hesse-Cassel and Brunswick. The American authorities induced some of them to desert through offers of land grants. Others of the Hessians, as they were indiscriminately called, decided to cast their fortunes with the foe when taken prisoners of war. Still others remained when peace came, or returned after going back to Europe with their companies. Exactly how many became permanent residents of the United States cannot be determined. Though it is known that approximately twelve thousand five hundred of the total number never went back to Germany, some of these had died of wounds and disease and others settled in Canada. But the evidence indicates that the majority stayed on in the land of whose opportunities they had learned from direct observation as soldiers. As peaceable invaders, however, they did not flock together, but scattered widely among the German communities already established.

The formation of the Constitution in 1787 raised the question whether a strong central authority, endowed with lands and charged with regulating commerce, would rise above the conflicting state rivalries and seek to increase the population by a positive encouragement of immigration. One project was soon under way which suggested that such hopes might materialize. Under the land ordinance of 1785 an extensive grant had been made to a company of Ohio Associates who, instead of competing with the neighboring Ohio Company for settlers from the seaboard states, turned to Europe. Hoping to facilitate matters by selling their lands in exchange for bonds that had been floated to finance the American Revolution, they chose France as the particular field for operations. Joel Barlow, sent to Paris as an agent, fostered the establishment of a company composed of Frenchmen who purchased a town site upon the Ohio and soon were deep in plans for their projected city of Gallipolis.[4]

When the Constitution went into effect in 1789 Congress hastened to pass such legislation as was immediately needed. Included were a naturalization law, which merely embodied previous colonial practice,[5] and a quarantine law, adopted solely as a health precaution.[6] Naturalization and quarantine might have been parts of a far-reaching program, but such was not the case. When Hamilton sat down, however, to draw up his reports on lands, public credit and manufactures, he could not avoid a conscious or unconscious decision as to a population policy for the Union. These documents, composed before the Federalist-Republican quarrel made the question of immigration a partisan issue, reflected the author's long-range views.

The mode of disposing of the lands was determined by the condition of the treasury. Since the new government had no fortune but the millions of acres of public domain, the prudent Secretary rejected the suggestion that the promise of a family grant be used to attract thousands of Europeans. Though the possessions were extensive, a few generations of native-born Americans would soon exhaust them; better to sell them at a price sufficient to replenish the official coffers and to insure that the settlers would have ample capital to tide over the first critical months. Not until the homestead act of 1862 did the government return to the principle discarded in these early days.

A different situation confronted industry. Alexander Hamilton's idea of a nation independent of the workshops of Europe at once raised the question of how to offset the inadequate supply of labor for hire by inducing foreign artisans to cast in their lot with the infant republic. Many pleas came to the Secretary's attention. Individual workers in England and Ireland, describing their desperate plight, begged him to provide means for transporting them and their families to America.[7] Let the navy, wrote others, carry the workers free of charge; or let an export tax on tobacco provide a fund with which to subsidize a merchant fleet for this purpose.[8] How seriously Hamilton considered these proposals it is impossible to say.

There was another side to the matter which certain of his American correspondents emphatically presented. They reported their experience that artisans whose coming had to be subsidized usually did not possess the skill which they claimed; that they were lazy at their tasks; and that, when once acclimated, they were apt to try industrial pioneering for themselves.[9] Evidently the recital of these opinions carried weight, for Hamilton in his report ignored all schemes involving a subsidy.[10] So the United States began its career with no encouragement to immigrants except that offered by its opportunities, and with no barriers except those confronting native and foreigner alike.

Events in Europe rather than in America governed the nature and size of the early immigration under the Constitution. A few months after Washington took office, the French people were in revolt; in a year western Europe was at war;

and by 1793 Great Britain had joined the conflict. The Atlantic was no longer a free highway of commerce. From that time until 1815 the politics of the United States centered about neutrality, impressment, proposals for economic sanctions and, finally, war. In the circumstances the flow of migration was determined, not by the opportunities of an undeveloped continent, but by the fortunes of the great contest. Political refugees of high degree, young men fleeing from conscription, peasants and yeomen flying from bloodshed, destruction and taxation, crossed the ocean, usually in haste and with no other thought than that any change would be for the better. It was a motley procession. The passengers of one season bore little resemblance in nationality or in social status to those of the year before. From a study of these twenty-five years there emerges no generalization valid for more than half a decade.

Following the outbreak of the French Revolution, half a million *emigrés* — lords and ladies, clergymen and conservatives — found shelter in the Netherlands and in the German principalities along the Rhine, where they hovered beside the French border confident that the Parisian mob would soon spend its fury, or disperse at the first show of force by the Continental monarchs. Instead, the revolution widened; and the mob was disciplined into an army which for a quarter of a century kept Europe in turmoil. The *emigrés*, obliged to resume their travels, sought more distant lands where family and property might be secure. Here they were joined in the succeeding months and years by more recent exiles, often humble in origin, who from being the rulers on one day found themselves the next, by a turn of the wheel of politics, in the shadow of the guillotine.

At the beginning of the troubles in the summer of 1789, many directed their thoughts toward the United States. Gouverneur Morris, then in Paris as the agent of some

American landowners, was besieged with requests for information and advice. He entered willingly into the plans which were soon under way, but no immediate action followed.[11] Two ships loaded with colonists were already crossing the sea to found the town of Gallipolis on the banks of the Ohio. If news of the settlers' experience proved encouraging, enthusiasm would sweep aside all obstacles.[12] Five hundred thousand Frenchmen, it was said, would follow the pioneers to the West; a new epoch in American colonization would begin. All hopes, however, were soon dissipated, for the Gallipolis project failed. In America it was mismanaged; its legal status was dubious; the settlers fell into the hands of sharpers. The six hundred Parisians who reached the Ohio survived in spite of fevers, unaccustomed labor and an Indian war.[13] But none of the contemporary schemes could overcome the pessimism excited by the fiasco.

Henceforth the flight of Frenchmen was an individual or a family matter. Most of the refugees were accustomed to official society and, possessing some modest remnants of their previous wealth, did not need to seek immediate employment. For the most part they flocked to Philadelphia, then the seat of government. Observers looking for the picturesque and the dramatic found rich material for their pens: noble ladies who conducted pensions for their fellow *emigrés*, and counts teaching awkward Quaker youths how to fence and dance. But the majority engaged in no occupation but that of quenching their nostalgia through a lively social life that reproduced a miniature Versailles.[14] Louis Philippe, later the "citizen king," held court in his residence on Fifth Street; Talleyrand increased his knowledge of intrigue and human nature during his two years' sojourn; and Brillat-Savarin, the great epicure, decided after a few months' experience in a boarding house to dedicate his life to improving the noble art of cooking.

But the body of Frenchmen included many whose background was not that of Paris or Versailles. The uprising in the homeland had had its reverberations in the West Indies. The Negroes of the French colony of Haiti rose in revolt, spreading bloodshed and destruction in their wake. The whites who escaped fled to the coast where they commandeered merchant vessels or embarked in any boats they could find for the only shore which guaranteed safety. In a few days they landed in Charleston, Norfolk, Baltimore, Philadelphia or New York. Lacking money and terrified by the scenes they had witnessed, they presented a pitiful spectacle. Since no existing private charities could provide for such numbers, additional measures of relief were organized. Besides the funds subscribed in various states and cities, Congress appropriated twenty thousand dollars. Altogether probably a quarter of a million was distributed.[15]

Americans were amazed at the ease with which these Frenchmen accommodated themselves to their new life. In Philadelphia they were the gayest of the inhabitants — visiting, dancing on the streets, and serenading Quaker maidens accustomed to more sedate methods of courtship. But beneath the frivolity serious adjustments were taking place. A few went back to the islands when the French measures of pacification seemed successful; many took up lands near the coast cities, providing market gardens for the growing urban communities; others scattered to the inland towns to set up as physicians and dentists.[16]

Indirectly the French Revolution was responsible for a new influx of Englishmen. The 1790's beheld one of those migrations from Britain which, though so easily lost in the mass of Americans, has served to keep the United States in closer social and intellectual communion with the country from which it politically sprang. At first the officials and citizens had viewed the events across the channel with sympathetic interest, but the revolution soon took a turn that many Englishmen could not condone. The liberal minority in English politics were stigmatized as "Jacobins," and officers and populace became watchful to catch the faintest whisper of sedition. As early as 1791 the "Birmingham Riots" revealed the reactionary state of public opinion. The homes of peaceful citizens were looted and their occupants mobbed in the streets.

Foremost among the victims in Birmingham was Dr. Joseph Priestley — clergyman, philosopher, scientist and political liberal — who narrowly escaped with his life. Though attributing his treatment at first to the ignorant rabble, Priestley presently discovered that his respectable neighbors avoided and criticized him. This led him to evolve a plan of emigration in the company of friends whose presence would ameliorate the hardships. The group so organized purchased lands in Pennsylvania on the banks of the Susquehanna, and in 1794 Priestley sailed for the New World. New York and Philadelphia welcomed him with open arms, but this reception made colony life seem a drear experience by contrast. The Englishmen who joined him belonged to that class of intellectual and bookish pioneers which in a hundred successive enterprises was to reveal its unfitness for pioneering. Their morale suffered further from their resentment at the aloofness and assumed superiority of their leader and a few favored associates. The settlement did not prosper. Priestley himself took up his residence at Northumberland, fifty miles away, and later abandoned the scheme completely when called to a professorship in Philadelphia.[17]

Although these hopes of a forest capital to which English liberals might resort collapsed, individual and group immigration continued. Encouraged by James Drowley, a New York merchant desirous of creating a refuge in a region far from the inhospitable frontier, many families of progressive tendency founded new homes near Sparta in Westchester County.[18] There was, in fact, a steady infiltration of propertied and thrifty farmers into the Middle Atlantic states, who bought the improved lands of Americans infected by the Western fever. Most of these purchasers were liberals of some stripe, and many of them combined religious fanaticism with political radicalism.

Meanwhile the unrest of the times passed from the cities and farms of England over the border into Wales where it was fed by the growing nationalism, religious fervor and economic distress. In the eighteenth century Wales had begun to awaken from its ancient lethargy. Its people recalled the glories of former days; the customs and language of the past were revived; religious enthusiasm filled the chapels of the Methodists and Baptists; and to the complaints of religious oppression were added the economic hardships caused by the inclosures of the commons and the industrialization of the valleys of South Wales. When the British government undertook its antirevolutionary campaign, the hand of the administration lay heavy upon Welsh agitators. Ministers and editors were charged with sedition; even the singing of the popular "Liberty Song" brought imprisonment.[19] As a measure of relief the Pulteney family, owners of a vast estate in western New York, and the American minister in London were asked to aid in organizing a colonization *en masse*. But no encouragement was extended and the project, far too ambitious, failed.[20] Smaller groups, however, found cooperative emigration feasible. Utica and its countryside, the hills of Cambria County in Pennsylvania and Paddy's Run in Ohio were the sites of settlements which long continued to attract families from Wales and in succeeding decades sent out bands of young people to plant new churches and communities in the West.[21]

The instinct toward colonies was natural among the French,

English and Welsh, who had not participated strongly in the movement of the preceding century and hence had not yet developed a technique of individual migration. The tendency was strengthened by the state of the land market in America. Though the federal government possessed vast tracts on the frontier, Indian difficulties and uncertainty regarding policy discouraged buyers. Those states which owned millions of acres realized the desirability of selling them before competition with the Western lands developed. A modern holding company is hardly more complicated than the maze of corporations, partnerships and individual estates built up to dispose of these possessions. Princely domains were sold to such groups as the North American Land Company and the Pennsylvania Population Company. Like tracts went to John Nicholson, Robert Morris, William Brigham and others able to make a down payment or whose credit was good. The principle upon which the new owners operated was simple. Most of the land was sold to settlers at a price which merely covered the original cost and the expense of administration; but scattered throughout the settlements were certain tracts reserved for a future rise in value. If few of the speculators should live to reap the harvest, at least their sons and daughters would come into a rich inheritance.

To facilitate the recruitment of settlers, the promoters decided to tap the population reservoir of Europe. Thus the Holland Land Company, which had bought up a large part of western New York, sent an agent abroad to enlist the type of German farmer that had proved so successful in Pennsylvania and parts of the South. Instead of proceeding into the interior, however, he spread his publicity in the city of Hamburg. The authorities of the port soon stopped him, and when the families reached the New York frontier, company officials probably regretted that the port authorities had not acted sooner. Unwilling to work, dissatisfied with the rough surroundings and organized by ambitious leaders, they presently decamped, seeking other opportunities in Canada. After this experience the company forgot about foreigners and concentrated upon securing native American settlers. The lesson was one which later corporations did not attempt to unlearn.[22] Robert Morris, who exerted a strong influence in all speculative circles, was emphatic in the belief that new lands could be successfully colonized only by people possessing a heritage of American pioneer resourcefulness.[23]

At about the same time Philadelphia capitalists underwent a somewhat similar experience. The French refugees in the city included a number who professed a willingness to seek a permanent home on the banks of the Susquehanna. Still faithful subjects of Louis XVI, they watched with growing concern his increasing difficulties at home, and it was rumored they contemplated establishing a community to which he might retire until called back to the throne. Perhaps for this reason they named the settlement Asylum. But Louis never came to Asylum, nor was the cause the premature loss of his head. Few besides the original group cared to join the venture, and these few put more energy into convivial hours at the local tavern and horse racing on the common than in clearing the forest, cultivating fields and harvesting crops. Within a few years the stately homes, some of them only half completed, were deserted; and a quarter of a century later Asylum had become a cornfield.[24]

The Brigham interests in New York also undertook a French colony, at Castorland in their lands in the northern part of the state, employing a subsidiary company for the purpose. This region of rivers and forests on a remote frontier offered a life rougher and ruder than prevailed in most rural sections. Though the pioneers seemed to be made of sterner stuff than their compatriots at Asylum, in the end the results were the same. One by one the settlers drifted back to New York or Paris, or disappeared in the depths of the wilderness.[25] The taming of this part of the frontier awaited the coming of a hardier, more persevering stock.

Much more successful was the group settlement of Englishmen at Ceres in northwestern Pennsylvania. William Knox of Philadelphia was the sponsor, John Keating his indefatigable agent, and English Quakers were the colonizers.[26] Under able direction they developed into experienced woodsmen. Had others followed their example, the English immigration of the period might have become what many had hoped — a transplantation of institutions and customs as well as of individuals. Few knew of the existence of the English township in the mountains, however, and beyond one somewhat similar community organized in eastern Ohio, which may have been patterned upon it, its influence was limited to the participants.

In the meantime, without the use of foreigners, the land barons had seen their wilderness domains pass into the hands of industrious farmers. From New England caravans of fellow townsmen set out for the "Genesee country" of western New York; Pennsylvania Germans and their New Jersey neighbors swarmed into the new counties beyond the Susquehanna; people of Scotch-Irish and German stock of the Shenandoah Valley pushed up into the surrounding hills. Speculators sold their lands and, under sway of a boom psychology, argued that, if ten thousand acres had yielded them a small fortune, a hundred thousand would yield a far greater one. Events of 1795 gilded the belief. Wayne's defeat of the northwestern Indians pacified the frontier; Pinckney's treaty with Spain opened a route between coast and interior by freeing the Mississippi from tolls. There were, however, no more fertile Genesee valleys to exploit. Hence promoters had to be content with the poorer Georgia, Carolina and Kentucky lands; and in the scramble to secure them, prices rose far beyond any value that Nature would ever justify.[27]

President Washington, always a man of business and himself a participant in some of the earlier ventures, decided in the spring of 1796, when the speculation was running at full tide, that the moment was opportune to "get out of the market." His example set others to selling their holdings. In the slower tempo of the eighteenth century no single fatal day signalized the debâcle, but the outcome proved as disastrous as any modern "Black Friday." Empires built upon spurious reputations and slender credit collapsed,[28] and there was no one to offer succor. Commercial houses and the associated banks might have saved some, but their ships were at that very time being seized by the French.[29] The bankrupts included many prominent men of the day; Robert Morris, greatest speculator of them all, went to the debtors' prison.[30] Along with the native-born, foreign newcomers felt the prevailing distress. The suspension of internal improvements meant fewer opportunities for day labor; and the French depredations on American commerce cut off the markets for grain, rendering farming unprofitable. Though statistics are lacking, ample evidence of the drop in the immigration appears in the accounts of "deluded emigrants" published in the Continental press as well as in the discouraging descriptions of the United States in the British newspapers.

As the influx of the English declined, that of the Irish rose. General conditions in Ireland were satisfactory during the 1790's, for the war created a demand for linen, and the removal of the last restrictions on the trade with England caused an expansion of grain production that provided work for all hands. But England's difficulties spelled opportunity for the United Irishmen intent on an independent Erin. In 1798 the most formidable of all Irish rebellions broke out.

Though its suppression inaugurated the legislative union with the British Parliament, it also caused the proscription of thousands of patriots in Ulster as well as in the south who saw in flight the only alternative to the gallows.

In reality the victors were not so vindictive. Apart from hanging a few of the chief trouble makers, they planned to deport the rest; as Americans had generally sympathized with a movement which reminded them of their own war for independence, the United States was the logical destination. Rufus King, American minister in London, hearing the rumor, at once sent a sharp note to the Foreign Office. America, he said, desired no more "wild Irish" and would resist their importation to the last.[31] In after years the recollection of this language was to cost him the governorship of New York, but for the time being it proved effective.[32] The Irish were not sent, though ultimately they came. By way of Newfoundland and France, disguised as priests and women, or passing boldly over the frontiers, the suspected ones crossed from Ireland to the United States. Within a few months every coast city had its lodge of United Irishmen who, expert in politics, lent effective aid to the Jeffersonian Democrats in their war upon the Federalists.

Caught by the prevailing hard times, the Federalist party already stood on the defensive. Now their enemies had allies who could write and speak in the style of professional agitators.[33] The Federalist defense took shape in a series of laws which temporarily threatened to crystallize into a policy of restricting immigration. The liberal act of 1790 had already been so modified in 1795 as to raise the term of residence for naturalization to five years.[34] But this change had not been a party issue — Federalists favored it because they feared the revolution in Europe would prompt an emigration of turbulent political refugees; Republicans, because they feared the revolution would drive out aristocrats who,

COMING TO AMERICA

RETURNING FOR A VISIT

THE OLD WORLD AND THE NEW

if citizens, would stifle American liberties. In 1798 the Federalists acted alone. By the new law an alien must wait fourteen years before becoming naturalized, and must make a declaration of intention five years before the final papers.[35] At about the same time an alien act, patterned upon a British statute of the same designation, gave the President authority to deport any undesirable foreigner. A sedition act, applicable to natives and foreigners alike, aimed to curb freedom of expression.[36]

This legislation, however, significant from other points of view, had no appreciable influence upon the course of immigration. For the time being, the movement had slackened, perhaps almost to cessation. Ireland was being "pacified" and its people were closely guarded. The persecution of English liberals had run its course. German states and Swiss cantons were conserving man power by prohibiting departures; and the French, now holding all the Dutch and North Sea German ports, successfully choked migration by a rigid system of passport inspection.[37] In time, the knowledge of the existence of the restrictive American laws would undoubtedly have dampened European ardor for going to the United States; but the political skies soon cleared. In March, 1801, Thomas Jefferson and his party came into power; the alien and sedition acts expired by limitation; and a new naturalization law restored the five-year term.[38] America again was the haven toward which thousands could now look. Moreover, with the coming of the new century, the European stalemate of arms dissolved into a peace. Although the Treaty of Amiens between England and France was not signed until 1802, the rigor of military and naval supervision over commerce relaxed more than a year before; and as a result the summer of 1801 beheld a phenomenally heavy emigration.[39]

A series of crop failures, affecting in successive years wheat, rye and potatoes, speeded the movement. A general shortage in the harvest of 1800 rendered the situation in Great Britain acute, and on the Continent at best uncomfortable. Vigorous efforts by the British authorities to regulate sellers and buyers fanned again the desire for emigration. Since privateering was at an end and the sea was safe, accommodations were plentiful and the rates reasonable. Before the close of summer the streets of New York and Philadelphia swarmed with newcomers offering to employers all the labor they needed and bargaining for any lands with which Americans would part.

The experiences of that year, however, proved exceptional. The peace signed at Amiens in the spring of 1802 harmed the farmers and shippers of America, for the one class lost a profitable export market and the other its privileged position as neutral carrier. The resulting economic stagnation rendered a large proportion of the immigrants superfluous, a condition which lasted until the congested population was drained off into the new state of Ohio and, after the acquisition of Louisiana in 1803, into the hopeful settlements on the banks of the Mississippi. Few opportunities existed for Europeans except those with independent means.

In Great Britain and on the Continent bountiful harvests, unknown for several seasons, made up for the peace-time industrial slack.[40] Peace, however, did not long continue. In the spring of 1803 the nations girded themselves for the final struggle. Press gangs filled up the navies, and armies and factories absorbed the unemployed. Now Europe had no surplus man power; and although the stream of migration flowed rather steadily, it consisted of persons whom the governments had no desire to keep: Irishmen whose loyalty was dubious, and German sectarians whose religion and temperament nullified them as military assets.

This even current, varying little from year to year, continued until the European encroachments upon neutral ships and the tightening network of French arms blocked all the routes of Continental and Atlantic travel. From Ireland alone access to North America seemed possible; and finally this avenue was also closed when President Jefferson's embargo of December, 1807, locked up the commercial fleets within American harbors. Until the spring of 1809 all maritime activity and with it the passenger trade ceased.

To no Europeans did the repeal of the embargo bring greater joy than to the farmers of north Ireland. Upon them had fallen the brunt of the distress which Jefferson had hoped to render so severe as to compel a repeal of all restrictive decrees and orders. Other groups in the warring countries had discovered alternative outlets for their labor and substitutes for their needs, but the Ulstermen and their immediate neighbors depended wholly upon the flaxseed of Pennsylvania. When the supply could no longer be obtained, the growers were caught with no reserves. In the spring of 1808 they planted some seed of doubtful quality, Dutch in origin, but before the summer was over its worthlessness was revealed, too late, however, to replant the acres with crops that would at least have provided food. A winter of distress followed. The spinners had no flax, the weavers no yarn; dyers and bleachers lacked work; financial institutions were weakened.[41] Rebellion was in the air when news arrived of the opening of the American ports.

As was always the case in Ireland, distress swelled the throng of emigrants. In 1809 a distinct wave began which continued until the War of 1812 again closed commercial intercourse. Two factors, however, tended to moderate what would otherwise have been a more extensive movement. British legislation passed in the year 1803 had imposed new restrictions on the carrying capacity of vessels, thereby raising the cost of passage.[42] Although professing to act in the name of humanity, Parliament probably aimed mainly at hampering the departures. At the same time, the activity of British cruisers upon the high seas operated as a deterrent. Impressment of hands was the only method by which the navy recruited its full complement; and when American ships were being stopped and naturalized American citizens were being seized, Irishmen fleeing to the United States could not expect to escape a similar fate.

Many were the stories of outrage poured into sympathetic ears when emigrants landed on the docks of Philadelphia or New York. Wives told of husbands seized from their sides, leaving them with a brood of small children to face the rigors of the strange country. Even those prudent travelers who had obtained from the officials at Dublin certificates authorizing their departure found these documents no protection if the navy desired their services. Particularly flagrant was the forcible removal of sixty-two passengers from the *Belisarius*, stopped off St. George's Bank. Nor was the indignation lessened by the manner in which the sailors executed their task. "Come along," they cried. "You shan't go into that damn'd Republican country; we are going to have a slap at them one of these days, and you shan't be there to fight against us . . . we shall suffer no more emigration to that damned Democratic country — into the boats!" [43]

The War of 1812 halted migration once more. Although war was not declared until June, only one shipload of passengers arrived from Germany during that year; and the voyage, according to the story of one of them, involved successive adventures with British and American warships and privateers.[44] A few Irishmen may have slipped over in the course of the next two years; but most awaited the coming of peace before embarking on the adventure. The Irishmen in America who were still aliens when the conflict began had a somewhat uncomfortable time. No "War Hawk" of the

West greeted the declaration of war with greater enthusiasm than these expatriates. A movement at once began to organize Irish regiments which would be fighting the battles of Erin as well as of the United States, but the necessary authority was not forthcoming.[45] On the contrary, the administration adopted the usual precautionary measures, requiring all enemy aliens, whatever their private opinions, to register, and applied particularly stringent tests to naturalization cases. Their lot was made no easier by the fact that popular opinion failed to discriminate between the English, Scots and Irish — all were subjects of the British Crown.[46]

The isolation of the United States during the war dramatized a condition which had been more or less true since the struggle for national independence. Eight years of the American Revolution, ten years of political uncertainty from 1783 to 1793, nineteen years of European turmoil, and three years of American involvement — these years comprised a period during which immigration was hardly more than a trickle. A society accustomed to constant infusions from abroad found time to adjust itself to a condition where its people were home-born and home-bred.

It is one of the fundamental facts of American history that after 1815 signs of nationalism, lacking before, became conspicuous. Literature, economic policy, international politics, all reflected this change. Though historians usually attribute this development of nationalism to the second war with Great Britain, it is unlikely that an event which received far from unanimous support and excited bitter sectional controversies could have been responsible. On the contrary, one may well believe that the course of hostilities and their unexpected happy ending served merely to accelerate tendencies already present and inevitable. The children of the Revolutionary period had reached adulthood, and their outlook and its expression were bound to be different. The purchase of the empire of Louisiana fastened interest more intently upon the American continent. And added to these factors was the falling off of immigration which not only allowed the melting pot to simmer gently, but also hastened the Americanization of those non-British groups which had not yet lost their distinctive identity.

Most obvious among these marks of identity was language. From 1790 to 1815 English won an almost complete victory over its rivals. Already before the Revolution the process had begun. The settlers at Gwynnyd and Bryn Mawr in Pennsylvania, while retaining the place names, found them increasingly difficult to pronounce. After 1750 no more sermons in the original tongue were preached in the Welsh Tract. French disappeared as rapidly in the Huguenot communities with the passing of the immigrant generation. Swedish proved more persistent, for the Lutheran churches of the farmers along the Delaware continued to be served by ministers sent over by the Swedish Crown. But the American Revolution ended this missionary activity, with the result that the congregations became Anglicized in speech and their administration was absorbed by the Protestant Episcopal Church.[47]

But as late as the Revolution two foreign tongues, Dutch and German, seemed firmly rooted in American society. With them the real battles of the English language were fought. Though the Knickerbocker strain in Manhattan had entered fully into the commercial life of the metropolis, elsewhere in New Netherland the English conquest of a century before had little affected inherited social customs. On western Long Island, in northern New Jersey, up the Hudson Valley to its capital at Albany, the rural empire of *boers* and *patroons* continued to pursue a peaceful and prosperous existence. Dutch was the language of the market, the church and the home.

These folk took a reluctant part in the political movements that became the Revolution; but whether lukewarm, patriotic or silently pro-English, they could not escape the new order which it created. The East River and the North River bustled with commerce, which lined their banks with warehouses and docks. Inevitably the Dutch communities on the opposite shores felt the effects; and as the Hudson River developed into the great commercial artery toward the north, the sleepy villages on either side awoke to the new opportunities. No longer was Dutch all-sufficient. Old merchants struggled to master the strange English words; the young more easily adopted the new speech. English became the language of trade.

But many a man of affairs who willingly employed English six days a week balked at its use in religious services. Yet here, too, progress was made. In the city of New York the action of the governing body of the Dutch Reformed Church in 1775 in refusing to exercise jurisdiction over what was declared to be a local matter speeded the change. The minutes of congregations and the memoirs of their minorities trace the course of the controversy. Whatever the local variations, compromise paved the way to solution: first one sermon a month in the new tongue, then one sermon each Sunday. Gradually the proportion increased until Dutch was reserved for those special occasions when the elderly attended in full force. In the meantime English Bibles, English hymn books and English catechisms supplanted the old. The children breathed an entirely new ecclesiastical atmosphere, and by 1815, except in the remoter rural parts, the new basis had been attained.[48]

The dislodgment of the Dutch language from the home was another matter. Long after it ceased to be spoken elsewhere, many families continued its use. Until the middle of the nineteenth century this practice prevailed in some places; and witnesses attest that even as late as 1900 it was not a forgotten tongue,[49] though this may have been due to association with individuals of later Dutch immigrations. In any case, after 1815 language no longer barred participation in those pursuits, social and intellectual, needful for a full assimilation to American life.

The fate of German, which was spoken by about three times as many persons, varied with the circumstances that surrounded the main groups. The descendants of the Palatines who had remained in Ulster County and on the Mohawk Flats in New York were subjected to the same influences and underwent the same transformation as the Dutch. The action of the New York Ministerium of the Lutheran Church in 1800 in declaring that henceforth English should be the language of its deliberations and records gave the movement a decisive official impetus.[50] With even greater facility the German colonies in the West and South, far distant from the main stem of their fellow countrymen in Pennsylvania and Maryland, adopted the new institutions and speech. To prevent the younger generation from going over to the popular frontier denominations, the churches and ministers perforce fell into line.[51]

Resistance to Americanization proved strongest in the old congregations on the plains between the Delaware and the Susquehanna. The bulk of their members were German-born and German-trained, knowing little of their adopted country apart from the rural parishes in which they lived, and these were as Teutonic as the villages in old Germany. Such persons dominated the Ministerium of Pennsylvania, and the Ministerium in turn controlled the congregations within its constituency. The language question first arose before the Ministerium in 1804 on appeal from the city of Philadelphia. For some years an "English party" had been pressing their demands but without satisfaction from their local church council. The Ministerium, however, rejected the petition, affirming that the congregation should settle the matter for itself. The following year a faction of the same organization asked point-blank whether a congregation calling itself "German" could permit "worship and instruction in the language of the country along side of the German." This led to a definite recommendation that, when the use of two languages had become necessary, the congregation should divide for the sake of internal peace.[52] At the same time, however, a resolution provided "That the present Lutheran Ministerium of Pennsylvania and the adjacent states must remain a German-speaking Ministerium, and that no regulation can be adopted, which would necessitate the use of another language beside the German in its Synodical Meetings and business." [53] The dispute now reverted to the constituency in Philadelphia where in the next decade the embittered feeling provoked riots and bloodshed (in which nonreligious differences probably also figured) and a tedious process in the courts. In the end the German and English congregations effected a satisfactory division of property.[54]

Such a solution, workable enough in a city where numbers were sufficient to support more than one organization, did not apply to country towns where there was not enough to divide. A few years after the Ministerium disposed of the Philadelphia difficulty, trouble arose at Hagerstown. In 1812 the Synod recommended a method which other local churches could also employ: English should not be used, even as a "subsidiary language," until the majority of the congregation had so voted and the Church Council had given approval.[55] As this higher body consisted of the most elderly and conservative members, it accorded its consent grudgingly. "God is my witness," wrote the venerated Dr. Muhlenberg at Lancaster, "I worked against the English as

long as I could . . . ." [56] Some congregations achieved the
new dispensation, but through most of the Pennsylvania-
German country the old tongue continued to hold sway.
This victory at a time when the general movement was
towards Anglicization was an important factor serving to
preserve down into the twentieth century an enclave of
colonial rural America in the heart of the urban and industrial East.

Besides the language question, other issues involving the
rising spirit of nationality confronted the various religious
groups. Following the Revolution, one denomination after
another declared its independence of European jurisdiction
by forming national organizations.[57] A widespread reaction
occurred against the rationalism of European churchmen,
with a corresponding emphasis upon what was considered
fundamental, a simplification of ritual and worship. Frontier
religion, with camp meetings and an untrained ministry,
took its historical form during these years. The cordiality
once extended ministers of European birth and education
now gave way to coolness and suspicion. The Methodist
Conference acted as early as 1784, voting to accept no "European preacher" unless recommended by Charles Wesley and
expressly subject to the directions of Francis Asbury, later
the first bishop.[58] The Reformed Protestant Dutch Church,
legislating on the matter in 1806, forbade the consistory of
any congregation to allow a foreigner to preach until the
officers of the Classis to which the congregation belonged had
accorded official approval.[59] The Lutheran Ministerium of
Pennsylvania, which in 1784 had discussed methods for obtaining more pastors from Germany, in 1812 considered the
advisability of refusing to accept any without a three years'
probation. Seven years later it decided to admit to immediate
fellowship only those whose recommendations entitled them
to this mark of confidence.[60]

The Presbyterians, however, took the most decisive action. The General Assembly in 1798 adopted a regulation requiring all foreign ministers to submit their credentials to a committee of the Presbytery and to undergo an oral examination covering matters of doctrine. If these tests were successfully met, a year's probation must precede a permanent license. As this step was taken the same year that Congress passed the famous alien act, the new regulation gained a repute as the "Reverend General Assembly's Alien Act." Nor did the parallelism end here. Just as Virginia and Kentucky protested the action of Congress, so the Presbytery of New York, the following year, sent up a resolution condemning the ordinance as "unnecessary, unconstitutional, uncharitable and inconsistent." Its power thus challenged, the Assembly did what Congress did not see fit to do: it referred the action to the Presbyteries for their opinion. The majority approved the regulation as constitutional and desirable under existing conditions. It therefore remained part of the permanent code of the Church.[61]

The growing nationalism of the churches expressed itself in one other way. Although the frontier readily accepted pastors with no formal training provided their theology was sound, older settled communities coupled their suspicion of foreigners with a demand for institutions of learning which would train American youth in American ways. Progress toward this goal was necessarily gradual, for educational endowments could be accumulated only slowly. In time, however, the hopes were realized. The many seminaries, academies and colleges founded between 1800 and 1830 may be considered products of the first Americanization.

Tradition reckons the number of immigrants during the quarter-century from 1790 to 1815 at less than two hundred and fifty thousand. This figure, though possessing official sanction,[62] rests upon the slimmest of evidence. Yet the impression created by an intensive study of the period and of fragmentary contemporary data substantiates this estimate. Perhaps a larger number actually entered American ports; but as many of them were temporary refugees from France, Ireland and the West Indies, the *bona-fide* immigrants were not more numerous. In their sentiments these latter were already reconciled to a permanent separation from Europe. The usual personal ties could not exist in a world so stormy with wars. Many had every reason to forget the life they had abandoned. And so, into a country making rapid strides towards national consciousness, came a class of foreigners whose presence did not hinder the process. It may even have contributed to it.

IV

A NEW BEGINNING

PROBABLY NO YEAR was ever greeted with more enthusiasm than 1815. After a quarter-century of wars, turmoil and fear the promise of a new era refreshed the hopes of mankind. The Corsican who, taking the sword in the name of France, had deluged the Continent with blood was a prisoner on a Mediterranean island. The forces of stability and appeasement gathered at Vienna were rebuilding the shattered political structure; and with security thus assured, commerce and industry laid plans for the conquests of peace. The interlude of the Hundred Days — from Napoleon's triumphal return from Elba to his defeat at Waterloo — cast a brief shadow over this auspicious scene, but midsummer brightened prospects again. For men everywhere it was a new beginning.

The disturbed commerce of a quarter of a century could not, however, at once return to the older channels. Few timber ships arrived in Ireland in 1815 because Canadian logging had been neglected, and the importation of Pennsylvania flaxseed was small.[1] Merchant vessels which hurried to Liverpool to load cargoes for America before the English wares glutted the market did not wait to secure a full complement of passengers.[2] Not until after the Waterloo campaign in June could the Low Countries seek to reëstablish their former empire of trade. Thus the summer passed without any large migration to the western continent. Newfoundland, however, which had attracted over seven thousand Irishmen to its shores in 1814 through its fishing and privateering prosperity, proved a strong magnet. Three thousand landed at St. John's, only to learn that peace meant depression. Their distress forced the British authorities to provide assistance and issue warnings.[3]

The autumn months, however, witnessed an increase in arrivals. As American buyers quickly exhausted the stocks of the importers, commercial agents swarmed to English industrial centers to order more. From September to December captains returned to the United States with steerage and cabin passengers whose numbers so late in the year astounded observers. English farmers, Scotch Highlanders and German redemptioners landed in New York and Philadelphia, and sailors catching the contagion deserted their ships, depleting the crews and dismaying the officers.[4] French artisans and refugees gladly turned their backs on the uncertain politics of their native land, while Irish peasants hastened to board the first American vessels that docked in the ports of Ulster. Notwithstanding this late increase, probably less than five thousand newcomers reached the United States in the whole year.

By 1816, however, other propulsive forces had come into play. The farmers of Great Britain and Ireland, anticipating a decline in the demand for their products, had induced Parliament in 1815 to pass a new corn law to protect them against foreign competition;[5] but no legislation could obviate the effects on the agricultural system produced by high rents, scarcity of labor and the cultivation of marginal lands. Moreover, as the workers demobilized from the war-time industries returned to their parishes, poor rates began to rise. Tenants with long-time leases struggled to meet their obligations, while landlords with leases to offer found it almost impossible to dispose of them to advantage. In the spring of 1816 farming prospects were exceedingly dark.[6]

On the Continent a different legal tenure and a more moderate agricultural expansion during the war prevented so complete a rural collapse. The principal distress stemmed from the depression of industry. In Switzerland and some of the south German states, France and the French armies had absorbed the products of the family workshops and village factories; but now France, striving for national recovery by protectionist methods, raised tariff barriers against her neighbors. Through Europe in general the governments sought to maintain their war-stimulated local industries by similar means. In the countries excluded from trade, hands became idle, spirits depressed, and even those who had as yet escaped saw disaster impending. Among such workers the spirit of emigration quickly spread.[7]

To these causes must be added the restlessness engendered by more than two decades of European conflict. The men in the armies had passed from country to country, viewing new scenes and living in an atmosphere of constant change. By contrast, life in the native village seemed narrow and dull, while the world across the sea offered fresh and interesting adventure. The peace treaty itself increased the number of those eager to move about. Article XVII allowed six years for the inhabitants of districts which had been transferred to a new allegiance to leave without paying a property emigration tax.[8] Many of the principalities along the Rhine belonged in this category, and thousands of those departing chose America as their destination.[9] This treaty provision compressed within a few years an emigration which under normal conditions might have spread over a much longer period.

Peace also brought to Europeans a clearer knowledge of American opportunities. Along with renewed commercial relations occurred a renewal of personal connections: communications from friends and relatives long silent, and oftentimes direct invitations to join the oversea settlements — invitations hard to refuse when extended in the form of prepaid passages. Pennsylvania Germans sent to the districts along the Rhine and the Main circulars describing the prospects of their new Germany, and the reported success of vineyards in Kentucky and Indiana awakened the ambitions of the discouraged Swiss.[10] The advantages of land, labor and liberty in the New World became everywhere a topic of village conversation.

Progress was made slowly in restoring the network of European land transportation. For twelve months after Waterloo battalions returning from France crowded the roads, and all conveyances were employed in transporting army baggage and supplies. But in 1816 a regular boat service commenced on the Rhine from Basel to the Dutch ports, with a passenger agency which attended to the details of emigration.[11] In the same year the first steamboat ascended the river from Rotterdam to Cologne, an event heralding a new period in navigation.[12] Even these facilities, however, were inadequate; and when the emigration season of 1816 got under way, bateaux had to be constructed in the shipyards of the upper Rhine to handle the traffic.[13]

At this date only one nation, Great Britain, had adopted policies designed to influence the volume and course of emigration. Events in Canada during the war had shown the doubtful loyalty of many communities along the international border. Obviously this situation might be avoided in the future if colonists were induced to settle in strategically located townships. To this end the British authorities decided to do some experimenting, and in the spring of 1815 imported into Canada at the government's cost several hundred Scots.[14] But the Waterloo campaign caused a suspension of the subsidies, which the Colonial Office made permanent in March, 1816.[15] Planned settlement came to an end.

Meanwhile the British officials placed brakes on emigration to the United States by resorting to a half-forgotten statute of 1803. This act allowed British ships to carry one passenger for every two tons of registry but limited foreign vessels to one for every five.[16] In December, 1815, John Quincy Adams, the American minister in London, began to hear complaints from American captains in Irish ports that the restrictions were to be enforced.[17] Adams, convinced that the real object was to check departures for the United States, pointed out to the Foreign Office that this discrimination violated the provisions of the commercial treaty of July 3, 1815.[18] For several months the negotiations continued, Lord Castlereagh hesitating to admit that passengers could be classified as articles of commerce. An order of April 27, 1816, however, granted American vessels in English and Scotch ports the same quota as the British, and Parliament confirmed this equality on July 1. Before this time the American ships in Ireland were at a disadvantage and, by the time the act became operative, the normal season for departure had passed.[19]

Nevertheless, no captain sailing the Atlantic from early in the spring until late in the fall lacked passengers. The rates ran high — ten pounds from Liverpool to New York — with nothing provided but fuel and water.[20] Only the more substantial small farmers could pay such fares, or those who, like the French refugees, sought America for reasons not wholly economic. Newspapers congratulated the United States upon the superior quality of the arrivals and called particular attention to the large number of French among them.[21] Popular imagination tended to class all the latter as Napoleonic exiles — military officers and statesmen fleeing from the Bourbon reaction. In fact, many of them had no concern with politics. They were artisans who feared for the future because of the industrial uncertainty, and French-speaking peasants from Alsace who emigrated for reasons akin to those which actuated their German neighbors across the Rhine.[22]

Aside from the French, the Continent contributed little to the westward tide. Several shiploads of Swiss and Württembergers disembarked at Philadelphia, the traditional German port, and the families and redemptioners among them were readily absorbed by the employers and farmers of Pennsylvania.[23] When the summer influx reached its height and gave promise of continuing unabated through the fall, Hezekiah Niles enthusiastically prophesied that the total would reach fifty thousand.[24] In later years on sober reflection he estimated the migration of the season 1816 at twenty thousand, a figure undoubtedly much nearer the mark.[25]

At first, employment opportunities abounded, for during the war many of the Eastern cities, New York in particular, had fallen behind in the construction of houses, warehouses, docks, stores and offices. Contractors needed masons, stonecutters, carpenters, woodworkers and hodcarriers, and they promised to pay in proportion to the need. Probably it was this assurance of jobs that induced so many Americans to provide prepaid passages; certainly the knowledge of these opportunities persuaded many of the immigrants to risk their last shilling as passage money.[26] Most of the workmen were Irishmen.[27] The Irish emigration of the year was, in fact, centered on the United States and the maritime provinces.[28] As the number of newcomers increased, however, contractors found they could not employ all the hands that offered themselves. New York became congested with workers without jobs or resources who were obliged to seek charity from their more fortunate fellow countrymen.[29] To deal with this situation, the leaders of the Irish community formed the Shamrock Friendly Association, which granted temporary assistance and endeavored through correspondence and newspaper publicity to discover opportunities for employment in the interior. To such places the immigrants were directed, and in the fall months, though the influx continued, the surplus rapidly diminished.[30]

Meanwhile, others among the distressed arrivals besieged the British consul who used their plight to urge on his government the desirability of attempting to deflect the current of immigration to the unpeopled lands of Canada. Before the end of the year he was authorized to expend as much as ten dollars a person in forwarding from New York such British subjects as agreed to take up land in the provinces.[31] During the next few months one thousand six hundred and thirty stranded arrivals received assistance.[32] Newspapers and periodicals in Great Britain pounced on this information to moralize on the hazards of emigration; and when the consular descriptions were substantiated by disappointed adventurers who were able to return to their native land, the prospects for the following spring indicated a great decline in numbers.[33]

Such did not prove to be the case, for a new factor now entered the situation. Before the autumn of 1816 came, public attention had been directed away from the perils of emigration to an emergency created by Nature. On both sides of the Atlantic 1816 was long remembered as "the year without a summer." Toward the close of September John Q. Adams wrote from London that there had been "not one evening and scarcely a day in 1816 when a fire would have been superfluous." [34] Throughout the Occidental world, from the mountains of central Europe to the great interior valley of North America, peasant and farmer struggled against cold and frosts, rains and floods. Everywhere new discontents and difficulties added to those inherited from the wars.

In Scotland the abnormal weather ruined all prospects. The previous winter had come early and the spring months brought little change. During the summer hail and sleet fell in the Lowlands, snow in the mountains. Reapers who went out to gather the slender crop of grain found boys coasting on their sleds in the fields.[35] Ireland also reported days that were wet, cold and cloudy. Whereas a year before the markets had been glutted with produce, now the farmer could spare little, and so wet were the bogs that he could not replenish the pile of turf beside his cottage.[36] On the Continent conditions were similar. To the disasters resulting from rain and cold were added the ravages of high water along the valley of the Rhine and its tributaries. Farms were inundated; livestock and buildings were swept away; and in early August, just when a few favorable days promised a break in the weather, a ferocious storm uprooted fruit and forest trees, killing animals and piling up the swollen streams.[37] Switzerland escaped these floods, but there avalanches and earthquakes took their toll.[38]

The "year without a summer" yielded, at best, a scanty harvest. The granaries of England and Scotland were not entirely depleted, and the expectation of large imports from America kept prices down. But in Ireland where the potato yield was short and the oat crop a failure, the people were spared a famine winter only through governmental relief and private charity.[39] The distressed inhabitants of the German states along the Rhine and the Swiss cantons proved less fortunate. Though the public authorities and grain merchants made extensive purchases in the Baltic ports and the governments prohibited the export of local supplies, these efforts did not prevent prices from rising. The last years of the war had depleted grain reserves, and wind and weather delayed the coming of vessels on the long route from the Baltic through the North Sea to Netherland ports. An early winter froze the rivers and canals and the spring of 1817 brought new rains. Not until July did the bulk of the foodstuffs ordered the previous autumn reach the upper Rhine, and by that time an early and bounteous harvest had relieved the emergency.[40]

The intervening winter and spring had been months of famine. A decade later the physique of the military conscripts entering the training camps seemed to reveal the privations of this season of hunger. Deaths by starvation were not unknown; fever claimed many victims; thousands kept alive only through the charity of "soup kitchens." Country roads were thronged with peasants who wandered aimlessly about, camping in the village markets and besieging houses and individuals for assistance.[41] The social unrest offered opportunities for the ever present agitators. Peasant prophets arose in nearly every community to foretell a continuation of misery and to preach repentance for a happy eternity in the next world.[42]

Among them appeared an evangelist of a different type, a remarkable woman who knew emperors and kings and who promised a paradise on earth. Accompanied by a suite of forty persons and many followers, Madame Krüdener traveled from parish to parish, from canton to canton, distributing food to the hungry and raising hopes of a distant land of plenty where rulers would govern by love and provide security from the disasters of western Europe. The less credulous suspected her of being a Russian agent engaged in drumming up settlers for the Caucasus; but before any definite plans were announced, the Swiss police paid her encampment a surprise midnight visit, escorted the foreigners to the border, and ordered the natives back to their homes.[43] Madame Krüdener was not molested but, deprived of her company, her influence quickly disappeared and no organized mass migration resulted.

Yet the agitation of the prophetess was not without effect upon the course of migration. During the summer of 1817 several bands of Mennonites, numbering seven hundred in all, began a long overland march from Württemberg to the plains of south Russia. Czar Alexander, continuing a traditional Russian policy, gave them lands and supplies and granted them military exemption.[44] Although the agents of the Czar enlisted these settlers, Madame Krüdener's vision of a Land of Promise to the east doubtless facilitated their decision.

Other emissaries had been busy in the circles where material advantages overshadowed considerations of religion and mysticism. During the winter of 1816–1817 representatives of Dutch shipping firms spread the story that at Rotterdam and Amsterdam free transportation across the Atlantic was available.[45] In direct conversation with prospective emigrants they undoubtedly made clear that payment would take the form of service under the usual redemptioner terms; but popular report, seizing upon the first part of the tale, induced thousands of families to hasten to Holland. In March the trek began. The boats trading up and down the Rhine proved unable to accommodate the horde. Soon the roads on both sides of the river were clogged with ragged and bewildered families hurrying to reach the ship's side before the berths were filled.[46] On arriving, however, they learned that the shipping agents would accept as redemptioners only the sturdiest and most skilled and then only on harsh conditions. Some had brought carefully treasured pieces of gold to pay for passage if that by any chance should be necessary, but even these resources proved inadequate when the unusual demand boosted the fares beyond reason. Finally, no accommodations were to be had at any price.

Ashamed to return to the lands they had forsworn, they crowded into tenements of Amsterdam and squatted upon the streets.[47] Though the city had the reputation of caring generously for strangers, private charity could not succor the thirty thousand prospective emigrants who, it was estimated,

were stranded there by June. The public authorities hastily
built barracks outside the walls to quarter the poorer families
until more ships should arrive and rates decline.[48] Many
were directed to leave; a royal decree discouraged later comers
by permitting only those to cross into Holland for whose
support some resident of the kingdom would assume responsibility during the period preliminary to embarking.[49]

Disillusioned and penniless, the majority of the derelicts
had to swallow their pride and find their way on foot "back
home." The return journey presented a pitiful spectacle.
Though few possessed any baggage, the weary parents were
burdened with a multitude of offspring — infants in arms
and ragged children scarcely able to keep up with their elders.
At night the wayfarers camped on the outskirts of villages,
begging assistance from the inhabitants while the local police
officers eyed them suspiciously. As the straggling columns
advanced, they met new contingents coming down the
Rhine, but many of the latter, dismayed by the gloomy reports, turned about in their tracks. When at last the native
village was reached, they became a problem to the authorities. Destitute and homeless, the unfortunates had to be
supported from public funds until they again found work.[50]

Though in Great Britain the desire for departure was
equally strong, no similar scenes of confusion took place.
The seaports were not so far away and the information available for emigrants was more complete and specific. Notwithstanding the fact that distress prevailed throughout the
United Kingdom, the principal exodus occurred in England
where the yeoman farmers still possessed resources sufficient
to defray the cost of transportation.[51] Welshmen, Scotchmen
and Irishmen, no matter how eager to leave, ran into difficulties because, despite the presence of many grain-carrying
vessels in port, the rates were high. Popular opinion ascribed
this condition to the restrictions of the British passenger act,

a view reënforced by the fact that a modification of the statute in the spring of 1817 had the effect of reducing the price of passage in the case of persons going to the St. Lawrence and the maritime provinces.[52] The large influx of settlers into British North America dates from this season, although many of the arrivals in Nova Scotia and New Brunswick at once boarded the coasting sloops and schooners to continue their journey to the United States.

Hezekiah Niles of the *Register*, perplexed by the fantastic estimates of his journalistic contemporaries, attempted to secure reliable figures by studying the shipping lists in the daily press. Early in September, 1817, when the season was practically at an end, he reckoned the number of arrivals during the year at thirty thousand — twenty thousand from the British Isles, eight thousand from Germany and two thousand from France.[53] In the following January definite reports for New York and Philadelphia revealed that about fifteen thousand had disembarked at those places.[54] This fact would seem to confirm Niles's original estimate, for in the first years after the federal government began keeping accurate figures, New York and Philadelphia usually accounted for about half the total number of immigrants.

Thirty thousand inhabitants formed a large addition for a single year. That they were received with less difficulty than smaller numbers had been in earlier seasons was due to the changed economic situation. The frontier war in 1812 had quieted the Indian menace, and the peace of 1815 had inaugurated a renewal of the westward flow of population. Moving slowly at first, the stream gathered volume, probably reaching its crest in 1817. Eastern farmers, eager to move to the new settlements beyond the mountains, disposed of lands and stock at bargain prices to immigrants who could make cash payments.[55] Those newcomers who themselves went west quickly discovered openings for their labor on

the larger farms and as smiths, carpenters and masons.[56] Most
of the new arrivals, however, who crossed into the Ohio Valley, wished to till their own farms.

Their experiences illustrate again the fundamental principle that pioneering was a specialized occupation in which
only a few could succeed. The route over the mountains was
longer and more difficult than the immigrants had foreseen;
the expenses of travel cut deeply into their funds; many were
stranded in cities and villages along the way. If they finally
reached their destination, they found the most fertile and
accessible tracts preëmpted by speculators. The prospect of
pressing on into remoter regions proved discouraging.[57]
Such difficulties turned attention to the desirability of collective colonization. Why could not associations of settlers
be formed whose joint resources and efforts would secure
desirable lands, overcome inexperience and dispel loneliness?

A precedent had already been established. Late in 1816
several prominent newcomers among the French, excited by
the deplorable condition and uncertain prospects of their
fellow countrymen, joined with some philanthropic citizens
in applying to Congress for the sale of a few townships of
land on terms so favorable that many spoke of it as a "grant."
The French, the petitioners said, could contribute much to
American agriculture; they knew how to grow the vine and
the olive tree, and Americans by learning the art would
at last free the country from the necessity of importing wine
and oil from the Mediterranean; this possibility would
justify a deviation from the existing land policy. Congress,
duly impressed, in 1817 sold on extended credit four townships on the Tombigbee River in Alabama to a hastily formed
organization known as the Society for the Olive and the
Vine.[58]

The society at once recruited scattered Frenchmen, many
of them without practical experience in vineyards and olive

groves and without capital. A first contingent was sent south
to build a town and begin the clearing. They found Alabama in a primitive condition. The Indians were not all
removed from ceded lands; and surveys were so incomplete
that boundaries were uncertain. Only after the town of
Aigleville was established did the pioneers learn that they
occupied ground to which they had no title. Forced to remove, they could not duplicate their first enthusiasm in a
second attempt. Nevertheless another village did arise, farms
were marked out and more adventurers joined the colony.
For the next decade about two hundred settlers struggled to
fulfill the obligations that they had undertaken.[59]

Long before their failure was evident, the attention of
American Frenchmen centered on a more spectacular scheme.
The large element of soldiers of fortune among them were
not content with a placid existence as vintners and orchard-
men. Beyond Alabama were opportunities not only for
settlement but for adventure and possibly wealth. When
the bolder spirits proposed a soldier colony on the plains
of Texas to be known as Champ d'Asile, some of the Alabama
leaders deserted their companions, and Texas became the
hope of the remaining refugees.[60] The first expedition sailed
in December, 1817, and was joined at Galveston the following
spring by the commander, General Lallement, and large
reënforcements. But Indians, Mexicans, climate and hurri-
canes ultimately ruined the ambitious project. The survivors
were saved only by assistance rendered by the romantic
Gulf pirate Jean Laffitte and by charitable subscriptions
obtained in France.[61]

This ill-starred venture discredited several other contemporary projects more practical in nature. Many rumors had
attended its launching. Some considered it another of the
filibustering expeditions to help revolting Spanish America;
others whispered that the United States government was

fostering it in order to strengthen its disputed claim to Texas; popular opinion generally believed that the leaders had profited greatly by manipulating their rights in the Alabama land grant and were using the fortunes thus acquired in a chimerical asylum for Napoleonic veterans.[62] If the last surmise were true, it involved the Alabama settlers in a flagrant violation of the agreement that they had accepted when the generous terms were extended. Any group which approached Congress with a similar request could expect to have their petition viewed with suspicion and their plan subjected to searching scrutiny.

The Irish were the first to discover this fact. Almost as soon as the French proposals had been made public, the editor of the *Shamrock*, which served as the organ of the Hibernian immigrant element, asked, why could not an Irish colony be started on the same terms? [63] The following summer the editor repeated his question and ridiculed the objection that the encouragement of compact national settlements would be an unwise policy. Would two or three thousand unarmed families, he inquired, "rush from their forests, and overthrow the government, surrounded and supported as it is by millions of loyal citizens?" Certainly, he declared, no such danger could attach to the Irish whose prejudices were already pro-American.[64] When Congress met in December, 1817, it was greeted with petitions from the Irish societies of New York, Philadelphia and Baltimore.[65] Let Congress, they asked, set aside the existing land regulations and sell on long-term credit, instead of the usual four years, a township in Illinois Territory to be settled by Irishmen. This action, they averred, would assist penniless immigrants and at the same time speed the development of the surrounding region.

The House committee on public lands reporting on these petitions in February, 1818, undoubtedly reflected a public sentiment that was overwhelming. Recommending against the petitioners, it pointed out that such a concession would lead to similar ones to other national groups and thus discriminate against native-born citizens by granting special privileges to persons of foreign birth.[66] The House in accepting the report put an end to the agitation; and editorial comment in this period of heightened nationality indicates a firm purpose to protect the distinctive character of the American people as well as the industry of the country.[67]

Among those who anxiously followed the course of these proceedings was an Englishman whose mind was also busy with an ambitious plan. Morris Birkbeck, a substantial English farmer who had applied with profit much of the new agricultural science, viewed the future in his own country with deep pessimism. Acquaintance with Americans — Washington had been one of his correspondents — naturally drew his attention to the possibilities of the newer parts of America.[68] As in similar instances, the obvious drawbacks that pioneering offered to a man habituated to the society of rural gentry suggested the particular scheme. He and his friends would locate in a place where wide stretches of unoccupied land would render possible an extensive settlement of Englishmen. The first comers, men of capital, would bring with them servants who would ultimately become owners and in turn provide for the transportation of others. In the course of a few years the life of an English county would be reproduced in the New World.[69]

Birkbeck, his family and a friend, George Flower, emigrated in 1817. Birkbeck had already met Edward Coles, now the Governor of Illinois Territory, and perhaps this fact led him to choose the prairie country as the most promising location. The actual site, however, was yet to be determined because the leaders hoped that they too might secure special legislation from Congress. If they could obtain several townships on deferred payments, the considerable capital they possessed would be set free for improvements and the transportation of settlers.[70] Though both Jefferson and Madison promised to use their influence with Congress, they could not overcome the trend of the times.[71] Birkbeck and Flower, who spent the winter at Princeton, Indiana, realized by spring that their petition would not succeed and therefore they set a modified plan into operation.

They used most of their capital to buy sixteen thousand acres of public land on the prairie west of the Wabash River, where the town of Albion was founded.[72] Since no funds remained for introducing settlers, a campaign of advertising proved necessary. For this task Birkbeck was well equipped. Like Crèvecœur before him and Duden a decade later, he possessed a talent for glorifying the routine of pioneer existence. A slim volume, *Notes on a Journey in America,* had been prepared before the fate of the petition was known; now his *Letters from Illinois* appeared. Both found a ready market. Eleven editions of the one and seven of the other were printed in the course of three years, and the romantic descriptions greatly stimulated interest in the possibilities of the West.[73]

Two other foreign groups displayed an interest in organizing national settlements. The Germans and the Swiss, more than any other people, had a tradition of colonization behind them; but in all previous efforts religion had been the inspiring motive. The emigrants of 1817 who rushed frantically down the Rhine only to return hungry and despairing did not possess any of the advantages that religious fellowship and leadership provided. Moreover, the economic distress which impelled each family was wholly an individual matter. Any supervision or organization would have to come from above.

While the confusion of that summer was still fresh in the

minds of observers, the representatives of the Swiss cantons held their annual meeting. The deputy from the canton of Appenzell, which had been deeply affected by the emigration movement, urged the Confederation to undertake its regulation. The problem, however, concerned only a part of the country, and for that reason the assemblage decided to leave the matter to the several cantons for action in accordance with their needs and revenues. Probably as a concession to the losing party, it was agreed that, upon the demand of one of the governments, the Directory would use its influence with foreign powers.[74] In thus throwing the initiative back to each canton, the way was opened for the colonial venture of New Freiburg, the Brazilian undertaking that for several years influenced the course of Swiss emigration.

Even before this action by Switzerland, a similar proposal was offered in the Diet of the German Confederation by Freiherr von Gagern. As the representative of Holland, his humanitarianism had been aroused by the deplorable state of the refugees in the Dutch ports. He suggested the appointment of a committee to consider the problem; but, as in Switzerland, the difficulty affected only certain communities, and his proposal failed.[75] Von Gagern, undaunted, decided that, if the movement could not be organized on the European side of the Atlantic, an effort should be made in America. Accordingly he charged his brother-in-law, the Baron von Fürstenwarther, to visit the United States, observe the condition of the Germans there, and negotiate with the American government for easier terms of acquiring land.[76] By the summer of 1818 von Fürstenwarther was in Washington where he interviewed John Quincy Adams, the Secretary of State.

Adams's letter of June 4, evidently written as a summary of their conversation, embodies the first formal expression of the immigration policy of the nation. By that time Congress had revealed its attitude, and he could make an unequivocal statement. The republic, he said, invites none to come; it will not keep out those who have the courage to cross the Atlantic; they will suffer no disabilities as aliens, but they can expect no special advantages; foreign-born and natives alike face the same opportunities and their success will depend upon their individual activity and good fortune.[77]

The thirty thousand immigrants who during 1818 entered the United States [78] had no relationship to the development of this policy. Less than their predecessors of the year before did they need guidance or practical assistance. Not only did the experiences of 1817 serve as a warning to the reckless, but several Continental states maintained regulations that made it practically impossible for persons without considerable resources to leave.[79] The French political exodus had come to an end, and some of the Bonapartist exiles were beginning to return with the announcement of a more lenient attitude toward them. Though the rates of transportation from the British Isles continued high, at Dublin so many berths were engaged by relatives and friends in America that the shipping agents could not accommodate all those who appeared with reservations.[80] In general, the migration of the season consisted of the more prosperous small farmers and prudent mechanics, a large proportion of whom continued on to the American West.[81]

In England, however, the skilled worker faced a difficult barrier to emigration, for the government sought jealously to guard the technical knowledge and experience that assured the nation its industrial supremacy.[82] The exportation of models of machinery was prohibited, even to Canada,[83] and every prospective emigrant had to present a certificate signed by the authorities of his native parish that he was not a "manufacturer" or "artificer." [84] Great ingenuity was used to evade this requirement. Many sailed for Canada and then passed over the line. Others crossed the channel where less vigilance was applied and embarked for the United States at a French port. Those who were willing to resort to fraud found certificates for sale at as low a price as five shillings.[85] By one method or another — perhaps also through the lax enforcement of laws that were unpopular — many weavers, in particular, reached Philadelphia where in some suburban streets the sound of the loom never ceased.[86] By the end of summer the complaint was heard that overpopulation and unemployment were resulting from the great numbers that had landed.[87]

Common laborers faced fewer difficulties. During 1818 activity in construction and shipping was at boom heights, and Eastern farmers were still profiting from the dearth apparent in the European market. Contractors needed workers and farmers wanted help.[88] Persons engaged in the redemptioner business, discovering that new arrivals were quickly taken off their hands, prosecuted the trade with more vigor.[89] Since captains who sailed out of Irish ports could make two or more trips a season, they accordingly possessed an advantage over their Continental rivals in responding to the demand.[90] From early spring until autumn agents actively enrolled servants in all parts of Ireland, including the southern counties where the tradition of emigration was less strong than in Ulster and the north. The terms of service tended to be harsh, for masters claimed that, with the opening of the West, the danger of loss by runaways was greater. The traffic, like any other labor relationship that suggested slavery, encountered severe criticism. So many were the alleged abuses that the Pennsylvania legislature at its winter session adopted a law to protect more effectively the rights of servants.[91]

The year 1818 also saw a considerable flow of immigrants into Canada.[92] Though public funds no longer subsidized

their transportation, and no equipment or supplies were provided, every arrival could apply for a grant of land propor-
tionate to the means he possessed for its cultivation.[93] Many
small farmer capitalists found Upper Canada an ideal location, English in government and society. Along with them
came soldier colonists, veterans of the war around the Lakes.
They had been promised concessions and special advantages
and now, having had time to be transported home and mustered out, they returned with their families for another sort
of wilderness campaigning.[94] The majority of common
laborers going to the maritime provinces, however, sooner
or later continued down the coast to the American cities;
while of those who landed at Quebec or Montreal probably a
third did likewise, attracted by the reports of plentiful and
profitable employment.

Canadian landowners and officials eager to populate the
provinces had to contend with the growing belief that Morris
Birkbeck was creating a new England in the Illinois prairies.[95]
Some four hundred settlers joined him during the first year
of the enterprise, people who impressed all observers as being
as superior to the average immigrant in intelligence as they
evidently were in property.[96] But just when the reputation
of the settlement was brightest and translations of Birkbeck's
writings were bringing it to Continental attention, misfortunes began. Birkbeck and his principal associate, Flower,
quarreled and each founded a village for his own group of
adherents. Many of the later arrivals, disgusted with the
schism, preferred the Indiana side of the Wabash River, and
although occasional settlers joined their acquaintances and
relatives on the "English Prairie," the colony ceased to be a
significant factor in influencing migration.[97]

This event was not entirely the result of internal dissension. Birkbeck's vigorous propaganda provoked counter-
attacks, and the first to enter the lists was one who knew

how to express his opinions effectively. In 1817 William Cobbett during a sojourn in the United States continued to edit the *Political Register* from the Long Island farm which he made his home.[98] The tendency of British immigrants to settle in the West quickly drew his adverse comment, and his criticism finally centered on the Illinois venture. His book, *A Year's Residence in America*, published in 1819, contained an appendix explaining the hardships of pioneering, describing the fevers that infested the West, and accusing Birkbeck of causing untold and needless suffering for private gain.[99] Birkbeck answered in a vigorous pamphlet which charged Cobbett with being the hireling of a group of Eastern land jobbers who needed to stem the westward trend.[100] The accusation could not be proved, but the suspicion gained credence from the fact that such a group did soon make its appearance.

Another volume, published the same year, also warned against the Western fever. This was the *Letters from the British Settlement in Pennsylvania*, edited by C. B. Johnson. Who Johnson was is unknown; in fact, his very existence is questioned; and the "British Emigrant Society," whose advice to avoid the West for the healthy and accessible Susquehanna Valley figured conspicuously in his pages, may have also been created for the purpose.[101] The owner of the recommended lands, Dr. Robert H. Rose of Montrose, Pennsylvania, possessed tracts of imperial proportions; at one time his holdings amounted to at least a hundred thousand acres along the Pennsylvania–New York boundary.[102] But land without people was not wealth, and to get people it was necessary to deflect the westward-moving current. Johnson's *Letters* were widely circulated and favorably reviewed. Prominent Englishmen in New York City — perhaps for disinterested reasons, perhaps because Rose had negotiated with them — advised their newly arrived countrymen to proceed at once to the settlement.[103] Moreover, Cobbett had coupled his violent denunciation of Birkbeck's prairie colony with a cautious approval of the Pennsylvania enterprise. But the efforts were a few years too late. Although several families took up farms and in time prospered, Rose was obliged to turn his ingenuity to other speculations.

The colony idea died hard. It persisted even after it was clear that no bounties of government land could be expected. Thus Ferdinand Ernst of Hanover, coming to the United States in 1819, settled at his own expense twenty or thirty families near Vandalia, Illinois. But frontier fevers killed so many of the group that he was obliged to give up his ambitions and settle down to the routine of a pioneer farmer.[104] A second German project, which did not achieve even the distinction of a trial, possessed greater historical significance. It arose among the students of the university town of Giessen. Discouraged by the Carlsbad decrees of 1819, some of the younger liberals proposed a community settlement in the New World where their ideals might be realized and whence their influence might spread. When the government proceeded against the leaders because of their political nonconformity, they fled, and the colony project, which was only a by-product of their liberalism, automatically came to an end. But the idea was not forgotten; fifteen years later Paul Follen, one of the original sponsors, revived it on a larger scale and made it one of the most significant chapters in the history of German migration.[105]

Though none of these settlement schemes received encouragement from native Americans, the general attitude toward incoming foreigners was tolerant, if not cordial. James Flint, commenting in 1818 on the number of immigrants seen on the streets, said, "I have never heard of another feeling than good wishes to them." [106] Had sentiment been hostile, it would have so expressed itself during the congres-

sional session of 1818–1819, which enacted the first federal
statute dealing with immigration as a national problem. This
legislation arose from a growing realization of the unsafe and
unsanitary conditions of transportation. Less complaint was
heard from passengers coming from the British Isles than
from the Continent because Parliament prescribed certain
regulations as to space and supervision. But no laws, American, Dutch, French or German, governed the Continental
traffic. German newcomers told gruesome stories of hunger,
filth, disease and death.[107]

If humane considerations had not entered in, the need
to keep out pestilence would have proved sufficient to induce
Congress to appoint an investigating committee. This committee confirmed the existence of many of the evils and
prepared a bill which, with a minimum of interference with
the habits of the passengers or the discipline of the vessels,
would put an end to the worst conditions.[108] To members
of Congress the proposals seemed reasonable. Had anti-
immigration sentiment existed, an attempt would undoubtedly have been made to fix requirements so as to check the
flow. In the absence of such provisions the law of March 4,
1819, was merely a regulatory, not a restrictive, measure.
Recognizing overcrowding as the fundamental trouble, it
forbade any transatlantic ship entering an American port to
carry more than two persons for every five tons of its registry.
Customs officers must record the number of passengers in
such vessels. Heavy penalties were inflicted on violators.[109]
As it was too late to apply these regulations during the coming
season, they were to go into effect on September 1, 1819. Accordingly, federal supervision and official statistics of immigration begin with that date.

The ease with which the newcomers of 1818 were absorbed
promised a continuation of the movement on the same or an
enlarged scale in 1819. With this prospect in mind, redemp-

tioner brokers during the winter actively spread the news of American prosperity and enrolled servants for the spring ships. Commercial houses also anticipated a brisk demand and provided an ample fleet. Everything was ready for the greatest human migration the Atlantic had yet seen.[110] Then came an unanticipated collapse of business; the boom had run its course. The trouble began in the West where the heaviness in the overvalued real-estate market toppled over local banks. The panic, spreading eastward, destroyed one financial institution after the other. In their train, factories shut down; farmers faced starvation prices as they learned that Europe no longer needed their products; shippers saw no prospect of cargoes; the great commercial speculation that had exaggerated possibilities in the revolting Spanish-American states was suddenly deflated. John Quincy Adams, fearing the worst, confided to his diary on April 24: "In the midst of peace, and of partial prosperity, we are approaching to a crisis which will shake the Union to its centre." [111]

News of the collapse reached Europe too late to affect the spring and early summer migration. Mechanics, farmers and servants departed as hopefully as any of their predecessors, only to face on arrival a disillusionment as bitter as it was unexpected. Farmers with savings could provide for themselves, but many of them, instead of proceeding into the interior, lingered in the ports, fearing for the future, wasting their funds and sighing for the country they had left. Still the passengers continued to disembark. Through June and July, even into September, the newspapers reported arrivals until the number equaled, perhaps surpassed, that which had entered in the prosperous year of 1818.[112]

Mechanics who had no resource but their skill were in a particularly deplorable plight. The cotton mills of Philadelphia and the vicinity, which in 1816 had worked 2325 hands, employed only 149 on October 2, 1819.[113] The following year, when agents collected data for the federal census, they commented on the widespread economic disaster with dramatic brevity: "Flourishing in 1816, but now useless to the owners"; "Does but little business, and that at a loss"; "Very much depressed and daily declining"; "Stopped by the pressure of the times"; "Ceased operation in 1819"; "Demand dull, manufacture principally disposed of in barter." [114] These laconic statements revealed a condition which meant less opportunity for recent comers and exposed them at once to competition with the native-born unemployed. Even the most skilled artisans seized whatever job presented itself, whether sawing wood in the cities or breaking stones on the highways. Many set out on aimless wanderings.

As the summer wore on and the incoming stream continued, the calls upon charity became insistent. "The time has been when we were pleased to see the progress of emigration," wrote Editor Niles on July 31. "It is now painful to observe it because of the want of employment for our own people." [115] The city of New York sought to take appropriate action. A state law required each master of a vessel to report his passengers at the mayor's office, and authorized the municipal officials at their discretion to demand a bond not exceeding three hundred dollars for each alien likely to become a public charge.[116] This provision they now attempted to enforce, but their efforts met with little success. Passengers were landed at night and upon obscure wharves; or they were transferred to coasting vessels, which were exempt from the regulation; or perhaps they disembarked a short distance away and walked into the city.[117] "It has not been uncommon during the summer," the mayor reported, "to meet droves of these foreigners, who have been landed some miles to the east, lugging their chests and beds towards the city. Many of these have sunk under the fatigue; and we have now some of them in the alms-house taken from the roads, where they could not be left to perish." [118]

To one class of immigrants the distress of the times brought an unexpected turn of fortune.[119] The economic breakdown affected no speculators more directly than the redemptioner brokers whose servants were waiting on board the ships lying in the harbors of Philadelphia and Baltimore. Since no buyers appeared and every day meant an added expense in feeding the laborers, the brokers sent them out like groups of slaves to the West and the South in the hope of peddling them off along the way. Others, who could not secure credit to maintain the servants any longer, set them free to shift for themselves and oftentimes to meet a fate which, if equally deplorable, was the more bearable because they were their own masters. From this blow the redemptioner trade never recovered. The established agents went bankrupt; and the lesson proved so severe that in the future no new operators dared to revive the system.

Some of the immigrants of 1819 remained only a few days or weeks in the New World. If they were able to do so, the temptation to return was too strong to resist. But those who felt the distress most keenly possessed no means. Crowds of disillusioned foreigners thronged the consulates, begging to be sent back to the happy land of their birth.[120] The British consul at Baltimore reported it was "painful to attend my office" because of the despairing tales that he heard and the sights he witnessed.[121] Letters describing these conditions reached Europe toward the end of the summer. At first doubted, they were confirmed when refugees from the disaster began to arrive. English newspapers which in the spring had neglected to mention the extent of the emigration now did not hesitate to report and moralize upon the returning tide.[122]

Five years of peace had provided the United States a varied experience: prosperity and depression, unlimited hopes and black despair. But there was also something constructive that this period passed on to the future. A policy of immigration had been evolved; a regulatory law had been adopted. In addition, about a hundred thousand new inhabitants had been received. They were to live through much and to learn much, and ultimately were to make clear to Europe the true promise of American life. For the time being, however, the venture seemed a ghastly failure. The new beginning had been a false start, and America, which for a few years had enjoyed a repute unequaled by any other nation, fell into a popular disfavor which turned the European migrant towards other lands and left the western republic to almost a decade of isolation.

V

AMERICA IN DISFAVOR

THE BITTERNESS OF HARD TIMES tinged the attitude both of Americans toward immigrants and of immigrants toward America. No longer did the native-born view newcomers as welcome additions to their ranks. Foreign visitors became quickly aware of this reversal of feeling. Thus, Ludwig Gall, landing at New York with pleasurable anticipations in July, 1819, was chilled to hear a bystander refer to him and his companion as "more damned emigrants." [1] Another arrival, who called upon a merchant to present letters of introduction, was greeted by a disquisition on the desirability of an absolute prohibition of immigration.[2] A third observed that the Yankee looked upon the newcomer "with the most sovereign contempt . . . a wretch, driven out of a wretched country, and seeking a subsistence in his glorious land." [3]

With equal fervor the expatriates expressed their disillusion. The United States, in their opinion, had nothing to offer but a wilderness; the once acclaimed opportunities were only bait for the unwary; the people, uncouth and turbulent, possessed a government that was ineffective; mail robberies, murders and incendiary fires occurred daily, though the culprits were never apprehended; great storms unknown in other parts of the world ravaged cities and fields; fevers arose from the prairie swamps and from the marshes that bordered the ports.[4] "England, with all thy faults I love thee still," a homesick immigrant wrote upon a Pennsylvania bridge where it struck a responsive chord in the hearts of wanderers already growing weary of their journey westward.[5]

When can a civilized European feel at home in this prepos-
terous land? was a question which an amateur versifier answered in the lines:

> When fields of corn spontaneous spring
> From woods and miry bogs
> And emigrants are all content
> To feed on snakes and frogs.[6]

However bitter the state of feeling, both the immigrant
and his reluctant host had to face the actualities of the situation. In its report of December, 1819, the New York Society
for the Prevention of Pauperism cited the jobless aliens as
an important source of poverty in that city. "We cannot
force them back upon the ocean; we cannot suffer them to
starve at our own doors; we cannot drive them by force to
the shades and fastnesses of the wilderness." [7] To meet the
emergency, the society provided the simplest form of charity
— the soup kitchen. In the spring and summer that followed,
only a slight accession to the ranks of the laborers came from
abroad, and those who had survived the hardship, destitution and prejudice gradually found employment in New
York or elsewhere. But the prejudice against immigrants
did not soon die. The political events of the years immediately succeeding illustrate the conviction that America was
a world apart, now happily free to go its own way. The
Monroe Doctrine of 1823 was the formal expression of this
spirit of continental independence.

The decline in the number of foreign arrivals during the
greater part of the decade of the twenties was not due to any
lack of potential emigrants in Europe. While immigration
fell off, emigration continued — but to other parts of the
world where attractions, for the time being, proved stronger.
Since the close of the war Russia had rivaled the United
States in popular interest, and its renown continued for
almost a decade. It had been playing an increasingly im-

portant rôle in the affairs of Europe for a quarter of a century. It was Russia which had delivered the nations from the tyrant's yoke: the ill-fated Moscow expedition had marked the beginning of Napoleon's downfall. It was Russia which had initiated the Holy Alliance — a solemn guarantee (so people thought) that never again would dynasties or upstarts slaughter husbands and sons to gratify their overweening ambition. In the troublous times of the wars holy men had said, "Salvation will come out of the East" — and so it had.[8]

In Russia itself a new day was dawning. Alexander did not let his interest in a new world order blind him to the conditions in his realm. Resolving to modernize the nation, and not content with a mere westernization of the court and aristocracy, he planned to make over all economic life according to the model of the more progressive Atlantic nations. Peter the Great had worked in the shipyards of Holland and had introduced into his kingdom the skill and technique of the master workmen. But it was impracticable to send great numbers of merchants, physicians and farmers abroad to learn new methods. Alexander proposed to reverse the process and plant colonies of foreigners in the midst of Russia from whom the people might learn by daily association. In the preceding century Catherine had followed the same policy on the imperial estates,[9] but now the attempt was to be more general.

Unfortunately the first experiment was prompted by the necessity of protecting the frontier. Along the mountains of the Caucasus stretched an area over which Russia exercised only a nominal authority. Tartars and Persians had repeatedly laid it waste while the Empire was preoccupied with western campaigns. Though ordinarily efforts to secure settlers for such an unattractive task would not have succeeded, now the agents could appeal to other than practical motives. During the second decade of the nineteenth century southern

Germany (Württemberg in particular) and the adjacent parts of Switzerland witnessed one of the recurring waves of "Pietism" that arose spontaneously among the people. The desire to avoid a catechism and prayer book containing unorthodox doctrines turned thoughts to emigration; and the religious toleration decreed by the Czar, along with the concessions of land and the accessibility of the region, caused a first party to be sent out from Württemberg in 1816.[10] A much larger group followed in 1817, consisting of fourteen columns of wagons which left Ulm from April to August. Unhappily, the journey led through the unhealthy region of the lower Danube where over two thousand persons died and it was necessary to undergo an extended quarantine imposed by the Russian authorities. Many families, discouraged by these delays, separated from the main body and scattered among the older German colonies in south Russia. The others wintered in Odessa, but the second summer's journey was as trying as the first. Of the fifteen hundred families which had started on the pilgrimage, only five hundred reached Tiflis. In view of the limited success of this enterprise, the Russian government in 1819 instructed its minister in Württemberg to visa no more passports for this region.[11]

Interest now shifted to another part of the Czar's domains, one not only more accessible, but where the conditions of life were European, not Asiatic, and German settlers, as in the Caucasus, might serve as a frontier buffer. The Congress of Vienna, instead of crushing the national spirit of the Poles by subjecting them to the autocratic rule of powerful neighbors, organized a large part of the ancient state into a new Kingdom of Poland with Alexander of Russia wearing the crown. Only fifteen years later this experiment was to close in a revolution of blood and pillage which was to discredit Russia among the liberals of the world; but in 1815 Alex-

ander's intentions accorded with the highest ideals of state-
craft. His plans called for a comprehensive improvement of
agriculture and a stimulation of industry.

To achieve these ends, emissaries were again sent to the
population-congested areas of the west to secure farmers and
skilled artisans. Although tentative proposals were made as
early as 1816, development of the full program awaited the
ukases issued in 1820, 1823 and 1824. Agents charged with
circulating these documents explained the advantages that
were offered — lands, exemption from military service, and
freedom from taxes for a period of years.[12] At exactly the
time that the bubble of false hopes regarding America burst,
a country that had so much to offer for the future opened its
doors. Here were untilled fields and rich opportunities in
mines and commerce — all to be reached without the expense
and discomfort of a transatlantic voyage.

The details of the policy were worked out through a maze
of administrative orders. With a little experience the methods demonstrated their practicality, and reports of good
fortune encouraged other settlers to follow. The movement
probably reached its peak in 1824. At a time for which statistics of even overseas migration are scanty, figures measuring
a continental movement must be entirely conjectural. The
earliest and perhaps most reliable estimate fixed the number
of German emigrants who established themselves in Poland
from 1818 to 1828 at two hundred and fifty thousand — an
average of twenty-five thousand a year. During these same
years Germans entering the United States annually numbered less than a thousand.[13]

The agricultural aspect of this enterprise developed in an
unexpected way. Not only the government but also extensive
landowners offered concessions to induce settlement.[14] In
some cases, however, they promised more than they could
fulfill. This fact, combined with agricultural conditions that

were even more primitive than anticipated, caused many to desert farming; but, instead of returning to Germany, they drifted into the small industrial villages.[15] Imperial Russia, shut off from the factories of western Europe by tariff walls, offered a market for these new Polish industries; and at first by the hundreds, then by the thousands, the weavers and artisans of Saxony and Prussia crossed over to take advantage of this situation.[16] The villages which they founded on the sandy wastes became the cities of Lodz, Zgierz, Tomaszów and many others whose names loom large in the textile history of the nineteenth century.[17]

This turn of affairs in Poland did not cause the agriculturally inclined to renew their interest in the United States. A new rival had appeared in Brazil. Its popularity was the more surprising in view of the dismal failure of the first organized attempt at colonization. In 1818, when Switzerland was troubled by hordes of wandering beggars and the increasing poverty of the industrious peasantry, the Portuguese consul suggested to several of the cantonal governments that arrangements be made to transport hundreds of families to Brazil. Only Freiburg acted favorably on the proposal. Aided by royal bounties and special privileges, the Colony of New Freiburg was to be established not far from Rio de Janeiro.[18] In June and July, 1819, over two thousand emigrants from Freiburg and the neighboring cantons embarked upon the Rhine.[19] In Holland confusion regarding ships caused a long delay during which temporary shacks provided the only shelter. Many were suffering from fever when at last embarkation took place.[20] Some of the voyagers recorded only the horrors of the journey, the ignorance of the captain who beat along the shore looking for his harbor, the strangeness of the surrounding life, the incompleteness of the plans for their reception.[21] Others, though sensible of the discomforts, praised the king's cordiality and the hospitality of the

Brazilian people, and believed that a short time would set all things right.[22]

Such, however, did not prove to be the case. For six months, until lands were allotted, the colonists were crowded into villages or the dense quarters of cities where hundreds of them succumbed to the diseases of the rainy season. Largely for this reason, only eight hundred of the twenty-two hundred who left Switzerland survived in September, 1821.[23] Moreover, the subsidies of the government were too small to support those whose resources had been depleted by the delay. Relations with the Brazilians became more and more unfriendly, and were intensified by religious differences. The colony began to break up. Those who still possessed some means struck out for themselves; others bound themselves in service to wealthy plantation owners; the majority were saved by charity from their homeland. The authorities of Bern and Freiburg, who felt a special responsibility, joined with the wealthy Swiss in London and Paris in contributing to a relief fund. In several cantons where collections were taken in the churches, the ministers did not neglect to emphasize the moral — the sinfulness of leaving one's native land. Many persons believed that the disaster would end all projects of emigration to the New World.[24]

Other factors, however, upset this prediction. At no time since the discovery of the southern continent had the imagination of Europe been so stirred by South America. The protracted struggles for independence acquired an epic character, for not only had more than twenty millions thrown off an unbearable yoke, but they had thereby opened to the world a terrestrial paradise: a fertile soil yielding exotic tropical fruits, a balmy climate, inspiring scenery, rich resources in mines and forests.[25] South America could offer what Europe needed in exchange for the products of her workshops.[26] And of these new nations Brazil stood foremost.

Revolution and bloodshed had left scars in the former Spanish possessions, but Brazil had been spared these evils while securing an independence from Portugal no less real. She only needed industrious workers to people her domains, and this object became a fundamental aspect of her national policy.

In spite of the discouraging experiences at New Freiburg, Germans and Swiss were still considered the most desirable pioneers,[27] and therefore the Brazilian government selected Major Georg von Schaeffer, a professional soldier of fortune, to organize a fresh migration. After military adventures under the flags of Turkey, Bohemia and Russia he had finally taken service in the Brazilian army. There his loyalty, his striking appearance, his ability to handle men, singled him out as a person who could overcome the prejudices of German peasants against a new Brazilian undertaking. In 1822 he went with dispatches to various European courts, and then established himself in Hamburg, apparently in the status of a consul.[28]

Through his activities Brazil became a household word. A song, "Brasilien ist nicht weit von hier," was distributed on broadsides, and soon children sang it on the streets to the accompaniment of hand organs.[29] As a matter of fact, Schaeffer had little to offer those who came to him. If they lacked financial resources and expected free transportation, he turned them away unless they were vigorous young men willing to serve in Brazil's military forces. In such cases they were promptly enlisted, their passports were taken from them so that they might not change their minds, and Schaeffer's lieutenants proceeded to give them preliminary training. He received inquirers possessing ready money in a spirit of gracious cordiality, enchanted them with stories of Brazil, and finally persuaded them to pay over what cash they had for passage to South America.[30]

Many features of this recruiting irritated the German governments. Young men who had not performed their military obligations were being tempted to leave; penniless families which congregated at Schaeffer's headquarters in the hope that he would transport them were obliged to straggle back to their native villages in direst distress; his presence in Hamburg lured adventurers and criminals to the city.[31] By the close of 1824 the coldness of the officials caused him to move to the rival port of Bremen where he conducted operations for a few years from the office of the Brazilian consulate.[32] Despite Schaeffer's energetic campaign, the Germans who emigrated to Brazil in the middle twenties did not total more than four or five thousand. About the same number went to the United States. Of greater importance was the fact that his efforts excited the interest of prospective emigrants for several years, and kept them waiting until the prospects of Brazil were clarified — for better or for worse.

As has been seen, these projects, in Russia and South America, appealed especially to Continental emigrants. The British, however, were not entirely unaffected by the desire to get away. A group of Scots were among the first to respond to the invitation that came from Poland, but the adjustment proved so difficult that their cries of distress brought repatriation at the expense of the British government.[33] Brazil also attracted attention, but organized emigration was thwarted by official discouragement. Although many hundreds did depart, they were principally restless professional soldiers who, finding no employment in a peaceful Europe, enlisted in the battalions of the South American states.

The British authorities were intent on turning the current of emigration into imperial channels. Just as Russia and Brazil sought to shunt the tide of Continental emigrants toward themselves, so these British efforts aimed to prevent the flow of English, Scots and Irish to the United States. An unexpected event brought the matter into sharp relief. In the catalogue of Irish tragedies the famine of 1822 is dwarfed by the greater calamity of a quarter of a century later. Yet the experience of that year should have served as a warning signal to show that Ireland's prosperity rested on the precarious fate of the potato. The linen industry might thrive; but if the potato failed, the food of the people was gone, and distress and financial ruin threatened not only the humble cottager, but the whole unstable pyramid which rested upon the rents that he paid.[34] The crop of 1821 was a failure, and by the spring of 1822 the misery of the peasantry made necessary an appeal to the generosity of the British people. The response to this call and a good potato crop the following summer prevented a complete collapse,[35] but in many parts the distress fanned into flame the hostility between landlord and tenant which was always latent. In some counties the civil authorities were rendered helpless, and agrarian outrages became more and more common.[36]

Partly in order to cope with this crisis, partly as an experiment in colonization, a scheme of controlled and assisted emigration was organized in 1823 by the Colonial Office, which had had experience in establishing military settlements. Peter Robinson was authorized to enroll five hundred settlers and convey them to Canada at public expense. He confined his activities to a part of County Cork where some of the worst disorders had occurred. Landlords and priests coöperated in selecting families and in overcoming their prejudice that this was only "transportation" in disguise. When the party sailed from Cork in July, public approval was so strong that the vessel was surrounded by boats filled with persons clamoring to be taken on board.[37] Although these pioneers received an indifferent welcome from their Scotch and English neighbors in Canada, the experiment left an impression upon the minds of the Irish poor, awakening an intense desire to migrate.[38] Accordingly a second and larger contingent, also under Robinson's supervision, went out in 1825. Of fifty thousand applicants only about two thousand were selected.[39] Of the successful applicants many on reaching Canada proved unfit for frontier life, and a considerable proportion, having received passage across the Atlantic, slipped over into the United States.[40]

However disappointing these results, a precedent had nevertheless been set: government aid had been extended. Not unnaturally it began to be asked: why not grant to the English and Scots the same opportunity offered to the Irish? At the suggestion of Robert Wilmot-Horton, an ambitious member of the Colonial Department, a select committee of the Lords and Commons on emigration was appointed. During 1825 and 1826 this committee questioned economists and philanthropists, Canadian officials, Irish landlords and clergymen, and it heard all the advocates of colonial development, poor relief and social betterment. It prepared three reports, the third containing definite proposals for a state-subsidized group emigration. It was now up to Parliament to appropriate the necessary funds in order to make the scheme an official policy, with all its far-reaching implications in national and imperial life.[41]

Such action seemed all the more desirable because a new act governing the passenger trade tended to restrict departures.[42] These new regulations, besides imposing stricter requirements regarding food and accommodations, obliged every emigrant vessel to carry a surgeon. Apart from the financial burden, sometimes a qualified person could not be secured. The consequence was that those who had engaged in the business only for the sake of a little additional profit abandoned it. A general increase in the cost of passage resulted, and many who had planned to depart turned back, for their savings or the proceeds from the sale of their property no longer covered the fare.[43]

While these various policies were being experimented with in other parts of the world, immigration into the United States remained at a low ebb. From 1820 to 1825 the recorded arrivals ranged from six to ten thousand, the smallest number entering in 1823. The descending spiral of the post-panic years emphasized the conditions which had begun to turn newcomers away in the bitter autumn of 1819. No longer did the country employ an annual army of laborers, artisans and farmers, though here and there an opportunity opened for an active youth or a skilled mechanic, and agriculturists with capital could readily find bargains in improved lands. Ships were laid up with the decline in transatlantic trade; agricultural overproduction became more acute as the newly settled Western lands began to produce a surplus; industrial enterprise and public improvements were stagnant.

The detailed figures of immigration reveal the individual character of the movement. The recording was done in a haphazard fashion, many of the officials failing to indicate nationality and others neglecting to specify occupations. Though an exact analysis is impossible, merchants, mariners, farmers and laborers seemed to predominate. Probably the merchants were visitors on business who, in a strict sense, should not be considered, and the mariners were seamen returning home. Then as later, the farmer or laborer was the typical immigrant. A surprising proportion were artisans — blacksmiths, weavers, "spinsters" and "spinstresses." "Schoolmasters" was also a constantly recurring item. "Gentlemen," "ladies" and "yeomen" were numerous. One "nobleman" and one "horse doctor" are recorded. Others did not object to being described as "speculators." Evidently some of the newcomers hoped that the Americans still had a little money left for amusements, for the passengers included "showmen,"

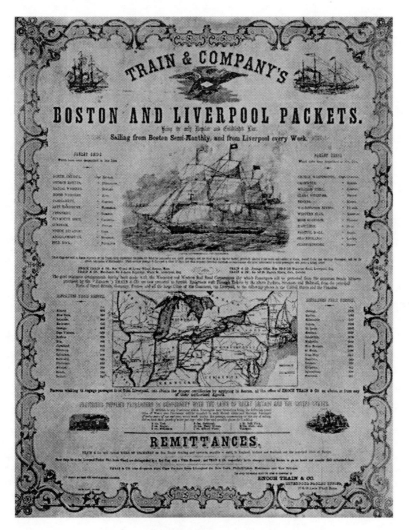

A POSTER FOR EMIGRANTS

"actors," "musicians," "comedians," two "rope-dancers" and one "elephant keeper." [44]

A slight increase of immigration occurred in 1824, and in 1825 the total passed ten thousand. This gain was due in part to the activities of Robert Owen of New Lanark, Scotland, famous for his philanthropy and social ideas, who decided to found a perfect community in the New World. Probably through Richard Flower of the Birkbeck settlement, he was induced to buy the lands and buildings of the Rappites on the Wabash River. This settlement, rechristened New Harmony, at once became the Mecca of persons from America and other lands. Owen had hoped that in three years the settlers might number a thousand, but within a month after the Rappites' departure about nine hundred were on hand, the village was "overflowing with people," and prospective members thronged the roads leading to the Wabash. By December, 1825, the inhabitants represented all but two states of the Union and most of the countries of northern Europe. Every word written about the experiment was a vivid advertisement for the West.

The increased influx of 1825 was also attributable to the inundations which during the previous winter had devastated the valley of the Rhine and its tributaries. The rush of waters had destroyed orchards and vineyards and swept away buildings and crops stacked in the fields. When the flood subsided the lowlands presented scenes of desolation. Mire, sand and débris covered the richest lands, and meadows were ruined. This catastrophe, though localized in its scope, started a new wave of German emigration towards the United States. The popular disrepute from which America had been suffering came to an end.

VI

PIONEERS OF THE GREAT MIGRATION

A S EVIDENCE of the favor with which the United States was now regarded by Europeans, thirty thousand registered passengers entered the United States in 1828, a figure more than twice that of two years before.[1] In 1832 over fifty thousand arrived, and henceforth on only two occasions did the annual total fall below that number.[2] A new movement was under way which was to culminate in the tidal wave of the 1850's. But between the emigrant of 1830 and his successor of 1850 there were pronounced differences. The former migrated in considerable doubt. Though America stood on the threshold of a great period of development, the labor system for this expansion was not yet devised, and emigration in the hope of securing work still seemed a precarious step. The later emigrant crossed the ocean, knowing a system existed which would hire him, distribute him, train him and, finally, assure him a better economic and social status than the one he had left. The working out of this system by the newcomers in the 1830's makes it appropriate to call them the pioneers of the great mid-century migration.

The years after 1825 brought an increasing realization abroad of the labor shortage in America. The depression following 1819 had come to an end. Projects for canals and turnpikes, for warehouses and mills, were being launched. Willing hands were needed. Foreign ship captains spread the word when they tied up at their home ports; and contractors sent agents abroad to recruit workers. This appeal fell upon fertile soil, for times were hard in Europe. The bitter winter of 1825–1826 was followed by one of greater severity, lasting well into the spring of 1827.[3] Prices kept within moderate bounds during 1826 because of the supplies still in storage, but with these exhausted, the second year of shortage witnessed a sharp rise.[4] As was usual at such periods, southwestern Germany, which never produced an abundance of grain, suffered most. Moreover, the extreme cold had injured the vineyards, depleting the cash income with which food might have been bought.

The marked upturn in American immigration in 1827 and 1828 mirrors these new factors. Those leaving Ireland were described as "the small, but industrious and comfortable farmers. These, having tasted of independence, valued it, and prefer, to an uncertain elevation from poverty at home, the effort to secure a permanency in another country." [5] Others were financed by relatives already established in Canada or the United States.[6] The proportion of poverty-stricken Germans was probably greater. They created a serious problem at Le Havre where many of them were stranded, unable to obtain ocean passage within their means.[7] Others became public charges in New York and Boston. The rush of newcomers proved so great as to cause a temporary glut in the labor market, and ship captains returning from the United States in the fall of 1828 spread pessimistic reports regarding the opportunities for work.[8] As a result, the number of passengers declined the following season.

But the pause was only momentary. Two events account for the resumption of European interest in America. The first was the winter of 1829–1830, one of the coldest on record. Its later weeks caused bitter complaints among those who suffered from lack of fuel. The prices of all necessities of life rose sharply on the Continent,[9] and June found Ireland in greater distress than in the famine summer of 1822.[10] On the earlier occasion men of means had aided the less fortunate; now they felt it prudent to conserve what they had. Before the summer was far advanced, a theme much more exciting than the price of rye or potatoes obtruded itself. The people of Paris (probably incited to violence by the high food prices) rose against the Bourbons, and from France the spirit of revolution spread to Belgium, Germany and Poland. These occurrences affected the emigration in a variety of ways.

As usual in Germany, students lent ready ear to the call of change. Forming secret societies, they studied constitutions and voiced radical theories. The authorities took stern measures to suppress such activities. Finally, on May 27, 1832, a great popular demonstration was held at Hambach to protest against the strict supervision. Thirty thousand visitors from all parts of southwest Germany collected in the village and listened to the spirited addresses. Many of the participants, returning to their homes, considered themselves apostles of the revolutionary gospel. Peasants who had gathered about the "liberty trees" refused in many communities to pay taxes and severely manhandled the officers who attempted to collect them. To cope with this situation, the government of Bavaria stationed soldiers through the Rhine districts, and presently peace returned to the countryside. An official investigation into the proceedings at Hambach led to many seizures and inquisitions, and scores of young enthusiasts recanted. Others, seeing the cause deserted by their companions and losing hope of ultimate success, fled the atmosphere of suspicion and espionage in which they lived for Switzerland.[11]

In Zürich, Bern and Basel where they joined the Polish patriots they plotted new uprisings, or awaited a general European war, which would completely change the aspect of Continental politics. For a time they lived on the charity of the Swiss, the secret contributions of such of their fellow countrymen as retained faith in the cause, and the funds collected by committees of liberals in other lands. But the ardor of these benefactors presently cooled, and the German expatriates, chafing under the inaction and economic hardship, began to disperse to more distant countries. Of the large number who established themselves in France and England, many ultimately crossed the Atlantic and assumed positions of political and cultural leadership in German-American communities.[12]

Numerically, however, this group was not great, and its influence on emigration was less than that exerted by other liberals whose protest had been expressed in a less violent manner. Many of these foes of reaction had long admired the government of the United States, and in addition usually had an interest in its economic opportunities. An uncertain future, dwindling property or growing families caused them to think of migration, but they were not living upon that ragged margin where any change would be for the better. A book published in 1829 by Gottfried Duden, a German who had settled in Missouri in 1824, was addressed to such persons. In this work, entitled *Bericht über eine Reise*, he proposed a plan. Let German initiative and capital, from both the United States and Germany, create a city in the American West to be a center of German-American culture and life; or let emigrants concentrate in one of the territories in sufficient numbers to control the organization of the new state government, and then by legislation establish the social customs and the language of the fatherland.[13]

Three attempts at group emigration were soon made. A society formed at Mulhouse distributed glowing literature, enrolled a few score enthusiasts, and departed in 1831. But almost as soon as they reached America dissension broke out and the members scattered to try their individual fortunes.[14] In the same summer an agitator, one "Proli of Offenbach," who had aroused intense religious and political zeal among his followers, sailed from Bremen with a party of about eighty who had pooled their funds in a common chest. This band suffered a secession of the younger members upon reaching New York. The remainder proceeded to western Pennsylvania, then to Ohio, losing families as they went; the remnant finally came to rest in Louisiana where the leader lived for many years in an obscurity that contrasted sharply with the publicity attending the beginning of the adventure.[15] A third group, made up of residents from Hesse and Bavaria, set out in the spring of 1833 for Arkansas, with popular interest following them to the place of embarkation.[16]

But the outcome of this third migration attracted little attention because a new project overshadowed these local and limited endeavors. It began with the publication in March, 1833, of a pamphlet at the small university town of Giessen. This publication reviewed the recent political developments and painted a pessimistic picture of the future. Though disclaiming any intention of inciting people to emigrate, the author or authors suggested a plan for joint action. To this end, interested parties were urged to form local organizations which should communicate with the provisional central committee in Giessen; when a sizable number had been heard from, a convention should be held and a permanent directory elected. Only persons able to finance transportation, the preliminary investigation of a site, and the purchase of lands were invited to participate. It was hoped that ultimately, after a demand for a laboring element appeared in the new settlement, the transportation of those with less property might be undertaken.[17]

The program proceeded as outlined. In September the general meeting was held and permanent officers were appointed. In the spring of 1834 a large and enthusiastic group gathered at Bremen ready for embarkation, but because of a misunderstanding with the shippers only one vessel was ready to depart immediately. A division of the personnel being made, the first shipload sailed for New Orleans.[18] Arkansas had early been chosen as the ultimate destination, but as a result of last-minute doubts the decision of the site was left to the leaders of the party. It would be somewhere in the Mississippi Valley — if not Arkansas, then Missouri or Illinois.[19] Those forced to await a later boat were dissatisfied and in doubt as to where their friends would be found. Their savings were wasted by the delay, and when at last the voyage was begun, the former high hopes had yielded to pessimism and the spirit of coöperation to petty feuds. The belief that their predecessors would have a site selected and some preparations made was the only comfort; [20] but in this also they were doomed to disappointment.

Upon landing at New Orleans the guides of the first group had decided to go to St. Louis and there await the arrival of the full company before making a final choice of a location. They chartered a Mississippi River steamer for the purpose; but the water was shallow, the ship could not proceed, and it was necessary to transfer the passengers to two smaller boats. Some now refused to proceed and struck out for themselves. When St. Louis was reached, the bonds of the organization broke completely, the remaining members scattering to a dozen different points. Near St. Charles, Missouri, a nucleus of several families planted themselves, the only community actually founded by the ambitious venture.[21] Meanwhile, when the second shipload reached Baltimore, they set out across the mountains to Wheeling where they boarded an Ohio River steamer. But the demoralization was complete; each head of a family followed that course which appealed to his interest; and only a remnant joined the waiting group at St. Charles.[22] Thus ended the *Giessener Gesellschaft*. Some observers ascribed the smaller German emigration in the following year, 1835, to the disappointing outcome of the undertaking.[23]

There was still another way in which the revolutions of 1830 influenced emigration. Aside from the political enthusiasts who were forced to leave and those who chose to leave, a much greater number of people received from the confusion of the times a finishing blow to their economic hopes. All internal trade on the Continent was halted; commercial and credit relationships were severed; and the heavier taxation needed to bear the burden of a larger police and military force wiped out whatever profit the scanty business transactions might yield.

The distress caused by such conditions was closely related to that which Nature produced. Crops continued poor; farm animals died from undernourishment and disease. In normal times the great surplus of grain which eastern Europe always had on hand would have rushed down the rivers and through the Baltic to the markets of the west, and prices would have moderated. But Poland, the greatest of these reservoirs, now was paralyzed, and western Europe had to depend on its own supplies. During the winter of 1831–1832 prices rose to excessive heights. In many cities occurred bread riots; in some rural parts the farms of the more prosperous were attacked, granaries opened and cattle killed. The spring of 1832 gave promise of even greater disturbances.[24] That these fears did not materialize was due partly to the bountiful harvests which came early in midsummer,[25] and partly to the fact that the large emigration of that spring drew off many who would have contributed leadership to popular demonstrations.

The emigration was larger — at least double that of the preceding year — and it continued late into the fall.[26] As commerce was caught unprepared, ships were not on hand to accommodate the rush and, except for those who had made advance arrangements and were fortified with contracts, the undertaking involved confusion, unsatisfactory quarters and high rates.[27] To make matters worse, 1832 was a cholera year. On some of the vessels the mortality was heavy; on all, the rumors and the disorders were terrifying; and upon reaching America the newcomers were chilled by the quarantine delays and the stagnant trade.[28] Some, taking the funds they had planned to use for other purposes, bought passage back to the ports from which they had come; others besieged the consulates, begging to be returned to the land of their birth.[29]

These discouraging reports soon became the subject of general conversation in the inns of Ireland, England and Germany; and a decided decline in the emigration from those countries during the following season resulted.[30] But by 1834 the harrowing tales of the cholera year were half-forgotten. The current word from America represented economic conditions as encouraging again and told of an increasing demand for laborers.[31] In Ireland the growth of emigration was especially noticeable, with a much larger proportion than usual going to the United States in preference to Canada. By April the quays of Waterford, Cork and Londonderry were choked with baggage carts and departing Irishmen.[32] Le Havre and Bremen witnessed somewhat similar scenes, but the higher passage rates kept down the numbers.[33] Cholera unexpectedly made its appearance again, though in 1834 its effects were overshadowed by wrecks at sea entailing the loss of several hundred emigrants.[34] It may have been these disasters that caused the number of aliens entering the United States and Canada in 1835 to decline a third and two thirds respectively.[35] The mortality on the Quebec route had been especially great.

Other factors exaggerated the zigzag course of migration. During the thirties the old system of group migration was giving way to a new one in which the individual made his own arrangements. His success was the result less of foresight and courage than of the state of commerce in a country which he did not know. As a consequence, success and failure, prospects and dangers, were all magnified. Resolve was followed by hesitation and hesitation by sudden resolve. A surge of arrivals one spring swamped the labor market, and the resulting unemployment caused a shortage of immigration in the next which in turn engendered an optimism that turned the tide again into full flood. By the close of the decade the system was improved, the annual variations lessened, and the periods of increased and decreased immigration conformed more closely to the swings of the longer cycles of prosperity and depression.

The peculiar conditions in the countries of supply helped to determine the personnel of migration. A generalization regarding rural England in 1830 would give an entirely false impression if cited for 1840. Between the two dates lay one of the most rapid transitions in the social history of the nineteenth century. At the opening of the decade parish life was dominated by the workings of the Elizabethan poor law of 1601, which practically bound the laborer to the place of his birth by assigning to the parish responsibility for his relief.[36] A necessary and effective piece of legislation when adopted, it had degenerated in the course of time.[37] By giving relief to all the able-bodied unemployed it fostered indolence; by restricting movement it destroyed ambition; by increasing the family dole at the birth of each child it encouraged improvident marriages that tended to propagate a permanent pauper population. The taxpayers of the parish, saddled with a steadily increasing burden of rates, saw no relief in prospect, for obviously the supply of laborers exceeded the opportunities offered.[38]

Certain parishes discovered that the emigration of only a few-score laborers greatly lessened their pauper problem and brought a marked decline in the poor rates.[39] The Horton

bill pending before Parliament would have made possible
group colonization with state aid; and when Parliament rejected the proposal, several parishes, beginning in 1829,
experimented unofficially with organized assistance. The
most notable undertaking was that of the Petworth Emigration Committee in 1832, embracing a group of adjoining
parishes. The large landowners bore the cost of passage to
Canada, and the vestries were persuaded to provide supplies
in the guise of advances of relief.[40] This effort proved so
successful both for the emigrants and for the parish that some
other communities did likewise, and the plan would probably
have found universal adoption but for a general revision of
the relief system by the poor-law amendment act in 1834.[41]

This legislation, which overturned a system of two hundred and fifty years' standing, stemmed from the disclosures
of a parliamentary investigation which revealed in glaring
publicity the many abuses, public and personal, that the
ancient law had fostered. The new plan took relief from the
paternal supervision of local boards and created "poor-law
unions" without reference to parish lines, to be governed by
guardians. Able-bodied persons and their families could
secure help only by taking up residence in the workhouses
where their activities would be supervised by overseers. The
act further authorized the use of local funds for assisted
emigration.[42]

The actual saving of money caused by the law was at first
less striking than the changed attitude of the rural laborer.
The grim walls of the workhouse were a constant reminder
that laziness and improvidence constituted crimes punished
by enforced labor. As the gangs of parish laborers were
broken up, the more prudent absented themselves from the
public houses and revived an interest in benefit clubs and
savings accounts, while the surly ones had no choice but to
take such employment as was available.[43] The population

of rural England, after more than two centuries of stagnation, found itself in motion.

Other conditions besides the new poor law contributed to the great internal shifting that characterized the latter part of the decade. The industrial and commercial expansion of the middle thirties demanded hands for the factories and docks, and, as was to be expected, the union guardians gave full publicity to this need. Their encouragement and actual financial support of transportation relieved local taxpayers, and helped to build up a market which soon absorbed all the grain and cattle that the English countryside could produce.[44] Already by 1841 more than half a million natives of agricultural districts had become residents of Lancashire.[45]

Partly as a result of this exodus into the cities, the large emigration to foreign shores which had been expected when the drastic poor law went into effect and for which it had made provision did not materialize. Other factors included the requirement that assisted emigrants must go to the colonies. In one parish where thirty laborers requested aid for transportation to the United States all but twelve refused to leave when the commissioners would help only those willing to change their destination to Canada. The improvement in rural England also acted as a deterrent. "The good days of the war are coming back," "It is Bonaparte's time again," [46] were common expressions at the country fairs, and the optimistic prospects led to projects of reclamation unknown for a generation. Ditching and draining converted bogs into meadows; hedges set off the fields of grain. There was employment for all, and into the cottages came new comforts that drove out thoughts of better lands beyond the sea.[47]

In Scotland different conditions prevailed. Emigration resulted from two factors: one, a transformation more or less constant in its operation; the other, an acute crisis. Late in the 1820's the process of depopulation, which had been so marked after the break-up of the clans in the eighteenth century, began again. The cause was the steady conversion of farm land into pasturage. The growing cities of England offered a market for meat, and the introduction of the steamboat made it possible to convey livestock to the London docks with practically no loss in weight. As quickly as possible, landlords replaced farm tenants with shepherds, and instead of wheat and oats the Highlands produced cattle and sheep.[48] "Heather is fast covering several places where good grain was wont to be raised," was the report from one mountain parish.[49] There was still a seasonal demand for labor, but no permanent supply of native workers was necessary as Irish immigrants could be readily secured. These newcomers with their lower standard of living replaced the Highlanders in the harvest fields of the Lowlands, building hovels in the lanes at the outskirts of the towns and living on potatoes, milk and herring.[50]

Though Scotland possessed no poor law, the landlords, fearing that the increase of poverty would involve them in a moral if not a legal obligation, set out to destroy the cottages that tempted the former lawful occupants to remain. Populous villages disappeared; mountain communities showed signs of decay; ruins overgrown with nettles and briars marked the site of many an erstwhile dwelling.[51] Observers missed the gayety and cheerfulness of earlier days. "The song of the milk-maid, and the whistling of the ploughman, which were so common in this land of poetry and song, are now seldom heard." [52] Emigration was the remedy of those who could afford it, but the majority found their way to the growing commercial and manufacturing towns in the Lowlands, or squatted on the banks of the locks in the vain hope that fishing and the manufacture of kelp would provide a decent livelihood.[53] The crisis came in 1836 and 1837 when a succession of inclement seasons destroyed the potato crop and placed the price of all other supplies out of reach. Public charity alone kept the people alive, and provided many with the means of emigration.[54]

In Ireland still other influences were at work. In 1829 Parliament had passed a bill which, while nominally concerned with Irish voting qualifications, was a land act of wide social significance. This law was the official answer to a revolt of the Irish voter. For half a century the Irish gentry had wielded political power through an elective system which gave the vote to each forty-shilling freeholder.[55] Every landlord could create as many such freeholders as he could provide with land which with any appearance of reason could be considered of this value; and over these voters he held the constant threat of eviction if they dared to oppose his will at the polls. But about the middle of the twenties a new spirit began to manifest itself in the ranks of the Catholic peasantry under the leadership of the eloquent Daniel O'Connell whose demand for Catholic emancipation was to succeed in 1829. The first revolt against the political overlords took place in the County of Waterford in 1826; two years later O'Connell was elected to Parliament by tenants defying the commands of the proprietors.[56] In this latter contest the powerful influence of the Church was strongly exerted. Appeals issued from every altar, and "the priests preached that the eternal salvation of the voter was at stake. If he lost his farm on account of his vote, he had earned the crown of martyrdom." [57] This successful assertion of class and religious feeling awoke the Irish peasants to a new sense of their power. The landlords knew their control was gone: the instrument they had created for their own uses had passed into other and abler hands. Powerless to use it, they proceeded to destroy it. The act of 1829, popularly known as the "disfranchisement act," abolished the forty-shilling freeholder as an elector by raising the qualification to ten pounds.[58]

Since the landlord now had no incentive to encourage subdivision, young men approaching maturity found it difficult to establish homes. The new policy also placed in jeopardy the many homes already created under the lord's patronage. Now that they ceased to yield political returns, these tenants were an encumbrance, a clog to any economic improvement of the estate.[59] The outcome was a consolidation or "clearing" of parcels into larger holdings. The landlord was under no obligation to make provisions for the dispossessed, with the result that a few became tenants on neighboring estates, or took refuge with relatives little better off than themselves, while others squatted on the waste lands or found a few acres in the bogs or on the mountain side. Still others became beggars or laborers in the cities; some migrated to England, and many drifted to the north of Ireland.[60] These evictions did not constitute an important direct cause for emigration, for the evicted did not have the means.[61] Only when a conscientious landlord provided passage or waited until his tenants had money ahead were they able to cross the sea.[62]

It is difficult to weigh the various factors making for emigration. These were the days of the White Boys, Blackfeet, Peep-of-Day Boys and Ribbon societies — secret organizations which burned, pillaged and murdered. Many of the emigrants from districts in which evictions were taking place were the "smaller gentry," Protestants by faith, who ascribed their departure to the prevailing disorders. They alleged a widespread conspiracy to deprive them of their property by force, or at least to terrorize them into abandoning their lands.[63] Their charges appear in petitions to the Colonial Department requesting transportation to America. According to one petitioner, "Any person bearing the name of Protestant is not safe in going a Mile from his own House even in the open Day, but in fact are in danger of being waylaid and half murdered merely because they are Protestants and don't go to Mass." [64] "I am a Protestant and about thirty years of age," wrote another. "In consequence of the present persecution I would be glad to go to America." [65] Many communities formed "Orange Lodges" to protect the Protestant inhabitants by the same methods by which they were being attacked.[66]

But in those parts of Ireland where Catholics formed a minority this motive did not operate. There the emigration of Protestants was entirely an economic phenomenon in which may be discovered indirect effects of the tenant evictions. Many of the dispossessed had gone into the north where a different system of land relationships prevailed. Accustomed to simple ways of living, they could offer a higher rent than those whose training had been according to the standards of the region. Consequently, as old leases expired, landlords welcomed them as tenants. No other course remained to the former occupant than to beat a dignified retreat by selling his improvements and belongings, and thereby securing the funds for passage to America.[67] This process resulted in a comparatively even exodus, as is illustrated by the report from one Ulster district that about forty-five of the best class of farmers departed annually, leaving their places to be taken by fifty "poor families from the mountains who came to labor." [68]

There is no way of determining how the total emigration from Ireland was divided among the various social and economic classes. Geographic origin, however, affords a clue. Contemporary evidence traces the bulk of it to the north, the government agent at Quebec estimating that five sixths of the incoming passengers were from Ulster.[69] The usual comment in describing the departure of a vessel, that two thirds of those on board were Protestants, affords additional evidence.[70] Since emigrants shipped from the nearest port

IRISH EMIGRANTS LEAVING HOME — THE PRIEST'S BLESSING

EMIGRANTS' ARRIVAL AT CORK — A SCENE ON THE QUAY

THE EMIGRANTS BEGIN THEIR JOURNEY

in order to avoid a long land journey, it is further relevant that most of them sailed from Newry, Belfast, Londonderry and Sligo. The committee which investigated the condition of the Irish poor asked the authorities of each parish for a statement regarding emigration. Though the replies were brief, a reading leaves the clear impression that only in Ulster and Connaught was it an important phenomenon.[71] Similar sources, however, indicate that it was increasing in the south — a condition to be expected in the light of subsequent developments.[72]

The special influences operating on emigration in these several countries were exerting their effect by the middle of the decade. In 1836 the current, which had been somewhat checked during the season of 1835, swelled to new proportions. The United States was experiencing another period of flush times; and the feverish prosperity drew to America not only the countless hands necessary to turn into brick and stone the dreams of capitalists, but also many small capitalists with dreams of their own.[73] Early in 1837, however, indications began to appear that all was not well at bottom. "The time has gone by for making money here," one person wrote to the *Freeman's Journal.* "We are so overrun with speculators from all quarters of the earth, that nothing can be done to advantage." [74]

But either the Europeans were unwilling to believe such reports, or conditions at home overcame their fears. Germans were expecting a famine as severe as that which followed 1816; [75] the Irish were living under dread of another rebellion; [76] and the Scots were starving. So into a nation verging on a financial collapse poured the largest immigration yet known. Most of the arrivals encountered dire suffering which extended well into the following year. German newcomers huddled in shacks, experiencing a degradation which they were ashamed to report to their friends at home.[77] British consuls were called on to relieve the Irish, English and Scots.[78] Little wonder that the movement fell off in the year 1838.[79]

In view of the experiences of these years the subsequent revival of emigration may seem surprising. Yet, though the hard times continued, favorable economic opportunities existed for persons with some means. Real estate was cheap, and improved farms were numerous upon the market.[80] Moreover, new classes and new nationalities now began to find their way to America, among them many religious sectarians whose resources enabled them to take advantage of the conditions. A complete history of their advent would entail a catalogue of congregations and ministers; and the doctrines and adventures of each group might have no significance beyond perhaps a single community in the Mississippi Valley. Yet some warrant attention because, as forerunners of the hosts to follow, they were the fathers of an exodus destined to people the broad prairies.

Few bands of emigrants have ever received the publicity that contemporary observers bestowed upon the Stephanists — followers of Martin Stephan, the religious mystic of Dresden. When he first attracted popular attention, it was as a magnetic speaker whose timely sermons and whose interest in workingmen's clubs gave him an influence that reached far beyond his parish. But Stephan was also a Pietist, the recognized sponsor of the many innovations in theology and ceremony that were disturbing the civil and religious authorities.[81] The police long suspected Stephan of conducting illegal meetings of his followers, not in the city, where supervision was close, but in the neighboring forests. Caught in the act, the minister and many of his people were arrested and, after an investigation, Stephan was suspended from his post in the fall of 1837.[82] To his adherents the doctrines he espoused overshadowed all other activities and relations of life. Stephan had long thought of founding a colony of the faithful, perhaps in Australia; now events forced his hand.[83]

During the winter the scheme took shape. With great skill and secrecy a company of prosperous peasants was enrolled from the vicinity, well-established artisans of Dresden and professional men.[84] A common fund was created to defray the cost of transportation and settlement, and a committee selected to look after the practical details.[85] In July, 1838, public announcement was made that the Stephanists would seek a refuge in America.[86] When the first contingent left Dresden in October, an artist commemorated the scene in a picture which later excited much attention when exhibited at the Leipzig fair.[87] For a while doubt existed as to whether Stephan himself could secure the necessary permission to depart, and he was held by the authorities even after the last groups had set out for Bremen, the port of embarkation. But at the last minute authorization was given, and a swift dash overland brought him to his awaiting people — all of which added a touch of the dramatic to the episode and served to heighten the interest with which journalists viewed it.[88] On November 19 five ships bearing seven hundred souls set sail for New Orleans.[89]

During the voyage Stephan was elected "bishop." Though there were dissenting voices, the fact that he was custodian of the emigration chest beat down all opposition. At St. Louis Bishop Jackson Kemper of the Episcopal Church granted the use of the cathedral for the ceremonies of installation. In the meantime ten thousand acres were purchased in Perry County, a hundred miles or more from St. Louis; and here the town of Stephansburg was founded, the outcome of many trials and the center of many hopes.[90] But new troubles promptly appeared. The long sea journey had bred gossip about the leader which caused stern moralists in the settlement to demand the truth. Stephan was brought

to trial by his subordinates; one witness after the other
testified against his moral character; and the evidence proved
so damaging that he was forced to leave in disgrace.[91] In a
few months Dresden hummed with the disclosures, with the
result that a great number of Saxons who were wavering
between the Old and the New World decided not to go.[92]
Though the incident put a temporary damper on emigration,
in the long run it stimulated interest, for by 1841 it was clear
that, in spite of their inauspicious start, the Stephanists were
making good.[93]

The Stephanists had not migrated because they were persecuted; they were fleeing as from a Sodom and Gomorrah.[94]
Another group, the "Old Lutherans" of Prussia, chose the
same course because of religious oppression. Frederick William III, tired of dissension among his people, sought to
effect a compromise between the Lutheran and the German
Reformed churches by creating a United Evangelical Church
based on a new prayer book. The strictly orthodox among
the Lutherans refused to conform in spite of the threat of
heavy penalties.[95] The result was an emigration to Australia
and America much larger than that of the Stephanists, affecting congregations in Pomerania, in Posen, in Magdeburg and
Berlin, regions which hitherto had contributed few families
to the outgoing stream.[96] The accession of Frederick William
IV in 1840 ended the active persecution, but by that time so
many contacts had been formed with lands overseas that the
movement showed no decrease.[97]

Australia, the destination of the first bands of Old Lutherans, quickly revealed its disadvantages. It was too remote
from Europe, too primitive a region and too expensive to
reach. By contrast, those who sought the United States prospered, soon developing flourishing communities in New
York and Michigan. Shortly after 1840 Wisconsin became
the particular haven, attracting settlers not only from Prus-

sia, but also from Mecklenburg, Baden and Württemberg.[98]
Many of them were actuated by economic and social as well
as by religious motives. In 1843 many of the Old Lutherans
departing from Silesia were weavers, and in view of the depression of the linen industry at that time it is evident that
unemployment was the predominant cause.[99]

The other important religious element which left Germany in marked numbers consisted of Jews. Their exodus
was due less to their religious zeal than to a desire to escape
anti-Semitism. In the eighteenth century the old medieval
disabilities from which the German Jews suffered had tended
to relax. Emancipation was the order of the day. But wars
changed matters and the official pendulum swung the other
way. The restoration policy of the states demanded conformity in political practice and theory; it also desired conformity in religion. The Jews were brought into special
prominence by the fact that they had helped to finance
many of the operations of the invaders during the French
occupation. These transactions with the enemy exposed
them to popular disfavor, and also yielded them a prosperity
which excited the envy of their neighbors.[100]

Several German states solved the Jewish problem by ban-
ishing the race from their dominions, but Bavaria faced a
more difficult situation. It was a complex of free cities and
ecclesiastical provinces, and many of these struggling principalities had found it profitable to have this industrious and
financially important class as subjects. The result was a
checkerboard distribution of the people. Villages entirely
Gentile in population were interspersed with others entirely
Hebrew, the legal status of the latter being fixed by a maze
of ordinances and regulations.[101] An edict of June 10, 1813,
had brought some order out of this chaos. Although some
of the provisions were liberal, those concerned with economic
activity were reactionary. Jews could be farmers, artisans

and manufacturers, but in order to engage in a business such as innkeeping or in a profession, a license was necessary, and the number of such licenses in any community was limited.[102] Württemberg followed the example of Bavaria in 1828 by adopting a law which prohibited the exchange or sale of property by Jews unless it had been occupied or farmed by the owner for at least three years.[103]

In the circumstances emigration was the only recourse of the youth. Jewish communities had long been accustomed to seeing their young men depart for other European countries or even America, and from time immemorial the young women had gone to Italy to serve as maids.[104] Now, however, thanks to the encouraging reports from across the Atlantic, a trend started in that direction, and every optimistic letter that reached a village prompted more to depart.[105] By 1839 ten thousand Bavarian Jews had emigrated, and the whole number in America was estimated at fifteen thousand.[106]

The fact that this exodus was one of tradespeople and professional men caused them to be widely distributed in the United States. The few with savings set themselves up at once as merchants in the cities; the majority trudged as peddlers through the length and breadth of the country until they had accumulated enough capital for a permanent establishment. The Jewish bands which came with the intention of buying adjacent lands usually held together only during the voyage. Jewish emigration, far from ending with the decade of the 1830's, continued with increasing force; but in the succeeding years it was caused not so much by persecution as by the prevailing depression which weighed upon Jew and Gentile alike.

The religious difficulties in Germany had their counterpart in Switzerland, the Netherlands and the Scandinavian countries. Switzerland, it is true, was the scene of no violent demonstrations; but Pietism had not burned itself out, and groups of Methodists and Baptists, which found it difficult to thrive in the restrictive atmosphere of the cantons, followed the traditional Swiss remedy of removal beyond the sea. In Norway and Sweden dissatisfaction with the established Lutheran Church also caused many to look to America, where religious freedom might be enjoyed along with superior economic opportunities. The first Norwegian migration, consisting of Quakers, took the form of the famous "sloop party" of 1825; whereas the Swedish movement began about 1841 with the settlement of Gustaf Unonius and his small band at Pine Lake, Wisconsin.[107]

Still another racial group helped to swell the flow of humanity across the Atlantic in the late 1830's. Wales had undergone the same program of legislation which had done so much to rehabilitate rural England; but these measures, successful because adapted to the conditions and psychology of the English farm laborers, had an unanticipated effect on a society and psychology fundamentally different. The Welsh had had little fault to find with the poor law of Elizabeth's reign: the scandals characteristic of English parishes did not trouble the Welsh guardians, nor was the financial outlay heavy.[108] True to the Celtic tradition, families and friends cared for their own when in distress, and local officers dispensed the poor funds jealously. Under the new régime outsiders acting as commissioners applied the "workhouse test" rigorously, separating husbands from wives, parents from children. Union workhouses were built at public expense, and salaries were paid to the officers to do what citizens had formerly done gratuitously. Contrary to English experience, the new poor law meant not less but more taxation.[109]

The commutation of tithes, another feature of the legislation, also produced special difficulties. Collecting the tithe in England, where most of the people maintained at least a conventional allegiance to the Anglican Church, had not

always been an easy matter; but in Wales, where the bulk
of the farmers were hot Dissenters, owners of the benefice
had given up the attempt to get all that the law allowed and
contented themselves with what they could get.[110] Under
the new system the tithe, when commuted to a money payment, was made part of the "county cess," and refusal to
pay involved summary legal action. Moreover, since the
commutation was computed to represent the value of the
payments previously made in kind, means were provided for
varying the cash payment with the rise and fall in prices; but
that variation was still an average, and a crop failure or
scanty harvest brought no reduction commensurate with the
farmers' actual distress. Furthermore, the averages were
reckoned for the kingdom at large, a system which worked
to the disadvantage of Wales where prices were usually
twenty per cent lower than elsewhere.[111]

This situation was further complicated by the growing
industrialization. The railroad builders of the world called
on South Wales for iron, and the resulting boom changed
the character of every valley that could yield coal or iron.
Shafts were sunk, sidings and inclined planes constructed,
and the mining lords took possession of the hilltops, which
hitherto had contributed to the support of the valley farmers,
as pasture for their draft animals.[112] Had the natives accepted
the inevitable, abandoned their farms and turned to mining,
their ultimate lot would have been happier; but the traditional dread of being "landless men" caused newly established families to rent a few stony acres and eke out this
income by day wages at the mines, walking perhaps a dozen
miles a day and reaping their meager harvests by candle-
light.[113] Being half-farmer and half-miner they endured the
disadvantages of each occupation. Thus, when after 1837
railroad building came to a standstill, the depression in the
coal and iron trades threw thousands upon their rural parishes

for relief, thereby increasing beyond all expectations the burden of the new poor rates.[114] And when progressively poor harvests led to two almost complete failures in 1840 and 1841, the inflexibility of the tithe demanded cash from farmers who had no cash to give.[115]

The sequel was a violent protest. In the summer and autumn of 1843 nocturnal bands disguised with feminine robes clattered through the valleys of South Wales, gathering recruits from the hillside farms and dispersing silently when the evening's work was done. Demolished gates, smoldering tollhouses, and bruised and frightened keepers marked their trail along the turnpikes. Notes of warning to prospective victims bore the signature, "Rebecca"; and about the family hearths and over the mugs of ale in the taverns the Welsh discussed in hushed tones the doings of "Rebecca and her daughters." [116] "I am a friend of peace, sir," said John Jones to George Borrow a decade later, "no head-breaker, house-breaker, nor gate-breaker, but I can hardly blame what was done at that time, under the name of Rebecca." [117] No one would acknowledge acquaintance with the marauders or reveal the identity of a single individual.

The bulk of the distressed population, however, consisted of devout Methodists and Baptists unwilling to vent their resentment in rowdyism. Believing in submission to the law, they saw no alternative but that of removal beyond its jurisdiction. Early in the century Welshmen had crossed the Atlantic to central New York; and after the war other family groups had settled in Ohio.[118] In the New World they had prospered, retaining the Welsh language and their religious customs. In 1835 the Reverend B. W. Chidlow, revisiting Wales, undertook in sermons, addresses and conversation to direct attention to the far country. Soon "the name of Ohio became a household word." [119] When he set out on his return voyage, many accompanied him and others followed. A second visit in 1840 rekindled interest, and a booklet that he published, *The American*, served as guide for the hundreds who took his advice.[120] The iron and coal regions of Pennsylvania offered excellent opportunities, and the Welsh era in the history of American mining dates from this influx of the thirties.

The stagnation and gloom that blanketed Wales after 1837 extended to the industrial areas of England. Blacksmiths, shoemakers, knitters and colliers wandered through the countryside, seeking work and begging. The cities of Lancashire provided soup kitchens, while empty streets testified to the general drain of population.[121] The war in China in which Great Britain was engaged prolonged the depression by closing some of the best markets for textiles. In deep discouragement large numbers of unemployed operatives bade farewell to their trade and to their native land. In the days of prosperity some of them had formed emigration societies whose accumulated funds now carried them across the sea.[122] Others less farsighted left their families behind, sailing by the cheapest route for the New World.[123]

Bare statistics fail to disclose the occupations and trades represented by the emigrants sailing from Liverpool; but observers reported that, whereas English farmers and Irish peasants had earlier predominated, now manufacturers and artisans constituted an increasingly large proportion.[124] The movement continued until 1842 when a downturn of American business conditions reversed the current of migration. Hundreds returned to Lancashire without expectation of an improvement of their condition. But the horizon soon brightened. In December church bells in town and country announced the end of the Chinese war, and by the spring of 1843, with the factories again in operation, the people went back to work.[125]

That spring saw a pronounced decrease of departures not

only from England, but from all the countries and districts that had been contributing to a migration which contemporaries regarded one of the wonders of the time.[126] The decline, however, was only a pause during which all the forces of expulsion were gathering new strength. Since 1828 half a million people had crossed the sea, and from this expanding network of relationships Europeans gained a fresh and lively knowledge of the New World which was to count for much in the future course of migration.

VII

AMERICA BECOMES THE COMMON MAN'S UTOPIA

FOR THREE CENTURIES prior to 1815 the consequences of Columbus's discovery were felt whenever European merchants discussed their markets, Atlantic shippers mapped their routes, or imperial statesmen formulated their policies. But into the humble cottages where the mass of Europeans lived and had their being, the western continent seldom made its way. They might hear, and perhaps on occasion speak, of exotic lands beyond the sea, but the image they conjured up was unreal and fantastic, not unlike the strange legends which entertained medieval fishermen and sailors. But just as in the years following 1492 these ancient myths dissolved into realities, so in the generation after 1815 the United States was discovered by the common man. Both its hardships and its blessings became known, and the Europeans, striking a balance between the two, did not hesitate to call the land a Utopia.

The migration of the eighteenth century had done little to dispel this ignorance of America. Religious communities separated themselves entirely from the Babylon they fled; criminals had no desire to communicate with the land of their birth; redemptioners did not possess the means. Though every immigrant in the decades that followed 1815 had his predecessors, he had little advance knowledge of the difficulties and mysteries that would confront him. Even as late as 1830 the simplest facts of American geography, government and life were clouded with misconception and perversion. Half a century after the American Revolution

Englishmen wrote to the British Colonial Office asking for grants of passage to "the Virginia Plantation." [1] There was a common misapprehension regarding sizes, distances and the general configuration of the country.[2] Although it is difficult to believe that several English families returned to their homes because upon gazing out to sea from Yarmouth they could not espy America, other evidences of geographic ignorance abound.[3] One Irishman requested a grant of land "in upper Kennedy in North America"; another, seeking the same destination, asked for passage "to an Island called Upper Canada." [4] An Englishman who had intended to remove to British America unwittingly settled in Ohio. A leading newspaper of Germany printed under the heading, "South America," news from Texas, Mexico and Virginia.[5]

Social and economic facts were as liable to misconception as political geography. Emmet warned his countrymen that all social relationships were so different that no Europeans could understand them without encountering them.[6] Some thought of America as a wild land infested with hostile Indians, poisonous snakes and tarantulas, and plagued with forest fires and racking fevers. To others it was a land of perfect equality, free from any of the miseries that perplexed the Old World. German emigrants passing through Le Havre, when asked what they expected to find beyond the Atlantic, had but one answer, *"Kein König dort."* [7] Yet some Englishmen upon arriving in the United States were amazed to learn that the country had no king.[8]

The polite literature of the time did little to correct the European perspective. The spirit of romanticism permeated fiction, poetry, philosophy and religion. The poets, Byron and Shelley, were romantic; likewise the novelists, Scott and Thackeray. They laid their scenes in far-off lands peopled with noble savages and virtuous seekers after the simple life. Many of these authors took their readers to America; and

Indians, frontiersmen and traders passed across their pages. Few writers enjoyed a greater popularity than the American Cooper. By 1830 his Leatherstocking tales had been translated into half a dozen languages, and his accounts of adventures in the northern woods and on the western prairies thrilled thousands of readers whose dissatisfaction with their own humdrum existence grew with every chapter.[9] Conceptions of the New World concocted out of such ingredients vanished before contact with its obvious materialism; but meanwhile the youthful curiosity which these dreams fired caused many to seek more solid information in the increasing volume of writings that purported to depict the real America.

As the questions of international politics growing out of the Napoleonic wars died down, public discussion turned to such matters as democracy, the control of industry and the protection of labor. Upon such discussions Americans looked with somewhat disdainful eyes, for the United States, they said, had already solved these problems: capital was secure, labor received a greater proportion of its product than elsewhere, rich and poor shared in the government. Although skeptical of these boasts, many Europeans believed that the western republic presented a laboratory of social experimentation from which the Old World could learn much. Beginning in the late twenties, a succession of observers crossed the Atlantic, visited Washington and talked to the President, mounted the Alleghenies and viewed the prairies and rivers, took notes on the bustling commerce of New York and Baltimore, and wrote their books on the voyage home. The literary success of the first travelers induced others to follow. If one was decidedly favorable in his appraisal, another felt obliged to be violently critical, whereupon a third took occasion to express a moderate view. Profiting by the vogue of such writings, landowners and emigrant agents learned to present their advertisements in travel form. The popularity of American travel literature was to continue for at least a century.

Although the output was largest in Great Britain and France, these writings probably exerted their greatest influence in Germany. Not only were all the important foreign works translated,[10] but an increasing number of Germans visited the New World to record their own impressions. Preëminent among them, as we have seen, was Gottfried Duden. After three years' residence upon a farm in Missouri he returned to his native land in 1829 and published in a periodical a series of letters describing his experiences. Collected in the volume entitled *Bericht über eine Reise nach den westlichen Staaten Nord Amerikas*, they constituted the most important piece of literature in the history of German emigration. The book's appeal lay in its informal nature. It contained no account of visits to the White House, no statistical tables of the growth of exports. Instead, it portrayed everyday life on a Missouri farm. One letter told of spring labor in the clearing, another of the bountiful harvests. Still others dwelt on pastimes in the forest and on the river, the glory of sunsets and moonlight nights, the absence of overbearing soldiers, haughty clergymen and inquisitive tax collectors. This was the existence for which the harassed peasant longed. The volume passed through several editions, one of which a Swiss emigration society distributed at cost.[11]

Popular interest in such books was greatly abetted by the ubiquitous village reading clubs. Although not unknown elsewhere in Europe, these organizations were most characteristic of Germany. The sponsor was generally a local minister who steered the discussion away from controversial religious and political topics and, in order to give the gathering an air of respectability, limited smoking to one or two pipes and drinking to a single glass of beer. Usually each member purchased one book each season or subscribed to a periodical. At the weekly meeting in the inn or the parish schoolroom the first part of the program consisted of reading chapters from some chosen work, after which followed a free exchange of opinions. Since history and travel formed the bulk of the material, America tended to be the center of interest. In some instances, the original purpose was to read about the United States with emigration in view; and in all instances a more accurate knowledge of the distant land and its opportunities resulted.[12] Many such societies existed among the Jewish people who found in a study of Jewish liberties in other parts of the world a source of encouragement.[13]

Groups of this nature were less necessary in Great Britain because of the abundance of cheap printed matter. Newspapers, it was said, were passed from hand to hand "as long as the texture of the paper holds together, or its color can be distinguished from that of the printer's ink." [14] Weekly journals appeared in increasing number. In particular, the publishing house of Chambers in Edinburgh did much to foster interest in emigration. *Chambers's Edinburgh Journal* and *Chambers's Information for the People* attained a phenomenal circulation, especially among farm servants and artisans who had hitherto read little.[15] These publications and their imitators described in detail the various countries and regions where Britons had settled and prospered, purveying information in a strictly realistic way and reprinting letters from actual emigrants. Many who decided to join their countrymen across the sea owed their first interest to a reading of these Edinburgh journals.[16]

The spread of facilities for public education in the British Isles and Germany at this time helped greatly to strengthen the influence of the printed word. In the case of Ireland the establishment of national schools in 1832 inaugurated a linguistic revolution. In 1822 approximately two million inhabitants spoke only Irish; by 1861 the number fell to less than one hundred and sixty-four thousand.[17] Many, of course, had emigrated, but acquisition of the tongue spoken in North America had facilitated their going. An even greater incentive was the knowledge of geography disseminated by the schools. Children at the most imaginative age saw the world unfolded on the maps upon the wall; the schoolmaster told them of distant countries with abundant land, no rent, no agent to steal away the produce of the fertile fields. Boys and girls living in rags and wretchedness dreamed of the day when they would seek their fortune across the sea; and when that happy time came, the whole family often went with them. Many emigrants acknowledged that in the schoolroom their first longing for a pioneer's life was born. So well was this fact recognized that parishes wanting to encourage emigration were urged to obtain a more abundant supply of maps.[18]

In the eighteen thirties and the early forties emigration was usually the result of careful planning. Those contemplating the step searched through gazetteers and geographies and ransacked bookshops for additional material. They consulted newspapers at the village inn for emigration notices and shipping advertisements. They visited neighbors to listen to letters from departed relatives.[19] According to a contemporary, the "reading families" were those most prone to depart.[20] The thoroughness of one family was surprising: "We even got a young man from the State of Ohio to stay a whole month in the house with us in order to insure a perfect practical knowledge of the country which was intended to become the theatre of our future destiny." [21] Often this interest continued over a period of years before emigration actually took place.

Agents and shippers realized the value of guidebooks and

travel literature in fanning the urge, but because of the expense they usually preferred to drum up interest through personal interviews. Philanthropic men and organizations, however, made such material available in order to cure many of the ills that attended the movement. Thus, an Irish clergyman kept in his home a library of approximately a thousand volumes of geographies, guidebooks, gazetteers and histories of foreign lands for persons who might care to consult them.[22] The Limerick Emigrants' Friend Society maintained a clearing house for information received from the Colonial Office and from the governors of the colonies, and pushed the sale of cheap emigrant literature in the neighboring villages and rural communities.[23]

Though the authority of printed matter was great, it paled before that of the personal letter. When a vessel left the quay no phrase in the chorus of shouts from the shore rang out more loudly than "Write soon!" Letters could not be expected in less than six months; then the correspondent wrote with the greatest care, for he knew every expression would be weighed about the home fireside and the future of a score of lives might depend upon the tone of one emigrant's first report. He wrote thoughtfully, moreover, because the high cost of postage discouraged frequent communications.

Judged by modern standards, the international postal service of a century ago hardly deserved to be called a "system." The United States had its organization; so did Canada and the countries of western Europe. But between lay three thousand miles of the Atlantic which belonged to no nation. The transportation of letters over the sea was a private commercial affair engaged in by as many concerns as there happened to be ships. A correspondent in the United States sent his letter by domestic mail to some shipping house on the coast, inclosing a sum to cover the ocean expense and the inland postage abroad.[24] The captain was the real agent, though passengers often advertised that they would carry correspondence in their baggage and so undercut the captain's charges. The price of this informal service, as advertised, varied from twenty-five to fifty cents a letter, a suggestion of the high rate charged by other forwarders.[25] If the sending of a single letter cost the equivalent of a day's wages, it is not surprising that letters were written only when necessary and that they spoke with authority.[26]

A persistent belief existed that letters were tampered with; that no communication derogatory to the country was allowed to leave; that to encourage immigration false letters of praise were concocted and signatures forged — a simple enough matter at a time when many of the senders, being illiterate, had to depend upon another's pen.[27] To guard against interference and to prevent fraud, ingenious devices were adopted. Before departure it would be agreed that the emigrant's letters should be written upon a certain variety of stationery, or bear a device pricked by pins in the corner, or have the sealing wax applied in a place agreed upon, or a bent pin or small coin hidden in the wax. Occasionally a code would be adopted in which words did not mean exactly what they said. Thus a departing Irishman arranged that, if he advised his brother not to follow him without their dear grandmother, then, in view of the fact that the venerable dame had been dead thirty years, the advice should be interpreted as an adverse report.[28]

Contents so safeguarded could be nothing but the truth. The arrival of such a letter was not merely a family but a community affair. Neighbors assembled, the schoolmaster was pressed into service, and the letter was read amidst a silence that bore eloquent testimony to the profound interest. Often copies were made and sent to other communities.[29] The spirit of these missives was overwhelmingly encouraging, partly perhaps because the emigrants usually postponed writing until they had surmounted the initial difficulties.[30] But when a pessimistic and discouraging letter arrived, it was taken most seriously and could offset the impression made by several of the opposite tenor.[31] The authenticity of each communication, however, had to be above suspicion. When the authorities attempted to stem the current of departures by publishing in official gazettes correspondence from disappointed emigrants, it was disregarded by the public as self-interested propaganda.[32]

Letters from departed friends and relatives contained not only information and advice, but also tangible evidences of a more abundant life — a bank note, an order on a commercial house, a prepaid passage. With international exchange in a rudimentary stage, the difficulties which attended the forwarding of mail increased when money was involved. Settlers sometimes walked several hundred miles to a seaport to find a ship captain or some passenger to whom they were willing to entrust the delivery of funds. When an immigrant died whose heirs resided in his native land, the distribution of the inheritance among brothers and cousins created a local sensation that was soon reflected in an increased migration of fortune hunters.[33] It also led to a deluge of inquiries that flooded European consulates in America, asking for assistance in tracing a bequest which it was understood was forthcoming.[34] The "rich uncle in America" thus started his romantic and elusive career.

Letters, remittances and legacies attested that emigrants were making a success, but the most convincing and unanswerable evidence was the reappearance of the expatriate himself. Sometimes he returned in so short a space of time as to be scarcely credible, as when the emigrant of one spring came back the following winter with earnings sufficient to transport the rest of his family. Usually several years elapsed, but then the transformation was all the more striking. No persons had ever departed in a more distressed condition than those of the years from 1815 to 1819. Many had had to sell their labor as redemptioners in order to defray the cost of passage. But now after ten or fifteen years poverty had given way to wealth; instead of slavery, an independence that few of their native countrymen could enjoy was theirs. The visit of one of these adventurers was a demonstration no village could ignore, and gave rise to many stories of the good fortune that had come to the once pitied fugitives of the "hunger years." [35] Conversation and the press repeated the stories of the penniless servant who was now a rich merchant, of the apprentice who was master of a hundred employees, of the poor tenant who owned scores of acres. Not only success, but a rapid success, was the recurring theme.[36]

European consuls in America, especially those from the Continent, felt bound to play up the tragic lot of the poor creatures whom the honeyed promises of emigrant agents had deluded; and in certain years examples were readily found. But they all realized that such cases were not typical.[37] The Prussian consul at Baltimore evaded a direct opinion by explaining that in so large a country people came and went without passes and there really was no way of ascertaining their fate.[38] With greater frankness the consul of Hesse stated in 1833 that in recent years immigrants had been successful and that even those who had come without resources had prospered.[39]

One other source of information about America consisted in the United States consuls abroad. The country's growing trade had caused the establishment of consulates in many ports and at many inland cities of Europe. Since most of the German states denied passports to departing subjects unless they could produce evidence that the country of their destination would not exclude them, applicants went to the consulates for the necessary certificates.[40] The procedure was a mere matter of form, which after a time was entirely neglected; but the habit of going to the consulate for information became established and some of the offices, notably those at Bremen and Frankfurt-am-Main, proved particularly helpful. Had the United States government worked out a policy for the purpose, it might have used these officials for securing the most desirable type of settler. As it was, the nature of the services rendered depended upon the information and public spirit of the individual consuls.[41]

Few emigrants departed as unattached individuals. The first to go was likely to be the chosen emissary of parents or neighbors; the later ones went to join the pioneers and round out the family circle. In the letters to relatives and friends back home the sentiment constantly recurred: if you were here, then joy would be complete. An Irishman wrote of his brother, "Had I him here, I would count myself the happiest of men." [42] "When we sit down to our meals," declared another correspondent, "I think how happy I would be to share them with my dear friends in Scotland." [43] Such writers took pains to explain that for their friends back home the way was now prepared: "You will not have the care on your mind as we had, not knowing where to go to, or what we was going to do, for you know that we tried the road for you, and I hope you will follow us." [44]

If information brought its disillusions, it also strengthened resolves. Europeans learned that America was a land of labor, but they also learned that there was work for all, particularly for the man who could handle a spade, the mason who could lay bricks, the carpenter who could erect a frame. To almost any of these pursuits the average peasant of northern Europe could turn his hand, and to the opportunity his attention was called by broadsides distributed through the country parishes, chance newspapers sent home by emigrants and the advertisements of agents and shippers.[45] Nor need the father of a family bear the entire burden, for, as letters explained, wives and daughters were in demand as domestics, and younger children might be apprenticed to farmers and mechanics without the premium which European employers usually asked.[46]

One day's labor, the European peasant learned, was equivalent to an acre fit to grow corn.[47] From two or three years' savings the industrious workman could buy a farm already cleared and provided with the necessary buildings. This condition in part indicated the high scale of wages; more directly it attested the abundance of available land. The land-hungry German understood only with difficulty a society in which the sum he now paid as annual rental would purchase complete title of a farm twice as large as his present holding. Or, if already a landholder, he was dazzled by the knowledge that he might sell his possessions, pay out two thirds of the proceeds for transporting his family to America, and yet have enough left to buy four times as much land as he had originally owned.[48] Even the discomforts of pioneering might be avoided because the American, with a lack of sentiment strange to a European, willingly parted with the fields that his industry had cleared, at a price far below that which he might legitimately have asked.[49]

The waste which European visitors to the United States denounced as the reckless squandering of a patrimony, the hungry peasant interpreted as proof of America's bounty. The messages sent across the Atlantic spoke a vivid language: the peaches and apples rotting in the orchards of Ohio were more "than would sink the British fleet"; the average farmer left ungleaned in his fields enough wheat to "keep a whole parish"; and kind-hearted housewives wished "that the poor people in England had the leavings of their tables, that goes to their dogs and hogs." [50] Feasting was not reserved for special occasions because every day resembled Christmas at home. For this plenty the farmer depended on no one; everything served in his household, with the exception of tea and coffee, came from his own fields. [51] Even the landless laborer shared in Nature's generosity. On the public works the fare included beef or pork at each meal, coffee or tea for breakfast and supper and, in addition, glasses of whisky at intervals during the day. [52] The worker who lived at home could keep his larder well stocked, being able to buy a whole hog at a time. [53] "Tell Thomas Arann to come to America;" wrote one immigrant, "and tell him to leave his strap what he wears when he has nothing to eat in England, for some other half-starved slave. Tell Miriam there's no sending children to bed without supper, or husbands to work without dinners in their bags." [54]

This prosperity, so the argument ran, rested in part upon the fact that what a man produced was his to enjoy. The per-capita expense of government was only one fourth that of the Netherlands and less than a tenth that of England. No percentage was deducted as tithes for the clergy or as rates for the poor. Though the United States had about the same population as Prussia, the standing army of the latter was fifty times as large. It was amazing that a farm that kept eight horses paid a tax in America of only twelve dollars. [55] The surplus in Jackson's treasury — the spectacle of a government having so much revenue that its disposition was a major problem — had no parallel in European annals. "Now for vermin," wrote an especially bitter correspondent, "there are plenty of common flies and other insects, but nothing to hurt you. I have found nothing as bad as the taxation and the Old Tories of England." [56]

Freedom from heavy taxation was only one of the many attractions of the American system of government. Adopted citizens noted with gratitude that there was no gendarmerie to pry into private affairs, no compulsory military service postponing marriage and an independent start in life, no enforced school attendance to deprive a parent of his child's services. Since there was no censorship, newspapers played a large part in political and social life. All citizens were equal before the law, and political distinctions did not take the place of respectability as the test of a man's worth.[57]

Perhaps Congress paid little attention as the clerk's voice droned out the President's annual message, but across the Atlantic it had eager listeners. "We read this document," wrote an Irish editor, "as if it related purely to our concerns,"[58] and many political agitators used it as a textbook of liberalism. At a time when a journalist's labor consisted largely of clipping his contemporaries, the message received a wide circulation throughout western Europe, reaching many households not yet influenced by personal letters. Especially during the Jackson régime these messages were influential. Their tone was self-congratulatory, setting off American blessings against conditions in decadent Europe. Every comparison strengthened the urge towards emigration and, since each document contained facts regarding the sale of lands, the removal of Indians, the progress of canals and roads, the whole constituted a summary of the current prospects of the republic.[59] In some alarm a conservative German journal urged that the republication of these presidential messages be banned by law on the ground that they publicized doctrines prohibited by the censors.[60]

On several occasions America's fair political repute suffered a temporary eclipse. The election of Jackson gave rise to gloomy prophecies. He represented, it was said, the half-wild men of the West against whom would be pitted the aristocracy of the East. The resulting social confusion would be not unlike that which attended the invasions of the Goths and the Huns. In the end Jackson, himself by profession a soldier, would overthrow the organization that had elevated him and become a dictator. But the early years of his administration passed without a social war, and the republic's staunchest protector turned out to be its military president.[61] The nullification controversy with its possibilities of secession suggested a different source of conflict. "We fear the dissolution of the American union," regretfully wrote the editor of the leading liberal paper of Ireland; [62] and the *Allgemeine Zeitung* heavily philosophized in characteristic vein. History, it said, teaches that only monarchies can long endure; republics when spread over great territories carry in themselves the seeds of dissolution; the American experiment is approaching its logical end.[63] But in a short time the Irish paper was able to announce jubilantly that the crisis was over and republicanism had scored another "splendid triumph." [64] There followed the controversy over the Bank, with disaster again foretold, and later the panic which passed over the land, ruining even conservative business enterprises. But the government survived these successive crises without great difficulty, and by the end of the decade the permanency of the republic was hardly subject to further question.[65]

To many, probably to the majority, economic freedom made an even greater appeal than political freedom. After a perfunctory customs examination on entering the country the continent lay open to the newcomer. He was free to move from place to place as he felt the inclination or need. He could carry on any trade or business unhindered by the regulations of local guilds. Whether he was naturalized or not made little difference as to his rights and privileges. There were no distinctions based on birth and, in so far as ranks existed, it was reported that the farmers belonged to the highest, with the artisans next and the professions and

the officeholders last — an order just the reverse of that prevailing in Europe.[66]

Laborers and servants were hardly to be regarded a distinct
class because their status was temporary. Moreover, while
thus employed, an immigrant enjoyed a position which European practice made it difficult to comprehend. Hired persons
were treated as one of the family, it being a common saying
among the farmers, "If a man is good enough to work for me,
he is good enough to eat with me." [67] Servants would not
admit they had a "master," always referring to their employer
as "Mister——." A traveler called at the home of a New Yorker
to whom he bore a letter of introduction and inquired of
the maid who answered his ring, "Is your master at home?"
She replied indignantly, "I have no master, sir!" and slammed
the door in his face.[68] All classes wore what appeared to be
the same quality of clothes; no sharp contrasts between
poverty and riches were evident; no beggars wandered along
the highways.[69] The only complaint one servant girl had
with her position was that her employer and his wife "talk
such very bad grammar!" [70]

How greatly the existence of religious freedom in America
affected prospective emigrants, it is impossible to measure.
It was the all-important fact to those congregations and sects
which sought relief from ecclesiastical domination. In the
life of the ordinary European peasant, however, religion did
not mean everything though it did mean something. By such
persons the question might be asked: since the United States
had no established church, did it have any religious life at
all? Clergymen of several denominations who visited the
Old World seeking missionary funds and recruits for the
ministry made reply. They declared that not only did religion flourish, but it was a more effective sentiment and a
stronger force for morality and justice than that which was
propped up by the state.[71] Although emphasizing the reli-

gious destitution in which immigrants found themselves until proper provision was made, they painted the future of the work most brightly. Probably many a pious soul who had no intention of leaving home was first stirred to investigate America by the glowing accounts that his religious periodical published under the guise of a missionary tour on the prairies.[72]

Knowledge of the many attractions of America registered all the more deeply because of the peculiarly receptive state of popular opinion in western Europe at the time. Peasants and artisans were swept by a longing for personal improvement. This desire to rise out of the situation in which they were born was a product of the mental and social upheaval of the Revolutionary period. The generation that began its career in that turmoil had now reached maturity. As the earliest scenes that surrounded them had been those of violent change and unprecedented progress, they chafed under the conservative prospects of the Restoration era. There was still hope for their ambitions in a new environment. In a direct sense, America fell heir to the progressive impulse of the Revolution.[73]

In most cases, perhaps, disappointment dulled the ambitions and reconciled the individual to his lot. But he then transferred his early dreams to his children. Establishing one's sons was an invariable family policy in Europe. It was a rule of society that parents should repay to the generation that followed what they had received from the preceding one. A man was a failure who did not leave each of his children as well off as he had been.[74] But by 1830 this aspiration involved problems and sacrifices unknown a few decades before. What was a civil or military officer with four or five sons to do when only with difficulty could he secure positions for two or three of them? Likewise the professions were crowded. In Hanover ten times as many candidates sought appointments in the Church as there were annual vacancies. Many a farmer could not provide his sons with tools, much less a respectable tract of land.[75]

To such parents the accounts from America spoke emphatically. Observers in the early 1830's noticed that emigration was changing in character. Instead of its bulk being made up of single young men — farm laborers, artisans and apprentices — or young couples going out to establish themselves, an increasing proportion now consisted of family groups in which several strong and active sons predominated. The explanation lay in the desire of parents to put their children and their capital in a land where both were needed and where a yield from each was assured. In Europe one often heard the phrase, "a poor man with many children"; in America the expression would have been an anomaly, for a man with many children soon ceased to be poor. "Mr. Malthus," wrote a settler, "would not be understood here." [76]

The family type of immigrant constituted the kind of newcomer most likely to succeed. Less mobile than the unattached settler, the family took quick and deep root. They patiently endured hardships from which the individual would have fled. All, young and old, contributed to the common undertaking for better or worse. If most of the reward went to the children, the father achieved a contentment which excited one contemporary to the following rhetorical flight:

The mind that was once the constant prey of fearful forebodings of coming wretchedness, is now peaceful and serene. The cloud that was dark and lowering, and threatened a coming storm, has now passed away, and the sun, which was thus for a time obscured, suddenly breaks forth in all his noonday brightness and brilliancy. Well may such persons (at least in so far as worldly circumstances are concerned) lay their heads down upon their dying pillow, and with their weeping family around their beds, commit their souls to God, and close their eyes in death, without a corroding thought of what is to become of their surviving relations, after they have gone the way from whence they shall never return.[77]

The fear for the family future reflected in part a vague feeling that Europe herself was doomed to destruction. The cares of age were creeping upon her; vigor and spirit were gone. Asia and Africa had had their day, and now the star of Europe was declining. Both philosophers and peasants felt this decadence. *"Amerika du hast es besser,"* wrote Goethe in a well-known poem of 1831; [78] and a few years before, a group of Scotch weavers, requesting government aid to migrate, declared they were "literally worn out in the feverish and fluctuating state of a commercial life. . . . To flee from this artificial existence to the calm and virtuous labours of a pastoral life, is the eager wish of your petitioners." [79] Moreover, though statesmen spoke of peace, thousands of regiments were under arms and, at best, peace was merely an armistice.[80] In language that suggests an acceptance of the principle underlying the Monroe Doctrine, writers emphasized the essential difference between the political systems prevailing on the two sides of the Atlantic. Ultimately they would conflict, with every advantage favoring the young and rising continent.[81] No wonder that farseeing men planted their family fortunes in a land where the future seemed assured.

The natural unwillingness to leave one's fatherland was mitigated by the fact that, in any case, old bonds of association were loosening. The common fields were being divided, and the feudal system with its joint obligations was being modernized, changes which entailed a weakening of sentimental ties as well. In this transitional period rose the vision of America with boundless opportunities for people like themselves. If they must have a new fatherland, why not the country across the sea? Love of country, they argued, was a laudable virtue, but what is one's native land? "It is not the ground on which we first saw the light of day, it is not the blue arch of heaven above us. No! It is of a higher nature — our habits and customs, the ties of family and friendship, our language — these constitute the true Fatherland." All these might be retained in America. Patriotism ceased to be a stumblingblock, and as imagination endowed this far country with all the traits of a wished-for land, a new patriotism tended to spur the peasants to migrate.[82]

Dread of the ocean gave some of the prospective settlers pause. Most of the emigrants came from the interior, and to them the Atlantic was a place of storms and shipwrecks. Agents and shippers, recognizing the strength of this prejudice, sought to dispel it in their advertisements and publicity. They stressed the seaworthiness of vessels, the skill and resourcefulness of the sailors, the accuracy of modern nautical science.[83] These assurances gained weight from the testimony of those who had crossed the waters. After having lived through the experience, wrote one, he would now have no more fear "than I should of going over the sheepwash."[84] Another, though attributing the success to Providence, was no less encouraging: "We have great reason to thank God for his kindness that we all got here safe, I should think it a great mercy that near 400 people came over in one ship and only one little infant died of them, and there were four births before we got there."[85]

This dread of the sea was most openly expressed by the women, but often their hesitation rested as much upon a fear of the life that would be theirs beyond the sea. They would lose domestic conveniences in exchanging the old home for a frontier cabin, and the loneliness of the backwoods loomed in sharp contrast to the pleasant society afforded by the village market place, the parish church and the neighbor's kitchen. While the father thought of the children's future, their mother dreaded a present in which illness would have to be fought without a physician's aid and death endured without a clergyman's comfort. Many a husband thus discovered a strong objection to emigration when the project was broached to the family council. Children would go anywhere for novelty, but the wife's reaction was a decided no. So chronic was this attitude that a popular emigrant guidebook prescribed the method for handling such obstinacy: be patient and temperate but firm and, if need be, plan to go without her.[86] Desertions of this nature, however, were uncommon. The marriage vow still called for more than love and honor. The woman who confessed she "should never have become an emigrant, if obedience to my husband's wishes had left me any alternative," spoke for many a wife and mother.[87]

In time feminine resistance tended to lessen. As America became better known, women learned that the backwoods were not the only destination, that America had its villages, markets and churches. Even more startling was the rumor that in the new land women's drudgery was less rather than more; that they did not hoe turnips, pull flax, make hay or milk cows; that the men chopped the wood and drew the water; that farmers' wives were ladies and farmers' daughters could "carry their heads high." Many a settler's wife was to be disillusioned and to experience all the loneliness and hardship that she had feared; but the desire for greater self-respect and more ease was alluring, and they obeyed cheerfully the command to depart.[88]

Reluctance to leave the pleasant community life to which they were accustomed affected men as well as women, though in less degree. The sentiment was most acute among non-British peoples, and the desire to avoid the necessity inspired the various schemes for a "German state" or a "German community" propounded about 1830. Persons acquainted with American conditions warned that success was impos-

sible.[89] Yet though failure greeted every one of these undertakings, the individuals concerned quickly learned to strike
out for themselves.[90] This outcome was not as strange as it
might seem. Groups had come to grief because they curbed
the most important single factor leading to success — individual enterprise. The moral was clear: a single person or
family could do better alone.[91] Thus by their failure these
ill-fated ventures probably induced a greater migration than
if they had succeeded.

Many signs pointed to the changed character of the German
newcomers. A decade before, the majority had been farmers
whom Americans lumped indiscriminately with the plodding
"Pennsylvania Dutch" of the eighteenth century. But the
immigration of ten years had introduced a different Teutonic atmosphere. Free from religious complexes, these later
arrivals soon lost their peasant characteristics. A few years
brought prosperity and a desire for social amenities. Their
communities attracted professional men of their own race —
doctors, ministers, musicians, teachers — and the presence of
this class in turn contributed to an improved cultural life.
In cities or townships, wherever a few thousand were to be
found, there blossomed schools, churches, bookstores, singing
societies and newspapers. In several parts of the country
local societies joined in forming state organizations,[92] and
in 1835 a movement began to bring the German Americans
together on a nation-wide basis. Pittsburgh Germans were
especially active in promoting this sentiment, and committees
of correspondence arranged the details. The first "German
Convention" gathered at Pittsburgh in October, 1837. The
delegates, holding that German feeling could be best maintained by giving the rising generation proper educational
facilities, recommended the founding of a seminary for the
training of teachers. Under this sponsorship an institution
was established at Philipsburg, Pennsylvania. The enthusi-

asm aroused by the first convention caused later ones to be held. The fifth and last met in August, 1843.[93]

Conventions, however, were not the principal means of exerting influence. The political importance of naturalized voters impressed itself on native politicians whenever military companies of German youth marched down the streets of New York, Baltimore, Pittsburgh or Cincinnati.[94] First in local, then in congressional and state, and finally in national elections, their favor was sought. Democrats told them that their coöperation had helped to overthrow the money power of New England and to place Jackson in the White House. Whigs ascribed to them the great victory of 1840. When the Democrats returned in 1844 Germans were led to believe that they were responsible.[95] The friendly attitude of all in office, from the President down, encouraged their group activities, while the failure of the nativist movement in the late thirties to spread beyond the ward politics of a few cities gave them renewed confidence.

By the end of the decade the Germans confidently held the belief that amalgamation with the Anglo-Americans and the submergence of their distinctive cultural traits need not be the inevitable outcome of participation in American political and social life.[96] Ties with Germany grew stronger with the constant accretion of new and vigorous blood, while closer trade relations resulted from the treaty with the Zollverein.[97] German customs, language, songs and institutions flourished in a hundred communities. A new Germany had come into existence, and the prospective emigrant was assured, "You will feel at home." [98]

For obvious reasons the situation of the Irish in America differed markedly from that of the Germans. They had prior familiarity with the language and many of the institutions, and with them political organization was an old story. The repeal movement of the early forties, however, increased their assertiveness. Organized at first to raise funds to help the agitation which Daniel O'Connell was conducting in Ireland, it promised for a time to develop into an uprising against the assumed superiority of the "original Americans." [99] Though the uprising never got beyond the stage of oratory, it consolidated many isolated evidences of Irish-American feeling and, through the deference exhibited by those in high authority, encouraged further collective activity in the political field in which they had already become adept.

As has been seen, the popular interest of Europeans in America varied with the diversity of circumstances. Broadly speaking, the interest was restricted to certain countries and to those parts from which emigration had taken place. In such regions hardly a village or hamlet or farmhouse could be found in which the pros and cons of the fateful step had not been thoroughly canvassed. Children grew up in an atmosphere of uncertainty and expectancy regarding the future. In one rural community in England it was reported that emigration was "almost the only topic of conversation. Many have ceased to take an interest in the discussion of home politics." [100] The departure of a group was the occasion for a general holiday while farewells were said. None could escape the impression of these recurrent occasions.[101]

To those who viewed such scenes disapprovingly the desire to emigrate seemed like a fever. Whole districts succumbed to the epidemic and, as if following a modern Pied Piper, streamed headlong to the seaports.[102] There, as on the quays of Ireland, they waited, "seeking to be transported to any part of America, they knew not whither, in any vessel, they cared not what, provided she bore them away from the poverty and destitution of their native land." [103] Occasionally the disease broke out mysteriously in some quiet country spot remote from the commercial connections that might explain the interest. In many such instances the responsible

agent was a villager who had returned from a visit to some
"fever-infested" region.[104]

The herd instinct was a powerful factor in these centrif-
ugal movements. Violent opposition on the part of the
authorities would have defeated its own purpose and for this
reason the governments refrained from positive prohibitory
action. They did, however, express their disapproval. In
many German states, as the interest grew, would-be emigrants
petitioned for treasury funds to help them, but the decision
was always unanimous that the good accomplished would not
warrant the expense and that the possibility of success was so
doubtful that no state had the moral right to encourage the
risk.[105] The official barriers to private emigration, however,
were not heightened. The policy was to let the movement
run its course while the authorities warned of the dangers
involved. Prussia alone leaned toward a more deliberate
curb. A law of 1820 made it a crime punishable by imprisonment to urge anyone to emigrate, and a further decree of
1845 sought to strike at the root of the trouble by prohibiting
the reading in public of any letter or paper which directly or
indirectly tended to the same effect.[106]

The philosophers of the time (and there were many of
them among the village clergymen and schoolmasters) followed a quite different line of reasoning. They thought of
America not as a place of bigger farms and higher wages,
but as a new country with a social mission divine in its
origin. America was the soil on which aging Europe would
rejuvenate its spirit. The childhood of the United States
was over; it had now achieved the full stature of a nation
able to receive all who came. In such troubled times in the
Old World, with business and society stagnant and artificial,
mankind could start again by embracing a simple life governed by a simple constitution. The American republic
provided the stage on which the great political and social

problems of the age would be solved.[107] It possessed abundant physical resources; man power and human intelligence alone were as yet insufficient, and now these were being supplied by the emigrants whose good fortune it was to partake in the process. Emigration was no evil: it was the "very pendulum of society." With two thirds of the world lying waste, talk of the necessity of checks upon the population was premature.[108]

Some sensitive souls imbued with that sentiment of love for country which is always associated with religion asked, "Is it a sin to emigrate, to leave the spot on this earth where God has put us?" To them a score of voices answered, "No!" The first commandment in Genesis had enjoined Adam and Eve to be "fruitful and multiply and replenish the earth." The confusion of tongues at the Tower of Babel afforded further proof that the spread of population was part of the divine plan.[109] But the best scriptural example was provided by Moses, who brought happiness to his people by leading the exodus from the land of Egypt. As one rural pastor elaborated the argument, now, as in Biblical times, the people are oppressed. Though there is no individual Pharaoh, there is a state of society which is the oppressor. The Israelites of today are the poor laborers and artisans whose burdens increase as their numbers increase. For them, no less than for the slaves of Egypt, emigration is the only salvation, and America is the New Canaan. Would that a Moses would arise to smite the waters of the Atlantic so they might part as the waters of the Red Sea had parted to permit the fleeing hosts to cross in safety! [110] Even as the good pastor wrote, the miracle was in process, for commerce was building a bridge over the Atlantic on which the sons and daughters of Europe might pass to their Promised Land.

VIII

COMMERCE BRIDGES THE ATLANTIC

FOR THE GENTLEMAN ADVENTURER the way to America had always been open. For the poor emigrant, however, the expense of stagecoaches and inns was high, the protracted wait at the port of embarkation cost him many pieces of gold, and the steerage accommodations entailed discomfort and suffering. The Atlantic crossing was not only expensive, but the chances of obtaining any passage at all were uncertain, for the movement of ships depended on the fluctuations of commerce rather than on the wishes of passengers. Sometimes America-bound ships thronged the ports of Europe; at other times the harbors were empty. A large-scale peasant emigration was possible only when the European demand for American products was so steady as to insure an adequate supply of vessels and when the tentacles of trade pushed inland to facilitate transportation on land. It was a commercial expansion of this nature that in the 1830's bridged the Atlantic and opened the doors of America to those countless individuals who must rely on their own resources, knowledge and courage for the great adventure.

The web of permanent intercontinental relationships which is called modern commerce had begun to form in the seventeenth century, but its strands had been confined by mercantilist legislation and repeatedly torn by wars. With the peace of 1815, however, the process resumed; and two decades later the German who smoked used American tobacco, the factories of Switzerland and France spun American cotton, and British houses and ships drew their timber from the Canadian forests. To satisfy these wants, steamboats threaded their way up and down European rivers, long-pointed barges glided through the canals, heavily laden wagons crawled along endless stretches of newly built roads, while on the Atlantic thousands of sails bound the two continents in a mutual dependence which no legislation could thwart and no wars destroy.

These developments rested in part on the experiences of the quarter-century of wars that closed in 1815. Privateers had swarmed the seas; navies had hunted one another on the broad oceans and along the island coasts; adventurous merchants had richly rewarded the captains who brought their cargoes safely through vigilant blockades. A generation of seamen had been trained to join boldness with caution, to develop speed and to devise new methods of navigation. With the return of peace they devoted their skill and enterprise to fighting the battles of rival shippers. The new commerce was not the child of steam: not for half a century would steam displace the sail.

Better instruments of navigation also increased the safety and speed of voyages. In three hundred years few new instruments had been added to the ship's equipment. Many a skipper of the North Atlantic ventured out to sea with nothing but experience, a collection of proverbs regarding the weather, and a thermometer with which to locate the Gulf Stream. For many of the appliances which textbooks on navigation deemed indispensable, the veteran sailor felt deep contempt, and in most cases the contempt was justified. Thus the compass could be relied upon only within limits. No satisfactory method had been devised of preventing or minimizing the influence that the magnetic pole or the ship's iron exerted upon the needle. As a result, vessels making a westward crossing of the Atlantic usually found themselves south and east of their reckoning. A report to the Admiralty in 1820 declared that half the compasses in the British navy were worthless. Though some improvements were made in the following years, an Admiralty Compass Committee undertook in 1837 to investigate the subject. Its report in July, 1840, proposed changes which were incorporated in the "Admiralty Compass," that, as then designed, remained the standard instrument not only in the British navy but in most shipping circles of the world until 1876.[1]

Another perplexing problem of the sea was the accurate determination of longitude. Latitude — distance north or south of the equator — was derived by a comparatively simple astronomical computation, but until the eighteenth century longitude — distance east and west of Greenwich — had involved a kind of guesswork known as dead reckoning. But it was almost impossible to make allowance for head winds, the drift of currents and faulty compass readings, with the result that longitude by dead reckoning was at best an approximation. A mechanical contrivance which checked off distance by means of a paddle wheel revolving at the stern provided a better solution except that it was likely to be torn from the vessel.[2] In the eighteenth century, especially built timepieces called chronometers had been devised to carry unchanged the hour of Greenwich so that it might be compared with the time at any position (noon, for instance) as determined by readings of the sextant. Every four minutes' difference represented a degree of longitude. The difficulty now was that the sea air and changes in temperature prevented that measure of accuracy which was essential, and "approximate location" was the best that could be attained. In order to perfect the chronometer the British Admiralty in 1820 began awarding generous prizes annually for improvements. By 1834 the principles had been so well worked out and the practice was so competent that the awards were discontinued. The instrument had become so accurate that a mariner could navigate his ship around the earth and show less than a mile's error in longitude at the conclusion of his voyage.[3]

With a trustworthy compass and chronometer seamanship developed into an exact science. Formerly sails were pulled at sunset and vessels lay by until morning; now they drove forward day and night. Besides the aid afforded by better scientific equipment, the vessels themselves embodied improvements that contributed to speed. Tradition lingers long at sea, and at the opening of the century ships still bore evidences of their origin from the medieval galleys of the Mediterranean. They were broad, top-heavy structures that offered constant resistance to water and air. But the long period of wars caused the sacrifice of many of the conventional features of marine architecture, and in the rivalry for speed that followed 1815, the Americans especially made one change after the other. Ships became longer and narrower, the impediments on deck were removed, and new masts and arrangements of sails were constructed to catch any current of air and offer the least obstruction to motion. Ultimately the historic clipper ship was evolved.[4]

The mariner, however, was interested not only in his vessel; he knew that beyond the horizon lay foreign shores, flanked with hidden rocks and changing shoals. By comparison the dangers of the deep seemed insignificant. Finding and entering a harbor called for more than seamanship; it called for coöperation from the authorities on shore. Hence the improvements made in lighthouses, charts and coast patrol proved as epoch-making as the new nautical technique. As late as 1807 the Eddystone Light, one of the most important in the English Channel, obtained its illumination from twenty-four candles. No reflector and no lens intensified or directed the beam; no code of flashes distinguished it from neighboring beacons.[5] When conditions had settled down after the peace of 1815, governments first gave serious attention to the question of the proper lighting of coasts. In 1819 the French minister of marine directed a commission to study the subject and experiment with new instruments.[6] Augustin Fresnel, one of the group, devised a lens on the principle of separate pieces together with a burner that produced a strong flame, and he also worked out a system for identifying stations by flashes at intervals of different duration. Although Fresnel's scientific career lasted hardly more than a dozen years, his improvements proved so basic that changes since then have concerned only mechanical details and the source of the light.[7]

The general application of these innovations was rapid. In 1825 the French government adopted the program of construction which its commission had proposed;[8] and in 1836 Parliament greatly improved the administration of all British lights by centralizing their control in the Corporation of Trinity House.[9] The United States in 1820 possessed only fifty-five lighthouses and a few buoys; by 1842 the number of lighthouses had grown to two hundred and fifty-six, lightboats to thirty and buoys to one thousand.[10] No longer need a skipper and his passengers fear an unexpected night approach to a dark shore, or an ominous fog with the silence unbroken by warning signals.

While the coast above the water line was being illuminated, the mysteries hidden in the shallows were being plumbed. The maps which most captains had long been accustomed to use revealed only the physical contour of a shore and some of the more important channels through the bars and shoals. No agency had systematically charted these lurking hazards, or engaged in checking the constant changes taking place below the waves. Americans especially needed such information because of the perpetual influence of tides and currents on their beaches. In 1816 the federal government commenced a survey of the New Jersey coast, but terminated it two years later for reasons of economy. The project, however, was resumed in 1832 with enlarged appropriations and was extended to other sections of the coast.[11] Meanwhile European nations undertook like activities. When Captain Francis Beaufort became hydrographer to the Admiralty in 1828, his interest followed British vessels into all parts of the globe. Wherever countries were unable to carry on surveys, his officers compiled the information. Their care and assiduity made the series of Admiralty Pilots the standard guidebooks for the seven seas.[12]

Though wrecks still occurred in spite of these precautions, they did not involve the same toll of lives or the bankruptcy of the skippers and merchants concerned. Life-saving crews and marine insurance now played a greater part in ocean trade. The Royal National Institution for the Preservation of Life from Shipwreck was founded in London in 1824, and in the following years all dangerous points about the British Isles were provided with boats, carriage and gear, under charge of a paid coxswain who mustered his crew from the neighboring residents.[13] In the United States the Humane Society of Massachusetts was the pioneer agency, and through its influence other Atlantic states took similar action, aided by funds from the state and national governments. Finally, these activities were merged into the coast-guard service under the direct supervision of Washington.[14] With the formation of Lloyd's Register of British and Foreign Shipping in 1834, the science of shipbuilding received an important practical impetus; and the system of insurance devised by that house removed from commerce the tragedy of individual ruin which had hitherto attended the loss of a ship and its cargo.[15]

The new era in Atlantic trade was signalized by the growth of the packet service. In the eighteenth century ships called packets had plied between England and the colonies, but they were government dispatch boats. Now the term desig-

nated vessels whose principal cargo was mail, cabin passengers and light freight, and whose sailing occurred at regular
intervals irrespective of whether cabins and hold were full.
The first packet went into operation in 1815, and by 1829
sailings occurred from New York to Liverpool and Le Havre
three times a month, from New York to London twice a
month, from Boston to Liverpool once a month, and from
New York to Hamburg and from Baltimore to Liverpool at
less frequent periods. A lively spirit of competition between
the ships resulted in improved service, greater speed and
more skillful seamanship.[16] As there were practically no accommodations for steerage passengers, the influence of these
lines on migration was indirect rather than direct. The
majority of departing Europeans continued to depend upon
ships whose principal occupation was the carrying of freight.
On the other hand, the methods of navigation and business
developed by the packets gradually affected all shipping
circles, and year by year the bridge of commerce was extended and broadened. Moreover, in the cabins of the packets
traveled a constant succession of the smaller capitalists, bringing funds to invest in American lands and industry, and also
the more prosperous professional and agricultural emigrants.

The number of passengers from Europe to the United
States in the ten years from 1830 to 1840 was five times that
of the preceding decade. The transport of emigrants had
become a regular feature of Atlantic trade. Violent fluctuations in the flow still appeared, but the scale had changed.
The season of 1843 was regarded one of depression and, compared with the years before and after, it was; yet the
number was about twice that of the year 1832, which only
ten years earlier had been considered an unprecedented outpouring. Commerce now accepted as a certainty that every
spring, irrespective of the prospects in the United States,
tens of thousands of persons would appear at the European

ports with money to pay their passage to America. With this assurance the trade took on a permanent form through establishing definite routes and schedules of sailing and through enlisting a special personnel. The emigrant had become a leading article of commerce.[17]

This transatlantic movement of European people filled a great need in the economy of ocean transportation. America had always had products to export to Europe, notably tobacco and then cotton. In return Europe sent its goods from factory and workshop. But this exchange involved an inequality of cargoes. Outward-bound vessels from America carried heavy freights; on the return the cargo, being finer in quality and smaller in bulk, left much of the space unoccupied save by ballast. In the colonial period this disparity had led many shippers into the African slave trade, which constituted the southern base of the New England triangular trade and built up the prosperity of the ports of western England. Under the new conditions it was emigration which saved the westbound traffic from being predominantly a transportation of ballast. Conversely, the increased shipment of tobacco, grain and cotton helped to reduce the price of passage to a level that the European peasant could afford. The brusque, hard-headed skippers did not realize that upon them had devolved the mission of spreading European culture. "I have no motive in it beyond a back freight to ships I am interested in," said a Liverpool forwarder to an investigating committee.[18] It was charged against American captains that they looked upon their passengers merely as packages to be delivered as quickly and in as good condition as possible.[19]

Consideration of the way in which shipping provided for emigration from a country involves first an inquiry into what markets that country offered as an attraction to ships from America. In the case of the eighteenth-century Irish, when the linen manufacture of Ulster was at its height and flax was too valuable to allow to run to seed, the people turned to the product of Pennsylvania for a satisfactory substitute. Ships from America discharging their cargoes at Londonderry, Belfast and Newry returned again to the ports on the Delaware, and Ulstermen wishing to travel at the cheapest rate went where the ships took them. In the early nineteenth century this exchange still continued, newspaper advertisements indicating that brokers engaged in dispatching emigrant vessels were also importers of flax and clover seed, pot and pearl ashes, tobacco and deerskins — characteristic products of the Middle Atlantic states.[20]

But by the fourth decade of the nineteenth century the trade in these commodities was largely displaced by the importation of lumber and woodenware. By that time the forests with which Nature had endowed primeval Ireland had disappeared. Though the peat bogs provided sufficient fuel for the laborers and cottiers, cottages could not be constructed entirely of mud and stones; some beams at least were essential. The growing population demanded a continual importation of timber, a demand intensified by the needs of the cooperage industry in the southern and central counties where Irish pork, eggs and butter were packed in barrels, firkins and crates. As the St. Lawrence region was the principal producer of the deals and staves with which the coopers worked, the number of vessels in the Quebec trade rapidly increased.[21] Spring was the time of year when emigrants desired to reach their new homes; it was also the season when the shipper could find the winter's timber cuttings awaiting him. Since the supply of ships was great and the competition keen, the rates of passage were forced down. In 1816 the English emigrant had paid ten pounds to reach the United States; in the early thirties the fare from Ireland to Quebec sometimes fell as low as fifteen shillings, though usually it hovered around two pounds ten shillings.[22] As this was just half the amount charged for the passage to New York, the difference had the effect of turning the Irish tide to British America.[23]

Arriving there, the newcomer found many inducements to keep him. The spring fleet, including the vessel in which he came, had to be loaded with timber, which meant that immediate employment was available. During the following winter he could engage in lumbering in the near-by forests or in shipbuilding along the Quebec water front. Farther inland, work might be found on the canals, roads and farms.[24] But many who had taken advantage of the cheaper rate to Quebec had done so with the intention of walking to the United States, and others whose plans were less definite "fell over the line."[25] What proportion of the whole number followed this course is uncertain. At the time some maintained that the majority departed.[26] Land in the United States was easier to acquire than in Canada, and opportunities for year-round employment were more plentiful.[27] It is clear, however, that until the forties this reëmigration was balanced by a countermovement which reached Canada via New York.[28] That lines of migration should cross in this way is not as surprising as it may seem. Canada was an attractive field for the settler with some means and a strong political attachment to the Empire. Many such made the voyage by way of New York on the packet ships, preferring the greater comfort and the quicker trip. The poor laborer, however, had no choice in the matter and, while directing himself to Quebec, considered "the States" his ultimate destination.[29]

Not all those who sailed from Ireland to British America went as far into the interior as Quebec, for as the demand for timber waxed, the exploitation of the forests of New Brunswick began. The journey was shorter to Halifax, St. John and St. Andrews, the competition greater, and the fares for passengers were even less than to Quebec. Hence this was the route chosen by the poorest. When they arrived, however, the future had little to promise them. Work was available in the forest and during part of the year at the docks, but there were few large landowners to assist the penniless immigrants to become settlers.[30] Consequently the maritime provinces were only one stage on the route to the United States. Some passed on immediately; others worked for a time to acquire the means.

Here, too, commerce had prepared the way, for at the line separating Maine and New Brunswick the British timber trade met the American coasting trade.[31] This coastal trade was brisk. Improved methods of farming in the Eastern states created a demand for the only mineral fertilizer with which agriculture was then acquainted, gypsum or plaster of Paris, of which Nova Scotia possessed large supplies. From the mines it was taken to Eastport and Passamaquoddy and there transferred to the American coastal vessels which conveyed it as far south as New Jersey and Pennsylvania. Since these craft also carried deck passengers, laborers found it possible for a small sum to reach the United States ports where their services were most in demand.[32]

But the States could also be reached overland. By following the road through the wilderness of northeastern Maine, the emigrants drifted on to the more populous areas of New England, working their way as occasion arose or begging their food and shelter. Many of these wayfarers attached themselves to the communities through which they passed, becoming the nuclei about which larger groups of their fellow countrymen later gathered. The pioneer Catholic churches in Maine clearly define the route. This infiltration of Irishmen from the maritime provinces helped to break up the Anglo-American character of New England. In this sense, it is probably no exaggeration to consider Hibernian

New England as the product of the New Brunswick timber trade.[33]

In the meantime the Irish current was turning toward what was to be its more permanent channel. Great as was the market for lumber in Ireland, it was not capable of indefinite expansion. Paralleling the route of the timber ships for a great part of their course was a rapidly growing branch of commerce. Through its gateway at Liverpool, Lancashire was importing American cotton and sending back the varied products of its factories. Although these ships took on much of their cotton at New Orleans and Charleston, they discharged their English wares at the more northern ports. Since the westbound freight consisted principally of ballast, these shipowners looked with jealous eyes upon the great human cargo that Ireland had to offer. At first they routed their vessels via Irish ports, stopping only to take on emigrants.[34] But in the era of sails this often involved serious delays. The winds in the Mersey were as variable as elsewhere; and when a favorable breeze rose, captains were eager to get clear of the land and through the channels as quickly as possible. To waste time beating around the Irish headlands or up the rivers on which the ports were located often entailed serious financial loss. It was more reasonable to convey the Irish to Liverpool, and the rapid extension of steam navigation between Ireland and Liverpool facilitated this plan. As an inducement, the brokers bore the cost of this first leg of the journey and, especially in southern Ireland, this roundabout course early became the standard route.[35] From 1832 on, British authorities calculated that nine tenths of the emigrants from Liverpool were Irish.[36]

Other circumstances also encouraged this development. Most of the carriers in the cotton trade were vessels of American ownership and registry because under the laws of the United States they enjoyed a monopoly of the coastal trade from the Northern ports to the Southern where cotton was laden, and hence could offer rates which the British found it difficult to match.[37] Since few American ships called at Irish ports, both sentiment and prudence inclined emigrants to go to Liverpool where they might be found. Even the English admitted that a Yankee skipper was superior to his British counterpart. In most cases the American was at least part owner of the ship; and even when the captains served on salary, greater care was exercised in their choice, for American insurance companies investigated their character minutely before taking a risk.[38] "Let the ship be American," advised the most popular emigrant guidebook, "remember he is going home, and the captain probably will never pull off his clothes to go to bed during the whole voyage." [39] The many accidents on the Quebec route continually gave point to this advice.[40] Undoubtedly, too, the American captains were better businessmen than their British rivals. They made alliances with Irish brokers, appointed keepers of public houses their agents and, through their extensive connections in America, obtained a large share of the passengers who traveled on prepaid fares.[41]

These same powerful forces concentrated at Liverpool the bulk of the English emigrant trade. In other ports the facilities were less certain. Only in exceptional years could those departing from the south find sufficient shipping in the channel ports. London had little passenger trade to the United States save by the regular and expensive packets. Occasionally a vessel sailed from Hull, but from this port, as from London, the necessity of passing through the channel or about Scotland made the journey of such variable length that the expense of feeding the human cargo rendered the profits uncertain.[42] Though Liverpool sometimes forwarded emigrants from Scotland,[43] usually Greenock, Glasgow, Cum-

THE DEPARTURE

SCENE BETWEEN DECKS

LIFE ABOARD AN EMIGRANT SHIP

arty and Aberdeen were able to meet the local demands. They were visited regularly by ships bringing in timber and cotton, and the exodus seldom exceeded the capacity of these craft. Most of the Scotch commercial connections, however, were with Canada, and it was to the frontier of Ontario that most of the Highlanders went.[44]

The first question asked by the prospective emigrants from the Continent was, "How can we reach the sea?" The bulk of them were farmers dwelling in the valleys of Switzerland and the adjacent states of Germany. Nature, it is true, had provided them with a highway. The Rhine was navigable from Basel to the ports of the Netherlands and, together with the Main and the Neckar, formed a route which tapped all the regions of German and Swiss emigration. Traditionally the Dutch shippers had made the most of this natural advantage, developing a passenger business with the redemptioner system as its center. But when that system was abrogated, they found it difficult to compete with ports which, maintaining steady commercial relations with the New World, were able to transport emigrants as an incident to their main purpose. The Dutch exchanged the products of northern Europe with those of southern, imported the spices of the Far East and sugar and coffee from South America; but since the interior of Holland was as thoroughly agricultural as the United States, the two countries had little to exchange. As late as the 1820's custom caused many emigrants to use the Rhine route as their relatives and friends had before them. But in the early thirties the Netherlands were in turmoil; Belgium won its independence and launched a separate existence. For a few years ordinary business was at a standstill. As this was just the time when German emigration was gathering force, the current, prevented from following its usual channel, created two new outlets on the sea, Le Havre and Bremen.[45]

Of these two Le Havre first gained prominence. The city was, in fact, a child of America. Francis the First in 1519 had built at the mouth of the Seine "The Harbor" from which to send expeditions to the New World. For three centuries explorers, privateers and colonists had set out from its quays. After the fall of Napoleon it began to play a different rôle. Back in the hills of Alsace a new industry, that of cotton manufacturing, was developing. Commerce had to feed these factories raw cotton from the Southern states of America; and although the Rhine was the natural route, the tariffs levied by the states through which it flowed heightened the cost unduly. As a result, the bales were imported through Le Havre and transported overland. Friedrich List was amazed at the extent of the business, noting that the value of the goods carried between Strasbourg and Le Havre surpassed five hundred million francs annually, with freight charges of almost fifty million.[46] To handle this trade, new transatlantic ships were built, the docks of Le Havre were enlarged, steamboats and barges multiplied upon the Seine, and hundreds of freight wagons were placed upon the roads of eastern France.[47]

The extension of this path of commerce to their doors soon affected the plans of emigrants. Freight wagons returning from Basel and Strasbourg to Le Havre carried passengers willing to travel the slow way, while persons with more means forwarded their heavy household belongings by the freighters, and themselves used the more rapid stage lines. Most of the emigrants, however, started towards the west in the style of their American contemporaries — in covered wagons. The family carriage was arched with sailcloth and the interior packed with the women, children and baggage. The men and older boys walked outside, leading the horses. In this fashion long caravans set out from the German–French border, camping each evening by the wayside and frugally consuming the supply of food that was to support them across the Atlantic.[48]

At Paris a wait of ten days or so occurred. There the horses were sold at the fairs held twice a week. During this delay the Germans bivouacked on the banks of the Seine or in the gardens of the Louvre, taking occasion to stroll through the museums and galleries and to visit the places where in their childhood so much history had been made. Sophisticated boulevardiers turned to gaze at the wandering groups of brightly clad peasants, and throngs of curious onlookers frequented their camps on the river.[49] In continuing the journey the majority embarked upon the steamboats on the Seine, or traveled as deck passengers upon the barges that these steamboats towed to the port. Three times a day stages set out for Le Havre, but such conveyance was usually too expensive. From the crossing of the Rhine until the waters of the Atlantic were sighted required a journey of several weeks. To be sure, some caravans avoided Paris entirely, traveling by road directly to Le Havre. In such instances, the wagons were oftentimes taken apart and packed in the hold of the ship, to be reassembled upon reaching the American shore for traveling over the mountains into the West.[50]

Thanks to this intercourse Le Havre took on the appearance of a German town. The combined influence of the cotton and emigrant trade drew to it not only representatives of the larger commercial houses, but also a host of German innkeepers, small merchants and ship agents. The emigrants themselves sometimes went no farther. A number were stranded by being cheated out of their property; some had miscalculated the cost; others feared to embark; and a few deliberately remained to prey upon their fellow countrymen. Every season left some to live upon the charity of the French, or to find a way back to their former home.[51] To cope with this problem the government decreed that all who entered the country must possess a contract ticket or adequate means of support. But the regulations were easily evaded and the authorities, recognizing the beneficial effects of the traffic in promoting French commerce, did not undertake a rigorous execution.[52]

During the active season there were always several thousand in the city awaiting the hour of departure. The delay might extend from one to six weeks or more if the winds were contrary or the congestion was great. In the meantime they lodged in the cheapest houses, sometimes several families to a room, cooking and washing and keeping as much as possible outdoors. When the ship finally sailed, they joyfully bade farewell to this enforced idleness and to the limited opportunities of the Old World.

Since the principal article of Le Havre's transatlantic commerce was cotton, and since its ships carried few manufactures on the return voyage to America, only occasional vessels made New York their destination. New Orleans was then the important cotton port, and it was there that thousands of Germans landed annually.[53] Because neither the climate nor the economic life of the lower South appealed to the German peasants, most of them went further inland. Passage up the river was cheap; to St. Louis and Cincinnati it varied from two to two dollars and a half, according to the stand of the water.[54] The Mississippi and its tributaries therefore became the great highway by which the Germans approached the states where they were to do so much to implant their culture. Just as the Canadian timber trade shunted into New England the pioneer Irish who later drew a greater exodus after them, so the cotton trade of Le Havre gave to many Mississippi Valley communities their Teutonic tinge.

In spite of its advantages, however, Le Havre was not to be preëminent in the great mid-century migration of Germans. The rise of Bremen as a world port attests the recu-

perative powers of her citizens. Though Nature had endowed
the city with a long estuary opening into the North Sea as
well as with the river Weser leading through the fields of
Hanover and Westphalia into the mountains of Thuringia,
these assets man had failed properly to capitalize. When the
nineteenth century began, the river trade was on the decline.
The ships were poor in construction, frequent tolls interfered with the flow of traffic, and the boatmen further hampered trade by arbitrary price agreements. Bremen, far from
drawing ocean commerce to her door, found it necessary to
ship her products around to Holland whence they passed
up the Rhine to south Germany. Her trade was confined to
the immediate vicinity; the hinterland carried on its business
largely through Hamburg, which overshadowed Bremen for
both historical and economic reasons.[55] After the Napoleonic
wars Bremen's prospects continued gloomy. Cut off from
the European system, she was compelled to engage in the
more risky transatlantic trade — and therein she found her
salvation.

Her first victory was the treaty with the United States in
1827.[56] By its terms each party extended to the citizens of
the other the privilege of doing business in its ports on the
same footing as nationals. In reality, this provision worked
to the particular advantage of Bremen, for the cost of con-
structing vessels and the wages of seamen were so low with
the Germans that the Americans could not afford to compete. Moreover, the merchants of Bremen knew the market
for which they were providing. As a result, the Yankee ships
lost the commerce with Bremen.[57] To take proper advantage
of her opportunity, however, Bremen had to improve her
connections with the sea. The mouth of the Weser had
gradually been silting up, and transatlantic vessels found it
impossible to approach the docks. Since it was impractical
to keep the channel open, steps were taken to create a new

harbor. By a treaty with Hanover a tract of land twenty miles down the river was secured, engineers skilled in dredging and dyking were obtained from Holland, and in 1830 Bremerhaven opened to the world's commerce.[58]

The way was now paved for the next step: the capture of the tobacco trade of central Europe. "Smoking is a natural want to the Germans," an American official reported,[59] and it was the satisfaction of this want that caused an exodus of young merchants to found branches or allied business houses in America where they studied local economic conditions with Teutonic thoroughness.[60] Asking no credit they bought tobacco in Baltimore, the entrepôt of the Maryland and Virginia trade. The cash prices and the simplicity of the transaction appealed to the planters, and the merchants soon secured control of the supply. After shipping it to Bremen it was there manufactured into cigars and the surplus forwarded in bulk to the interior. In a few years Bremen supplied Germany, Austria and Switzerland with tobacco and disposed of half of the export from the United States.[61]

Thus was created a situation parallel to that which confronted the timber merchants of Ireland and the cotton importers of Le Havre. How could a return freight be found? Again emigrants provided the answer. Hitherto Bremen had paid little attention to them, and those who came to the port often endured a long wait before obtaining accommodations for the United States.[62] Now the conditions changed. Tobacco could be imported more cheaply and sold at a price that drove out competitors. By the same token, emigrants could be transported more regularly and at a rate comparable to that of other ports.[63] The recruiting staff of the emigrant forwarders consisted of the many small dealers through whom the interior tobacco trade was carried on.

Opportune troubles in the Netherlands helped to boom

the passenger business. The independence of Belgium and the subsequent hostilities and blockades forced the commerce that formerly entered the Continent by way of the Rhine to seek an entrance through the North Sea ports. As a result emigrants, forced to go where ships were to be found, flooded Bremen.[64] So profitable was this unexpected traffic that houses formerly skeptical turned to it with enthusiasm, and this participation of established firms gave Bremen vessels a reputation for safe and fair dealing that was lacking at places where the trade had fallen into the hands of speculators. Moreover, ordinances in 1832 and 1834 provided for an official examination of the seaworthiness of ships, a guarantee of forwarding by other means in case of mishap, and regulations governing the appointment of agents. A few years later when several small German states decided to transport their prisoners to America, such persons were forbidden conveyance in Bremen ships in order to retain the good name of the trade. These regulations and the news of the safe arrival of vessels in America received wide publicity throughout Germany. By 1843 Bremen equaled, if it did not surpass, Le Havre in popularity.[65]

Arrangements for reaching Bremen from the interior steadily improved. Emigration had formerly been confined chiefly to southwest Germany, but in the thirties it made headway in the more northern states, notably in the kingdom of Hanover. This development provided Bremen with a supply on which to draw while contacts were being established further to the south. Not until 1843 was the natural highway of the Weser utilized to a marked extent. After 1832, when the twenty-two toll stations on this comparatively short river were reduced to nine, an increasing number of emigrants began to use it,[66] but early attempts to establish regular steamboat traffic were blocked by Hanover's refusal to permit passage through her territory before 1843–1844. Hence the majority proceeded by land. Those going via Le Havre could travel in their own vehicles because of the facilities offered by the horse market in Paris, but there was no such opportunity on the northern route. However, the great freight wagons that had once returned to Bremen empty provided accommodations.[67] In addition, a wagon service was organized for emigrants from the south. In Stuttgart a carriage capable of conveying two families and their goods could be rented with a driver who, when the two weeks' journey ended, returned with what southbound freight he could secure. Such arrangements were cumbersome, however, and Bremen did not realize the full benefit of her position until the era of railroads and steamships.[68]

Baltimore, as the shipping point for Virginia and Maryland tobacco, was the natural destination of the Bremen ships.[69] But since there were few opportunities in Baltimore or the vicinity for immigrants, only those with commercial interests or without money stayed there. The majority passed over the mountains, giving the upper part of the Mississippi Valley its German pioneers, among whom the natives of the north German states predominated.

This exchange of tobacco for men constituted a lucrative business. The old Hanseatic city of Bremen prospered. Up and down the lower Weser, in the creeks and bays, ships were built to handle the traffic and, being constructed primarily for carrying passengers, offered the best accommodations that the times afforded.[70] But the smoking capacity of the German people was limited, and the supply of men available for exportation overbalanced the amount of tobacco that could be profitably imported.[71] Not until the repeal of the British navigation acts in 1849 made it legal for Bremen ships to participate in feeding and supplying Great Britain was the fullest development reached.

A few miles to the east, at the mouth of the Elbe, lay the

city of Hamburg, a great emporium which at first looked with interested disdain upon the efforts of its weaker neighbor. Content with an established position, it did not for some time appreciate the opportunities offered by the transportation of human beings. It possessed a packet communication with the United States; and when on rare occasions the number seeking passage exceeded the ship's capacity, a vessel or two were hired for their accommodation.[72] The emigrant traffic seemed too uncertain; it was based upon a demand which sprang from circumstances too special to appeal to practical businessmen whose fortunes were already made. They objected to having their city repeatedly overrun by rabbles, and discouraged the trade by prohibiting the entrance of persons "in troop formation." [73] Even the later regulation of 1837, which established safeguards for emigrants, subjected their stay in the port to strict police surveillance.[74]

But when they observed men in Bremen whom they had always considered poor attain their own standard of wealth and saw Bremen itself turn into a bustling port, the Hamburg merchants were surprised to discover that the despised trade had become one of the staples of modern commerce which they had let slip through their fingers.[75] Meanwhile, the extension of the movement of German emigration into the north and east was bringing an increasing number of passengers to Hamburg's docks. But they could not be taken care of; and in any case the fare across the Atlantic was higher. Six hundred Saxons who came down the Elbe in 1838 were obliged to proceed overland to Bremen for ocean accommodations. That Hamburg's own river should be a feeder to a rival's prosperity caused resentment. Something must be done, the merchants said; but unable to grasp the nature of the movement going on before their eyes, they thought in terms of colonies, dallying with an obsolete hope until the fire of 1842 forced them to reconstruct both their city and their ideas.[76]

A fundamental difficulty existed in the geography of Hamburg's trade. In 1840, 2484 ships entered the harbor, of which 1038 came from Great Britain, 268 from the West Indies and South America, and only 85 from scattered ports of North America.[77] In the trade with the United States there was no extensive or organized branch of commerce for which emigration could form a counterpoise, as elsewhere it had with timber, cotton and tobacco. Yet the emigrants who came to the port had to be provided for. Since they could not travel directly, they must travel indirectly. The thousand ships from Great Britain pointed the way. Connections between Hamburg and England had always been close. In 1838 steamships crossed three or four times a week from Hamburg to Hull, which was reached on the third day. Another three days' journey brought the travelers to Liverpool where usually they could embark at once for New York, a voyage of thirty-five or forty days. Never was the total duration more than fifty days, whereas directly from Hamburg or Bremen the voyage to America averaged between fifty and sixty, and in some years more. The "Hull route" offered a saving in time and money as well as experiences more interesting and varied.[78]

At Hamburg, agencies sold the necessary tickets, and at Hull German guides who spoke English met the parties and conducted them across the island to the waiting ships at Liverpool.[79] On each of the three laps of the journey — the North Sea, the canals from Hull to Liverpool, and the ocean crossing — the passengers profited by being the complement of an already established movement of commerce. The route, however, was subject to possible inconveniences and irregularities; in vain the authorities of Hamburg tried to obviate them.[80] In later years it was to enjoy a phenomenal development and to prove a significant factor in the great mid-century exodus.

Thus by 1842 Le Havre, Bremen and Hamburg had become the sluice gates through which the rising flood of Continental emigration moved. The outward flow was expedited by a freeing of the navigation of the Rhine. For hundreds of years this great natural route had been blocked by numerous tolls. Although the Congress of Vienna in 1815 had appointed a commission to remove them, the divergent interests of the Dutch and Prussian representatives caused action to be postponed. Finally, a treaty providing for unrestricted passage to the sea was agreed upon. "With one mighty stride the Rhine, in the year 1831, stepped forth from the Middle Ages." [81] A similar removal of barriers occurred on the Rhine's two great tributaries — the Main, which cuts through Hesse and Bavaria, and the Neckar, the highway of Württemberg. By the middle of the thirties direct and regular communication existed between the remote cities of south Germany and the Dutch ports. [82] Between Cologne and Rotterdam the steamship service was daily, and vessels operated in close connection with the stage lines. [83]

The Dutch ports, however, profited little from the emigrants who used the Rhine route. In 1842 Antwerp completed rail connections with Cologne; and by offering special rates, maintaining a supervisor of emigrants and issuing regulations for safety and hygiene, it succeeded in drawing off an appreciable proportion of the travelers. [84] At Düsseldorf and Cologne still others were attracted northward to Bremen. [85] Those who did reach Rotterdam usually went by coastal steamer on to Le Havre for embarkation. [86] So the freeing of the Rhine proved more of a boon to the emigrant traffic of Bremen and Le Havre than to the old cities at the mouth of the river.

In these various ways commerce not only placed at the

disposal of the emigrant a fleet of ships, but it also recruited for his service an army of men. The confused individual who traveled from the Old World to the New was apt to consider the tavern keepers, freight forwarders, ship brokers, captains, crews and land agents whom he encountered as so many villains, each of whom handed him on to the next when he had extracted what gold he could. In many instances this opinion was well founded; but the function they performed for society at large was indispensable, and collectively they deserve to rank high among those who hastened the peopling of America's unoccupied spaces. They tore the emigrant loose from his old environment, bore him across the Atlantic and, after rudely shuffling him about, forced him into proper relationship with the new social group. The emigrant agent was not a new creation. In the previous century he had appeared as the trafficker in souls, the *Seelenverkaufer*, who had visited village after village on the upper Rhine and with his siren songs and promises filled Dutch ships with redemptioners. In the nineteenth century he acted as the intermediary between the peasant with his parochial outlook and commerce with its world-wide sweep.

At first it was the captain who concluded the bargain with the emigrant. Advertisements in the newspapers repeatedly advised, "Apply to the captain on board." [87] Similarly the early guidebooks warned their readers against dealing with intermediaries. Negotiate with the master only, they said; then if accommodations are not as promised, there can be no plea of misunderstanding. Perhaps because many of the vessels were commanded by the owners, a closer personal connection seems to have existed between captain and passengers on ships departing from Ireland than elsewhere. Notices tell of the services he undertook to perform, such as personal care of the seasick and the giving of recommendations to American business acquaintances. [88] One can often detect in these philanthropic declarations carefully concealed alliances with employers of labor and owners of land.

The Irish trade remained comparatively unorganized, though Liverpool houses endeavored through agents to turn the stream in their direction. The Irish, distrusting paper receipts, would not hand over their hard-earned shillings until they reached Liverpool and had seen the vessel with their own eyes. Even then they were in no hurry, for postponement often yielded a decided advantage since Liverpool rates sometimes "broke" at the last moment. A hundred passengers were often booked within two hours of departure, and fare reductions of fifty per cent were not uncommon.[89]

But on the Continent no emigrant could lawfully leave his parish until he had signed a dozen documents. In doing so he surrendered all claims upon his community and his fatherland. Therefore the prospective emigrant found it prudent to think his way carefully through all the steps of his journey, and it was an advantage to know in advance what his passage would cost. The master of a ship tied up at a distant port could not well provide this information and, in any case, an American captain with no knowledge of a foreign tongue was at a disadvantage in negotiating with Germans and Swiss. As a go-between the ship broker made his appearance. At first he usually acted merely as a "runner," bringing the passengers to the captain and receiving a commission for each.[90] But as time went on, the shipowner (captain or business firm) sold outright the space available for a flat sum to one of the recruiting houses. There his responsibility ceased. He had nothing to do with the rates charged by the broker, and if the emigrants did not appear in time for the sailing, he left without them.[91]

At first the scramble for passengers centered in the ports, but as competition increased, greater enterprise proved needful. At Le Havre agents would journey a day or two along the road to meet the advancing Germans, and finally they extended their operations by opening local offices within Germany and Switzerland. This practice received impetus from a French regulation in 1837 which required each emigrant to present at the border a contract ticket issued by some responsible concern of Le Havre.[92] Similar action by the city of Bremen caused the employment of several hundred local representatives.[93] Not only did these agents attend to the mechanics of emigration, but they stimulated the movement to their own private gain, printing letters in the newspapers, distributing circulars and conversing in the public houses and market places. Many mistakenly saw in their activities the principal cause of the exodus.[94]

Thus the powerful forces of commerce smoothed the path of the emigrant. They rendered the journey financially possible for that class from which the redemptioners had formerly been recruited. In the years 1816–1819 steerage passage from British ports cost from ten to twelve pounds;[95] by 1832 accommodations could be obtained in the regular New York packets at six pounds and on ordinary trading vessels at about four.[96] In 1818 passage from Le Havre was quoted at from 350 to 400 francs, and in the early thirties at from 120 to 150.[97] These figures agree with the contemporary opinion that the extension of commercial relationships had produced a substantial cut in rates. It is no exaggeration to say that in the course of fifteen years they had been halved.[98]

As a result, millions of Europeans might reasonably hope to find fortune and happiness in the New World. Commerce had by 1845 put America within their reach in such a way that they need not surrender the individuality without which, political philosophy was teaching them, no happiness was possible and no fortune worth-while.

HOPES AND FEARS OF THE THIRTY YEARS' PEACE

FOR THREE DECADES after the defeat of Napoleon Europe enjoyed unbroken peace. No marching hosts devastated the countryside; no encamped armies bred pestilence and plague; no military levies burdened shops and homes with taxes. Time and again rumors foretold an impending conflict. Yet, though a dozen diplomatic crises brought nations to the verge of war, year after year passed without a call to arms. Never since the days of Augustus had the western world known a peace so general and so prolonged. But where were the blessings that should have come in its train?

In the foreground of public policy, overshadowing all other questions of the day, loomed the specter of poverty. It was not merely the pauperism of city slums growing out of the factory system; it was a creeping paralysis that affected the countryside as well. Agriculture was decaying, and a rural proletariat filled the villages with a rabble of the young and unemployed. When harvests were good, all suffered because of low selling prices; when crops were short, all suffered because of hunger. With each decade conditions grew worse. The multitudes of children swarming in every household had no prospects of land or employment. The ancient Roman civilization had been destroyed by barbarians who overran the country from without; the present civilization was producing its own barbarians. When one entire social class was impoverished, the order of society could not be maintained; and Europe seemed to be rushing toward catastrophe.

For many, "overpopulation" was a sufficient explanation

of the prevailing misery. The physiocrats of the preceding century had taught that a nation's wealth grew as the number of its people grew, and that furthering this increase was an obligation of the state. But now a complete revolution in theory occurred: Malthus was the prophet of the new age. Whereas the seventeenth century had had to find food and work for thirty million new Europeans and the eighteenth for sixty, the nineteenth added two hundred and thirteen million to the total.[1] A hundred and eighty-seven million saw the century begin, four hundred million saw it end.[2]

Some contemporaries accounted for this phenomenon by the "good times" during the wars which, they said, had made earlier marriages possible and hence larger families. Others attributed it to the peace when there were no campaigns to take husbands away from their firesides and break the continuity of family life.[3] But war and peace had less to do with the matter than the scientific advances of the nineteenth century. Sanitation made sickness more unlikely; surgery and medicine cured it. Transportation brought the resources of the world to the very doors of famine-stricken areas. In the war against plagues, prayers and fasts were subordinated to cleanliness, quarantines and the use of vaccination. New methods and a new conscience reduced the appalling rates of infant mortality, and the gradually increasing excess of births over deaths exercised a cumulative effect.[4] Generalities regarding population growth are in themselves, however, barren of significance. Every country and in some countries every district underwent its own peculiar development. The effects on rural life appear vividly in the reports and discussions that attended the efforts of statesmen and humanitarians to fix on appropriate remedies.

Ireland was the object of special attention. With the establishment of the Irish Parliament in 1782, a new spirit had for a time quickened the life of the nation. In the cities arose impressive public buildings; the provinces were connected by a network of canals; the new markets thus brought into reach stimulated agricultural development. In 1783 Parliament began a system of bounties upon exported grain, and the increased production that followed received fresh impetus from the war-time demand of English cities and the British army.[5] In 1805 Newenham reported that the tillage was, "at least, six times more extensive than it was about one-and-twenty years ago." [6] At last the Irish cottier, earning high wages on a neighboring estate and enjoying a profitable outlet for whatever surplus food he raised, attained prosperity. Many became tenants of larger holdings; and counting on the long continuance of the war, they incurred obligations at extravagant rents. Looking back from 1851, a newspaper editor sighed, "Oh, those were great days for old Ireland." [7]

Peace came with chilling effect and a deflation of land values. The increased population that abundant work and food had supported was doomed to almost half a century of painful adjustment, an adjustment all the more difficult because the growth of population continued. The light-heartedness with which young people undertook family obligations, although they possessed no acres to feed them, no roof to shelter them, no wages to support them, amazed visitors from other lands.[8] Some contemporaries ascribed this attitude to the influence of Catholic priests who for reasons of private morality and church policy encouraged early marriage; [9] others blamed the recklessness engendered by poverty, the feeling that "our condition can't be worse." [10] Probably it was only a natural phenomenon in communities where public opinion, the standard of living and the laws did not stand in the way. Moreover, relatives were kind and Nature was generous.

The generosity of Nature was exhibited in the fields where

the potato vine flourished. For better or for worse, the potato had become an indispensable element of living; and out of an estimated population of nine million in 1845 at least four million relied on it.[11] During the famine the Irish looked back to the good old days: "Och, we sure had everything we wanted in the potato, God bless it; we had only to throw a few of them in the hot ashes and then turn them, and we had our supper." [12] The Irish appetite, trained over a pot of potatoes, had little yearning for bread and meat. In amazement captains of emigrant vessels saw their passengers throw overboard the chocolate, plum pudding and cheese which formed part of the ship's fare on special occasions, and down in the steerage sick children cried constantly for potatoes.[13]

Not only was the potato wholesome and nutritious and easier to prepare for the table than other field products, but every part could be used. The haulm thatched the cabin; the peelings fed the pig, the cow and the chickens. An acre or an acre and a half supported a family. A particular variety known as the "lumper" throve on stubble and unfertilized ground and, by its prodigious yield, encouraged a much wider planting than would otherwise have occurred.[14] The potato, said its ardent supporters, has insured Ireland against those frightful famines that formerly were a periodic scourge.[15]

Such optimism was shortsighted, for the potato was a hazardous food. Since it could not be preserved longer than a few months, the superabundance of one year could not make up for the deficiency of another. Its bulk rendered transportation uneconomic, with the result that a local shortage might bring disaster to hundreds of families.[16] Moreover, the ultimate effect upon the soil was ruinous. The cultivation of the potato alternated with that of grain, and the former gradually wore out the land, causing a steady falling-off of the yield of wheat and oats.[17] Though agricultural improvements had many advocates in Ireland, landlords and farm agents found the people apathetic. The turnip, they reported, was regarded an interloper and treated much as a stepchild in the agricultural family circle.[18]

With the potato was associated intense family and communal feeling. The tuber occupied a secure position in popular literature. One of its protagonists wrote,

. . . and on winter nights, when the storm is sweeping over the hills, and the rain pattering furiously against the door, how happy, how truly felicitous to sit in a circle all round the fire, to hear the pot boiling, to see the beautiful roots bursting their coats, and showing their fair faces, to hold the herring on the point of a fork till it fizzes into an eating condition, to see the milk poured out into all the jugs, and to see the happy faces, and listen to the loud laughter of the children — Oh! give me a winter night, a turf fire, a rasher of bacon, and a mealy potatoe! [19]

The central importance of the humble root gave to land and land relationships the predominant position they held in the Irish scene. It was the aspiration of every man to become master of a patch of soil, for a lifetime if possible but at least for the few months of the planting season. In the thirties, however, the movement toward consolidation of holdings made the fulfillment of this ambition increasingly difficult. Moreover waste lands, peat bogs and mountain sides no longer offered opportunities for pioneering. In other words, with a greater pressure of population the supply of land grew steadily slimmer. Accordingly, the peasants' dread of being left landless caused them to promise almost any rent when they bid for leases. But once the land was secured, trouble arose in a new form as the tenant sought to evade the obligations of his contract. The agrarian outrages that constantly disturbed the country grew out of this mutual fear and distrust of landlord and tenant.[20]

The search for a solution encountered a maze of legal and

extralegal practices embraced in the term, "local relationships." Five stout tomes with ten thousand columns of testimony record the findings of the Devon Commission which in
1845 inquired into the tenure that prevailed in rural Ireland.
The roots of the system ran back into history. Henry II,
Elizabeth, Cromwell, William III, had confiscated provinces
and baronies with which to reward followers or pay off debts.
These possessors in turn colonized their lands with settlers
from Scotland and England, or became landlords themselves.
Custom as well as law fixed the status of the peasants. By
the eighteenth century the Ulster system of "tenant right"
permitted the tenant certain privileges which the law did not
recognize — privileges which made it possible for him to hold
his land intact during his lifetime and which created an
interest that he might ordinarily pass on to his heir. This
custom, however, did not prevail throughout Ulster, and it
existed in some places outside the province.[21]

Elsewhere in Ireland, rebellions and the lack of sympathy
between Protestant landlord and Catholic tenant had generally prevented the peasant from acquiring an assurance of
long tenure based upon custom. The majority were tenants
at will, which usually meant, whatever the law said to the
contrary, that they were entirely subject to the will of the
landowners. As a result the peasant, uncertain of the length
of his stay, put the land to maximum use, ignoring all considerations of soil conservation, and perhaps subletting part
of it to other tenants at will with the help of whose payments
he often met his own rent. In this fashion tenants became
landlords until in some instances the hierarchy was "six
deep." [22] The census of 1841 revealed that over forty-two per
cent of the holdings in Ireland were between one and five
acres in extent.[23] Smaller holdings the census did not enu-
merate, but thousands of them existed as a result of the rapidly
increasing class of the landless, made up of persons ejected

from consolidated estates and of the sons of five-acre cottiers.

To accommodate them, the conacre system was devised. This scheme rested on the belief that, whereas the credit of any single individual might be worthless, a partnership of such persons, in which each assumed responsibility for the total rent, constituted a reasonable risk.[24] Under direction of a "collector" (because no respectable agent or landlord was willing to meddle in the sordid business), an association of ten or fifteen villagers would be formed to whom would be leased an acre of rich, newly broken pasture land or one that had been highly fertilized. Since the normal yield of potatoes would be prodigious, so was the rent, usually ranging from seven to ten pounds an acre.[25] Seed secured on credit had to be paid back at from fifty to one-hundred-per-cent increase at the harvest.[26] In ordinary years the conacre system worked: the laborers got their food and the renter his money. But like all Irish economic life, it was a hand-to-mouth gamble, more discredited than other systems because it encouraged squalor and perpetual bickering within the group, and because failure brought appalling distress and harsh legal measures to enforce payment of the rent. Many possessors of lands permitted conacre only because they feared the resentment of the people if they refused.[27]

The Irish absentee landlord and the conacre peasant formed parts of the same economic scheme; and although differing in worldly circumstances and modes of thought, they had one thing in common: rent. It was the chain that bound together the many-jointed structure. The principal concern of the laborer and the small holder, it was the perpetual worry of the intermediate landlord who depended on the payments of his tenants, and it alone made possible the luxurious society of the Irish circles in London. If once the chain broke and remained broken, collapse was unavoidable. Fortunately a certain flexibility had developed, for it

was customary to permit a year's delay in the payment of
rent and, as long as prospect existed of the arrears being met,
no action was taken. In the meantime the larger holders,
while extending mercy to their debtors below, paid interest
to their creditors above.[28]

Among the farmers who possessed five acres or so the field
rotation of wheat and potatoes provided a steady income.
The production and export of Irish wheat enjoyed a constant
increase, the latter rising from an average of one hundred
and fifty thousand quarters annually in the period 1815–1820
to six hundred thousand in the years 1827–1830.[29] During
the thirties the advance continued. This was due in part to
the lower costs in Ireland, which made it possible to undersell
English-grown grain in England; but more fundamentally it
was the result of increased consumption, thanks to the growth
of cities in Great Britain. Importation was a necessity; and
since the British Isles were surrounded by the tariff wall of
the corn laws, with Ireland the only region inside the in-
closure capable of much expansion, the Irish profited from
the waxing demand.[30] Moors and bogs, hillsides and mountain valleys were prepared for the cultivation of wheat; old
pastures were broken up and sown.[31] Wherever falling water
existed a mill was erected. Soon two thousand mills were
grinding out flour whose high quality won it an assured
market in England.[32] Every shilling contributed to the prosperity of the Irish tenant, and every two or three acres of
wheat meant also an acre of potatoes for supporting another
family of sons and daughters.

Those whose holdings were too small for raising wheat
obtained their cash income from the so-called provision trade.
If a peasant were so fortunate as to own a cow, he could
count on a generous supply of milk, and from his hard-
worked churn came a steady output of butter which found
a ready sale in England. Dutch butter, which had hitherto

monopolized the London market, now met severe competition from the article which the new steam packets brought to the wharves from Ireland.[33] But the cow represented a capital investment beyond the reach of most tenants. Their money-maker was a more humble animal. No visitor returned from the Emerald Isle without a vivid impression of the Irish pig. The attention bestowed upon its care to the seeming neglect of hungry and ragged children aroused the traveler's indignation. He did not realize what every father knew — that without a fat hog to slaughter in the autumn the very life of his sons and daughters would be in jeopardy. The pig was easily fed, rooting out unseen food in the barnyard and neighboring bog and devouring the refuse from the potato pot. It repaid its owner by being the savings bank from which the rent was paid. Even the conacre men managed to keep at least one pig.

The English worker, when employed, demanded ham and bacon for his breakfast. The Irish product was universally good, English breeders admitting that its quality equaled that of their own. Irish pork formed the staple food of the British navy, and the packers of Cork supplied the fleet, as well as many merchant vessels, with countless barrels of the salted meat. Every fall the animals, rounded up from several hundred thousand houses, were driven in herds to the seaports, and there they were either bought by the local packing houses or shipped to Liverpool. In England they were transported by rail to the provincial markets where they commanded a price which, while lower than an English stockman could accept, involved neat profits for all the Irish concerned.[34]

With his ham the English worker required eggs, and again the Irish cottier responded. The barnyard hen, even more of a scavenger than the pig, was a liberal producer when carefully tended by the housewife and her children.

In the hinterland of the ports commission merchants organized a network of collectors, usually boys who, covering a regular daily route, gathered up basketfuls of eggs and left money at the cottagers' doors. From this supply eggs were exported by the ton. The shillings and pence which this trade yielded went into the precious hoard which the peasant patiently accumulated piece by piece.[35]

The round of these agricultural tasks left an interval in the summer for a further search for cash. The grain harvest came a month later than in England, and potatoes might be left in the ground until early winter. There was thus offered an opportunity to seek temporary employment as harvest hands in England. The practice was not unknown before 1825, but these casual laborers had found little welcome in a country already filled with unemployed workers, and, in any case, the journey across the Irish Sea was uncomfortable and costly.[36] But thereafter the scene altered. Steam practically annihilated the channel. With forty-two packets plying between the two islands by 1830, competition beat down the fare to as low as six or nine pence.[37] Moreover, the new poor law and the growth of industrialism drained the English villages of their surplus men and created a shortage of farm laborers.

The Irishmen rushed in to fill the gap. In July the bands would gather — thousands of tenants and their sons who left the potato fields to their women and children and trekked to the ports. Crossing to Liverpool, they fared forth in groups of eight or ten, armed with sickles, to bargain with the farmers to cut the grain or mow the meadows. Six pounds was a small return for the trip; most managed to clear eight pounds or more. With this little fortune hidden in their ragged garments, the workers went back home ready to enjoy the advantages in clothing, shelter and feasting which their enterprise had made possible.[38]

Economically, the Ireland of 1845 differed markedly from that of 1815. Its classes, still exhibiting extremes of wealth and poverty, were more tightly knit together in a common economic life; and the structure as a whole was more closely interwoven with that of England. A great pioneering work had been accomplished; waste lands of vast extent had been put under the plow and the hoe. If the Irishman was often shiftless, untidy, improvident, so also was the American backwoodsman of the same period and the latter's log cabin was hardly more habitable than the former's mud hut. With moderate luck the Irish would outgrow their primitive ways just as the American frontiersmen usually did.[39]

The outlook in 1845 was distinctly promising. The thoroughgoing inquiry conducted by Lord Devon's commission clearly indicated that any changes in the land system would aim at bettering the condition of the horde of small tenants. Irishmen themselves displayed greater interest in their future. County agricultural societies, in the face of prejudice and ignorance, agitated for improvements in crops and farm practices.[40] The temperance crusade of Father Mathew was helping to destroy one of the chief incentives to idleness and to encourage a healthier and higher standard of living.[41] In 1838, as a result of the success of the new poor law in England, legislation provided for workhouses in newly organized "unions" and sought ultimately to eradicate the vagrancy and begging that perpetually paraded Ireland's woes on the public highways. Although many paupers preferred the old system of charity and continued their aimless wanderings, a feeling of satisfaction stemmed from the belief that an emergency would find the authorities prepared and that never again would the horrifying scenes of 1822 be enacted.

Other aspects of the economic situation were less encouraging. At a most critical time, when all attention should have been focused on self-help, Daniel O'Connell's agitation for repeal of the political union with England swept the land. Listening to fascinating oratory and blaming England for Erin's ills was a beguiling occupation, but it diverted thought and energy from more immediate, practical measures of improvement. British politics also held a threat for Irish well-being in that the Anti-Corn Law League was rapidly gaining strength. Any breach in the protective wall presaged difficulties for the Irish grain grower. A modification in 1842, making it easier for foreign livestock to enter the United Kingdom, caused a flurry of emigration among the more substantial tenants and suggested graphically the results of repeal.[42] This law of 1842 occasioned further alarm by lowering the duties on salted and cured provisions from foreign countries. American pork quickly reached the English market where it undersold the Irish product. Though it did not find favor, not being prepared for the British taste, all realized that ultimately the Irish provision trade must face competition which, if successful, would ruin more than just the market for swine.[43]

A matter of more fundamental concern was the problem of food. The harvest of one year never fully tided over the cottiers' families until the next potato crop was out of the ground. The summer months regularly witnessed hunger and misery that sometimes drove half-starved households to eat nettles and weeds.[44] Communities whose patches suffered from blight found themselves in an even more desperate plight. "During the whole summer," wrote one intimately connected with peasant hardships,

the potato-fields were watched with the utmost solicitude. The lightning and the east wind that withered the stalks, the drought that retarded their growth, or the rain that prevented their ripening, were noted with anxious care, till the wished-for day arrived when they were brought to the markets in cart-loads, and joy and thanksgiving were in every heart.[45]

Summer after summer passed with suspense followed by rejoicing, but everyone knew that if Nature withheld her favor for even a single season the whole economic structure of the island would collapse.

Other parts of the British Isles seemed more fortunately circumstanced. In Wales and Scotland scenes of distress still continued, but these appeared to be the aftermath of economic maladjustments now happily removed, not the evidence of a growing poverty eating upward into the ranks of the landed classes. England's troubles, it is true, were not at an end. Hunger and riots often broke out in the city slums when temporary depressions slowed the factory wheels; but after the mid-thirties country life became sounder, with markets for grain, ample employment, and a system of poor relief which cared for the unfortunate while disciplining the indolent. When peace and plenty generally reigned, occasional industrial slumps did not dim the optimism of publicists and statesmen.

But across the channel and up the Rhine there were pessimists whose forebodings were as gloomy as any that Ireland could offer. The parallel need not be pushed too far, but in certain respects southwestern Germany and southern Ireland presented conditions strikingly similar. In Germany also an increasing agricultural population, pressing hard upon the available land, had split it up into tiny holdings. There, too, the potato was rapidly becoming the food of millions whose fortunes depended upon its continued yield. Moreover, a complicated system of money payments, due from one class to another, formed as vital a strand in the economic fabric as the ever present Irish rent.

Ever since the Germanic migration in the early Middle Ages, the land bordering the upper Rhine had been known for its small holdings. In fact, however, they were small only as compared with the large estates of northern and eastern

Germany, France and Italy. The average farm was of comfortable size, and usually adjoined extensive domains, the property of ducal families and religious foundations. But the first two generations of the nineteenth century saw the small farms degenerate to that condition vividly termed "fragmentation." The land was torn into shreds, and subdivision carried to a point where in recorded instances a daughter was given in marriage with a few fruit trees as her dowry and two heirs shared a living room in the family home.[46]

Fragmentation was the fruit of several circumstances. During the period of French domination the social ideas of the Revolution had been introduced, with the result that the estates of the monasteries were confiscated and parceled out among the landless. Many large landowners, finding it advisable to leave, accelerated the process by selling their property to speculators who passed it on to a dozen or more purchasers.[47] Attempts to curb this speculation by legislation failed.[48] Another factor was the removal of all obstacles to marriage (except those erected by the Church or the conscription laws), which speeded the growth of population, filling households with sons who twenty years later demanded lands of their own. Though the return of absolutism after the expulsion of the French caused a modification of the liberal edicts, the restrictions were less drastic than in earlier times and, in any case, could not affect the population increase which had already taken place.[49]

Whatever the contributing influences, fragmentation was, in fact, the only method by which the rising generation could be provided with land. It was impossible for a son even of boundless energy to do what his father had usually done — acquire a farm by draining a swamp or leveling a hillside. Careful investigation revealed that all the tillable land had already been put to use; the sand patches, moors and mountain slopes still lying idle were not suited to cultivation.[50] To provide an acre or two for each of his children became the great care of the head of the family. The principal rift in the cloud came from the knowledge that a smaller area now sufficed to support a household than a generation before.

Two circumstances had made this possible. One was primarily political. After the peace settlement of 1815 the central region of the valley of the Rhine belonged to Prussia; and at once a market for wine, safeguarded by tariffs from the producers of France, lay open to exploitation. Later the formation of the Zollverein extended the advantages of this protected market to the south German states. A boom in vineyards resulted. Every peasant whose land possessed a sunny exposure concentrated on grape growing. Ground was cleared, hills were terraced, loam was laboriously transported up the rocky slopes, and retaining walls were built. When the crop was normal, the product, however small, yielded an income that met living needs and often left a surplus.[51]

The other factor was the cultivation of the potato with its many advantages as a cheap, space-saving and nutritious food product. Not until the latter part of the eighteenth century did the potato era of the Continent begin. First used extensively during the years of scarcity in the 1770's, the root gained rapidly in popular favor, effecting a revolution in the peasant menu.[52] In some places it formed the chief nourishment of the family and fed the cow, the sheep and the pigs as well. "Potatoes are half the life of Germany," commented an observer, "the foundation of peace and of the people's well-being." [53] If a monument is erected to Jenner as a public benefactor, inquired another, why not one to Drake who first introduced the tuber to Europe? [54] The peasants welcomed it as an ally in their struggle for land; and season after season the potato patch with its green vines occupied an ever larger share of the family's time and interest.

By the middle of the century fragmentation had reached a point that made it an important factor in emigration. Many a substantial farmer with foresight realized that in the absence of available land his children were doomed to the status of "potato eaters." Thus, if a man with fifty *morgen* of land (somewhat more than thirty acres) had six children, an equal division on his death would give each less than ten *morgen*. This was not enough for subsistance without engaging in day labor, which violated their training and pride. So to prevent this outcome the estate was sold, all embarked for America, and the family savings sufficed to buy for every child a farm as large as the paternal estate in Germany.[55] Especially in the early forties, when the United States offered few opportunities for laborers and mechanics, the German emigration consisted largely of such parents and their unmarried sons.

But the majority of the peasants, lacking the necessary foresight, remained in the fatherland where their troubles thickened. With the increasing demand for private lands, covetous eyes were cast upon the common lands which adjoined each village; and in the first quarter of the century steps were taken for their division.[56] Though the action afforded a measure of immediate relief, longer experience revealed countless disadvantages, for the division completely overturned the economic scheme of the peasants' life. Benefits which they had taken for granted now ceased to exist. The pasture for the cow, sheep and geese was lost; and since feeding in stalls and pens called for more produce than the small landholder could provide, he had to send his livestock to private pastures and pay rent for what formerly had cost him nothing.[57] The acre or two that he gained did not offset the loss. Usually this land was in a position where it could not be put to the best use, the temptation to sell was great, and the money thus obtained was soon spent. Often legal complications and lawsuits swallowed up the full value of the acquisition. The division of commons tended to bring to the more substantial peasants land which they did not need or want, and take from the less favored what was an absolute necessity.[58]

Another change affected other fundamental conditions of life. Traditionally the scheme of community living had rested on a balance of field and forest. Every village had its woodland, every castle its hunting preserve. From its depths came fur for winter clothing, deer and wild boar for the table, logs and faggots for the fireplace. So essential were these products that use of the forest was strictly regulated. On certain days of the year lords and communes allowed swarms of peasant men, women and children to cut down the dead trees and gather the fallen branches for the season's firewood.[59]

This balance was maintained until the epoch of the Napoleonic wars. Troops moved slowly. Advancing and retreating armies, often camping in a single spot for months, laid forests bare before they departed. At the same time uncertainty as to the future caused many private owners to dispose of their holdings at any price, and in the closing years of the struggle many villages preserved their solvency in the face of heavy taxation only by selling their woodland.[60] The balance thus lost was never regained. In the years following the peace, growing city populations demanded more houses, and since coal was too bulky for long-distance transportation, the rapidly increasing factories used wood for fuel. When railroads were built, they consumed the stoutest and straightest timbers for ties and rails.[61] But the peasants suffered who had to buy what their ancestors had freely enjoyed by immemorial right. To such persons the tales of the boundless forests in America made a powerful appeal.

Even those more fortunately situated found themselves

drawn into a scheme of life which upset traditional social arrangements. The philosophy of the Revolutionary era helped to supplant the theory of a class privileged by birth with the idea of a class privileged by wealth. Money now could buy the rank and pleasures which formerly blood and patronage alone had provided. Realizing that a higher status was attainable, peasants with savings strove to shuffle off the visible signs of their age-long lot.[62] "What has become of our peasantry — the kernel of the German nation?" moralists anxiously asked. Once clothing spun at home and dyed in bright colors revealed both the province and the profession of the wearer.[63] Now this costume and the simple virtues it signified were cast aside. Peasants visited the taverns, which multiplied rapidly; they patronized the dealers in "colonial wares," who opened stores in every village, for all must drink coffee and cocoa. Even laborers now wore shoes and stockings at work and carried watches.[64] The standard of living was rising, and whether they could afford it or not, sons and daughters deemed as necessities many things which their parents had gone without.

This desire for better things expressed a characteristic trait of the times.[65] Unfortunately many were willing to risk their future in the pursuit of this ambition. If we need money, they argued, our lands can be made to produce it, and the additional capital for this purpose can be secured through mortgages. Capital was plentiful and interest rates were low. State debts contracted during the wars had been paid off, extensive industrial development had not begun, and investment in lands was encouraged by law and tradition.[66] As a result, farmers borrowed to drain the lands, buy blooded stock, build better barns and fertilize the soil, thinking they would recoup their outlays by the enlarged production. But the lands were mortgaged at figures beyond any reasonable expectation of a profitable return. The pessimistic journalist who asserted that every peasant home in Germany was encumbered no doubt exaggerated, but his allegation evoked no protesting replies.[67]

In a life becoming so progressive and modern, the continued existence of many agrarian relics of feudalism presented an anomaly. The German small holder in the eighteenth century had owed obligations to three lords. From one he received his law, from another his land, and to a third he was bound by the place or condition of his birth. The nature of the allegiance had little bearing upon the nature of the obligation. All yielded the lord economic advantages: payment in money, in service and in kind. In some localities, following the Middle Ages, services had been commuted to money payments, and, thanks to favorable changes in the value of money, such peasants derived a distinct benefit. But the majority continued to render service with their arms and their agricultural labor at the lord's bidding.[68] Although sometimes the tribute amounted to nothing more than the token delivery of a dozen eggs or a hen, usually the peasant had to give up part of his crop — a payment which, once considered slight, now constituted a serious loss in view of the narrowing surplus that separated his family from starvation.

The most grievous of the payments, however, was the one to the Church. Since the "tithe" varied with the size of the crop (usually a tenth, sometimes as low as a twentieth, occasionally as high as a fourth), it was more just than many other exactions. In good seasons both parties prospered; in bad, both suffered. The right to the tithe had, in many instances, passed out of the hands of the Church, but even when the clergy were the recipients, no generous or indulgent spirit prevailed. Collection usually excited strife. Quarreling occurred over the number and size of sheaves; and since the lord was also entitled to a "blood tithe" (a percentage of all animals produced), he sometimes enforced his rights by breaking open pens and stalls forcibly removing calves, lambs and pigs. His agents even ransacked cellars and carried off cheeses and eggs as animal produce.[69]

Aside from the actual loss of time, money and food, the economic results of the régime were bad. The peasant was robbed of his most precious hours; his fields were neglected; his initiative was dulled. Not unnaturally, the tenth he must deliver loomed greater than the nine tenths he retained. Moreover, the services he rendered to the lord were unsatisfactory and listless. The Revolutionary ideas of the Napoleonic period, however, gave an impetus to projects of reform, causing Prussia through the Stein-Hardenburg legislation to adopt a program of modernization.[70] But in southeastern Germany change encountered stout resistance. The counts and dukes, returning with the Restoration, exerted themselves to preserve the long-established economic and legal system. Crop shortages and growing poverty, however, caused bitter complaints in the representative assemblies, with the result that many of the states took action making it possible for lords and peasants, when both were so inclined, to provide for abolishing or transforming the feudal obligations. But these enactments involved no compulsion, no assistance from the governments, no detailed regulation of the process. Only a few of the richer peasants entered into such agreements, leaving those who bore the heaviest burdens unaffected.[71]

The halting course of legislation resulted, in part, from the fact that, when Germans spoke of "abolishing feudal dues," they did not contemplate the drastic step of declaring all payments henceforth at an end without compensation to the petty dukes, counts and landlords who had hitherto enjoyed them. On the contrary, these beneficiaries were to be indemnified in an amount that represented the capitalization of the annual money value of the services and payments. But what was the annual value, for example, of a sheaf of wheat or a basket of grapes? There were local and yearly variations, and the period of years chosen for an average might yield highly different results according to its length. Agreement could be reached only by compromise. But even when these matters were decided, the financial problem remained. How could the peasants meet their new obligations? Public assistance was obviously necessary, but hard-pressed governments shrank from a policy that entailed considerable expenditures.[72] When laws which seemed satisfactory were placed upon the statute books, aversion to change together with uncertainty regarding the legality of the enactments prevented their widespread application. Real reform slumbered until the revolutionary year of 1848.

As in Ireland, the pessimism of social commentators deepened with the marked aggravation of all the unfavorable conditions in the late thirties and early forties. The credit situation was changing. Hitherto farmers had been encouraged to incur debts by the low interest rates and easy terms of renewal, but now bankers were being besieged by hundreds of railroad projects promising them twice as large a profit. They took every opportunity to withdraw from agricultural loans. The resultant mortgage proceedings precipitated many a personal tragedy.[73] Some peasants struggled stubbornly on, disposing of part of their property and trying to farm successfully what was left; or in their financial plight they borrowed from money lenders who charged them ruinous rates of interest.[74] Thus, while the governments sought to better the peasants' legal status in order to improve their economic situation, unanticipated factors were sinking the people in a mire of indebtedness. An official Prussian report in 1845 emphasized the relationship of this growing stringency in rural finances to the increase in emigration.[75]

Nature was also raising her hand against the husbandman. A drought in the year 1842 withered the pasturage, and cattle had to be killed, thus removing an important source of meat, milk and cheese. The potato crop was small, and by spring the principal supplies were exhausted. As a result, many who could find purchasers for their holdings emigrated in haste.[76] The season of 1843 proved unusually wet until August when a prolonged drought set in. Though crops turned out somewhat better than in 1842, some localities suffered from actual starvation.[77] The following year proved comparatively satisfactory except that the yield of wine, which had been declining since 1840, was small and of poor quality.[78] The principal cause of apprehension, however, centered in the potato. The potato disease (whatever it was — contemporaries discussed it bitterly) had first appeared along the Rhine in 1829, and since then had been present each season in some part of Germany.[79] The thought of its becoming general suggested a picture of universal ruin because of the peasants' basic dependence on the root.

No natural boundary separated southwestern Germany from its political neighbors and, in these regions, economic life tended to follow a similar pattern, being modified principally by differing legal policies. In Switzerland household manufactures and trade were the main occupations in some parts, herding in others; but in about a third of the cantons agriculture predominated, and there rural institutions resembling those across the Rhine existed.[80] Long before, however, the maximum of inhabitants had been attained. As a result, in most cantons the system of one child inheriting the family estate prevailed, leaving the others to engage in trade or emigrate either to some other country of Europe or to America. In this way a balance between estates and heirs was maintained, and most of the holdings continued to be sufficiently large to insure a comfortable living.[81] As in

Germany, a crisis in agriculture was feared, but it was an event for which more careful provision had been made.

In France the legislation of the Revolution had opened the lands of the Church and the nobles and some of the common possessions to the peasants' use; and the principle of equal partition among heirs had been subsequently written into the Code Napoleon. Under the new dispensation the landscape became cut up in an illogical and unexpected manner. "The fields seen from a distance," according to one description of a rural commune, "resemble a robe striped with a thousand rays. Each strip of land looks like a narrow ribbon; and the shadow of a big tree often covers its whole extent." [82] In 1826 there was one *cote* for every four inhabitants; in 1842 one for every three — and this in a population that was increasing but slowly.[83] The British economist McCulloch prophesied that France would degenerate into a "pauper warren" of creatures who, like the Irish, would become the beasts of burden of foreign nations.[84] The saving element in the situation lay in the fact that the potato was not the all-important food and in the further circumstance that the far-reaching acts of August, 1789, had once and for all swept away the peasants' financial and labor dues.

In some regions special conditions aroused just apprehension. In northeastern France, rising from the left bank of the Rhine, stretched the foothills and mountains of the Vosges repeating the economic life characteristic of the opposite-lying Baden: vineyards, small holdings and mountain industries. Rich soil and thrifty peasants had brought the system to a high state of development, but the future was to show that they, no more than their German neighbors, were proof against an agricultural crisis.[85] To the southeast, in an offshoot of the Alps, lay small valley farms and highland pastures with a population that could support itself only through seasonal migrations to more favored areas.[86] Simi-

larly in the Pyrenees the inhabitants were living on marginal
lands, and in the central highlands of France poverty was
apparent to all who penetrated to the isolated villages.[87]

To the north of France, Belgium was undergoing a difficult
transition. Serfdom had disappeared early, and the French
domination had swept away the last feudal obligations resting
upon the peasants. The same period saw the introduction
of the principle of the transferability of real and personal
property by testation; and although the courts tried to avoid
the logical consequences of this system, a great parceling of
the land resulted — an outcome facilitated by the fact that
weaving, spinning, nail-making and gunsmithing were vigorously carried on in isolated cottages or at wayside forges.[88]
With the tremendous strides of the linen industry in the
first decade of the nineteenth century the lands were further
divided by sale and lease to accommodate the workers.
By 1840 observers and peasants alike felt occasion for worry.
Machine competition was causing difficulties for the spinners
and weavers; the potato had become the staple crop; and the
agitation for dividing the still remaining common lands
threatened the peasants with the loss of accustomed rights.[89]

For various reasons the people of the Netherlands escaped
the troubles of their next-door neighbor. Although the practice of dividing the soil among all the heirs had early been
adopted, physical conditions and Saxon influence prevented
the custom from reaching, as elsewhere, an extreme development. From the eleventh century on occurred a systematic
reclamation of the coast lands to take care of the increasing
population, and with the revival of commerce the Netherlands pursued an agrarian course unlike that of its neighbors.
As a result of the desire to retain the paternal estate intact
in the bequeathing of property, methods were devised to
avoid the logical outcome of the law of succession. The
holdings were small, but scientifically cultivated; and soil,

climate and near-by markets had caused the early development of the cattle industries. The agricultural régime was favorably balanced, and the forties and fifties witnessed no violent crisis.[90]

Meanwhile the plain of northern and eastern Germany, bordering the North and Baltic seas and drained by the Weser, the Elbe and the Oder, experienced an agrarian evolution distinctly different from that of the Rhine Valley. In the second quarter of the nineteenth century an isolated, self-centered life was the most evident feature of its civilization. Customs, dialect and existence itself seemed to be limited within the manor bounds of the various kingdoms, duchies and provinces. But this apparent self-sufficiency was not real. Agriculture to be prosperous required an outlet; and as the cost of overland and river transport of bulky freight to the industrial regions of central Germany was prohibitive, the broad estuaries opening upon the North Sea pointed to England as the natural market. As the British Isles became increasingly industrial, their food was secured more and more from the German fields. This trade brought wealth to the dukes and lords, but it rendered their well-being dependent upon a legislature in which they had no voice. As the English duties on corn, cattle and dairy products varied, so the economic conditions of these Germans rose and fell.[91]

Not only were the peasants subject to these vicissitudes, but they suffered from other disabilities according to where they lived. In Hanover, Oldenburg and parts of Westphalia there had developed a type of labor which depended upon annual tours to Holland for summer work. By 1840 this seasonal migration formed a vital part of rural existence. Fathers and sons spent several months on the dykes and in the brickyards and harvest fields and returned with eighty or a hundred *gulden*. These earnings constituted an essential contribution to the family's support, for, though a cottage and a few acres at home provided food, the lord could demand for their use, not a certain number of days a month, as elsewhere, but an indefinite amount of labor — whatever he needed to sow his fields and gather his crops. In the absence of the men this work was performed by the women and children.[92] In Mecklenburg and Schleswig-Holstein, where large-scale farming prevailed, the emancipation decrees had the effect of turning the serfs, for whose support the lord had been responsible, into day laborers dependent entirely on their own resources.[93] As long as harvests were plentiful and the market for grain was secure, the peasantry was fed, but there was no assurance that these favorable conditions would last. Should Holland cease to demand foreign workers or the corn laws of England be fundamentally changed, the lord would have no alternative but to turn adrift the superfluous families.

Denmark followed a development analogous to that of eastern Germany. The free peasant proprietors of earlier times had gradually been reduced to serfdom in the course of the nation's many long wars, and by the middle of the eighteenth century the country had become a domain of large estates. No landed property could be divided without express permission of the minister of the interior. Though some reforms in defining feudal obligations and encouraging emancipation had been effected, the old system remained virtually unchanged until after the commotions of 1848. On the whole, the problem of poverty was under control, and publicists were troubled more by the intellectual and cultural backwardness of the people than by any dangers to their material welfare.[94]

In Sweden and Norway the peasant proprietors had not disappeared, as in Denmark, and serfdom did not exist. The greater proportion of the soil belonged to the peasants and, as divisibility of inheritances was a principle of law, the

Scandinavian peninsula tended to be a region of small holdings.[95] The evil effects of this system were less noticeable than elsewhere, for the younger generation found opportunities in shipping, in the forest and in the mines. Yet all was not well. The potato had made its entry into the agricultural economy; debts had been incurred in the days of easy credit; and whatever danger threatened these elements of rural life forecast a misery deeper than either country had recently known.[96]

Beyond the Elbe lay yet another world of peasants and lords, whose relations had not developed to the stage where change was imminent and whose situation attracted little attention. Western Europe had troubles enough of its own. Overpopulation, hunger and unemployment were the topics that dominated all discussions of social conditions. Hope struggled with fear as people viewed the future, with fear gradually gaining the mastery.

X

COLONIZATION NO REMEDY

THOUGH HUNDREDS OF THOUSANDS of Europeans emigrated during the 1830's, the ranks of the laborers
were not thinned. There were more hands seeking
work, more mouths waiting to be fed, more misery apparent
at the close of the decade than at its beginning. Many observers believed that emigration made matters worse, for
the father took with him the proceeds from the sale of his
farm and the young man carried his patrimony — resources
slender enough individually, but aggregating a total which
constituted a serious loss to the countries concerned. In any
case, this channel of escape did not benefit the class in greatest
immediate need: the family whose larder was empty, the
laborer whose children were in tatters. They could not
finance their removal to the other side of the globe. Society
must help them, argued the philanthropists. The outlay,
though great, would be only temporary, for the wealth which
they produced would in time come back to enrich their
native land.

World events persuaded the theorists that they were right.
The globe was full of prizes waiting to be grasped. The
Turkish Empire, hard pressed by Russia and suffering from
internal dissensions, was falling apart. British gunboats were
blowing their way up the rivers of China, with political
results no one could foresee. France was winning an empire
in Algeria, returning sailors told stories of new islands in the
South Seas, the republics of Central and South America were
in turmoil. Great Britain was changing New Zealand and
Australia from naval stations and penal camps into outposts

of white domination in the Pacific. On the shores of the Pacific also lay an unprotected California looking across to the fabulous Orient. In these lands awaited richer opportunities than even the sixteenth century had offered. And so the argument ran: plant in them the hardy laborers that Europe cannot support and, by so doing, solve the social problem and at the same time assure an inflow of wealth greater than the earlier dreams of Spain and Portugal.

Most of these theorists were German, for the French and the British were too deeply engaged in the task of empire to speculate much about it. Both countries recognized emigration as an instrument of effective occupation. France undertook the peopling of Algeria with Europeans on as extensive a scale as the war with the elusive native leaders allowed. In Great Britain, statesmen, publicists and colonial administrators urged emigration to New Zealand and Australia as a patriotic duty and, by offering practical inducements in the form of passage and land grants, the government facilitated the departure of that yeoman class which had always formed England's most successful colonial pioneers. A German observer in London wrote that hardly a month passed without the organization of some new society to foster colonial expansion.[1]

The Germans themselves engaged in the same pastime. It was an age of societies [2] — philanthropic, social and political — and all took an interest in emigration. Though history credits these organizations with few accomplishments, their existence dominated emigration discussion from 1840 to 1845. The hope that some of the contemplated enterprises held forth caused many families, who otherwise would have left, to postpone their going. On the other hand, popular recognition of the failure of these schemes, coming at the time when the urge toward emigration was growing intense, turned the current decisively to the United States.

In Germany the search for colonies could not be other than popular. Thirty years later Germany was to be united politically; intellectually and socially it already was a unit. Thoughtful men deemed the expatriation of tens of thousands of countrymen too serious a cultural drain. The emigrants, they complained, generally gave up their heritage and hastened to become Americanized, regarding it an honor to be considered a "Yankee ass." [3] The sea, which to other nations marked the pathway to immortal renown and glory, was a River Styx in crossing which the Germans forever cut themselves off from the ways of the fatherland. Even when they clung to their culture, they injected it into new surroundings and contributed the stuff that would enrich an alien civilization. Why should Germans be the fertilizers of other civilizations?

Such views commanded increasing support among the trading classes. Although they were divided geographically by customs barriers and local regulations, all realized that emigration not only decreased the number of customers in the home market, but also strengthened Germany's competitors. Germans who went to America stimulated temporarily the flow of goods across the Atlantic, but in time their tastes grew to be like those of their neighbors; and instead of the great ally which sentimentalists claimed was being built up out of Teutonic blood, the United States would ultimately be a deadly rival with unbounded resources on which to draw.[4] If this looked to the future, there were other rivals whose efforts involved a more immediate threat. A German, going to the colony of another European power, became subject to the exclusive colonial policy of that nation and at once an economic foe of his former home.[5] Backed by their navies, these powers were seizing more territories than they knew how to develop. They were looking about for some hardy stock to suffer the pains of experimental pioneering.

Now that slavery was becoming obsolete and the slave trade abolished, they were turning to Germans as a substitute for Negroes. Germans were cheaper to obtain and, if they survived, would offer a profitable market.[6]

The historian may question the motive alleged, but the fact cannot be denied. French agents were busy along the Rhine and in the ports, and they had already induced emigrants to change their intended destination and go to the sands of Algeria.[7] When peace was established in northern Africa, an intensification of such efforts might be expected. Two powerful English organizations, the South Australia Company and the New Zealand Company, were also advertising lands and recruiting settlers in Germany. As early as 1837 a band of Silesian sectarians, who feared the religious atmosphere prevailing in America, had been persuaded by agents of the South Australia Company to accept free transportation to its settlements. Though the first discomforts were acute, the settlers soon attained a moderate prosperity, repaying the company for the cost of passage. For the company this investment proved an unusual success. It determined to secure more settlers of the same type and its efforts were seconded by the personal invitations which the emigrants sent back to their friends at home. Profiting by this example, the more recently organized New Zealand Company decided to offer similar inducements.[8]

Alarmed by the situation, many Germans urged the Zollverein to sponsor colonial enterprises. Under its leadership Germany was advancing along industrial lines, and it seemed logical that the agency should manifest similar energy in widening the market for exports. But already preoccupied with the difficult business of holding together territorial states of such divergent interests and traditions, the Zollverein had no desire to assume further responsibilities.[9] In the circumstances one of the maritime city-states of the North Sea took the lead. A combination of conditions caused Hamburg to become the colonial pioneer of modern Germany. For one thing, the merchants feared that, if some Zollverein proposal materialized, they would lose the trade in colonial products which had long been Hamburg's staple.[10] For another, many of the citizens saw in the project a means of capturing part of the trade in emigrants which was enriching Bremen.[11] But the most powerful factor was the man who presided over Hamburg's affairs.

Karl Sieveking was one of those Hanseatic statesmen who might have won greater international renown had their local patriotism not restricted their activities. While sojourning in South America in the diplomatic service of his city, he had interested himself in the German settlers there. Now, as syndic or chief magistrate of Hamburg, he proceeded to develop his ideas, taking advantage of the fact that the New Zealand Company was short of funds and experiencing difficulty in securing colonists. Through John Ward, an officer of the British company, he arranged in the fall of 1841 for the sale of the Chatham Islands (a group lying to the east of its main possessions) to a company which Sieveking would organize. The syndic regarded the project merely as a first step, for he hoped ultimately to secure other places — possibly Brazil, South Africa, Samoa or Palestine — and to bind these colonies to one another and to the fatherland by a systematic packet service.[12] The German settlers in these lands would retain cultural and commercial connections with home and hence, instead of being merely articles transported across the sea, would be a constant source of wealth to Hamburg. After the contract had been made and the society had undertaken a nation-wide agitation for emigrants, the British government unexpectedly annulled the sale.[13] The promoters might now have turned to other possibilities, but before this could be done, a fire completely destroyed the business sections of

Hamburg, and for several years the city did not concern itself with external interests.

The Chatham Islands proposal had not been without its critics in Germany. Many objections were raised in the press: the long sea journey, the expense of transportation, ignorance regarding the resources of the region, the impossibility of defending a distant possession.[14] The method of acquisition, it was further argued, was dangerous. Should patriotic Germans risk their lives and fortunes in a venture clandestinely conducted under the aegis of Great Britain? [15] None of the burghers of Hamburg, it was pointed out, planned to emigrate. That city would risk only its intelligence and reap all the benefits. The proposed colonization society with branches throughout south Germany was merely a scheme of Hamburgers to secure money and people.[16]

Some of this criticism was prompted by a growing interest in colonization manifested in the rising manufacturing districts along the Rhine, whose leaders recognized Bremen as their German port. In April, 1842, the very month which saw the end of the South Sea attempt, a group of nobles and princes gathered at a village on the Rhine to consider plans for an organized emigration. A society popularly known as the *Mainzer Adelsverein* was formed with the avowed object of peopling Texas with Germans. In this manner it purposed to alleviate social misery by a systematic and directed emigration. Skeptics, however, charged that the princes, fast losing their hold on the German peasantry, hoped for a feudal state overseas. Others saw the secret hand of England seeking to erect a bulwark against Yankee imperialism, or to check the spread of slavery. Still others considered the project a purely financial undertaking, cloaked with benevolent phrases because princes could not as openly avow their desire for gain as the merchants of Hamburg.[17]

Once the plan of a concerted emigration was announced,

the society was approached by various countries with tempting inducements — Central America, Brazil, the La Plata states. But the Republic of Texas remained the choice; and in September, 1843, the Adelsverein purchased the rights of a French promoter who had made a colonization contract with the Texan government the preceding year. Next, a committee was sent to Texas to provide for the reception of the first contingent; and in June, 1844, a formal manifesto detailed the steps to be taken by prospective settlers.[18] Popular interest in the project had been growing. The preceding autumn a traveler in the mountains had found Texas the principal topic of conversation among the poor.[19] Individual families, able to establish themselves, had already departed. Therefore the first group was quickly collected, and as the contract for their transportation was made with Bremen shippers, that city waxed enthusiastic over the scheme.[20] At once the Adelsverein began a campaign of publicity for the following year.[21]

Meanwhile a blow had befallen the undertaking in Texas. Upon his arrival in July, 1844, the principal agent, Baron von Solms-Braunfels, learned to his dismay that the rights which the society had purchased from the French promoter had lapsed in the preceding December. The President of the Republic refused to renew them, and the political faction advocating annexation to the United States opposed a new and direct grant.[22] Solms-Braunfels, however, succeeded in buying the rights of two other promoters. Nevertheless, when the first expedition of about seven hundred arrived toward the close of the year, no preparations had been completed, and they were forced to camp during the winter. Finally, in the spring, they were settled at a frontier station named New Braunfels. Undoubtedly this disposition was the best that could be made; but the colonists, aggrieved by their long encampment, felt they had been deceived because, instead of the three hundred and twenty acres promised them in Germany, the resources of the company permitted each family to receive only half an acre in the town and ten acres in the country.[23]

Unaware of the situation that awaited them, colonists in the homeland eagerly enrolled for the fleet that was to sail in 1845. In Hesse local administration officers were directed to urge upon prospective emigrants the advantages offered by the Texas project.[24] Prussia, however, fearing lest trade relations with Mexico be prejudiced, warned against any formal support.[25] Twenty-eight ships were dispatched. When the society met in July, 1846, it was openly admitted that more settlers had gone to Texas than could be properly cared for,[26] but the confession came too late. Disillusioned colonists were returning to Germany; others, stranded in a part of America where labor was in little demand, felt obliged to enlist for the Mexican War. Bitter and deluded refugees scattered to all parts of the United States.[27] The collapse was complete, and the company went into bankruptcy. An attempt to retrieve the financial losses by a lottery met with no popular response. On the last day of 1847 announcement was made that no further official responsibility for the settlers would be accepted.[28]

The Adelsverein was not wholly responsible for the failure. The annexation of Texas by the United States in March, 1845, removed all possibility of those special privileges which an independent Texas might have offered and upon which the hope for success rested. No support or encouragement or advice was received from experienced Germans already in America. The political and aristocratic tendencies of the princes dampened the interest of expatriates already boasting of their republicanism. Policy, geography and untoward circumstances wrecked an enterprise which might have deeply influenced the subsequent course of emigration.

The enthusiasm with which the Germans hailed the Texas scheme and the faith which led them to risk their fortunes in it evidenced the pitch of colonial interest which kept two other projects alive. These, too, were the products of business rivalry. Three of the great ports of western Europe — Le Havre, Amsterdam and Rotterdam — belonged to nations that already held distant possessions from which these cities derived increasing wealth. The colonial agitation of the early forties in its commercial aspects represented an effort on the part of less favored ports to secure similar sources of trade. The Chatham Islands were to be an appendage of Hamburg; Texas was to enrich Bremen. The proposed colony of Santo Thomas was the protégé of the merchants of Brussels and Antwerp, and the corresponding movement in Prussia expressed itself through Königsberg's venture on the Mosquito Coast.

The Belgians realized that, lacking people, a navy and political importance, they would find it difficult to appropriate any of the rich undeveloped areas of the non-European world. But if they could become masters of some outlying strategic spot destined to become a crossroads of trade, there tribute might be exacted. Events in China were centering attention on the Pacific; prophetic eyes had already foreseen the future of Central America. Somewhere on that neck of land in the New World the Atlantic and the Pacific would exchange their wares.

A few years before, an English company had secured from Guatemala a grant of proprietary rights to the coast and hinterland of Santo Thomas on the Gulf of Honduras. This company, having skimmed the superficial riches by cutting the logwood, now willingly transferred its remaining rights to the recently organized *Compagnie Belge de Colonisation*, a transfer confirmed by the government of Guatemala in 1842. In return for exclusive privileges of trade the new company undertook a program of development involving the introduction of ten thousand colonists within three years.[29] So large a number could be obtained only in Germany; and there an army of agents, fortified by favorable scientific reports, enthusiastic press notices and the patronage of the Belgian king, waged the campaign. Their efforts bore fruit in the enrollment of eight thousand families, and on a festive day in March, 1843, three ships sailed out of the harbor of Antwerp, the roofs and quays black with crowds to herald the dawn of a new commercial era.[30]

The first private reports that came back proved discouraging,[31] but the company, deeming the misfortunes merely the hardships of beginning, sent out nine ships in 1844 and three more in 1845. By the latter year, however, the completeness of the failure was apparent. The three-year term had passed. Santo Thomas, instead of a colony of ten thousand souls, was a village of a dozen wooden houses and fifty straw huts, sheltering about three hundred people.[32] The government of Belgium withdrew its support. Ponderous official documents detail the reasons for the failure; but, apart from the specific aspects of mismanagement, they were such as characterized all overseas pioneering: sickness, scanty supplies, personal feuds and resentment against iron discipline. The settlement melted away as its survivors returned to Europe, or crossed over to the United States, or cast their lot with the Caribbean lands.[33]

The Königsberg venture ran a somewhat similar course. In 1820 Prussia had taken an uncompromising position against such schemes in a law imposing heavy penalties upon anyone found guilty of inducing citizens to emigrate. The issue arose later in a different guise when the government considered the possibility of securing California as a colony. How far the negotiations proceeded it is impossible to determine. Some contemporaries believed that Mexico definitely offered to sell the province. It is certain that Baron von Bunsen, the Prussian minister in London, continually urged its acquisition.[34] But a memoir of February 17, 1845, ended the matter, the opinion being expressed that the advantages in trade and settlement would be offset by the cost of the military régime necessary to control the hostile Indians and hold back the advancing American settlers. California would be as great a burden to Prussia as Algeria was to France.[35]

Despite this decision the Prussian colonial enthusiasts persisted. They cherished the same ambitious scheme of controlling the Central American transit trade that spurred the promoters in Königsberg. A special impulse for the endeavor resulted from the distress caused by a local crop failure in 1844. Under the patronage of Prince Karl of Prussia, a commission visited that part of Central America known as the Mosquito Coast in order to investigate its possibilities for settlement. The report, published in 1845, was favorable; and in Berlin and Königsberg societies were formed to foster a systematic colonization. At this point the government intervened under the law of 1820. The public meetings called to arouse interest were banned, and Prince Karl and others high in the scientific and political world were forced to withdraw their support.[36] Though this ended the open activities in Berlin, a small group persisted and, joining with the society at Königsberg, purchased from English traders a tract of land near Bluefields on the east coast of Nicaragua.[37] In high hope a ship was dispatched in the spring of 1846. Disaster did not await its arrival. The ship was wrecked farther up the coast and, when the passengers finally reached Bluefields, their spirit of adventure had evaporated. The prospective settlers died or dispersed, and the traders secured an annulment of the grant.[38] The project was, as had been foretold, not a colony but a graveyard.[39]

Texas, Santo Thomas and the Mosquito Coast — these names predominated in the German emigration literature of the early forties. Their constant repetition indicates that the colonization movement, although disowned by the several governments, expressed a national aspiration. When one project failed, all eyes turned toward another, hopeful that the lessons of experience would insure a more promising outcome.[40] Success, however, would have been a miracle. Empires that had cost maritime nations centuries of striving and fighting could hardly be won by inexperienced commercial companies no matter how great their enthusiasm. It is true that colonization might have taken another form, and that the concentration of German settlers in regions industrially undeveloped might have yielded as rich returns as the political domination of semicivilized peoples.[41] But such concentration was impossible in view of the existing rivalries within Germany itself.

Not only did the supporters of each experiment face the combined jealousy of all the others, but as a group they were opposed by the upholders of a quite different policy. These men favored expansion within Europe. From their early home on the banks of the Rhine, they pointed out, the German people had occupied the forests and swamps east of the Elbe. Now let them continue — on to the valley of the Danube, into the mountains of the Balkans, beyond to the shores of the Black Sea, and across the Hellespont to the once prosperous lands of the Near East. Although these theorists never crystallized their plans, they included the greatest German economist, Friedrich List, and the editor of the most influential journal, G. Höfken of the Augsburg *Allgemeine Zeitung*; and they successfully dried up the only springs from which the political power and the financial resources, essential for the development of transatlantic colonies, might have come.[42]

Still another group, rejecting collective colonization whether in America or Europe, sought to adapt German policy to the inescapable actualities of the situation. Realists in their approach to the problem, they recognized that individuals emigrated not to benefit those left behind but themselves; that they had little interest in politics or culture except as the one concerned taxation and the other affected everyday affairs; and that, above all things, they wanted land of their own.[43] The lessons learned from the experience of countless German pioneers should not be ignored.[44] Advocates of this view urged, therefore, that no effort be made to maintain political connections with the emigrants, but that all energy be devoted to developing them into cultural and business colonies. The germs of such colonies already existed in the scattered settlements of the Ohio and Mississippi valleys. Let the most promising ones be extended by directing to their vicinity the bulk of the future emigration.[45] Encourage trade by appointing consuls; strengthen intellectual and social ties by subsidizing missionary activities and fostering the use of the German language.[46] If perchance the Union should fall apart, some states would then be wholly Teutonic and free to determine their political destiny.[47]

The arguments of this school of opinion gained strength from the conditions in the United States. The early forties signalized an extensive movement to the land on the part of Germans already in America. The continued industrial depression caused many native Americans to leave the older settled regions for the West, and filled the real-estate market with conveniently located and reasonably priced farms. Societies for joint settlement were formed by the German Americans;[48] and as a means of assisting the movement, Francis Grund, who had served as United States consul at Bremen, traveled through the regions of emigration, enlisting the coöperation of individuals and groups.[49] To the King of

EMIGRANT-LANDING IN NEW YORK

INTERIOR OF CASTLE GARDEN

ARRIVING IN AMERICA

Württemberg he proposed the creation of an official emigration agency, but Württemberg, like the other German governments, shunned any open participation. V. Werner, a minister of state, was sufficiently interested, however, to organize a private society for the purpose of buying lands in the United States, sending out settlers and using the repayments as a revolving fund to continue the process. But capital was timid at a time when railroad investments promised a surer return, and in the course of two years hardly more than fifty shares were sold.[50] Though this effort failed, the years from 1843 to 1846 beheld a substantial spontaneous emigration from other parts of Germany — from the province of Silesia, from Münster and Minden in Prussia, from Osnabrück in Hanover and from Oldenburg. All these were regions of the household manufacture of linen, and the contemporary crisis in that trade accounts for the size of the outpouring.

The crisis might have been foreseen and remedial measures undertaken, as was done contemporaneously in Belgium. There the government took decisive action. Following an extended inquiry into the evils of the existing system, a committee was appointed in every commune of Belgium to supervise production and maintain the old standards. Public and private charity acted as a stabilizing force during the period of transition to machine methods,[51] and meanwhile the recently founded technical schools taught the new science of textiles, and capitalists were encouraged to invest in factory enterprises. Within fifteen years a modern system had arisen. There was no pronounced "linen period" in the history of Belgian emigration.[52]

The Germans, however, adopted no policy but to work harder and longer under the old system. In the fever of competition standards were lowered. The product of the spinners degenerated to such a degree that it could not be used on machine looms. England, hitherto a valuable customer, preferred the yarns spun in her own mills. As weaving machines were introduced slowly into Germany, these manufacturers also passed over the native product and imported English yarns. In the year 1841 about a million and a half pounds entered the port of Hamburg. Thus the spinners lost not only their foreign but their domestic market as well.[53] The decline of the weavers was almost as spectacular. Latin-American slaveholders, who had hitherto bought freely, discarded linen and clothed their Negroes in cotton; neighboring European states protected their own industry by tariff barriers; and at home the product of the gradually expanding factories undersold that of the household weavers.[54]

The blow fell hardest on the spinners and weavers of Silesia. There the workers in their huts had long been little better than the slaves of merchants who sold them yarn and bought their cloth. Though a few had tried to secure land, they became bogged in debt; and now, with hardly a potato patch to feed them, their only recourse was charity.[55] Though some of the more prosperous weavers managed to leave,[56] as a class this landless proletariat was too poor to emigrate. Some ambitious ones trudged to Poland and Hungary, only to return in the autumn with tales of woe.[57] An attempt by the government to locate the unemployed on lands in the less populous districts of the province failed when heavy spring rains and freshets flooded out those already settled and discouraged further enthusiasm for the project.[58] The majority spent their energy in riots, lived off the doles and were gradually absorbed in the building of railroads and cotton factories.[59]

Hanover and the western provinces of Prussia, making a finer product than Silesia, did not suffer so acutely. Yet adjustment was necessary. Fortunately, most of the textile workers had not completely lost their inheritance of land.

Its sale provided them with the necessary capital for emigration, and in the late thirties and again from 1842 to 1845 the linen districts of western Germany sent out a steady stream of families.[60] One lesson the events of the period had made unmistakably clear: colonization was no remedy.

XI

THE FLIGHT FROM HUNGER

THE SUCCESSION OF EVENTS beginning in the autumn of 1845 settled the issue between those who argued that the social condition of western Europe was improving and those who regarded it with apprehension. The summer had been encouraging to the optimists. More land than ever before had been planted with potatoes, and the luxuriant fields promised a bountiful harvest. July and August produced the usual seasonal rumors of the presence of the potato disease; but even when trustworthy information confirmed the reports of crop failures along the lower Rhine and in parts of England and Scotland, hope still predominated over fear. As long as Ireland escaped a visitation, no feeling of alarm could be general.[1] October, however, brought news that the dreaded rot was ravaging Ireland and in a most virulent form. Not only potatoes in the ground but those already stored exhibited a mysterious degeneration.[2] In the judgment of later years Ireland suffered a loss of from a third to a half its normal crop.[3] In England and Scotland the yield fell off about a sixth.[4] Though no accurate estimate can be made for the Continent, complaints of a shortage came all the way from Holland and Belgium to the mountains of Switzerland.[5]

Ireland endured a winter of deep distress. In many instances neighborly kindliness and British philanthropy prevented outright starvation.[6] The government also lent a helping hand. The legislation for poor relief, adopted in 1837, had made provision for public works in hard times, but only after application by local officers and an investigation of the utility of the proposed improvements.[7] To speed up the process a new act was hastily passed early in 1846.[8] The immediate results proved disappointing, however, for only a few communities and a few thousand persons were benefited. More effective was the action of the ministry in London in permitting the importation of maize or Indian corn duty free.[9] Since the wheat harvest had been normal and in the north the supplies of oatmeal were large,[10] the purpose of the act was to enable the farmers to sell these foodstuffs at high prices in the markets of Europe while buying for their own consumption a larger quantity of cheap food.[11] This explains the paradox — which agitators were not slow in pointing out — that, while Ireland was starving, its quays were thronged with ships bearing its products to the docks of London and Liverpool.

The approach of spring brought further relief in the form of emigration. The size of the movement, however, was not remarkable. Observers agreed that, if means had not been wanting, the volume would have been considerably larger.[12] The people departing consisted mainly of small farmers whose resources had not been exhausted by the struggle of the preceding months and who, fearing for the future, resolved to leave before inevitable poverty engulfed them. Young, active and industrious, they struck out to save themselves while time permitted.[13]

In Germany the winter passed with relatively little suffering. The supplies of grain proved sufficient for the needs; and although high prices at first threatened to cause distress in the factory regions, organized charity succeeded in handling the emergency. Nevertheless, savings were exhausted and reserves of capital expended which were essential to help society weather a second similar crisis.[14] In England, also, the immediate outcome was more favorable than had been expected. The construction of railroads continued, and the demand for laborers provided employment. The agricultural regions complained of a shortage of hands.[15]

That emigration from the German countries should be proportionately greater than that from Ireland was natural. Apprehension regarding the future was as widespread, and private resources were greater. So extensive was the demand for accommodations that the shipping houses at the Continental ports, which had previously devoted their efforts to securing passengers, now found difficulty in securing an adequate fleet. Bremen bookers published warnings advising no one to come to the city who did not already have a contract in his pocket.[16] Hamburg merchants were also active in the trade.[17] At Rotterdam and Amsterdam the congestion was so great that no attempt was made to find freight cargoes. Coastal steamers, packed with Swiss and Germans, discharged their passengers at Le Havre where many of them had to camp a good part of the summer until they could obtain passage.[18] In Norway and Sweden similar incidents occurred. Even the southern provinces of Denmark displayed a growing interest in emigration.

But during the summer of 1846 popular interest did not center in the troubles of ship brokers, nor did it concern itself much with the delays and hardships of emigrants. One question overshadowed all others: what would be the fate of Ireland? In May and June the country seemed completely exhausted. Those who were not in debt for food owed the landlord a year's rent and faced the likelihood of eviction. Many could not secure seeds for planting; others lacked the physical vigor to perform the needed tasks, or were listless in the hope that government aid, having been once extended, would continue and increase.[19] Most discouraging of all was the ever present fear that the disaster of the preceding season might be repeated. Oftentimes in the past the people had survived a year of shortage; never had they been obliged to endure two in succession. "If the next crop fails us," declared a peasant, "it will be the end of the world with us." [20] Despite favorable conditions early in the season the crop did fail, and it was the end of that world which they and their forefathers had known and loved.

The destruction was the work of a few days, some said of a single night.[21] An article in the *Irish Farmer's Gazette* on July 12, announcing the failure of the crop, may be taken as dating the beginning of the new catastrophe. A letter of Father Mathew records the swiftness of the disaster. Traveling one day from Cork to Dublin, he saw the potato patches in bloom and rejoiced at the abundance of the coming harvest. Returning a week later, he saw the same fields "one wide waste of putrifying vegetation. In many places the wretched people were seated on the fences of their decaying gardens, wringing their hands and wailing bitterly the destruction that had left them foodless." [22] For a while a certain calmness prevailed among the people at large, then came panic and terror, and finally a sullen resignation.

The popular attitude reflected political despair as well as economic tragedy.[23] The repeal movement had raised the hopes of the Irish. Even in the trying times of the previous winter communities on the verge of starvation had sent contributions to the cause. But now their inspiring leader, Daniel O'Connell, lingered at the door of death. The battle had been lost on two fronts. The feeling was inescapable that Ireland would never again be able to feed its people. The usual agricultural labors of the autumn were neglected; fields were deserted. The only hope now lay in that government from whose rule the Irish had so persistently tried to free themselves.[24]

If Ireland had been alone in its misery, an immediate mobilization of all the humanitarian forces of Europe might have instilled new confidence. But no country had at first much concern for what was happening beyond the national boundaries, for there was trouble at home. Germany had passed through a cycle of hope and disappointment not unlike that which the Irish had experienced. A hot summer had covered the fields with a rich verdure. Speculative grain merchants who had kept supplies in storage were so confident of an ample harvest that they threw their wares upon the market.[25] But such expectations proved premature. The fruit withered on the trees; the early potatoes were afflicted with rot; the rye had suffered from the heat; the yield of grain was small. All hopes then centered upon the late potatoes, but they also proved disappointing.[26]

These German communities had progressed beyond the stage where the failure of a particular agricultural product spelled starvation. They sold and bought and had some capital upon which to draw; local financial institutions were willing to extend credit for adequate security. The principal hardship was the high price of food. These high prices resulted partly from the local shortage and partly from the activities of town and country officials in buying up grain for storage in the medieval magazines.[27] The upward trend was increased by the lively demand in France, which caused German produce to be exported whenever the Germans would not pay what the dealers asked.[28]

In the fall and winter that followed there developed an international grain panic that greatly hampered relief in the stricken countries. Crop failures had not been universal. On the plains of northern and eastern Germany the yield was about normal. Though no one knew the exact situation in the Baltic or Black Sea provinces of Russia, there came no reports of a shortage. Agricultural America, which always produced a surplus, could ultimately deliver an unknown quantity, but statesmen were concerned with immediacies. Countries like France, Spain and Portugal, which tradition-

ally had encouraged the export of grain, now suddenly prohibited sales to foreign houses.[29] Great Britain repealed its
century-old corn laws partly in an effort to meet the Irish
crisis.[30]

Irish grain had not been affected, but the authorities hoped
that the high prices which it would bring in foreign markets
would make possible the importation of sufficient quantities
of maize to feed the people.[31] This hope, however, overlooked
two facts: less wheat had been planted; and maize could not
reach Ireland until the canals in the interior of America
opened for transportation in the spring. It would thus be
summer before it would be available for food. With autumn
the real famine began. Though the potato failure had probably not exceeded that of the previous year, there were now
no other resources on which to draw. A few pigs had survived the slaughter of 1845–1846, but the blighted fields
foretold their doom. The swine were driven half-fed to
market — a pathetic reminder of the six or seven hundred
thousand which were usually sent across the Irish Channel
to England. Nor did dug patches now supply forage for the
farmyard hen. Consequently it also disappeared and, with it,
the supply of eggs that had varied the peasant's diet, or contributed to his meager cash income.[32]

No Englishman has ever written the history of those famine
months, and no Irishman has ever thought it necessary. They
were vividly recalled at every Irish fireside in the decades
that followed; they became part of the tradition of British
misgovernment that nourished the growing sense of nationalism. A description of one famine presents a description of all,
whether in India, China or Ireland. Some, when they realized
the inevitable, withdrew to their cottages to die in patient
resignation. Whole families took to the road, straying from
parish to parish and leaving the enfeebled old or young to
perish by the wayside. Many who escaped actual starvation

died of "famine fever," a form of typhus induced by under-nourishment and spread by the wandering population. The dead were buried unrecorded in pits.[33]

As the winter progressed, the system of relief, too tardily organized, became more effective. Also by January cargoes of maize from the United States appeared in the harbors.[34] Other supplies arrived from the Mediterranean and the lower valley of the Danube.[35] Wheat which had been shipped from Ireland a few months before came back to be distributed by the government to the starving.[36] By February there was ample food in the country. The emergency was not over, however, for the food had to be quickly distributed in a land of still primitive communications. The rivers were frozen, and horses and carts were too few for adequate conveyance by land.[37] Even when meal and flour reached their destination difficulties remained. Many of the inhabitants had never tasted bread; their kitchens had no ovens; the housewives did not know how to bake the loaves.[38] These disadvantages were in time overcome; and by March the imports swelled to unimagined proportions. In one week a hundred vessels laden with corn and breadstuffs arrived at the port of Cork.[39] In "anything that could float" — small coastal schooners that had never ventured away from the American shore and vessels hastily launched in the shipyards — the New York commission agents sent the surplus of the New World to the starving Irishman.[40] In so doing they fed not only his body but also his imagination, for he learned convincingly of a land where there was an abundance of food to spare.[41]

This distribution of food represented the more successful aspect of British policy. A new piece of legislation, commonly called the "labour-rate act," provided the basis for emergency employment.[42] It did away with local initiative, and empowered the lord lieutenant or his subordinates to decide when and where public works should be undertaken. The cost should be jointly borne by the owners and occupiers of the land in that district. The law was well-intentioned, but its effects proved disastrous. The improvements consisted chiefly of roads which were little used. Property acquired no profit while saddled with the charge. Since the wages were too small to support the worker and his family, charity continued to be necessary. At one time approximately a tenth of the people were nominally engaged in this labor, neglecting the farm tasks of the winter and spring, and heaping new financial burdens on a society already breaking beneath the strain.[43] Perhaps most unfortunate of all were the physical consequences. Many of the workers were already weakened by hunger and exposure; the work was heavy; sanitary arrangements in the camps were primitive. Fever soon appeared and found a fertile breeding ground.[44]

Probably few of those who decided on emigration in 1847 reasoned consciously regarding their state. Their impulse was merely to get away. A curse rested upon the land. Misfortunes had been great; they might become greater. "Poor Ireland's done," "The country's gone forever," "It can never again recover" — these were the expressions heard wherever emigrants congregated. Even in parts of the country which had escaped the severest blows the sentiment prevailed, for they feared their turn might come next.

A great impetus to the movement was given by the abundance of shipping in the Irish ports. This was due to the forehandedness of the commercial houses of Liverpool, which anticipated a throng of passengers and, in this belief, raised their rates from three pounds to five. When the increase proved no deterrent, the brokers asked for seven, and the amount was readily paid.[45] Only the activity of government agents prevented them from canceling contracts made at the lower figure and offering the accommodations to the highest bidders.[46] But seven pounds, or even five, exceeded the resources of the departing laborer. Only the "more respect-able" emigrants, those who had planned some time in ad-vance, went via Liverpool.[47] For the poorer sort, however, opportunities abounded in almost every Irish harbor. Wher-ever an American or Canadian schooner landed its cargo of grain, a bargain might be made; and on such vessels they set out from home.[48]

Throughout the spring and early summer the village streets and country roads bustled with activity. A few carts, prob-ably lent by philanthropic neighbors, helped to transport the baggage from home to the sea. Most of the wayfarers found no difficulty in carrying their meager belongings on their shoulders. On every hand crowds of neighbors, often totaling hundreds, streamed toward the ports where they camped in confusion upon the quays, contested for passage and finally embarked on the great adventure.[49] Newspaper editors, little dreaming this was but the vanguard of the mighty army that would depart in the next decade, declared the land was being depopulated.[50]

But how could people on the ragged edge of starvation finance such a migration? The sources of their funds were many. Hidden in the thatch of many a poor cottage in Munster and Connaught were a few sovereigns, put aside for an emergency; and the emergency had now ·come. The sale of furniture netted a few pounds more.[51] Landlords complained that out of pity for the obvious distress of their tenants they had not pressed them for the last year's rent, and now this rent was taking them forever out of their reach. Others did not hesitate to beg, and those who con-tributed believed they were giving to the most worthy of causes.[52]

Another important source of money consisted of drafts sent from Canada and the United States by relatives who were aroused to action by the news of the disaster. Though such funds may have been intended for relief, the recipient hastened to buy passage — the most effective relief of which he could conceive.[53] Landlords did their part, often sending tenants at their own expense. In many such cases the motive was self-interest, not charity, for in a few months the tenants might become paupers and thus a perpetual charge upon the estate.[54] Some landlords organized a migration *en masse*, chartering a ship, hiring an agent to supervise the transportation, buying supplies for the journey, and giving to each a few shillings with which to start the new life.[55]

Not all the emigrants of 1847 crossed the Atlantic. When the difficulties grew acute, many laborers recalled a prosperous land, distant only a day's sail. Familiar with England from having visited it annually during the harvest season, they decided to take wife and children there and make it their permanent home. Five or six shillings paid the fare, and they landed in uncounted numbers at Bristol and Liverpool and at the villages on the Welsh coast. Here they at once fell a burden upon charity. Some of the parishes considered sending them back to Ireland, but under the conditions that seemed like returning them to inevitable starvation. So the newcomers were encouraged to move inland and beg their way from city to city until they found work or a kindly disposed community.[56] During 1847 more than a quarter of a million reached Liverpool alone.[57] Some of these ultimately went to Canada or the United States; but the majority settled in the great factory cities of the north where they became the ancestors of a large proportion of their present-day inhabitants.

The stagnation of trade and the high prices induced by the scarcity aroused fears in England during the winter of 1846–1847 that ultimately the distress would equal that of Ireland. But the spring brought improvement. Railroads were still being built; farmers, as yet unaware of the threat to them involved in the repeal of the corn laws, continued to ditch and drain; and Canada and the United States, enriched by the pounds secured from selling their food products, became such good customers that the manufacturing plants of Lancashire enjoyed a spirited revival.[58]

Although the German emigration reflected no such social crisis as that which afflicted Ireland, nevertheless the prevailing hunger swelled it to a new height, and an almost accidental circumstance gave to it the character of a flight. The winter of 1846–1847 was one of suffering, with food supplies short and speculators busy. Many factory districts were obliged to depend upon charity, and almost all but the most prosperous farmers felt the pinch of high prices when buying the food their fields had failed to yield. A vague fear that current troubles portended greater difficulties gained ground; and in the autumn the American consul at Amsterdam, reporting the sentiments of German emigrants passing through his port, declared, "All well informed persons express the belief that the present crisis is so deeply interwoven in the events of the present period, that 'it' is but the commencement of that great Revolution, which they consider sooner or later is to dissolve the present constitution of things . . . ." [59] Many persons testified to the intensity of the eagerness to leave. George Bancroft, the minister at Berlin, wrote that "all Germany is alive on the subject"; that the movement would be "enormous, and limited only by the amount of the transports . . . ." [60] One consul told of villagers preparing to depart in a body; [61] another described the public as "seized with a Panic." [62] Newspapers added their testimony, not only in news items, but also in the official declarations of intention required by the laws of many of the states.

The evidence is conflicting, however, as to the economic status of the emigrants, the class to which they belonged, and the material resources they took with them. Some accounts bewailed the departure of the most desirable: farm families of the middle class with many sons and daughters and comfortable means.[63] The indications of poverty, however, were more pointed. The city of Cologne found it necessary to provide cheap lodgings for those who could afford no others; [64] and the Belgian authorities forbade emigrants to enter the kingdom who could not show a sum sufficient for support and passage.[65] Many communes sent their beggars and their chronic poor to America.[66]

As early as the first of February, 1847, Bremen was filled with waiting persons fearful lest the demand for transportation exceed the supply. Many vessels normally employed in the passenger trade were out searching for cargoes of grain, and the time of their return was uncertain.[67] This fact contributed to the chaos into which the entire business was soon thrown; but the most important factor was one beyond the shippers' control, one injected into the situation from a source which they had always felt it safe to ignore.

Hitherto the law of 1819 had been the only American federal regulation governing immigration. When Congress gathered in December, 1846, petitions from officials of the state and city of New York and from charitable organizations urged a more effective control in view of the conditions abroad. The outcome was the act of February, 1847, supported by all political factions and evidently actuated by humanitarian considerations. This law left unchanged the principle established in 1819; but in view of the great changes in marine architecture since that time it specified that on the lower deck fourteen "clear superficial feet" must be allowed for each person, and on the bottom or orlop deck thirty.[68] It also prescribed the length and width of beds and continued the food requirements of the older law. Vessels arriving in the United States after May 31 with more passengers than the new system permitted should be subject to confiscation.[69]

Though this date allowed sufficient time for the information to reach Europe before such ships sailed, it ignored the system of contracts under which most of the Continental trade was conducted. The German and Dutch merchants hardly knew what to do. If they should dispatch a ship with all the passengers they had agreed to take, it would be confiscated upon arriving in the United States; if they should refuse to transport all the persons with whom they had entered contracts, German laws carried penalties so heavy as to ruin them.[70] The obvious way out was to hire more ships, but in the mercantile world in the spring of 1847 no more vessels were to be had.

Confronted with this situation someone started a rumor. Its origin was never traced, but circumstances suggest that it came from an interested source in Bremen. A circular, widely spread throughout those regions in Germany where the emigration fever raged, deliberately gave the impression that the new American law amounted to a prohibition of immigration.[71] If, as seems likely, the object was to influence holders of tickets to annul their passage, it had no such effect. On the contrary, it seems to have encouraged many to make a sudden resolve to emigrate in the belief that only by hastening could they reach America before the door was finally shut. Learning it was useless to seek accommodations at Bremen and Hamburg, they flocked down the Rhine to the Dutch and Belgian ports. Because of the stiffer price of passage there, many were obliged to return to their homes.[72]

In the meantime the shippers of northern Germany discovered a way round the American law. Hitherto they had avoided trade with Canada because of the difficulty of obtaining return cargoes; but the emergency rendered this a minor consideration. Accordingly the advertised vessels sailed to Quebec, carrying their full complement of passengers, and accompanied by agents who conducted the emigrants upon arrival overland to New York, or directed them by the shortest route to the American West.[73] This diversion of the immigrant trade occasioned alarm among the various American interests concerned with the traffic and also among European shippers. In response to the flood of protests the government took action. The law could not be repealed in a moment, but it could be construed. To this end the Secretary of the Treasury issued a circular which allowed the space occupied by the berths to be included among the "clear superficial feet" assigned to each passenger. Although such an interpretation lay within the letter, it certainly did not comply with the intention of the law. Its adoption made inevitable further legislation.[74]

Despite the effort to improve the conditions of ocean passage the emigrants encountered dreadful suffering on the congested vessels. The crowds of Irishmen, sailing hopefully from their stricken island, believed that they were leaving misery behind; but in the six or eight weeks of their voyage the pestilence which they were fleeing broke out again with a lethal fury that shocked even those who had witnessed the scenes of the preceding winter. Physicians called it "ship fever," though it was probably a modified form of the "famine fever" or hunger typhus, a fact indicated by its absence from vessels coming from the Continent.[75] The disease in some cases originated among passengers already suffering from a mild form of it when they boarded the ship; oftentimes the germs were carried by lice in clothing that had been salvaged from persons who had died.[76]

Ships sailing from Liverpool usually discovered the plague before leaving the shores of Ireland, and were able to place the patients in the fever hospitals of Cork.[77] But vessels departing directly from Ireland could not do this. Once out upon the Atlantic they continued their course whether the passengers were sick or well. Carrying the poorest peasants, those who had had closest contact with the pestilence, they exhibited gruesome scenes. The worst were enacted on the boats bound for the British provinces. Of the 89,738 emigrants who embarked in 1847 for the St. Lawrence ports of Canada 5293 died during the voyage. Of the 17,074 headed for New Brunswick 823 perished.[78] The mortality at sea amounted to approximately six per cent.

Though the toll of death was heavy, the disease had not yet run its course when a vessel reached port. Sick and dying passengers were brought on shore at quarantine. The first lot were admitted to the hospital at Grosse Isle, thirty miles below Quebec, on May 14. By the end of the month 1200 were accommodated in beds and tents, and thirty-five vessels were waiting to discharge their sick. Though new buildings were hastily constructed and an attempt was made to separate the dying from the less infected and to reserve a part of the island for convalescents, 10,037 died in the ships at quarantine or in the hospitals at Grosse Isle.[79] The total mortality among those embarking for Canada was therefore approximately sixteen per cent. Even this figure is conservative, for many families, detained in Quebec because one of their number was kept at Grosse Isle, readily fell prey, if not to ship fever, to other diseases induced by temporary housing and undernourishment. At St. John and St. Andrews the mortality was also great, 1292 recorded deaths taking place at quarantine and in the hospitals.[80]

American officials stationed along the inland frontier tried to prevent those whom they suspected of having participated in this migration from crossing Upper Canada into the United States.[81] In the absence of similar vigilance along the seacoast many of the unfortunates who landed in New Brunswick entered the New England states. Usually the husband and father went ahead, while the wife and children waited until he found work.[82] When the family arrived in tatters and rags, the effects of starvation still visible on their gaunt faces, the Bostonians believed that all the misery of Ireland had been emptied on their shores.

The advent of these refugees together with the greater number who came directly from Ireland caused Massachusetts to revise her legislation against pauper newcomers. Though a bonding system had been established in 1837, it had not worked well.[83] Sick and aged had been allowed to land without the required guarantee being given; the officer in charge justified his laxness by declaring, "My only plea is humanity." A legislative committee early in 1847 discovered that not a single prosecution for breaches of the law had been pressed to a final judgment.[84] The events of the summer dramatized the need for more effective legislation. So great was the influx of human wrecks that a receiving room for invalids just off the ships was constructed at Boston Long Wharf, and a carriage was kept constantly busy conveying them to the boat for transportation to the hospitals on Deer Island.[85] In the face of a flood of petitions the legislature delayed action no longer when it met in January, 1848. The new law made no change in the capitation tax, nor did it increase the amount of the bond; but the bond was no longer limited to ten years, heavier penalties were attached, and more effective methods of enforcement provided.[86]

Although New York City witnessed less appalling scenes, the people were keenly aware of the dangers to which their geographic position exposed them. The neighboring coast of New Jersey offered convenient opportunities for disembarkment. Shipmasters anchored off these ports went through the form of bonding and then left the emigrants to find their way across the Hudson as best they could.[87] Even honest skippers, with no intention of violating the New York re-

quirements, patronized a class of professional bondsmen who
for a per-capita charge relieved the captains of all the petty
details and assumed financial obligation for pauper immigrants. Though the bonds were legally drawn, in time these
men became responsible for fabulous sums which rested upon
security of dubious value.[88] This general situation, strengthened by popular opinion expressed in public meetings, led
the legislature on May 5, 1847, to create an administrative
body of six commissioners of emigration, appointed by the
governor, who served together with the mayors of New York
and Brooklyn and the presidents of the German and Irish
emigrant societies. The act required the master of a vessel
to pay a fee of one dollar for every passenger he landed in
the harbor. The distribution of the funds so acquired was
left to the commissioners, who were also given extensive
powers in appointing and removing the administrative officers.[89] The New Yorkers believed they had made adequate
provision against any evils the future might bring forth.

The people of Baltimore also felt the necessity for protective measures. The traditional immigration into that port
had consisted almost entirely of Germans who passed on to
the agricultural West; but now the famine sent over its hordes
of Irishmen. Though the local Hibernian Society collected
funds to relieve the distress, the newcomers brought with
them disease that quickly spread through the city.[90] Existing
laws proving inadequate, the mayor urged prompt action on
the city government. An ordinance, hastily adopted, desig-
nated a quarantine ground, and directed the health officer
to inspect all arrivals and send those who were sick to the
hospital, the cost of treatment to be borne by the master or
owner of the vessel.[91] Evidently this municipal regulation
proved effective, for the newspapers of the summer and
autumn, although noting the arrival of numerous immigrant
ships, made no further complaint of disease-spreading
paupers.[92]

Louisiana, also prompted to action, used a combination of state and municipal legislation in dealing with the problem. Laws of 1842 and 1843 had authorized a head tax on each passenger arriving from foreign ports or on coastal vessels from the Atlantic seaboard. These funds were administered by the charity hospital of the city of New Orleans.[93] Such was the situation when the fateful spring of 1847 brought its deluge of stricken Europeans. On one April day nearly a hundred starving people were admitted to the charity hospital. Fifty new arrivals, discovered lodging in a small house, were so diseased that they were unable to work; some of them were living on straw gathered in the streets.[94] To make matters worse, an epidemic of yellow fever was raging in New Orleans, the worst it had ever known. Against this new terror the immigrants had no powers of resistance.[95] Public officials did what they could in the distribution of relief, and buildings were hired as temporary shelters for the sick. The chief burden, however, fell on private charity.

Since existing legislation fell short of the need, city ordinances gave the mayor discretionary power over the landing of immigrants and imposed a flat fee of ten dollars upon every vessel which had sickness on board.[96] Because the legal right of municipal officials to control matters of quarantine was questioned, the legislature created a state board for the purpose. Unfortunately it was given insufficient power, and in disgust the municipality of New Orleans passed an ordinance taxing all incoming passengers. Only the veto of the mayor prevented its application.[97]

Such was the harvest of legislation produced by the crisis. The people in four states had been aroused to action and had set up barriers which, though not prohibitive, indicated their belief that no longer should all classes of Europeans pass unrestricted through their gates. This legislation formed the basis of immigration regulation until the federal government in 1882 assumed control. In one respect, however, the legislation ran into immediate difficulties. Shipping interests objected strenuously to the requirement of a flat fee. Though small in the case of each individual passenger, it amounted to thousands of dollars in the course of the year, and shipowners could not shift the tax to the emigrant by increasing the price of passage 'because conditions of competition rendered this inexpedient. As a result, the shippers in Massachusetts and New York brought action in the courts to test the constitutionality of the laws in those states. In due course the cases reached the federal Supreme Court, which in 1848 sustained the litigants. The decision in the "Passenger Cases" held that the legislation in question involved a regulation of foreign commerce and hence invaded the domain of action reserved to Congress.[98] In the face of this decision the states reverted to the system which an earlier judgment had declared to be within their competence. They required masters of vessels to give a bond to indemnify them for any expenses incurred by an immigrant who became a public charge, and specified further that this bond might be commuted by the payment of a cash fee for each passenger. In everyday operation therefore the practice remained the same.[99]

As a result of the bad consequences of the interpretation placed by the Secretary of the Treasury upon the act of 1847, the federal government took additional action regarding the carriage of passengers at sea. The law of 1848 repealed the old "two-passengers-to-five-tons" provision, and provided that the number of "clear superficial feet" allowed each passenger should be determined by the height between decks. It also prescribed a diet of greater variety, including wheat, potatoes and rice, and held the captain responsible for the general cleanliness and discipline on board the ship.[100]

Meanwhile the peasant farmers in Europe who had not joined the emigration of 1847 anxiously watched the prospects of the coming season. "The very life of the country," wrote an Irish observer in June, "seems to be bound up in the results of the coming harvest." [101] The people of the island set out only a small quantity of potatoes. Seeds were lacking and, in any case, faith in the treacherous root was wanting. Instead, they planted green crops, especially turnips, and the more substantial farmers, encouraged by the prevailing prices, extended their acreage of wheat and oats.[102] The potato planting fared well, however. The fields did not wither, and the potatoes when taken from the soil were sound. Optimism returned, and a cheerfulness unknown for many months reappeared in the countryside. It was clear, however, that until another year could bring its yield from the ground the food supply would be deficient.[103] In Germany the outcome was essentially the same. The crop of grain was abundant though that of potatoes was short. Prices remained high and a food scarcity still threatened.[104] But elsewhere in Europe and America the granaries were full, and the fleets of the world were ready to bring those in want the surplus of the fortunate.[105]

Thus ended the year 1847. The great disaster, long feared, had come and had gone. Hunger had written a chapter of death and suffering into the history of western Europe. It had sent tens of thousands fleeing across the sea. But the future promised to be different. Mankind looked forward with renewed hope.

XII

NEW FORCES AT WORK

THE FEELING OF OPTIMISM with which the old year closed seemed confirmed by the events of the opening months of the new. Eighteen hundred and forty-eight was a year of political wonders. In some countries men died fighting behind the barricades for the cause of popular rights. In others, obstacles that had seemed insuperable fell before the simple threat of force. The French monarchy gave way to a republic; Metternich fled an exile from Vienna; Hungarian patriots struggled for an independence that seemed almost within reach. Every German state and every Scandinavian kingdom witnessed tumults in its streets and ultimate reforms in its government. But after revolution came reaction. The year 1849 dispelled most of the bright dreams that its predecessor had evoked. The Hungarian uprising was crushed by the Austrians. The unified Germany which the people tried to create at Frankfurt failed of realization. In Baden a new revolution brought armies into the field, and the defeat of the insurgents sent hundreds to prison and thousands fleeing over the frontier. There were plenty of new constitutions that served as reminders of the victories of 1848, but bureaucratic administration knew well how to temper the concessions. These happenings were paralleled by others of a different order. The British Parliament and the Diet of almost every German state altered their laws in regard to land and commerce. An American army fought its way to Mexico City and effected a peace that added a new empire to the Union. Gold was picked up in the sands of California.

Events followed one another with such rapidity that contemporaries could not see them in their proper relationship. But the confusion gradually resolved itself into the outlines of a different order. There emerged a new Europe and a new America, soon to be bound together by the intimate ties of more than a million persons who crossed the Atlantic to cast their lot with the western republic. Some of the changes in the years 1848 and 1849 marked the culmination of an evolution long under way; some were precipitated by the agitation of reformers; some were concessions hastily made by frightened monarchs; and a few represented the unheralded workings of Nature. In the light of these happenings the motives of the emigrants and the immediate causes for their departure stand clearly revealed.

Indirectly, Parliament's repeal of the corn laws in 1846 proved an important factor in stimulating interest in emigration. The act signalized the adoption of free trade as a permanent policy, and its repercussions were felt far and wide. The supplying of England with food had hitherto been a branch of trade international in its scope. The existence of a "sliding scale," which permitted the importation of grain when the domestic price reached a certain level, kept the traders of western Europe in a constant state of expectancy. In particular, these opportunities profited the patriarchal lords whose large estates on the fertile plains of north Germany always produced a surplus of wheat and rye. Receiving early word of the repeal from their agents at Hamburg, they landed their supplies in London before the grain merchants of the eastern Baltic or the lower Danube knew of the possibilities.[1] Much of the comparative prosperity that had distinguished the farmers of north Germany from those in the south centered in this exportation. How would they fare now that the English market was to be open all the time, with the advantage falling to those who could sell most cheaply?

In particular, Russia loomed as a menacing rival, for its broad steppes offered a boundless area for expansion. The Greek merchants who had hitherto acted as middlemen in the limited shipments from the Black Sea through the Mediterranean entered energetically into its development. But effective competition could not be called into existence in a year. Russia possessed primitive roads and vehicles. Away from the sea and the navigable rivers, transportation was so rudimentary that a journey to Odessa with a cartload of grain required eight or ten weeks, though the distance did not exceed two hundred miles.[2] Railways would have cured the difficulty, but before any could be built, Russia was involved in war; and it remained for a later generation to enjoy the fruits of the trade.

For a few years the old producers of Germany were safe, even from competitors whose products could reach the English market. The high prices prevailing since 1845 had exhausted the usual Continental surplus carried over from season to season.[3] With the crop of 1849 the stocks began to be replenished; but again in 1850 the yield fell short.[4] Only France might have offered a serious threat, for the high prices that began in 1847 caused an increased planting of wheat. But no new system of cultivation was adopted; and as conditions became more normal, France fell back to the position of a nation in which the domestic supply and demand maintained an even balance.[5]

Whatever the fears felt by the north Germans, they were small compared with the terror that gripped the English farmer when he realized that his wall of protection had been razed. The Englishman worried about competition not only from the Continent, but also from across the Atlantic — from the clearings of Upper Canada and the prairies of the Missis-

sippi Valley. Every word that had been written inviting
Europeans to pioneer beyond the sea had stressed the in-
exhaustible possibilities offered by the virgin soil, and those
descriptions had sunk deep into their consciousness. The
English yeoman expected to be overwhelmed by a flood of
wheat that would sweep away his comforts and destroy his
independence. History looks back upon that consternation
with surprise. Although the tide increased, the flood did not
come. America was not yet ready to seize what England
offered. Until the Civil War, the American price for grain
so closely approximated that offered in Liverpool that exportation was not a profitable venture. Four years of war
and its aftermath delayed for another decade the inevitable
results of the British legislation, and not until the 1870's did
the gloomy prophecies come true.[6]

But people are influenced by what they think is going to
happen; and the consensus of opinion from 1848 to 1850 was
that every English landowner, tenant and agricultural laborer
was headed for ruin. As if to confirm such fears, the laborers
soon found themselves in difficulty. The ending of the era
of railroad construction threw men out of work, sending
them back to the rural villages.[7] To make matters worse,
farmers, convinced that crop prices would be so low as not to
justify further capital investments, generally put a stop to
continued improvement; and on estates where employment
was still available, immigrating Irishmen often underbid the
local residents.[8] As a result, the union workhouses rapidly
filled with families in need of relief, and a mounting food tax
added another terror to the farmers' fears. "They are fast
approaching the same state as in Ireland," reported a gloomy
correspondent.[9]

This widespread anxiety in regard to the future explains
the sudden revival of interest in emigration in 1848 and 1849.
The press sent forth a library of "settlers' guides" that drove

all other literature from the windows of the village stationers. Short-lived emigrant journals attempted to direct the current. Emigrant societies flourished wherever persons, who had the desire but not the means, believed they might jointly secure funds for transportation.[10] Agricultural laborers who had savings or financial help from friends already in America left in surprising numbers. In a similar spirit tenant farmers, scraping together their resources, resolved to take their remaining capital to a part of the world where agriculture promised better.[11] In these two years the volume of the departing English and Scots probably exceeded that of the Irish. Scotch emigration from the Lowlands was induced by the same forebodings that haunted the English farmer. From the mountains of the north and the western isles it marked a continuation of the process of "clearing" which, starting in the eighteenth century, had sent out successive clans of Highlanders as the great lords pushed forward the modernization of their domains.[12]

In Ireland, also, the repeal of the corn laws threw the landlords and the intermediate tenants into a panic of despair. Wheat had been the rent-paying crop, but how could the farmer now compete with foreign growers for the English market? His land was weighed down with taxation, and its productivity impaired by the break in the simple system of rotation.[13] For some of the medium farmers emigration was the answer, but the majority found a solution at home. Temperature, soil, rainfall and geographic location had fitted Ireland for grazing. The industrial workers of England, demanding roast beef in times of prosperity, provided a profitable market for all the cattle that the neighboring island could raise.[14] Consequently these landlords and farmers decided to do away with the host of cottiers and their tiny holdings. Thus they fell in with the program of the government which, consciously or unconsciously, had the same end in view.

By 1848 the smallest cottiers were practically extinct. They had constituted the bulk of the emigrants to England and America in the flight of 1847; many were lodged in the poor-houses; others had died of starvation. Along with them had disappeared all who had facilitated the system of exchange of which the cottiers had formed a part — the petty shop-keeper who sold a yard or two of cloth or a pound of sugar, the wandering trader who collected and marketed the eggs and pork, the artisan who put the finishing touches on the cabin or built a piece of furniture for the newly wed. The removal of a type of person who was not an independent farmer or an independent laborer, but a laborer paid with a patch of land to gamble on the cultivation of a treacherous root, was a healthy purgative. But his extinction involved the welfare of other classes whose interests had been entwined with his lowly position; and he left behind a load of community debt that rested heavily upon his more fortunate neighbors.

This burden was established by the Irish poor law of 1847, which replaced the statute whose shortcomings the crisis of 1846 had revealed.[15] That emergency had been met by the out-and-out contribution of private and governmental charity and by the system of employment relief. The new act was less ambitious in its scope. It did away with work relief, aimed to reduce the number of those entitled to the dole and redistributed the cost of relief.[16] Two features of the system are of fundamental importance in accounting for the emigration that followed.

Small holders read with dismay the "quarter-acre clause" which denied to individuals leasing a quarter of an acre or more the right to receive assistance, no matter how deplorable their temporary situation might be. Presumably persons with three sixteenths of an acre might retain their holdings and be allowed help; but this class had already disappeared. Those who were hungry in the autumn of 1847 held up to five or even ten acres.[17] Such persons could relinquish their lease and thereby get rid of the obstacle that stood between them and aid. It is likely that this is what the framers of the law intended. The new Ireland which they wanted to build upon the ruins of the old would be one which would sharply separate farmers from agricultural laborers. If this was their purpose, they were disappointed. Land was surrendered, but the former three or five-acre man had no desire to remain a servant in a land where he had once been free, particularly since he had no prospect of steady work.[18] He bade farewell to his native soil, also to his wife and children. If he had the means, he went to America; if not, he crossed over to England. In either case he left his family to be supported in the workhouse while he saved his earnings to bring them together again.[19]

This circumstance emphasizes the second significant feature of the law. Who should pay the rates to care for these deserted wives and children? The taxes could not be levied directly upon the landlords, for not one among them would have been solvent at the end of the first year. Nor could they be spread indiscriminately over all tenants great and small, for that would have obliged many to contribute to their own support. Therefore a classification was made which exempted tenants whose yearly rent amounted to four pounds or less. Those not in the exempted class saw themselves singled out to shoulder the back-breaking burden of Ireland's poverty. Rather than see their remaining capital gradually drained into the treasury of the poor-law union, the farseeing among them used it to finance their journey beyond the reach of the rate collectors. Thus a second class of emigrants was set in motion by the law.[20]

Apart from the statute itself, the urge to depart was accelerated by the heartless process known as "clearing." Most of those affected had not met any of their obligations since

EJECTMENT OF IRISH TENANTRY

the autumn of 1845; and when called upon, the sheriff had no choice but to perform his official duty though it was little to his liking. When families were evicted and their dwellings razed lest they move back in, it was the landlord's bailiffs and his agents who wielded the crowbars.[21] A person passing through these districts and observing the broken gables and the skeleton frames of what had once been cottages, or the heaps of dirt that had once been mud hovels, exclaimed, "I seemed to be tracking the course of an invading army." [22] Not all this wreckage was due to heartless landlords, however. Many of the homes were already unoccupied. "Leveling" was the sequel to emigration; and in 1849, the year from which most of the accounts date, the outgoing current was again flowing in a rapid stream.

The decline of numbers in 1848 evoked little surprise. The violent convulsion of the preceding year had shaken loose nearly all of those not rooted in the more permanent foundations of Irish life. The distinguishing feature of the movement was the advent of the vanguard of that army of middle-class farmers and tenants who were to evacuate the land during the next half-decade.[23] A much larger proportion of the emigrants than in 1847 sailed to the United States, for Quebec and the St. Lawrence route with their memories of Grosse Isle were in disrepute. Passage thence was also more costly because the legislators of Lower Canada had placed a tax of twenty shillings upon every arrival. As this was the approximate difference in the usual rate from Ireland to the two countries, its addition brought about an equalization that made New York and Boston as accessible as the Canadian ports.[24] Though ship fever broke out again as in the previous year, it was not of such character as to fill ships with dead and hospitals with dying.

One more factor contributed to the Irish decline of 1848. The surprising success of those who had risked a potato planting in 1847 encouraged others to make the effort in the following spring. The price of seed potatoes was high, but no sacrifice proved too great in order to secure them. The family cow, the household furniture, all the clothing but a few rags, were sold. Everyone watched the growing crop with anxious attention.[25] In July, when it was too late to lay plans for emigrating, the disease appeared; in August it spread at an alarming pace; in September the failure turned out to be as extensive as in 1846.[26]

The majority knew that this was their last effort. No longer could they struggle against the revolution that Nature and the British government had wrought. Despondency sank to its lowest depths in the winter of 1848–1849. A continuation of disease, hunger and unemployment seemed the predestined lot of those who tarried in the land of their fathers. Even many Catholic clergymen, who had hitherto urged their flock to remain at home, recommended departure.[27] From America came letters telling of plenty to eat, to drink and to spend. The famine refugees had surmounted the initial difficulties and their unanimous advice was, "Follow us!"

In these circumstances all classes found in emigration the only topic of interesting conversation. People neglected preparations for spring tillage in order to debate the question of when and how to go. They resorted to the pawnbrokers for the last few shillings needed to complete the family's "emigration fund," pledging such articles as bridles, saddles, pewter plates and dishes, brass candlesticks and pieces of furniture.[28] From America came a swelling stream of remittances that firmly established the principle that "emigration begets emigration." As in 1847, vessels, unloading the supplies needed to offset the deficiency of the harvest, afforded an abundance of accommodations that could be readily and cheaply secured.[29] The great wave of departing

Irishmen which was to reach its crest three years later began in the season of 1849.

Meanwhile a new act of Parliament added to agrarian un-settlement and served to speed the outflow of people. A new set of landlords was desirable for the proper development of Ireland — men free of the burden of inherited debts, with capital to improve the land and replenish the depleted live-stock. But the forms of property conveyance were clumsy, and the uncertainty regarding accumulated debts and un-paid taxes rendered it almost impossible for a prospective buyer to secure a clear title.[30] To remedy this situation the encumbered-estates act, passed in 1849, created a special court with almost despotic powers over the transfer of land. Any arrangements which the judges sanctioned wiped away all previous claims.[31] In the next few years this court did its work. The purchasers were English and Scots seeking a profitable investment. The new proprietors felt no senti-mental attachment to the dwellers on the estate; they had no associations with the community; they did not have sufficient surplus capital to tolerate tardy payments. Moreover, they were convinced that Ireland's future lay in pasture. Like the proverbial new broom, they swept clean, increasing the number of evictions to an extent which the mounting figures of emigration reflected.[32]

One more legislative act had its indirect effects on emigra-tion. The corn laws had been repealed in order to assure the workers of England cheaper food prices than those re-sulting from the monopoly enjoyed by the agricultural class of the country. One other monopoly still remained, that of the shipping interests. As the next logical step, Parliament in 1849 put an end to the navigation acts, thereby interna-tionalizing the carrying trade of Great Britain.[33] Although it was not a motive in the repeal, Parliament's action in-sured a low price of passage for the emigrants from the country. It was on the Continent, however, as later discussion will reveal, that the step exerted its most far-reaching effects.

On the surface it seemed that political conditions rather than economic maladjustments were responsible for the surge of emigration from Germany in the years after 1848. At no time before or since have the institutions of the western republic been held in higher esteem among its inhabitants. Every letter from a happily settled emigrant with its comparison between government by princes and that by the people served as political propaganda.[34] When liberal journalists described their Utopia, it was the United States in disguise. When self-appointed statesmen suggested changes in government, they looked to America for their models. A Prussian minister of the interior, calling attention to the doctrines and funds coming from New York and St. Louis, suggested that an effort be made to direct the stream of emigration to countries possessing monarchical institutions.[35] An ultraconservative editor even urged that a Prussian army corps be dispatched over the sea in order to remove the Yankee menace forever.[36]

But admiration of American republicanism did not mean that it constituted a dominating, or even an influential, motive for taking the momentous and practical step of transferring one's family and allegiance to an alien land. The history of those who were involved in the uprisings is significant in this connection. The sporadic and unorganized movements of 1848 and the more serious outbreak of 1849 in Baden created a grave problem for the authorities. To keep the thousands of political prisoners in custody was an expense; to set them at liberty entailed danger and loss of prestige. As a way out of the dilemma, the government of Baden offered to send the rank and file at its own expense to America. The striking fact is that only a dozen or more accepted. The overwhelming majority preferred jail and martyrdom at home.[37]

The same hesitation characterized the ten thousand rebels who escaped the pursuing troops and found an asylum in Switzerland. Their welcome there was not the most cordial. Committees in the United States and in certain places in Europe collected funds for their temporary maintenance; [38] and the interest and sympathy which Americans profusely expressed recommended the United States as the ideal place for continuing the work for a German republic. To this end a call was sent out for a meeting of interested persons in Zürich in late July, 1849, to draw up a concerted plan of action. But only a handful appeared. None of the recognized leaders would commit themselves to the scheme.[39]

That many of the refugees eventually went to America was due to other circumstances. Some of the obscure offenders slipped back into Germany where the police ignored them.[40] Others, whose names and exploits were known, received personal invitations to go to America and, when money was sent, accepted. By the summer of 1850 the Swiss cantons, eager to get rid of their uninvited guests, induced the federal council to establish a credit of ten thousand francs to facilitate their departure. This caused a more general exodus.[41] Many, loath to leave Europe, settled in London, but this often proved a way station for a more distant destination. Thus one by one, and in scattered groups, the immigration of the heroes of 1848–1849 took place.

The roll call of those who settled in the United States repeats some illustrious names: Kinkel, Hecker, Schurz, Sigel. What they accomplished in politics and culture has no place in these pages that recount merely the story of why they came. Of those who had nothing to offer but their reminiscences, Americans soon tired. The self-importance which they assumed and their naïve belief that they could live off their past alienated from them the sympathy of even their own compatriots. As opposition had been their only occupation, in America they became religious and social radicals as they had been radicals in politics at home; and the Know-Nothing agitation of the fifties was in part a revolt against them and their ideas.

Taken all together, the political refugees who emigrated to America numbered only a few thousand. What, then, was the motive that caused three quarters of a million others to desert their fatherland? The bulk of them were peasants with solemn faces, workers with calloused hands, artisans with worried expressions — classes which had been little concerned with politics, and with revolution not at all. They came from regions where reaction had not always been the most pronounced, but where business was poor and the future of trade and agriculture unpromising.[42] It was the desire to improve their economic station that actuated them.

The fact that the total of German departures in 1848 was less than in 1847 might seem proof that freedom was the motive: the year when it appeared to be within reach, the current hesitated as if awaiting the outcome of the struggle. But other influences were potent. Conditions at neither of the two important ports through which emigration flowed were normal. The February revolution in Paris completely disrupted French trade; neighboring governments by declaring martial law interrupted travel over the border in the usually busy spring weeks.[43] Bremen might have taken over the lucrative passenger traffic of its French rival as it had once profited by the embarrassment of the Dutch merchants; but the Hanseatic cities had their own troubles. War was raging in the Danish duchies of Schleswig and Holstein; and as a precautionary measure against possible unneutral acts by Hamburg and Bremen, the Danish fleet established a blockade of the German North Sea coast. Passing through this squadron was such a hazardous venture that few ships took the risk, and bookers chose to send the persons with whom they had contracted on American vessels hired from London, or by way of Antwerp.[44] It is true the demand for passage was less than usual, but this grew out of the difficulty that prospective emigrants experienced in finding purchasers for their real estate in a time of war and rumors of war.[45]

By 1849 the affairs of commerce returned to a more normal state, although after an armistice during the winter war again broke out in the North Sea and for a second time a blockade was proclaimed. But Bremen, foreseeing this eventuality, had anchored its emigrant vessels off the Ems in Oldenburg, to which point the passengers were dispatched overland.[46] In spite of an increase in numbers, persistent complaints emphasized the continuing difficulty of selling property. Incidentally, this fact indicates that in material possessions and social standing those departing belonged to a higher class than the persons who usually undertook the journey.[47] Their willingness to sacrifice their belongings in order to effect an immediate escape suggests the dread with which they viewed the future in Germany.

For a generation the peasant proprietors had sought the modification of those obligations derived from law and custom, which necessitated the delivery to landlord and Church of a part of the yield of every harvest. The champions of reform took the position that, at a time when all other agricultural transactions were being put on a money basis, it would be desirable to include these burdens as well. For twenty years some of the states, Saxony in particular, had wrestled with the countless legal and financial problems that this change involved, and had evolved certain principles and practices which were accepted models. But until 1848 other states had hesitated to take the step.

The uprisings of that year began among artisans and laborers in the cities. They could hope for success only if the rural population, angered by the lagging course of agrarian reform, would join forces with them. Fully aware of the danger, kings, dukes and ministers of state hastened to give the agricultural element all that it asked. Legislators were summoned, bills were laid before the deputies, and by the close of the year they were adopted. This legislation provided ways and means of commuting payments in kind into gold and silver and of capitalizing them at fifteen or twenty years' money payments. He who would be free need only pay to the lord this capital sum. Since even thrifty Germans did not have that much money and no existing institutions of agricultural credit could provide it, the legislation established official land banks for lending the necessary amounts in return for mortgages on the property concerned. To this bank the peasant owed an annual payment which in the course of time discharged all his obligations of principal and interest.[48]

This was a deliberate adjustment to the spirit of the age which, if all had continued normal, would have been hailed as one of the great victories of peaceful revolution. But neither the present nor the immediate future proved to be normal. The money market was disturbed by the political shocks in every center of finance; crops which formed the only possible sources of repayment failed to maintain an average yield; and the ardor with which all rushed to mortgage their lands belied the traditional caution of the German farmer. The Irish tenant had a new landlord to whom he owed his annual rent; the German peasant had obtained a new master whose yearly demands would be enforced by the strong arm of an impersonal institution. For both the Irish and the Germans tragic days lay ahead.

Athwart this confused European scene events in California cast a golden glow early in 1849 as tales of fabulous fortunes made overnight spread rapidly from port to port and village to village. Among those who embarked on the long voyage round the Horn were young gentlemen whose hands had never known toil, poets who expected to record the exploits of the argonauts, obscure men from remote communities hungry for far adventure. Not only Germans and Irish, but Swedes, French, Bohemians and Danes — people of almost every nationality — succumbed to the contagion. All of them found excitement, some of them gold; but otherwise they accomplished surprisingly little. They were not typical of the multitudes of plain men who during the next decade were to bring their families to the labors and hardships of the pioneer West. They opened no new paths of migration, started no continuing exodus, and most of them ultimately returned, in poverty or wealth, to the homes they had left.[49]

In even greater numbers the Americans thronged to California, trekking across the plains or struggling through the jungles of Panama or sailing round Cape Horn. For every one who departed, business and industry in the older parts of the country had to discover a substitute; and the able-bodied European, no matter what his trade or his tongue, found a place awaiting him. Factories, shipyards and labor contractors hung out the sign, "Help wanted"; and if the immigrant disliked the city and its slums, he could obtain employment in the household of a farmer whose "hired hand" had slipped off to California.[50]

Other influences also speeded the westward movement of the native population and made opportunities for the foreign arrivals. The territorial acquisitions of the Mexican War, the Mormon occupation of Utah, the flourishing settlements in the valleys of Oregon, aroused the American public to a vision of new lands of promise which were theirs to possess. Moreover, the war brought the inevitable demand for a "bonus," to which Congress responded in 1847 by granting every veteran, even if he had served only in a local militia company, one hundred and sixty acres of land in any part of the public domain.[51] Every section of the country contributed to the westward-moving tide. The Old South sent its sons to occupy the new cotton lands of the Southwest, and the New England farmers poured down from their hills into the fertile prairies.

The European immigrant did not have the means to become a plantation capitalist, nor the desire to till the stony farm lands of Connecticut and Vermont. But in the Old Northwest many a British, German and Norwegian farmer found just the lands and establishments that he sought, and with the modest capital he had hoarded he took possession. Forty or eighty acres of mingled forest, meadow and cultivated fields, a frame house and a log barn with a well and an orchard, satisfied the deepest cravings of his heart and his ambitions for his posterity. Whenever a farmer of Ohio, Indiana or Wisconsin loaded his wagon and set out toward the Mississippi, it usually meant that a foreign family would soon take his place.[52]

Still other opportunities came to the immigrant as a result of the opening up of northern Michigan. This region had hitherto suffered a strange neglect. Climate, water, taxes and soil had all borne the blame for this aversion, but probably the lack of any natural communication with the interior of the peninsula was the chief reason. Settlement had been limited to patches along the shore line and to the neighborhood of the historic trail connecting Detroit with Chicago. When this road was paralleled with the rails of the Michigan Central and branch lines reached their fingers up toward the big woods in the north, the old fears vanished. The fifties beheld a northward movement of the population of Michigan, creating bargains in farm lands for European newcomers in the southern tiers of counties.[53]

Similar openings occurred in northern Pennsylvania and

southern New York as a result of the building of the Erie
Railroad — a short cut between the lower Hudson and the
waters of the Great Lakes. Before this time many fertile
valleys in the mountains had been only sparsely peopled
because of the difficulties of transportation. Now, as the
tunnels of the Erie cut through the mountains and its bridges
spanned the valleys, the lands attracted eager settlers, including immigrants whose savings from work in the cities at
last enabled them to achieve their fondest ambition. This
undeveloped country, lying at the door of half a dozen cities,
was as far toward the frontier as most of them desired to
venture; and it was a common opinion that, judged by results, they fared better than many who went farther into the
interior.[54]

Farms for those who wanted farms, work for those who
had no capital but their hands — this was what mid-century
America offered those for whom Europe could find no place.
The stage was set for the greatest migration the world had
ever known.

XIII

THE GREAT MIGRATION

TO MANY OF THE MIGRATIONS in ancient and modern times the adjective, "great," has been applied. It aptly characterizes that westward movement of Europeans which began with the discovery of the New World and has continued until our era. More narrowly, it describes the rush of people into the United States in the century following the close of the Napoleonic wars. In these pages it denotes an even more restricted period — the years from 1850 to 1860 when something like 2,600,000 aliens poured into the country and the foreign-born inhabitants increased from 2,244,600 to well over 4,000,000. The number of Irish grew from 962,000 to 1,611,000, of Germans from 584,000 to 1,276,000, of English from 279,000 to 433,500, of French from 54,000 to 110,000, of Swiss from 13,000 to 53,000, and of Scandinavians from 18,000 to 72,500 or probably more.[1] This migration was great in comparison with the native American population, great in the trails of settlement it broke, great in the cultural foundations it laid. Subsequent decades were to see a larger volume of arrivals, but no later migration paid richer dividends to American civilization.

In Ireland more emigrants departed in 1851 than in 1850, while the year 1852 established a record that stood for all time.[2] "The poor law is the great and permanent depopulator of Ireland," declared an editorial writer.[3] The burden of the poor rates diminished but little from year to year.[4] Although the men who had flocked into the workhouses at the height of the calamity were gradually drained off by death and emigration, they left their wives and children behind. Those who betook themselves out of the island usually sent for their families after two or three years, and this caused a reduction in expense; but an appallingly large number of orphan children remained a public charge. As they grew in age and appetite, the cost of their maintenance increased, and ratepayers could anticipate little relief for perhaps a decade. The continued strain at last broke many farmers who at first had hoped to weather the storm. Though prices and markets improved, the extra charge consumed the expected profit.[5] With every year a more comfortable class gave up the struggle to join the exodus across the Atlantic.

In many unions the farmers sought to solve their difficulties by subsidizing the transportation of paupers. Although the immediate outlay was great, the plan involved an ultimate economy. The system would have been applied much more widely had not protests poured in from the ports of the United States and Canada. The few shillings which the parish put in the emigrant's hands supported him for less than a week after arrival.[6] He had no friends to help adjust him to the new life. He lacked the initiative and energy of the newcomer who paid his own way. From being a pauper in Ireland he became a pauper in America.

More successful was the assistance extended to emigrants by those who wanted them to come instead of those who wanted them to go. Despite the evidence of bankers, clergymen and others, no one knows with even approximate certainty the amount of these personal remittances; but the increasing effectiveness of this form of help is clear. American currency inclosed in a letter, a draft sent in care of the parish priest, an order upon a shipping firm of Liverpool — each contributed a part of the total.[7] The young man sent out by the pooled resources of his family discharged the obligation at the earliest possible moment, knowing that the sooner it was done the more brilliant his former neighbors would deem his success. Therefore he took the first job that came to hand, accepted whatever wages were offered and lodged in the cheapest rooms. His low standard of living antagonized native American workers, yet in many cases it was prompted by this spirit of self-sacrifice.[8] By 1854 some commentators went so far as to assert that the process of "sending for relatives" was the sole explanation of the continuance of emigration.[9]

Certainly by that time the original causes had spent their force. The tenant known as the "small holder" in the old régime had disappeared. The landlord who had formerly leased patches of from four to ten acres now maintained farms of from twenty to fifty.[10] The cottier who had resigned himself to the status of laborer had no trouble in finding work. As early as the harvest season of 1851 complaints began arising of a shortage of hands. In 1852 farmers paid a wage which few could remember had ever been equaled; in 1853 the difficulty of securing extra help delayed the gathering of crops; and in 1854 the demand was so great "as almost to require solicitation hat in hand."[11]

Even the potato regained its position as a dependable and popular food. At first with hesitation, then with growing confidence, the small farmers planted the root. In spite of their betrayal in the recent past, it formed an indispensable part of their way of life. They looked upon turnips, grazing and wheat and all the other new-fangled notions that government and journalism urged upon them as merely a last resort, to be discarded as soon as Nature smiled again. Though every July brought its alarm and a considerable proportion of the crop continued to suffer from the pernicious disease, its virulence gradually diminished; and when the planting of 1853 yielded a healthy and abundant supply, even the skeptical seemed convinced. "There's meat and drink in them this year," said a tenant whom a landlord had interrupted at his work. The next spring, carefully hoarded savings went into the purchase of seeds, and a breadth of potato land was sown that recalled the years before 1846.[12]

In spite of this steady improvement emigration continued. Critics explained it as a mania that had afflicted the people. Certainly no one could escape the ever present reminders: handbills of the shipping agents distributed wherever crowds assembled, notices of sailings on the billboards, personal letters that kept the interest alive.[13] The higher wages only made fulfillment possible. If conditions at home were good, elsewhere they were better. The emigrants merely did what seemed rational — what many had done so successfully before them.[14] Not all of them went to America, however. As early as 1852 a congestion of unskilled laborers was reported in the Eastern cities of the United States and this fact, coupled with the growing nativist movement in such centers, may have had something to do with increasing the number of persons who settled in the busy manufacturing districts of Lancashire. The attractions there were not unlike those which beckoned them to the industrial regions of America.[15]

In England also the reasons for emigration tended to become less acute after the first few years of the decade. The complete ruin of agriculture, so freely prophesied, did not take place. At first, however, it seemed as if the worst would happen. In 1851 thousands of yeoman farmers, tired of the struggle with low prices and high rents, left for America.[16] But in 1852, with local prospects no better, the hope held out to agriculturists by Australia, combined with the lure of gold discoveries there, shifted this current to a land under the British flag which they could reach with little more cost than was necessary for transporting a family to the interior of the United States.[17] The demand for ships in this distant trade withdrew many vessels from the Atlantic lanes with a consequent rise of the price of passage to American shores.[18] The

stimulus of Australian gold also quickened the lagging manufactures of England, and this in turn aided the farmer by
increasing the food demands of the urban wage-earners. So
the farmer took hope and resumed his improvements; and
at harvest time he looked in vain for the bands of reapers who
had formerly begged for work. He had to pay higher wages;
the laborers were cheerful and well-fed; and in the general
improvement of conditions the poorhouses lost many of their
women and children.[19] By 1854 scarcity of help rather than
redundancy formed the problem of rural England. No
longer was emigration indispensable as the only means of
procuring employment and bread, though, of course, other
reasons for emigration remained.[20]

In Germany conditions were less favorable for the farming
population. In 1850 emigration temporarily declined, a fact
which the American consuls in the country ascribed to the
continuing difficulty of peasants in disposing of their property.[21] The disturbed state of domestic politics, the uncertainty of the grain market, the unsettled questions of foreign
policy with their constant threat of war, rendered impossible
the sale of real estate at what had hitherto been considered
a fair valuation. Only those left who were willing to sell their
lands at a sacrifice.

The next few years, however, brought such discouragement that increasing numbers of peasants were willing to
dispose of their holdings at any price. Germany had escaped
the catastrophe that ravaged Ireland only because its economic structure did not rest so exclusively upon a single
crop. But like the Irish cottier, the peasant along the upper
Rhine clung tenaciously to his field of potatoes; and in the
seasons following 1848 his hope and despair varied with the
success of his carefully cultivated patch. The excellent harvest of 1849 brightened his hopes; the widely extended planting of 1850, yielding little more than the seed, returned him

to despair. As a result, only a third of the normal acreage was planted the next year in many places with an outcome no more encouraging. The crop in 1852, however, restored confidence in the potato; and when the season of 1853 again proved satisfactory, the people generally considered their troubles over.[22] Other crops also had fared poorly. In 1850 the yield of rye proved discouraging and the wine of poor quality; and in 1852 the results were no better.[23] During the next two years disease and pests, hailstorms and floods ruined whatever prospects the early months of summer had offered. Only with the autumn of 1854 did the agricultural crisis end.[24]

Artisans and mechanics also suffered acutely from the uncertainty of the times. Revolution had disturbed internal trade; rumors of wars limited exports; the rural poverty cut down the home market. The brightest hope of industry lay in the future of the Zollverein; but that future depended largely upon the course of foreign affairs, and Austria's growing jealousy of the increasing commercial strength of her neighbor boded ill. Though accurate statistics of the occupations of the emigrant are lacking, the opinions of those concerned with their transportation and some fragmentary figures kept by agencies and bureaus indicate that a greater proportion of skilled laborers than hitherto turned to America as a haven.[25]

In the meantime the problems of scarcity and poverty had burdened every administrative officer and every charitable organization. Crowds of beggars traveled the highways, reminding observers of the grim scenes of 1846–1847. The winter that followed the harvest of 1851 was notably harsh in its effects because of the shortage of both grain and potatoes. Only the most vigorous efforts of relief kept famine away from industrial cities and rural villages.[26] That Germany should go the way of Ireland and the agricultural population perish of starvation seemed a not impossible outcome. The fortunate recovery of the potato from 1852 on removed this specter.

Nevertheless the credit of the small farmers cracked under the strain, and the financial ruin harried them out of Germany as ruthlessly as though actual starvation confronted them. The indebtedness which in the early fifties rested upon this class is traceable to three sources. In the first place, many of them were involved in mortgages from the years before 1845 when an abundance of capital and low rates of interest had encouraged extensive and often reckless improvements. In the second place, many farmers in the hard times between 1845 and 1847 had saved themselves only by piling up debts which they found impossible to shake off before greater disaster overcame them in 1851–1852. Finally, the annual payments they had assumed after 1848 in order to free themselves from feudal obligations were no less a threat because due to the government.

Just as necessity forced the Irish tenant to default in the payment of his rent, the German peasant could not meet his notes; and just as eviction "cleared" the Irish countryside, foreclosure put German lands up to forced sale and sent the owners across the sea.[27] In many cases, perhaps in the majority, the father did not await this last disgrace. Realizing his impending fate, he saved both self-respect and a remnant of his possessions by selling his land at any price he could get, effecting an honorable agreement with his creditors, and then taking his family of stalwart sons to the American West.[28] That he set out upon the journey not entirely devoid of capital illustrates another parallel between the German and Irish migration.

Despair in Europe, hope in America: these two attitudes, the one complementary to the other, overcame any lingering doubts the German emigrant may have felt as to the wisdom of his course.[29] The events of the day intensified the distrust which had been born during the political reaction. Never did the commune's regulation of personal and business affairs seem so heavy as when times were hard and individual ingenuity was not allowed to find a way out. The kaleidoscopic changes in France that turned a Napoleon into a president and the president into an emperor raised grave apprehensions as to the future peace of Europe. Would Germany fall victim to that upsurge of chauvinism?

Such considerations, however, exerted less influence than the increasing volume of personal letters which arrived each year as the number of German settlers in America enlarged.[30] A passenger who mingled with the travelers in the steerage asked one after the other why he had left the fatherland. Without exception each took from his pocket a letter from a brother, cousin, son, daughter, friend or acquaintance, and handing it to him said, "Read this." [31] Such letters painted shadows as well as lights, disappointments as well as successes, but universally the writers declared they had no desire to give up the new for the sake of returning to the old.[32]

The peak of the German emigration was attained in the years 1853 and 1854. Although peasant farmers predominated, other ranks of society, high and low, figured in the movement. Among them were the poor, sent out at the expense of the communes to which they belonged, or perhaps subsidized by the government when the local organization could not meet the charge. Most of the states along the upper Rhine made appropriations for this purpose, though the size of the amounts indicates that only in unusual cases was this source available.[33] Baden developed a system of state, local and individual coöperation which assisted the annual departure of a few hundreds.[34] American objections, however, limited the scope of such efforts. Of the horde of

Germans who emigrated during the decade only a few thousands can be described as paupers.

At the other extreme were families not merely in comfortable circumstances but unquestionably wealthy.[35] Neither hunger, financial ruin, nor political disaffection impelled them to leave. Rather, they represented one aspect of that migration of capital that always accompanies a migration of labor. They saw in America the possibility of multiplying a fortune measured in thousands to one of millions. In part also they reflected the intensity of the distrust with which many people judged the social and political future of Europe. Many of them, however, were merely responding to the current craze, being intent on getting off because everyone else was going.

Of the prevalence of that craze there can be no question. Emigration represented the cure for all ills, private and public. The decision to depart was entered upon with a lightheartedness that little comported with the traditional stolidity of the German householder. According to a newspaper correspondent, one night the thought entered the peasant's mind that emigration might be a desirable step; the next day he talked it over with his friends and each strengthened the resolution of the other; on the morning of the third day they all engaged passage.[36] A thirteen-year-old boy shouldered his pack and set out on foot for Le Havre, determined to avail himself of the opportunities of the new land even if his parents remained at home.[37] Old people, however, were not immune to the fever and, despite the manifest difficulties of adjustment, undertook the adventure in the hope that they might enjoy a few years of unsullied happiness.[38]

The governments reversed their attitude of a decade before when they had looked upon every emigrant as a national loss and had hindered departure by a multitude of regulations. A strong motive was doubtless the belief that a "bloodletting" would preclude a revival of social disorders. Among the concessions made in 1848–1849 was a simplification of all the legal formalities which preceded emigration. In the interests of military defense, however, the authorities kept an eye

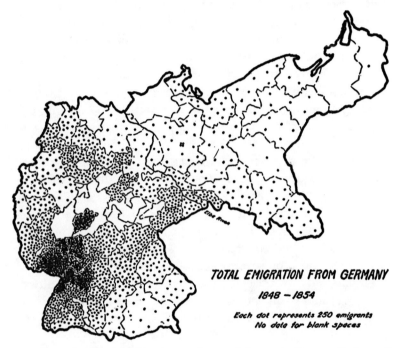

TOTAL EMIGRATION FROM GERMANY

1848 – 1854

Each dot represents 250 emigrants
No data for blank spaces

on the young men whose services might soon be needed; and as the horizon clouded with the first threats that were to culminate in the Crimean War, the efforts became more active.[39] But it was easy for the person who wanted to avoid this obligation to slip over the Rhine into France where passport formalities were more or less perfunctory; and the long newspaper lists of those who failed to respond to the call for military registration indicate the popularity of this way of escape.[40] Only via Hamburg and Bremen were the difficulties serious. These cities, anxious to keep on good terms with the officials of the interior states, instituted a strict police supervision over prospective passengers and reported the suspects to the respective consuls.[41]

On the other hand, the German governments took protective measures on behalf of emigrants through supervising the activities of the agents. Though the business of these men was lucrative, it involved many risks and might entail much suffering for those with whom they dealt. The secret of success consisted in keeping a proper balance between the number of ships that the agent hired and the number of passengers with whom he made contracts.[42] When this balance was disturbed, as often happened, he usually sought the quickest way out by hastily turning emigrant himself. In order to counteract such abuses, most states now licensed agents, demanding a heavy bond as a guarantee against default, and they prohibited certain practices such as the sale of "through tickets" into the interior of the United States on the ground that they lacked means of punishing breaches of contract on the American side.[43] So strong was the competition among the several agencies that they also improved their methods by adopting a system of couriers for guiding the emigrants from the villages to the ports and thus seeing them through the first and often most difficult stage of the journey.[44]

Large numbers continued to travel by way of Le Havre, thanks to the enterprise of the businessmen there. When the Hanseatic cities, with their efficient agencies and their arguments of better service, began to attract the south German traffic which Le Havre had always considered its own, the shippers at the French port demanded aid from the government. Their case was strengthened by the fact that the continued development of cotton manufacturing required the cheapest possible transportation of the raw fiber to the factories, an object which could be accomplished only through the retention of the passenger trade. Therefore the state railways granted reduced fares to emigrants, ranging from a third to a half of the customary charge, and ran special trains during the spring season.[45] As a result of these concessions, Le Havre retained a large share of the German trade and an almost complete monopoly of the Swiss. It also fell heir to much of the emigration down the Rhine, which, unable to find accommodations at Antwerp, continued by coast steamer to the French port. Efforts made by the Belgian government to develop its merchant marine by stimulating the passenger traffic failed because of the nature of its transatlantic connections.[46]

It was, however, at Hamburg and Bremen that the trade in human beings, which many moralists of the time reprobated as a shameful business, really centered. The completion of several important links in the rail connections of these ports with the interior occurred just as the great movement began, and in the contest to secure passengers special trains and reduced rates played a part. One circumstance rendered this achievement more difficult than in the case of the French. The railroads were Prussian and Saxon, and the good will of these governments was essential. On the whole, coöperation was achieved, although in 1853 the Saxon authorities declined to grant a desired reduction on the ground that far too many encouragements to emigration already existed.[47]

On the days preceding the regular sailings on the first and fifteenth of every month the streets of Bremen and the banks of the Weser bustled with confusion. The town was not large and its inns were neither commodious nor many. To expect hotels to be constructed for the sake of two months' patronage was out of the question; and therefore the merchants erected a special lodging house at Bremerhaven. For a generation it was a model of its kind and the last roof that sheltered many of the emigrants on Europe's soil.[48] As a further assistance to the travelers, the municipal authorities sponsored a society which maintained booths at the railroad station, the river dock and the market place, where lists of rooming houses were posted and bewildered peasants were given advice.[49] Often five thousand passengers arrived and disappeared in forty-eight hours. Their coming and going were handled with a dispatch that illustrates how businesslike the arrangements had become.[50]

The chief difficulties at Hamburg sprang from the inability of the shippers to provide space for the incoming throngs who, having no contract, acted on the belief that in a harbor crowded with ships there was always room for one more. Only a small part of Hamburg's merchant ships, however, were bound for the United States, and the packets catered to cabin passengers. The situation gave an impetus to the construction of vessels, but this was too tardy a solution to take care of the immediate need.[51] As a result, the merchants forwarded the surplus passengers by way of England, a route already well established and one capable of indefinite expansion.

For this trade the merchants of Liverpool were more than eager. The prosperity of that city was so closely bound up with the carriage of emigrants that the shippers viewed with growing apprehension the inevitable decline of the Irish exodus. In the Hamburg connection they saw a means of tapping new reservoirs of humanity. In the winter of 1851–1852 the campaign got under way. Hundreds of agents were appointed throughout the German hinterland with the promise of a liberal commission for every contract made.[52] Public houses were flooded with broadsides, and newspapers were enlisted in the cause. This propaganda focused on a vigorous attack upon Bremen, stressing the length of the journey as compared with the passage by steam over the North Sea, by rail through England and the shorter ocean crossing from Liverpool.[53] The counterattack, which quickly appeared, emphasized the many chances for deception that transshipment made possible and painted the dangers inherent in a trip across the Atlantic in the company of Irishmen.[54] Though every succeeding year provided an abundance of personal incidents in confirmation of these warnings, the English companies, for the time being, had the advantage. The increasing emigration via Hamburg yielded a rich toll to Liverpool.

But the growing patronage of this route stemmed only in part from propaganda. A new emigration was getting started while the old was yet at its height, and for these people from the plains of northern Germany Hamburg was the obvious port. Great numbers came from the provinces of Schleswig and Holstein where the defeated soldiers in the Three Years' War, though granted a general pardon, could expect no promising future at home. Groups of officers and men formed natural traveling companions; and their compact settlement in eastern Iowa was long known as New Holstein. With them went farmers worried by the war's aftermath of taxes, and agricultural laborers rendered desperate by a deepening depression.[55] These latter held no land, enjoyed but few rights in the common and derived a scanty income from working on the lord's estate. When the hard times blanketed these old grain-exporting regions of the north, there was no commune to help the people, and the lord had no legal obligations in the matter. In Mecklenburg conditions were particularly bad: the percentage of the unemployed was great and their resources were small. Medieval laws of settlement and the fact that all trades were controlled by local monopolies prevented a natural redistribution of the population.[56] Unfortunately the repeal of the English corn laws had had little beneficial effect because of

the war and the general European scarcity; and by the beginning of the fifties competition with more fertile acres
was being felt.[57]

A "landlords' panic" not unlike that which struck England and Ireland seized the rural nobility. Seeking to reduce
expenses, they exacted every possible service from their economic vassals, and encouraged those to leave of whom they
had no need. Since neighboring estates and villages would
not receive them, there was only one place for them to go —
America. Thus began a movement which increased in intensity during the decade and continued with almost unabated
force even when other parts of Germany showed a decline.[58]
How they obtained the means is obscure. Unlike the peasants
of the southwest, they had no land to sell and their personal
possessions were few. In many cases, especially at first, the
lords paid the fare; and as these emigrants began to earn
money, they extended help to those behind.[59] Such family
assistance must have been generous because in many places
the emigration comprehended almost as large a proportion
of the inhabitants as in Ireland, causing the landlords to
change their complaint from overpopulation to excessive
wages.[60] In the neighboring Prussian province of Pomerania
a few districts witnessed a similar outpouring; and to the
south, in Hanover and Oldenburg, the condition of the grain
farmers accelerated a current already running strong.[61]

Of the Continental emigration during the 1850's fully
ninety per cent originated in those states and principalities
that later comprised the German Empire. The other ten per
cent derived from the countries bordering on Germany.
The movement from these latter regions resulted in part
from conditions that mirrored on a smaller scale the agrarian
situation in the fatherland, and in part it was the outgrowth
of local developments. Switzerland offered the closest parallel to the German situation. In the valleys and mountains

that sloped down toward the Rhine the people had experienced similar conditions: a growing rural population and agricultural indebtedness, hasty agrarian reform and political disturbances, crop shortages and financial distress.

In two respects, however, the Swiss emigration was distinctive. One was the systematic resort to subsidization. Legislative councils discussed ways and means, and the newspapers reported the departure of the groups.[62] The American consul at Basel insisted that the practice was employed as a means of getting rid of paupers,[63] but the Swiss authorities denied the charge. Almost every commune possessed a mountain pasture or a plot of woodland jointly owned by the inhabitants, and impoverished persons who desired to depart were given a sum which was supposed to represent the purchase price of the rights they relinquished.[64] Though doubtless only a subterfuge, the device gave the transaction an air of respectability, and was not without a psychological effect upon the individuals. The second characteristic, though less important, involved action by the federal union itself. Plans of colonization had continued to be agitated in Switzerland despite the discouraging outcome of the attempts made at New Freiburg in Brazil and New Glarus in Wisconsin. Though the general government still refused to aid such schemes either with money or through diplomatic channels, it did understand the desirability of official guidance and protection and therefore stationed an agent at Le Havre to whom persons in distress might appeal.[65]

Despite the fact that geographically the peninsula and islands of Denmark are a continuation of the north German plain, the rural evolution of the preceding century had been different there. The agricultural laborers enjoyed a more secure position, and for only a little more than a decade had the farmers taken an interest in the possibilities of the English grain market. The repeal of the corn laws therefore meant opportunity rather than deflation; and when the war ended in 1851, they turned with energy to exploiting the new trade openings. Improvement was the order of the day — better agriculture and better roads. The city of Copenhagen, sharing the spirit of enterprise that swept all the Baltic coasts, entered upon a period of brisk development. Not only did work exist for every Dane in town and country, but newcomers from Sweden and Germany found ready employment.[66]

That emigration nevertheless occurred was hence not due to bad economic conditions.[67] It resulted from the advent of Mormon missionaries. Fifteen years before, when Mormon emissaries first reached England, many of the converts had chosen to join their coreligionists in Missouri and Illinois. Now that the Church was permanently established in the Valley of the Salt Lake where every acre demanded labor, the Mormon authorities adopted the colonization of converts as a systematic policy. Special attention was directed to northern Europe where workers in iron and stone as well as hardy farmers could be obtained. To this end two missionaries were sent in 1850 to Copenhagen, which was intended to serve as a base of operations for the three Scandinavian countries.[68] Though Denmark was at the time the only one of these states to permit Mormon preaching unmolested, legal freedom did not insure popular freedom. The missionaries were pelted with stones on the street, and converts were likely to find the windows of their homes broken.

But the religion had an appeal, as did also the descriptions of the paradise in the far-off mountains. In 1852 the first small band set out, and in the succeeding years conversion and emigration were almost synonymous.[69] By the spring of 1860 twelve organized parties numbering more than three thousand had started from Copenhagen, traveling via Hamburg and Liverpool. The majority paid their own expenses, but a few were aided by the Church's emigration fund. All profited from the special lodging accommodations in Hamburg and Liverpool, the chartered ships across the Atlantic, and the assistance of agents who welcomed them at New York and New Orleans. Though the Mormons encountered much greater difficulty in starting their work in Sweden, among the groups leaving Copenhagen were also occasional bands of Swedes.

For the most part, however, the emigration from that kingdom was of a more traditional nature. Internal religious dissension continued to be an important factor, so important and obvious that many commentators deemed it the only significant motive. As earlier, the bulk of the Swedish emigrants came from the north-central provinces, where the state Church vigorously combated nonconformity, and where the less fertile soil produced a recurrent scarcity and want that strengthened, and in some cases overshadowed, the complaints of ecclesiastical tyranny.[70] But when the movement made its appearance, as it did with increasing force, upon the fecund plains to the south, other explanations proved necessary; and contemporaries cited heavy taxation, the antiquated laws that governed land and labor, and the enthusiastic letters from settlers in the Mississippi Valley.[71] Among these, the last carried special weight, as the prosperity of the Swedish pioneers contrasted brightly with the bitter hardships they had first endured. During 1853 and 1854 the shippers of Göteborg were overwhelmed with people clamoring for passage. Since direct sailing vessels could not convey the throng, the overflow made their way via Hamburg or Hull to Liverpool.[72] As yet, however, the outpouring from Sweden, though great in the opinion of the startled officials, did not approach the proportions of a folk migration. That was to come twenty years later.

In the Norwegian part of the king's domains, however,

such a migration was already under way. As a result of the repeal of the English navigation acts, the new facilities offered by the Quebec route put the passenger trade on such a sure commercial footing that the captains engaged energetically in stirring up interest. They repeated encouraging reports of earlier Norwegian migrants and adduced confirmatory evidence in the many hopeful letters they brought back with them, while the newspapers also spread the tidings far and wide.[73] The rapid institutional development of the American settlements — the springing up of Norwegian churches, schools and newspapers — signified a social maturity which appealed to many who had hesitated to take their families into an unbroken wilderness. Now that a "secondary migration" was taking place and Norwegian settlers were shifting from northern Illinois and Wisconsin into Iowa and Minnesota, opportunities existed to buy cultivated farms within sight of the steeple of a Lutheran church.[74] The presence of ten vessels with outbound passengers at Kristiania Fjord in April, 1853, provided sufficient evidence that emigration no longer consisted of the sporadic departure of religious or political malcontents.[75]

As in other countries where the outgoing tide bore a high ratio to the population, the movement was given impetus by changes in the conditions of the most humble tillers of the soil. Recent times had not been easy for the *husmænd*, or cottiers. Their mountain-side clearings, stony and unfertile, had never produced more than a bare living. Now, three years of hunger left debts and dissatisfaction; no legislation had improved their lot; and their cottages thronged with sons who asked, "Where are we to find a few acres for our household?" [76] The answer came from across the Atlantic in the form of money and encouragement. The owners of Norwegian ships no longer needed to seek freights on every quay in Europe; they loaded their living cargoes in the home ports and landed them under the bluffs of Quebec, where commissioners of the state of Wisconsin saw them safely through the swarms of land agents and labor contractors.

To the southeast of Germany, in Austria-Hungary, emigration during the fifties came predominantly from the province of Bohemia. Gold seekers formed the van of the movement, yet it was not their path-breaking activities as much as the newly granted right of unrestricted departure that was responsible. The many bonds, commercial and intellectual, connecting Bohemia with Germany helped to disseminate the idea that emigration provided a cure for the troubles of agriculture and industry. But not many were affected, for the ten thousand Bohemians who sought the New World formed but a small proportion of the total population.[77] They were, however, the pioneers of the countless thousands who were to follow; and the location of their communities strongly influenced the future distribution of the stock in the United States.

All nationalities benefited from the improved conditions of ocean travel. Although perils remained, they were not such as might earlier have deterred the faint-hearted. Immediately after the repeal of the British navigation acts, the sailboat passenger trade reached its highest development. The westbound carriage of emigrants and the eastbound transportation of American staples were tied together in an international network of communication. The mechanical perfection of the ships and the expert seamanship of the crews made possible the establishment of schedules that reduced congestion in the European ports and facilitated distribution of the emigrants through the United States.[78] Some imaginative souls suggested that steam would replace sails and even the steerage traveler would spend only two weeks on the water. In less than two decades this revolution was to occur. For the time, however, the increasing number of transatlantic steamers exerted an influence only by turning the packets from their more select service to the emigrant trade and thereby providing better accommodations as well as stiffer competition.

Further improvement came from legislation. The British and American laws of 1848–1849 had banished absolute hunger and greatly reduced the danger of pestilence. But many discomforts and unsanitary conditions remained, a state of affairs which one did not need to be a Victorian to stigmatize as indecent. Two long parliamentary reports exposed the details of the shady side of life on board emigrant vessels; and the resulting act of 1855, with its specific regulations as to space, food and arrangements, long remained the controlling statute.[79]

The United States tightened its restrictions the same year. The abuses that had arisen were not due to lax enforcement of the older regulations. At Baltimore on one occasion eight vessels, and in New York eighteen, had been libeled and their captains fined. In other instances ships had been seized and sold.[80] It was the inadequacy of the legislation that was at fault. Marine architecture had made rapid strides; "three deckers," unheard-of in 1848, had been introduced, and there was perpetual controversy between shippers and custom-house officials regarding the interpretation of the provisions. Congress accordingly appointed a committee whose inquiries added to the catalogue of horrors; and a public meeting of the merchants of New York urged that the confusion be ended by law.[81] In 1855 Congress passed a comprehensive statute regulating the tonnage and space requirements in accordance with the number of decks and the intervening height.[82] To the aid of the British and American laws came the great commercial decline of 1855, which caused shippers out of self-interest to make conditions more attractive to passengers.

The thriving city at the mouth of the Hudson drew an

enlarging number of immigrant vessels to its spacious harbor. Increasingly, those embarking in Europe had no idea in mind but to get to New York, which they knew bore some sort of relationship to the rest of America.[83] Many ships destined to load cotton in New Orleans or timber at Quebec were obliged to heed the popular desire and first land their passengers in New York.[84] There were, however, two exceptions. The main body of the Norwegians reached the West by way of the St. Lawrence and the Great Lakes; and as a result the American figures for the decade give an inadequate notion of the size of the Norwegian immigration. Also, many Germans landed at New Orleans where the German Society, eager to get them out of the unhealthy quarters of the city, speeded their departure north.[85]

Some Americans — and not only land agents — urged that the South offered many opportunities which the Germans should seize. They had flourished in the Carolinas and Georgia in colonial days, why not in Texas and Tennessee now? [86] The twenty-five thousand who settled during the decade in Texas achieved a success comparable to that of their compatriots in the old Northwest; but Tennessee was another story. The speculations of a land company known as the Wartburg Colony disillusioned many who had invested their capital in it; and its failure discouraged other attempts at group settlement in the region.[87] In the South the immigrant who tried to make his own way encountered many hindrances: a roundabout line of communications, difficulty in buying the small amount of land that alone he could afford, and the presence of slavery — an objection the weight of which it is impossible to judge.[88]

In the face of these discouragements the main stream of German migration continued to flow along the channels already established. Its direction was due chiefly to geography and mass attraction, but conscious direction played a part.

After the failure of the colonization schemes of the forties German thought adjusted itself to the inevitable. Lovers of the fatherland adopted a new policy: facilitate the concentration of Germans in those parts of the United States where they are already numerous; keep sentiment alive by fostering churches, schools and intellectual bonds; then let the home country draw whatever profit it can from these commercial and cultural ties.[89] As a means to this end, the National Society for German Emigration was organized in 1847.[90] It printed a guidebook for general distribution, published a weekly journal for three years, and established local branches in Frankfurt, Leipzig and elsewhere. It also carried on activities in America, forming connections with existing German societies and prompting the establishment of new ones. By such means it kept up-to-date its information regarding routes, land and economic opportunities. After his arrival the immigrant could proceed from city to city, receiving advice at each stage.[91]

Irish societies also existed in many places, but they were local in organization and used their meager funds in the alleviation of distress. Had they desired to concentrate their fellow countrymen geographically, it is unlikely they could have accomplished much, for the distribution of the Irish depended upon the opportunities for work. On landing in Boston or New York the immigrant had nothing but his hands, and a visit to the labor contractor's office preceded his hunt for shelter or a meal. Obtaining a job, he left his family in a tenement room and went to Illinois or Maine, wherever his "gang" was sent. Sometimes he found the village or the countryside to his liking and, settling down as an odd-jobs man or occasionally as a farmer's helper, he sent for his family. More often he returned to the city where church and companions reproduced the pleasant social life of the old country and where he might find factory employment.

Unfortunately, the boisterous urban life of the 1850's placed few restraints upon convivial drinking, and Irish intemperance shocked staid Americans who made no allowance for the laborious and frugal existence which most of these immigrants led. The Irish also competed with native workers for jobs, and offended further because of their attachment to a religion which was traditionally distrusted and feared in America. These factors are usually accounted the reasons for the growing antiforeign feeling that culminated in the Know-Nothing agitation of 1852–1856. But to them must be added American resentment at the attempts made by refugees to embroil the country in the various European political quarrels and the religious reaction against the atheism which many German liberals flaunted in the sight of churchgoers. Legislators went to the state assemblies with bills to protect American labor; Congressmen took to Washington proposals for drastic changes in the naturalization laws; and workmen evidenced their displeasure by rioting and violence whenever elections, picnics, funerals or fires brought them into contact with the immigrants.

This intolerance contributed to halving the incoming tide in 1855, but other factors were more fundamental. In 1854 immigration had reached a volume not to be equaled again until 1873. Nearly four hundred and twenty-eight thousand foreigners entered the United States. The labor market was well-stocked before the first spring ships arrived; and despite the effect of the Crimean War in reducing Atlantic shipping and thus raising the price of transportation, vast numbers landed in the succeeding months.[92] Having paid a higher fare than they had planned, many were unable to move farther and added to the congestion in the coast cities. To make matters worse, a sharp contraction took place in business as news from the West reported a drought and then a general shortage in the wheat and corn crops.[93] If agriculture were to fail, railroad construction and other improvements must cease. Hence back to the cities poured the discharged laborers to crowd into the already overflowing slums and to increase the wrath of the Know Nothings.

Little wonder that the hopeful arrivals of the year longed for the security of the old home; and many of those who could afford it actually returned.[94] No record of these departures was kept, but by February an unofficial estimate placed the total at six per cent of the immigration of the preceding season.[95] The first-hand accounts they took back with them and the information culled from letters were seized upon by governments that had been alarmed by the magnitude of the 1854 emigration. Prussia distributed thousands of handbills publicizing the distress of its misguided subjects, and Saxony plastered the street corners with placards that reported the Know-Nothing riots in which Germans fell as victims.[96]

In any case, the war situation in Europe would have discouraged emigration in 1855. Every ship not engaged in importing necessities from America was needed for carrying troops and provisions through the Mediterranean to the Crimean battle-fields. The transatlantic fares rose to unheard-of heights, far beyond the purses of those classes that had always supplied the largest contingent to the exodus. Moreover, recruiting parties in every Irish village offered more adventures in the British army than even the American West promised. Although the German states were still clear of war entanglements, nervousness about the future made them keep an unusually watchful eye upon every able-bodied man of military age. To slip away was no longer possible.[97] Norway and Sweden experienced the prosperity that always falls to neutrals; and with Russian wheat off the market, the English farmers and their tenants enjoyed good prices. Every economic motive for departing had been suspended. Though peace returned in the spring of 1856, the armies had to be brought back home, and the high prices continued throughout the summer. Emigration to America remained at the level of 1855.

But with the opening of the season of 1857 the emigrant ships were back on the usual routes; agents were again at work. Innkeepers and land promoters were happy, and ports on both sides of the Atlantic resumed their usual bustle. Large groups departed in the spring, and over two hundred and fifty thousand landed in America before the year closed. The increase in numbers would have been far greater except for the fact that the summer brought discouraging news from the United States. The war in Europe had halted the business recession in America only to prepare the way for a greater collapse. The overexpansion and overfinancing of the years before 1854 inflicted the customary penalty of a commercial and agricultural depression. The year 1857 beheld a repetition of the scenes of 1819 and 1837: wage cuts, unemployment, hunger demonstrations. European governments did not need to warn their people against leaving, for every letter and every newspaper dispatch told of the disaster.

The great mid-century movement slowed to a halt. In 1858 the number of arrivals fell off a half and continued at that level the next year with a slight pick-up in 1860. Those who came consisted largely of separated families reuniting in a new home and of persons joining their former neighbors in the Western prairies.[98] On both sides of the Atlantic the Great Migration had done its work. In Ireland and Germany prosperity had replaced rural poverty, and cheerfulness reigned where gloom and dread had once held sway.[99] Two million new Americans, in the factory and on the farm, built their hopes into the future of their adopted country. Hardships were many and disappointments not few; but they confidently peered into the future, little dreaming of the impending conflict between North and South in which their arms were to bear so noble a part.

The four years of bloody strife destroyed not only the old South but also, in a less obvious way, the varied immigrant America of the North. The Civil War changed the ideals of the foreign group and substituted a new leadership. Immigrant homes were filled to overflowing with young people when the war began. Sons joined the regiments and went to the front, if not because of patriotism, then because it was good business: bounties and promises of land. When that happened, parents spent less time thinking about the far-off land of their fathers, more in thinking about the land of their children. Dreams of the past gave way to the realities of the present. Immigrant newspapers subordinated news of the Old World to dispatches from the battle lines, while clergymen neglected ancient theological differences in order to minister religion to persons stricken with sorrow. Editors and clergymen who failed to conform lost prestige and following. When the war ended, foreign languages and foreign customs had not disappeared, but ideals had changed. All who lived in America, alien-born and native-born, were resolved to become one people.

BIBLIOGRAPHY AND NOTES

BIBLIOGRAPHY AND NOTES

THIS VOLUME is based on a wide variety of first-hand materials most of which are unavailable in the United States. The principal sources consist of unprinted archival records, official and private correspondence, government reports and contemporaneous newspapers, magazines and books. Among the more important European newspapers are, for Germany: the *Abendzeitung* (Dresden), the *Agronomische Zeitung* (Leipzig), the *Allgemeine Auswanderungs Zeitung* (Rudolstadt), the *Allgemeine Preussische Staats-Zeitung* (Berlin), the *Allgemeine Zeitung* (Augsburg), the *Allgemeine Zeitung für die deutschen Land- und Forstwirthe* (Berlin), the *Bremer Handelsblatt*, the *Deutsche Tribüne* (Munich), the *Freisinnige* (Nuremberg), the *Kölnische Zeitung*, the *Leipziger Allgemeine Zeitung*, the *Morgenblatt für gebildete Stände* (or *Leser*) (Stuttgart), the *Münchener Politische Zeitung*, the *Neckar Zeitung*, the *Weser Zeitung* (Bremen) and the *Zollvereinsblatt* (Stuttgart); for Great Britain: the *Australasian Record and Indian Observer* (London), the *Emigrant and Colonial Advocate* (London), the *Emigration Gazette, and Colonial Settlers' Universal Guide* (London), the *Emigration Record and Colonial Journal* (London), the *Hull Advertiser and Exchange Gazette*, the *London Chronicle*, the *Mark Lane Express* (London) and the *Times* (London); for Ireland: *Carrick's Morning Post* (Dublin), the *Dublin Mercantile Advertiser*, the *Dublin Morning Post*, the *Dublin Penny Journal*, the *Farmer's Gazette* (Dublin), the *Freeman's Journal* (Dublin), the *Galway Free Press*, the *Leinster Express* (Maryborough), the *Londonderry Sentinel*, the *Newry Telegraph*, the *Sligo Journal* and the *World* (Dublin); and for Switzerland: the *Baseler Zeitung*, the *Gazette de Lausanne* and the *Neue Zürcher Zeitung*. The relevant archival materials, collections of letters, public documents and other sources are listed in the footnotes in connection with the particular subject under discussion. There, too, will be found references to some of the more significant monographic treatments as well as to general historical works.

CHAPTER I. THE WESTWARD IMPULSE

1. *Allgemeine Zeitung* (Augsburg), Dec. 9, 1816.

2. See, for example, Harry Jerome, *Migration and Business Cycles* (N. Y., 1926).

3. On this whole matter, see R. R. Kuczynski, "Population: History and Statistics," *Encyclopaedia of the Social Sciences*, XII, 240–248, and the references he cites.

4. O. D. Lütken, *Untersøgninger angaaende Statens almindelige Oeconomie* (Sorøe, 1760), 87.

CHAPTER II. THE PEOPLING OF THE COLONIES

1. Richard Hakluyt, *A Discourse on Western Planting* (*Documentary History of the State of Maine*, II; Cambridge, 1877), 21.

2. *A Century of Population Growth* (Wash., 1909), 9.

3. H. L. Osgood, *The American Colonies in the Seventeenth Century* (N. Y., 1904–1907), I, 58–59.

4. Captain John Smith, *Travels and Works* (Edward Arber and A. G. Bradley, eds., Edinburgh, 1910), I, 263.

5. Alexander Brown, *The First Republic in America* (Boston, 1898), 106; J. A. Williamson, *The Caribbee Islands under the Proprietary Patents* (London, 1926), 7.

6. Smith, *Travels*, II, 444.

7. Brown, *First Republic*, 97, 172.

8. C. M. Andrews, *The Colonial Period of American History* (New Haven, 1934–1938), I, 123–124.

9. Virginia Company of London, *Records* (Susan M. Kingsbury, ed., Wash., 1906–1935), I, 34, 269.

10. Virginia Company, *Records*, I, 566.

11. Brown, *First Republic*, 243.

12. Brown, *First Republic*, 275–276; Virginia Company, *Records*, I, 95.

13. Virginia Company, *Records*, I, 57.

14. E. I. McCormac, *White Servitude in Maryland, 1634–1820* (Balt., 1904), 11–14.

15. *Ibid.*, 29.

16. *America and West Indies, 1574–1660* (*Calendar of State Papers, Colonial Series*, London, 1860–1939, I), 137, 174, 180, 266.

17. John Winthrop, *The History of New England from 1630 to 1649* (James Savage, ed., Boston, 1853), 206.

18. Governor and Company of the Massachusetts Bay, *Records* (N. B. Shurtleff, ed., Boston, 1853–1854), I, 109, 123.

19. Melville Egleston, *The Land System of the New England Colonies* (Balt., 1886), 48; Winthrop, *History of New England*, I, 278; Governor and Company of Massachusetts, *Records*, I, 83, 196, 228.

20. Colony of Rhode Island and Providence Plantations in New England, *Records* (J. R. Bartlett, ed., Providence, 1856–1865), I, 28, 53.

21. Colony and Plantations of New Haven, *Records, 1638–1649* (C. J. Hoadley, ed., Hartford, 1857), 25, 28–29, 35, 38, 40.

22. Winthrop, *History of New England*, II, 37.

23. *Ibid.*, I, 399; II, 8, 21, 25, 103.

24. T. J. Wertenbaker, *Patrician and Plebeian in Virginia* (Charlottesville, 1910).

25. "Colonial History Debunked," *Tyler's Quar. Hist. and Geneal. Mag.*, VIII (1927), 3–4.

26. "Land Certificates for Northampton County," *Va. Mag. of Hist. and Biog.*, XXVIII (1920), 142–151.

27. John Burk, *The History of Virginia from Its First Settlement to the Present Day* (Petersburg, Va., 1805), II, 87.

28. Virginia Company, *Records*, I, 25.

29. Smith, *Travels*, I, 263.

30. *America and West Indies, 1574–1660*, 30, 31, 37; McCormac, *White Servitude*, 9.

31. *America and West Indies, 1574–1660*, 19.

32. Contemporary extracts on Virginia history, 1650–1656, *Va. Mag. of Hist. and Biog.*, XVII (1909), 279, 360; XVIII (1910), 49.

33. "Virginia in 1656–1658," *ibid.*, XVIII, 151; *America and West Indies, 1574–1660*, 412, 447.

34. *America and West Indies, 1697–1698* (Calendar of State Papers, Colonial Series, XVI), 1.

35. Governor and Company of Massachusetts, *Records*, III, 415.

36. *Ibid.*, III, 415; IV, pt. i, 308, 385.

37. Conway Robinson, "Notes from the Council and General Court Records," *Va. Mag. of Hist. and Biog.*, VIII (1900–1901), 166.

38. Colony of Rhode Island, *Records*, I, 377.

312   BIBLIOGRAPHY AND NOTES

39. *The Winthrop Papers* (Mass. Hist. Soc., *Colls.*, ser. 5, VIII, 1882), pt. iv, 67–68.

40. *America and West Indies, 1677–1680* (*Calendar of State Papers, Colonial Series*, X), 529.

41. *Ibid.*, 577.

42. *Winthrop Papers*, pt. iv, 450.

43. *America and West Indies, 1689–1692* (*Calendar of State Papers, Colonial Series*, XIII), 40.

44. Andrews, *Colonial Period of American History*, IV, 159, 231.

45. *America and West Indies* (*Calendar of State Papers, Colonial Series*): *1661–1668* (V), 559; *1669–1674* (VII), 144, 257; *1677–1680*, 491; *1681–1685* (XI), 105, 294; *1697–1698*, 554.

46. *Ibid.*, *1681–1685*, 372.

47. *Ibid.*, *1677–1680*, 311.

48. V. T. Harlow, *A History of Barbados, 1625–1685* (Oxford, 1926), 301; *America and West Indies, 1661–1668*, 220, 555; *1693–1696* (*Calendar of State Papers, Colonial Series*, XIV), 182.

49. *America and West Indies, 1681–1685*, 430; McCormac, *White Servitude*, 17, 21–23, 33–34, 46.

50. *America and West Indies, 1669–1674*, 58.

51. James Ford and others, *Slums and Housing* (Cambridge, 1936), I, 26–27.

52. *America and West Indies, 1669–1674*, 17, 526.

53. R. P. Powell, "Transportation and Travel in Colonial New Jersey," N. J. Hist. Soc., *Procs.*, n. s., XVI (1931), 285.

54. E. C. Stokes, "The Quakers and Early Citizens of Burlington," *ibid.*, XIII (1928), 172–173, 175; G. S. Pryde, "The Scots in East New Jersey," *ibid.*, XV (1930), 1–39; A. V. D. Honeyman, "The Early Scotch Element of Somerset, Middlesex and Monmouth Counties," *Somerset County Hist. Quar.*, VI (1917), 1–23.

55. *America and West Indies, 1685–1688* (*Calendar of State Papers, Colonial Series*, XII), 327; *1689–1692*, 201, 266; *1693–1696*, 119.

56. *Ibid.*, *1669–1674*, 40.

57. *Ibid.*, *1669–1674*, 324; *1675–1676* (*Calendar of State Papers, Colonial Series*, IX), 240; *1677–1680*, 360; *1681–1685*, 131.

58. *Ibid.*, *1675–1676*, 238; *1681–1685*, 338–339, 510; *1685–1688*, 92, 233; *1689–1692*, 331.

59. Harlow, *History of Barbados*, 36, 42, 44; Williamson, *Caribbee Islands*, 10, 21, 38, 66–67.

60. Williamson, *Caribbee Islands*, 183–184.

61. Harlow, *History of Barbados*, 45.

62. *Ibid.*, 42–44, 292, 309, 338; Williamson, *Caribbee Islands*, 154; *America and West Indies, 1661–1668*, 529; *1675–1676*, 421–422; *1696–1697* (*Calendar of State Papers, Colonial Series*, XV), 392.

63. *America and West Indies, 1661–1668*, 153; *1669–1674*, 86, 88, 90, 92, 124, 132, 278, 295; *1677–1680*, 619.

64. A. C. Gregg, "The Land Policy and System of the Penn Family in Early Pennsylvania," *Western Pa. Hist. Mag.*, VI (1923), 151, 153–154, 156–158; Marcia C. Bready, "The Colonists of William Penn," *ibid.*, V (1922), 259–261; Robert Proud, *The History of Pennsylvania, in North America* (Phila., 1797–1798), I, 191, 216, 218–220, 229, 304.

65. *America and West Indies, 1689–1692*, 201, 266; *1693–1696*, 630, 651; *1696–1697*, 2, 11–12, 420–421.

66. McCormac, *White Servitude*, 17, 21–22, 46; *America and West Indies, 1696–1697*, 422.

67. McCormac, *White Servitude*, 22, 26; *America and West Indies, 1681–1685*, 430; *1696–1697*, 646; *1697–1698*, 9, 389.

68. Virginia Company, *Records*, I, 251, 368, 392, 466, 499, 633.

69. *America and West Indies, 1574–1660*, 26.

70. McCormac, *White Servitude*, 29.

71. *America and West Indies, 1574–1660*, 113.

72. *Ibid., 1689–1692*, 368.

73. A. H. Hirsch, *The Huguenots of Colonial South Carolina* (Durham, 1928), chs. ii, iv, viii–ix; *America and West Indies, 1661–1668*, 350; *1677–1680*, 336, 364, 428; *1685–1688*, 179, 322, 398; Province of Massachusetts Bay, *Acts and Resolves, Public and Private* (Boston, 1869–1922), I, 90.

74. Commissioners for Trade and Plantations, *Journal, 1704–1708/09*, 26, 28, 32, 35, 37, 42, 58, 60, 63, 65, 98, 226, 230, 232, 518; *1708/09–1714/15*, 319, 443; "A General View of the Conduct of the French in America," *Gentleman's Mag.* (London), XXV (1755), 17.

75. Oscar Kuhns, *The German and Swiss Settlements of Colonial Pennsylvania* (N. Y., 1914), 49–51, 53–54, 57; Provincial Council of Pennsylvania, *Minutes* (Phila., 1851–1852), III, 322.

76. C. A. Herrick, *White Servitude in Pennsylvania* (Phila., 1921), is a general study of the redemptioner system in the colony of its greatest development.

77. J. P. MacLean, *An Historical Account of the Settlements of Scotch Highlanders* (Cleveland, 1900), 102, 105, 107–108, 176, 442;

South Carolina. Resources and Population. Institutions and Industries (Charleston, 1883), 383.

78. H. J. Ford, *The Scotch Irish in America* (Princeton, 1915), 186–192, 229–233, 247–248.

79. C. K. Bolton, *Scotch Irish Pioneers in Ulster and America* (Boston, 1910), 180–181.

80. S. G. Fisher, *The Making of Pennsylvania* (Phila., 1896), 162–165; J. T. Adams, *Provincial Society, 1690–1763* (N. Y., 1927), 172.

81. S. C. Johnson, *A History of Emigration from the United Kingdom to North America, 1763–1912* (London, 1913), 1–3.

CHAPTER III.   THE FIRST AMERICANIZATION

1. *Journals of Congress* (Phila., 1800–1801), X, 118–123.

2. 25 Geo. III, ch. 67.

3. E. J. Lowell, *The Hessians and the Other German Auxiliaries of Great Britain in the Revolutionary War* (N. Y., 1884), 20–21, 285–291; A. B. Faust, *The German Element in the United States* (rev. edn., N. Y., 1927), I, 349–356.

4. D. J. Ryan, "The Scioto Company and Its Purchase," Ohio Archaeol. and Hist. Soc., *Publs.*, III (1890), 122–123; T. T. Belote, ed., "Selections from the Gallipolis Papers," Hist. and Philos. Soc. of Ohio, *Quar. Publ.*, II, no. 2 (1907), 60, 62, 79.

5. *U. S. Statutes at Large*, I, 103–104.

6. *Ibid.*, 474.

7. Alexander Hamilton, Papers (Library of Congress), VIII, 1073, is an example of a plea for transportation.

8. Hamilton, Papers, XI, 1395–1396.

9. One such letter may be found in Hamilton, Papers, XII, 1597–1599.

10. Alexander Hamilton, *Works* (J. A. Hamilton, ed., N. Y., 1851), III, 192 ff.

11. Gouverneur Morris, *Diary and Letters* (Anne C. Morris, ed., London, 1889), I, 19, 260–261, 324, 342.

12. Belote, "Selections from Gallipolis Papers," 60, 62.

13. W. H. Smith, ed., *The St. Clair Papers* (Cin., 1882), II, 190–191, 195, 206–207; J. B. McMaster, *A History of the People of the United States* (N. Y., 1883–1913), II, 147–151.

14. J. F. Watson, ed., *Annals of Philadelphia and Pennsylvania in the Olden Times* (Phila., 1870), I, 181–182; [William Sullivan], *Familiar*

Letters on Public Characters, and Public Events (Boston, 1834), 126; Samuel Breck, *Recollections* (H. E. Scudder, ed., Phila., 1877), 196.

15. Moreau de Saint Méry, *Voyage aux États-Unis de l'Amérique, 1793–1798* (S. L. Mims, ed., New Haven, 1913), 55, 66, 89, 285–286, 294; Duc de la Rochefoucault Liancourt, *Travels through the United States of North America* (London, 1799), II, 462, 668.

16. Rochefoucault Liancourt, *Travels*, I, 45, 50, 54, 582, 584; II, 250; Isaac Weld, *Travels through the States of North America* (4th edn., London, 1800), 132–133; Watson, *Annals*, II, 41–42.

17. J. T. Rutt, *Life and Correspondence of Joseph Priestley* (London, 1832), II, 228, 239, 244, 300; Dumas Malone, *The Public Life of Thomas Cooper, 1783–1839* (New Haven, 1926), 80–81; Rochefoucault Liancourt, *Travels*, I, 74, 76; Anne Holt, *A Life of Joseph Priestley* (London, 1931), 144–188.

18. J. T. Scharf, *History of Westchester Co., N. Y.* (Phila., 1886), II, 338.

19. C. G. Sommers, *Memoir of the Rev. John Stanford, D. D.* (N. Y., 1835), 349; J. T. Griffith, *Rev. Morgan John Rhys* (Lansford, Pa., 1899), 11; note on Thomas Evans in *Bye-Gones, Relating to Wales and the Border Counties* (Oswestry), n. s., X (1907–1908), 321.

20. "A Sketch of the Life of William Jones," *Cambrian Register* (London), II (1796), 247–251.

21. B. W. Chidlaw, *An Historical Sketch of Paddy's Run, Butler Co., Ohio* (Hamilton, 1876), 1, 4–5; Isaac Smucker, *History of the Welsh Settlements in Licking Co., Ohio* (Newark, n.d.), 4, 12; M. M. Bagg, *The Pioneers of Utica* (Utica, 1877), 133–135; Griffith, *Rhys*, 60–61, 63, 65; E. W. Jones, "The Early Welsh Settlers of Oneida County," Oneida Hist. Soc., *Trans.*, no. 5 (1889–1892), 61, 63.

22. Rochefoucault Liancourt, *Travels*, I, 130; P. D. Evans, "The Pulteney Purchase," N. Y. Hist. Assoc., *Quar. Jour.*, III (1922), 90.

23. Robert Morris, Private Letter Book (Library of Congress), I, 253–254.

24. Louise W. Murray, *The Story of Some French Refugees and Their "Azilum"* (2nd edn., n.p., 1917), 20, 47, 55, 57, 60; J. W. Ingham, *A Short History of Asylum, Pennsylvania* (n.p., 1916), 20, 65; W. H. Egle, *An Illustrated History of the Commonwealth of Pennsylvania* (Phila., 1880), 424–426; D. von Bülow, *Der Freistaat von Nordamerika in seinem neuesten Zustand* (Berlin, 1797), I, 67.

25. F. B. Hough, *A History of Lewis County in the State of New York* (Albany, 1860), 34–73, 78, 104.

26. M. A. Leeson, *History of the Counties of McKean, Elk and Forest* (Chicago, 1890), 443; same author, *History of the Counties of McKean, Elk, Cameron and Potter* (Chicago, 1890), 227; R. B. Stone, *McKean, the Governor's County* (N. Y., 1926), 33; Egle, *History of Pennsylvania*, 925–926.

27. Morris, Private Letter Book, I, 12, 15, 18, 81, 133–134, 232.

28. Weld, *Travels*, 284–285.

29. Rutt, *Priestley*, II, 371, 373.

30. Watson, *Annals*, III, 257.

31. Rufus King, *Life and Correspondence* (C. R. King, ed., N. Y., 1894–1900), II, 635–647.

32. *Shamrock* (N. Y.), May 4, 1816.

33. W. G. Bleyer, *Main Currents in the History of American Journalism* (Boston, 1927), 127–128.

34. *U. S. Statutes at Large*, I, 103–104, 414.

35. *Ibid.*, 566.

36. *Ibid.*, 570–571, 596–597.

37. *Bell's Weekly Messenger* (London), Jan. 10, 1802.

38. *U. S. Statutes at Large*, II, 153–155.

39. *Paulson's American Daily Advertiser* (Phila.), June 16, July 3, 21, Aug. 24, 1801; John Lambert, *Travels through Canada and the United States of North America* (3rd edn., London, 1816), 147; C. W. Janson, *The Stranger in America* (London, 1807), 452.

40. *Bell's Weekly Messenger*, July 11, Oct. 3, 1802.

41. *Belfast Monthly Magazine*, II (1809), 75, 155, 254, 405, 485; W. S. Mason, *A Statistical Account, or Parochial Survey of Ireland* (Dublin, 1814–1819), I, 272–273.

42. 43 Geo. III, ch. 56.

43. *Shamrock*, July 6, 1811.

44. Adelaide L. Fries, tr., "Account of the Journey of Br. and Sr. Ludwig v. Schweinitz from Herrnhut to Bethlehem in Pennsylvania," *Pa. Mag. of Hist. and Biog.*, XLVI (1922), 312–333.

45. *Shamrock*, Sept. 14, 1812; *Irish Magazine and Monthly Asylum for Neglected Biography* (Dublin, 1812), 95, 530–531.

46. *Shamrock*, Oct. 24, 1812.

47. *Lutherans in Berks County* (n.p., n.d.), 29; A. B. Benson and Naboth Hedin, eds., *Swedes in America, 1638–1938* (New Haven, 1938), 52–54, 58.

48. H. A. Stoutenburgh, *A Documentary History of the Dutch Congregation of Oyster Bay* (N. Y., 1902), 39; Henry Onderdonk, *History of the First Reformed Dutch Church of Jamaica, L. I.* (Jamaica, 1884), 75; B. C. Taylor, *Annals of the Classis of Bergen of the Reformed Dutch Church* (3rd edn., N. Y., 1857), 26, 130, 168, 305; *A History of the Classis of Paramus of the Reformed Church in America* (N. Y., 1902), 71; G. S. Roberts, *Old Schenectady* (Schenectady, 1904), 88–89; General Synod of the Reformed Protestant Dutch Church in North America, *Acts and Proceedings* (N. Y., 1859), I, 257.

49. Ralph Le Fevre, *History of New Paltz, New York* (Albany, 1903), 59; Daniel Van Winkle, *Old Bergen, History and Reminiscences* (Jersey City, 1902), 318–319; B. M. Brink, *The Early History of Saugerties* (Kingston, 1902), 119; G. L. Vanderbilt, *The Social History of Flatbush* (N. Y., 1881), 54–55; "The Passing of the Dutch Language," *Olde Ulster* (Kingston, N. Y.), X (1914), 111–114.

50. J. Nicum, *Geschichte des Evangelisch-Lutherischen Ministeriums vom Staate New York* (N. Y., 1888), 33.

51. G. D. Bernheim, *History of the German Settlements and of the Lutheran Church in North and South Carolina* (Phila., 1872), 359, 365, 384, 406, 409, 420, 432; C. W. Cassell, W. J. Finck and E. O. Hankel, eds., *History of the Lutheran Church in Virginia and East Tennessee* (Strasburg, Va., 1930), 23.

52. A. Spaeth, H. E. Jacobs and G. F. Spieker, eds., *Documentary History of the Evangelical Lutheran Ministerium of Pennsylvania and Adjacent States* (Phila., 1898), 342, 344, 352; *Evangelisches Magazin, unter der Aufsicht der Deutschen Evangelisch-Lutherischen Synode* (Phila.), I (1811–1812), 106.

53. Spaeth and others, *Documentary History*, 353.

54. Watson, *Annals*, III, 313.

55. Spaeth and others, *Documentary History*, 438; *Evangelisches Magazin*, II (1812–1813), 8.

56. G. J. Krotel, ed., *Memorial Volume of the Evangelical Lutheran Church of the Holy Trinity, Lancaster, Pa.* (Lancaster, 1861), 87.

57. E. F. Humphrey, *Nationalism and Religion in America, 1774–1789* (Boston, 1924).

58. Annual Conferences of the Methodist Episcopal Church, *Minutes* (N. Y., 1840), I, 21.

59. General Synod of the Reformed Protestant Dutch Church, *Acts and Proceedings*, I, 360.

60. Spaeth and others, *Documentary History*, 195, 444, 539.

61. General Assembly of the Presbyterian Church in the United States, *Acts and Proceedings for 1798*, 7–9; *for 1799*, 8–9, 16–18. See also T. L. Birch, *Seemingly Experimental Religion, Instructors Unexperienced — Converters Unconverted — Revivals Killing Religion — Missionaries in Need of Teaching — or, War against the Gospel by Its Friends* (Wash., 1806), 33–36.

62. U. S. Bureau of Statistics, *Special Report on Immigration* (Wash., 1872), v.

CHAPTER IV. A NEW BEGINNING

1. W. F. Adams, *Ireland and Irish Emigration to the New World from 1815 to the Famine* (New Haven, 1932), 72.

2. Adams, *Ireland and Irish Emigration*, 70–71.

3. Charles Pedley, *The History of Newfoundland from the Earliest Times to the Year 1860* (London, 1863), 289, 304–305; Adams, *Ireland and Irish Emigration*, 71, 109–110.

4. *Niles' Weekly Register*, VIII (1815), 245, 320; IX (1815–1816), 150, 258, 299.

5. 55 Geo. III, ch. 26.

6. Joseph Pickering, *Emigration or No Emigration; Being the Narrative of the Author (an English Farmer) from the Year 1824 to 1830* (London, 1830), 1; *Farmer's Magazine* (Edinburgh), XVII (1816), 257, 381; XVIII (1817), 119; XXII (1821), 144.

7. *Gazette de Lausanne*, June 28, 1816; Ruprecht Zollikofer, *Der Osten meines Vaterlands oder die Kantone St. Gallen und Appenzell im Hungerjahre 1817* (St. Gallen, 1818), 189.

8. "Traité de paix signé entre la France et l'Autriche et ses alliés," G. F. de Martens, ed., *Nouveau recueil de traités d'alliance, de paix, de trève* (Gottingue, 1817–1842), II, 9.

9. Marion D. Learned, *Guide to the Manuscript Materials Relating to American History in the German State Archives* (Wash., 1912), 49, lists a great number of documents bearing on this emigration.

10. *Times* (London), March 24, 1817; "Neu-Schweizerland in Nord-Amerika," *Schweizerische Monathschronik* (Zurich), I (1816), 30–32, 45–48; H. C. E. von Gagern, *Mein Antheil an der Politik* (Stuttgart, 1823–1845), III, 146.

11. Eugen Philippovich, *Auswanderung und Auswanderungspolitik in Deutschland* (Leipzig, 1892), 109–110.

12. Christian Eckert, "Rheinschiffahrt im XIX Jahrhundert," *Staats- und socialwissenschaftliche Forschungen*, XVIII (Leipzig, 1900), pt. v, 198.

13. *Gazette de Lausanne*, May 24, 1816.

14. Helen I. Cowan, *British Emigration to British North America, 1783–1837* (Toronto, 1928), 66–74.

15. A. R. M. Lower, "Immigration and Settlement in Canada, 1812–1820," *Canadian Hist. Rev.*, III (1922), 45.

16. 43 Geo. III, ch. 56.

17. John Quincy Adams, *Writings* (W. C. Ford, ed., N. Y., 1913–1917), V, 526; VI, 54.

18. W. M. Malloy, comp., *Treaties, Conventions, International Acts, Protocols and Agreements between the United States of America and Other Powers, 1778–1909* (Wash., 1910), I, 624–627.

19. Adams, *Writings*, VI, 54–105; 56 Geo. III, ch. 114.

20. *Noble's Instructions to Emigrants* (Boston, Eng., 1819), 55.

21. *Niles' Weekly Register*, X (1816), 352, 431; XI (1816–1817), 208.

22. *Hull Advertiser and Exchange Gazette*, Aug. 17, 1816; *London Chronicle*, Oct. 10–11, 1815; *Niles' Weekly Register*, IX, 151, 258; X, 92, 316, 384; *Shamrock* (N. Y.), Dec. 30, 1815; J. S. Reeves, *The Napoleonic Exiles in America* (Balt., 1905), 9–10.

23. *Niles' Weekly Register*, X, 334, 401, 412.

24. *Ibid.*, XI, 115.

25. *Ibid.*, XX (1821), 192.

26. An Observer, *pseud.*, *A Review of the Trade and Commerce of New York from 1815 to the Present Time* (N. Y., 1820), 29; John Palmer, *Journal of Travels in the United States of North America and in Lower Canada Performed in the Year 1817* (London, 1818), 26, 34; *Niles' Weekly Register*, VIII, 234; IX, 171; *Carrick's Morning Post* (Dublin), June 24, 1818; *Amerika, dargestellt durch sich selbst* (Leipzig), no. 20, Aug. 1818; no. 23, March 1819.

27. John Melish, *Travels through the United States of America* (Belfast, 1818), 622; John Bristed, *America and Her Resources* (London, 1818), 387.

28. Adams, *Ireland and Irish Emigration*, 87.

29. *Ibid.*, 89.

30. *Shamrock*, Aug. 3, 17, Dec. 7, 1816. The volume of advice published by the society is *Hints to Emigrants from Europe, Who Intend to Make a Permanent Residence in the United States* (London, 1817).

31. F. O. to J. Buchanan, Dec. 4, 1816, F. O. (Foreign Office, Great Britain) 5/116.

32. Letter of J. Buchanan, Nov. 5, 1817, *ibid.*, 5/125.

33. *London Chronicle*, Sept. 19–20, Oct. 1–2, 19–21, 1816; April 22–23, July 19–21, Aug. 7–8, 1817.

34. Adams, *Writings*, VI, 89.

35. *Farmer's Magazine*, XVII (1816), 483–484, 491, 495, 500; XVIII (1817), 121.

36. F. Barker, *Medical Report of the House of Recovery and Fever-Hospital in Cork-Street, Dublin* (Dublin, 1818), 6, 44; William Harty, *An Historic Sketch of the Causes, Progress, Extent, and Mortality of the Contagious Fever Epidemic in Ireland during the Years 1817, 1818, and 1819* (Dublin, 1820), 113, 115.

37. *Allgemeine Zeitung* (Augsburg), July 14, 25, Aug. 12, 1816; [J. U. Buechler], *Land- und Seereisen eines St. Gallischen Kantonsbürgers nach Nordamerika und Westindien* (St. Gallen, 1820), 10; Wilhelm Sandkaulen, *Das Notjahre 1816/17 mit besonderer Berücksichtigung der Verhältnisse am Niederrhein* (n.p., 1927), 5.

38. *Gazette de Lausanne*, March 28, 1817.

39. *Farmer's Magazine*, XVII (1817), 482.

40. *Allgemeine Zeitung*, Nov. 13, 1816; Jan. 14, Feb. 11, Nov. 29, 1817; "Theurung der Lebensmittel in Folge von Misswachs," *Deutsche Vierteljahrs Schrift* (Stuttgart), 1843, no. 4, 224, 226–227; Sandkaulen, *Das Notjahre 1816/17*.

41. Zollikofer, *Der Osten meines Vaterlands*, I, 9–11, 20, 48; *Neckar Zeitung*, March 1, 1828.

42. *Allgemeine Zeitung*, Feb. 22, April 6, Oct. 26, Nov. 30, 1816; Feb. 24, Oct. 22, 1817; Feb. 13, 1818; *Gazette de Lausanne*, May 13, 27, 1817.

43. *Morgenblatt für gebildete Stände* (Stuttgart), July 16, 19, Aug. 11, 1817; *Allgemeine Zeitung*, July 6, 1816; July 12, Aug. 15, 1817.

44. C. H. Smith, *The Coming of the Russian Mennonites* (Berne, Ind., 1927), ch. ii.

45. Amt der Auswärtigen Angelegenheiten (Department of Foreign Affairs, Prussian Archives, Berlin, hereafter cited as A. A.), III, R. (Repositur) I, Aus. gen. (Auswanderungen, Generalia) 2, Vol. II, no. 5276.

46. *Allgemeine Zeitung*, March 27, April 17, May 9, 29, 1817; *London Chronicle*, June 5–6, 14–16, 1817; *Gazette de Lausanne*, April 4, 1817.

47. A. A. III, R. I, Aus. gen. 2, Vol. II, nos. 5276, 5667.

48. *Gazette de Lausanne*, July 18, 1817; *Allgemeine Zeitung*, June 11, 1817; *London Chronicle*, June 14–16, 1817.

49. *Allgemeine Zeitung*, June 10, 1817; *Gazette de Lausanne*, June 13, 1817.

50. *Gazette de Lausanne*, July 15, 18, 1817; *Allgemeine Zeitung*, May 27, June 11, July 2, 1817; A. A. III, R. I, Aus. gen. 2, Vol. II, nos. 3747, 5276.

51. C. O. (Colonial Office, Great Britain) 384/1, 141–143, 315–348; 384/3, 1089–1090; *Niles' Weekly Register*, XII (1817), 185; XIII (1817–1818), 59; *Farmer's Magazine*, XVII (1817), 111; XVIII (1818), 222.

52. *Carrick's Morning Post*, March 5, 1818; Adams, *Ireland and Irish Emigration*, 79, 88–89, 92–94.

53. *Niles' Weekly Register*, XIII, 35.

54. *Ibid.*, 314, 360.

55. John Knight, *Important Extracts from Original and Recent Letters Written by Englishmen in U. S. of America to Their Friends in England* (Manchester, 1818), ser. 2, 41; James Flint, *Letters from America* (Edinburgh, 1822), 54; H. B. Fearon, *Sketches of America* (London, 1818), 198; Palmer, *Journal*, 15.

56. Francis Hall, *Travels in Canada and the United States* (London, 1818), 11; Palmer, *Journal*, 103; Fearon, *Sketches*, 228; *Carrick's Morning Post*, June 24, 1818.

57. Knight, *Important Extracts*, ser. 1, 12; ser. 2, 37; W. T. Harris, *Remarks Made during a Tour through the United States of America, in the Years 1817, 1818, and 1819* (London, 1821), 123, 143.

58. *Annals of Congress* (Wash., 1834–1856), XXX (14 Cong., 1 sess.), app., 1313–1314; P. J. Treat, *The National Land System, 1785–1820* (N. Y., 1910), 309. The members of the Society for the Vine and Olive are listed in 18 Cong., 2 sess., *House Exec. Doc.*, no. 87.

59. Treat, *National Land System*, 309–315; Reeves, *Napoleonic Exiles*, 35–36, 38, 42; *Abeille américaine, journal historique, politique et littéraire* (Phila.), IV, 239, 335; V, 130, 241, 277–284.

60. [L. F. L'Hériter], *Le Champ-d'Asile, tableau topographique et historique du Texas* (Paris, 1819), 15–16.

61. *Abeille américaine*, VI, 237, 333, 367; Hartmann and Millard, *Le Texas; ou Notice historique sur le Champ d'Asile* (Paris, 1819), *passim*.

62. *Moniteur universel* (Paris), Sept. 29, 1818; *London Chronicle*, Oct. 10–12, 1818; *Niles' Weekly Register*, XV (1818–1819), 80; *Amerika*, no. 6, Jan. 1819.

63. *Shamrock*, Jan. 25, 1817.

64. *Ibid.*, July 5, 1817.

65. *Niles' Weekly Register*, XIV (1818), 211–215.

66. 15 Cong., 1 sess., *House Doc.*, no. 119; *Annals of Congress*, XXXI (15 Cong., 1 sess.), 1013–1014, 1053–1054.

67. *Niles' Weekly Register*, XIV, 393; *National Intelligencer* (Wash.), Aug. 20, 1818; Morris Birkbeck, *Letters from Illinois* (Phila., 1818), 149–150.

68. C. W. Alvord, *Governor Edward Coles* (Springfield, Ill., 1920), 366–367.

69. Morris Birkbeck, *Notes on a Journey in America, from the Coast of Virginia to the Territory of Illinois* (Dublin, 1818), v–vii.

70. Birkbeck, *Letters*, 77, 147–149; Alvord, *Coles*, 140, 371.

71. George Flower, *History of the English Settlement in Edwards County, Illinois* (Chicago, 1882), 78; Alvord, *Coles*, 371.

72. J. E. Iglehart, "The Coming of the English to Indiana in 1817 and Their Hoosier Neighbors," *Ind. Mag. of Hist.*, XV (1919), 93, 104, 117.

73. *Ibid.*, 103–104.

74. *Moniteur universel*, Aug. 3, 1817; *Morgenblatt für gebildete Stände*, Aug. 29, 1818.

75. *Moniteur universel*, July 13, 1817; Gagern, *Mein Antheil an der Politik*, IV, 296; "Der deutsche Bundestag," *Chronik des neunzehnten Jahrhunderts* (Altona), XIV (1817), 110.

76. *Philadelphia Register and National Recorder*, I (1819), 317.

77. This letter is published in *Niles' Weekly Register*, XVIII (1820), 157–158.

78. There are two contemporary estimates which approximate this figure: Matthew Carey, *Essays on Political Economy* (Phila., 1822), 451–452; and *Niles' Weekly Register*, XVII (1819–1820), 36.

79. A. A. III, R. I, Aus. gen. 2, Vol. II, no. 96; *Allgemeine Zeitung*, Aug. 30, 1817.

80. *Carrick's Morning Post*, March 5, May 12, 1818; Melish, *Travels*, xi.

81. *Niles' Weekly Register*, XIV, 408; XV, 33; *Carrick's Morning Post*, May 12, 1818.

82. The laws which regulated the emigration of artisans and mechanics from Great Britain are: 5 Geo. I, ch. 27; 23 Geo. II, ch. 13; 22 Geo. III, ch. 60; 25 Geo. III, ch. 67.

83. C. O. 384/3, 985.

84. *Hints to Emigrants to the United States of America with Copious Extracts from the Journal of Thomas Hulme, Esq.* (Liverpool, 1817), 34; Robert Holditch, *The Emigrant's Guide to the United States of America* (London, 1818), 40.

85. Letter of George Manners, Nov. 7, 1818, F. O. 5/135; William Amphlett, *The Emigrant's Directory to the Western States of North America* (London, 1819), 39–40.

86. Knight, *Important Extracts*, ser. 2, 22; E. T. Freedley, *Philadelphia and Its Manufacturers* (Phila., 1859), 233, 252, 300.

87. Knight, *Important Extracts*, ser. 2, 21.

88. *Niles' Weekly Register*, XIV, 310; XV, 110–112, 139; *Carrick's Morning Post*, June 24, 1818.

89. *Carrick's Morning Post*, April 15, 1818; Adams, *Ireland and Irish Emigration*, 113.

90. *Carrick's Morning Post*, Feb. 18, 1819.

91. *Laws of Pennsylvania for 1820*, ch. 4803.

92. Lower, "Immigration and Settlement in Canada," 46.

93. *London Chronicle*, Sept. 8–9, 1818, gives the information as to terms of settlement in Canada. See also Cowan, *British Emigration*, 74–75.

94. C. O. 384/3 contains many letters from ex-soldiers who had served in Canada and now wished to settle there.

95. An Emigrant, *pseud.*, *Things as They Are, or America in 1819* (Manchester, 1819), 7; Eneas Mackenzie, *An Historical, Topographical and Descriptive View of the United States* (Newcastle-on-Tyne, 1819), 299; *Emigration Gazette, and Colonial Settlers' Universal Guide* (London), no. 9, Dec. 18, 1841.

96. *Niles' Weekly Register*, XV, 33; *National Intelligencer*, Sept. 15, 1818; Amphlett, *Emigrant's Directory*, 172; Flower, *History of English Settlement*, 94.

97. Alvord, *Coles*, 372; Flower, *History of English Settlement*, 287; Iglehart, "Coming of the English," 108.

98. [Francis W. D'Arusmont], *Views of Society and Manners in America* (N. Y., 1821), 191.

99. William Cobbett, *A Year's Residence in the United States of America* (3rd edn., London, 1822), 300–344.

100. Morris Birkbeck, *Extracts from a Supplementary Letter from the Illinois; an Address to British Emigrants; and a Reply to the Remarks of William Cobbett, Esq.* (2nd edn., London, 1819).

101. C. B. Johnson, *Letters from the British Settlement in Pennsylvania* (London, 1819), iv–v, 39, 116–128.

102. W. W. Egle, *An Illustrated History of the Commonwealth of Pennsylvania* (Harrisburg, 1876), 1100.

103. Emanuel Howitt, *Selections from Letters Written during a*

Tour through the United States in the Summer and Autumn of 1819 (Nottingham, 1820), 51, 53–54; F. C. Johnson, "Pioneer Physician of Wyoming Valley, 1771–1825," Wyom. Hist. and Geol. Soc., *Procs. and Colls.*, IX (1905), 96–98.

104. Ferdinand Ernst, *Bemerkungen auf einer Reise durch das Innere der Vereinigten Staaten von Nord-Amerika im Jahre 1819* (Hildesheim, 1820), 110; Newton Bateman and Paul Selby, *Historical Encyclopedia of Illinois and History of Fayette County* (Chicago, 1910), II, 621–622.

105. Herman Haupt, "Die geplante Gründung einer deutsch-amerikanischen Republik," *Deutsche Revue* (Stuttgart), XXXII (1907), no. 3, 117–118.

106. Flint, *Letters*, 40.

107. The most painful of these cases is that given in Fearon, *Sketches*, 342–344.

108. *Annals of Congress*, XXXIII (15 Cong., 2 sess.), 414–415.

109. *U. S. Statutes at Large*, III, 488–489.

110. Adams, *Ireland and Irish Emigration*, 103.

111. John Quincy Adams, *Memoirs* (C. F. Adams, ed., Phila., 1874–1877), IV, 349.

112. *Niles' Weekly Register*, XVI (1819), 286, 295, 298, 319, 336, 368, 419; XVII, 36, 63.

113. "Documents Accompanying the Report on the State of the Commonwealth," *Register of Pennsylvania*, IV (1829), 168.

114. *American State Papers — Finance* (Wash., 1858), IV, 28–223.

115. *Niles' Weekly Register*, XVI, 378.

116. *Laws of the State of New York Revised and Passed at the Thirty-Sixth Session of the Legislature* (Albany, 1813), II, 440–442.

117. Managers of the Society for the Prevention of Pauperism in the City of New-York, *Second Annual Report, Dec. 29, 1819* (N. Y., 1820), 57.

118. *Ibid.*, 58.

119. Ludwig Gall, *Meine Auswanderung nach den Vereinigten-Staaten in Nord-Amerika* (Trier, 1822), II, 110.

120. Letters of William Dawson, June 1, Sept. 1, 1819, George Manners, Feb. 4, 1819, and Gilbert Robertson, July 1, 1819, F. O. 5/144.

121. Letter of William Dawson, Sept. 1, 1819.

122. *London Chronicle*, Sept. 9–10, Oct. 9–11, 1819.

CHAPTER V. AMERICA IN DISFAVOR

1. Ludwig Gall, *Meine Auswanderung nach den Vereinigten-Staaten in Nord-Amerika* (Trier, 1822), II, 6.

2. *Ibid.*, 12.

3. Emanuel Howitt, *Selections from Letters Written during a Tour through the United States in the Summer and Autumn of 1819* (Nottingham, 1820), 217.

4. *Morgenblatt für gebildete Stände* (Stuttgart), Jan. 4, 1827; G. H. von Langsdorf, *Bemerkungen über Brasilien* (Heidelberg, 1821), 19–21.

5. John Pearson, *Notes Made during a Journey in 1821 in the United States of America* (London, 1822), 12.

6. *A Clear and Concise Statement of New York and the Surrounding Country* (N. Y., 1819), 27–30.

7. Managers of the Society for the Prevention of Pauperism in the City of New York, *Second Annual Report* (N. Y., 1820), 24.

8. *Allgemeine Zeitung* (Augsburg), Jan. 19, 1818; W. Hesse, *Rheinhessen in seiner Entwicklung von 1798 bis Ende 1834* (Mainz, 1835), 117.

9. Gottlieb Bauer, *Geschichte der deutschen Ansiedler an der Volga* (Saratov, 1908), 7–8, 10–16, 19, 21. Catherine (1762–1796) had colonized 75,000. A. Soulange-Bodin, "L'Avant-Guerre allemande en Russie," *Revue hebdomadaire* (Paris), 1917, pt. vi, 231.

10. *Gazette de Lausanne*, April 18, 1817; *Germania, Archiv zur Kenntniss des deutschen Elements in allen Ländern der Erde* (Frankfurt-am-Main), I (1847), 204.

11. "Die Russische Regierungspolitik inbezug auf die Einwanderung," *Baltische Monatsschrift* (Riga), LXXI (1911), 18, 20, 22; "Die deutschen Kolonien in Transkaukasien," *Weltpost* (Leipzig), III (1883), 44–46, 64–65.

12. Bachschi Ischchanian, *Die ausländischen Elemente in der russischen Volkswirtschaft* (Berlin, 1913), 37; Frida Bielschowsky, "Die Textilindustrie des Lodzer Rayons," *Staats- und sozialwissenschaftliche Forschungen*, no. 160 (Leipzig, 1912), 11; Rosa Luxemburg, *Die industrielle Entwicklung Polens* (Leipzig, 1898), 3–4.

13. Ischchanian, *Die ausländischen Elemente*, 38; M. von Koschitzky, *Deutsche Kolonialgeschichte* (Leipzig, 1887–1888), 79.

14. Adolf Eichler, *Die Deutschen in Kongresspolen* (Berlin, 1919), 3; Hildegarde Rosenthal, *Die Auswanderung aus Sachsen im 19. Jahrhundert* (Stuttgart, 1931), 63.

15. E. H. Busch, *Beiträge zur Geschichte und Statistik* (Leipzig, 1867), 209.

16. Ischchanian, *Die ausländischen Elemente*, 38; [N. I. Pavlischev], *Königreich Polen* (Leipzig, 1864), 74–75; *Gesellschafter, oder Blätter für Geist und Herz* (Berlin), Nov. 5, 1828.

17. Ischchanian, *Die ausländischen Elemente*, 39.

18. *Gazette de Lausanne*, Nov. 20, 27, 1818.

19. *Ibid.*, July 23, Aug. 7, 1819; *Morgenblatt für gebildete Stände*, June 19, 1819.

20. *Gazette de Lausanne*, Aug. 17, 31, Sept. 3, 1819.

21. *Morgenblatt für gebildete Stände*, July 14, Oct. 16, 1820.

22. *Ibid.*, April 1, June 28–29, 1820.

23. *Gazette de Lausanne*, May 1, Nov. 13, 1821; *Morgenblatt für gebildete Stände*, Oct. 20, 1821.

24. *Gazette de Lausanne*, Aug. 28, Sept. 18, Oct. 30, Nov. 9, Dec. 7, 1821; Jan. 18, Aug. 16, 1822; *Allgemeine Zeitung*, Nov. 20, 1821; *Morgenblatt für gebildete Stände*, Dec. 18, 1821; April 20, 1822.

25. *Allgemeine Preussische Staats-Zeitung* (Berlin), Feb. 10, 1824; *Morgenblatt für gebildete Stände*, June 26, 1824; Alexander Lips, *Statistik von Amerika* (Frankfurt-am-Main, 1828), 3.

26. James Cleghorn, *On the Depressed State of Agriculture* (Edinburgh, 1822), 137; *Allgemeine Zeitung*, Jan. 25, Aug. 16, Dec. 14, 1827.

27. Langsdorf, *Bemerkungen über Brasilien*, 6.

28. *Abendzeitung* (Dresden), March 5, 1828; *Gesellschafter*, June 2, 1826; *Allgemeine Zeitung*, Dec. 3, 1823.

29. *Abendzeitung*, Oct. 11, 1825; *Kölnische Zeitung*, Sept. 26, 1852; *Gesellschafter*, June 2, 1826.

30. A. A. III, R. I, Aus. gen. 2, Vol. III, no. 6650 (Hamburg, Nov. 28, 1824); *ibid.*, Vol. V, no. 89 (letter of President of Senate, Bremen, to Grote, May 7, 1828); Carl Schlichthorst, *Rio de Janeiro wie es ist* (Hanover, 1829), 17–18; Julius Mansfeldt, *Meine Reise nach Brasilien im Jahre 1826* (Magdeburg, 1828), 11–12.

31. A. A. III, R. I, Aus. gen. 2, Vol. IV, no. 5590 (Berlin, Oct. 17, 1825); *Gesellschafter*, June 3, 1826; Mansfeldt, *Meine Reise*, 18–19; *Allgemeine Preussiche Staats-Zeitung*, Jan. 31, 1826.

32. A. A. III, R. I, Aus. gen. 2, Vol. III, no. 6649; *ibid.*, Vol. V, no. 89.

33. *Carrick's Morning Post* (Dublin), July 17, 1817; *Morgenblatt für gebildete Stände*, Dec. 15, 1817.

34. *Dublin Morning Post*, July 5, Oct. 1, 1821; Jan. 1, June 1, July 26, Aug. 26, Oct. 7, 1822.

35. *Freeman's Journal* (Dublin), April 26, 1822; *Farmer's Magazine* (Edinburgh), XXIII (1822), 364; William Sturch, *The Grievances of Ireland* (London, 1826), 30.

36. [John Wiggins], *Hints to Irish Landlords* (London, 1824), 8.

37. Letters of Peter Robinson, June 9, 12, 14, July 6, 8, 1823, C. O. 384/12, 41–43, 46, 51, 93, 97.

38. Report of Peter Robinson, April 2, 1824, *ibid.*, 219, 221–222; letter from a magistrate at Passage West, May 2, 1825, *ibid.*, 384/13.

39. Letter of Peter Robinson, May 31, 1825, *ibid.*, 384/13, 501, 503, 515.

40. *Quebec Mercury*, Jan. 10, Aug. 26, 1826.

41. Select Committee on Emigration from the United Kingdom, *Report* (*Parliamentary Papers*, 1826, IV; 1826–1827, V).

42. 4 Geo. IV, ch. 84.

43. Petition of March 22, 1824, C. O. 384/10, 657–658; letter of March 6, 1824, *ibid.*, 384/12, 614–615; letter of March 16, 1827, *ibid.*, 384/16, 153.

44. The recorded statistics of the United States are to be found in 16 Cong., 2 sess., *Sen. Doc.*, no. 118; 17 Cong., 1 sess., *House Exec. Doc.*, no. 134; 17 Cong., 2 sess., *House Doc.*, no. 107; 18 Cong., 1 sess., *House Doc.*, no. 161; 18 Cong., 2 sess., *House Exec. Doc.*, no. 108; 19 Cong., 1 sess., *House Exec. Doc.*, no. 175; 19 Cong., 2 sess., *House Exec. Doc.*, no. 143.

CHAPTER VI. PIONEERS OF THE GREAT MIGRATION

1. Compiled from 20 Cong., 2 sess., *House Doc.*, no. 141.

2. Compiled from 22 Cong., 2 sess., *House Exec. Doc.*, no. 119.

3. *Allgemeine Zeitung* (Augsburg), Feb. 19, March 28, 1827; *Allgemeine Preussische Staats-Zeitung* (Berlin), Feb. 10, May 25, 1826; March 7–8, 1827.

4. *Allgemeine Preussische Staats-Zeitung*, Sept. 18, 1826; April 5, 1827; Jan. 18, 1828.

5. *Dublin Morning Post*, May 2, 1827.

6. Letter of A. C. Buchanan, April 21, 1828, C. O. 384/20, 469–470.

7. *Journal du Havre*, Jan. 24, 29, Feb. 3, 10, 21, March 3, 1829.

8. *Ibid.*, Oct. 1, 1828.

9. *Abendzeitung* (Dresden), April 15, 23, May 4, 1830.

10. *Sligo Observer*, June 24, 1830.

11. Carl Bösel, "Einwanderers Reiseabenteuer," *Deutsche Pionier* (Cincinnati), III (1871–1872), 215; "Das Hambacher Fest," *ibid.*, XIV

(1882–1883), 110–113; "Das Königreich Baiern im Jahre 1832," *Chronik des neunzehnten Jahrhunderts* (Leipzig), n. s., VII (1832), 313–321; "Das Königreich Baiern im Jahre 1833," *ibid.*, VIII (1833), 141.

12. *Leipziger Allgemeine Zeitung*, Oct. 14, 1846; *Allgemeine Zeitung*, June 7, Aug. 13, 1836; Heinrich von Martels, *Briefe über die westlichen Theile der Vereinigten Staaten von Nordamerika* (Osnabrück, 1834), 20; Heinrich Schmidt, *Die deutsche Flüchtlinge in der Schweiz* (Zurich, 1899), 17–21.

13. Gottfried Duden, *Bericht über eine Reise nach den westlichen Staaten Nordamerikas* (Elberfeld, 1829), 234–236, 326.

14. "Plan zur gemeinschaftlichen Auswanderung nach Nord-Amerika," *Columbus. Amerikanische Miscellen* (Hamburg), 1830, II, 446–451; D. H. Hupfeld, *Briefe eines deutschen Ausgewanderten aus Nordamerika besonders eine Ansiedlung in Alabama betreffend* (Machig, 1834), ix, 86; Martels, *Briefe über die westlichen Theile*, 3–4.

15. *Allgemeine Zeitung*, Dec. 24, 1830; March 19, June 13, July 21, 1831; *Morgenblatt für gebildete Stände* (Stuttgart), April 6–7, 1832; Fritz Hermann, "Maximilian Ludwig Proli, der Prophet von Offenbach," *Archiv für hessische Geschichte und Altertumskunde* (Darmstadt), n. s., XIII (1922), 202–265.

16. *Baseler Zeitung*, Dec. 22, 1832; *Kölnische Zeitung*, Aug. 6, 1833; letter of Ernest Schwendler, March 31, 1833, Consular Letters (Department of State, Washington, D. C.), Frankfort-on-the-Main, I (1829–1851).

17. A. A. III, R. I, Aus. gen. 2, Vol. VI, no. 4162 [*Aufforderung und Erklärung in betreff einer Auswanderung in grossen aus Deutschland in die nordamerikanischen Freistaaten* (Giessen, 1833), 6–7, 12–13, 15, 21, 23–24].

18. *Briefe von Deutschen aus Nord-Amerika mit besonderer Beziehung auf die Giessener Auswanderer-Gesellschaft vom Jahre 1834* (Altenburg, 1836), xii–xiii.

19. *Aufforderung und Erklärung*, 16; A. A. III, R. I., Aus. gen. 2, Vol. VII, no. 2979.

20. *Briefe von Deutschen aus Nord-Amerika*, xv.

21. *Ibid.*, xvi–xx, 60–61.

22. *Ibid.*, xxi–xxiii, xxv, 2, 6–8, 11–12, 15–17, 23, 32, 35.

23. *Die alte und die neue Welt* (Phila.), May 16, 1835.

24. *Kölnische Zeitung*, April 15, May 1, 1832; *Baseler Zeitung*, June 4, 18, 1832; *Hannoverisches Magazin*, Feb. 8, May 30, Dec. 26, 1832.

25. *Baseler Zeitung*, June 23, 25, July 26, 1832.

26. *Kölnische Zeitung,* May 9, 1832; *Allgemeine Zeitung,* May 28, July 17, 1832; *Journal du Havre,* Sept. 14, 1832; A. A. III, R. I, Aus. gen. 2, Vol. VI, no. 4182.

27. *Kölnische Zeitung,* May 24, 27, 1832; *Liverpool Commercial Chronicle,* May 5, 1832; *Journal du Havre,* April 2, 1832.

28. *Freisinnige* (Nuremberg), May 1, 1832; *Allgemeine Zeitung,* April 10, 1832; *Journal du Havre,* Nov. 3, 1832; *Dublin Mercantile Advertiser,* Oct. 15, 1832; *Galway Free Press,* May 26, 1832; *Quebec Mercury,* June 9, 26, 30, Aug. 4, 1832; letter of J. Buchanan, Aug. 15, 1832, F. O. 5/274.

29. *Didaskalia, oder Blätter für Geist, Gemüth und Publizität* (Frankfurt-am-Main), Nov. 25, 1833; *Quebec Mercury,* Aug. 9, 1832; letter of J. Buchanan, Feb. 15, 1833, F. O. 5/284; *Dublin Mercantile Advertiser,* Oct. 15, 1832.

30. *Quebec Mercury,* May 25, Oct. 10, 1832; *Dublin Mercantile Advertiser,* April 21, 1834; letter of Richard Keating, C. O. 384/36; Select Committee on Agriculture, *Report (Parliamentary Papers,* 1833, V), 366, 501.

31. *Kölnische Zeitung,* Jan. 25, 1834; *Baseler Zeitung,* Oct. 16, 1834; *Mark Lane Express* (London), Sept. 24, 1834; letter of Richard Keating, C. O. 384/36.

32. *Freeman's Journal* (Dublin), April 5, 9–11, 14, 19, 25, 1834.

33. Letter of Ernest Schwendler, Sept. 30, 1834, Consular Letters, Frankfort-on-the-Main, I.

34. *Quebec Mercury,* Sept. 6, 1834; *Nautical Magazine* (London), IV (1835), 371; Special Sanitary Committee of Montreal, *Report upon Cholera and Emigration for the Year 1834* (Montreal, 1835); report of A. C. Buchanan, Dec. 12, 1834, C. O. 384/41.

35. *Quebec Mercury,* July 23, 1835; letters of Lieutenant Haddon, April 2, 1835, and Lieutenant Miller, Aug. 29, 1835, C. O. 384/38.

36. 43 Eliz., ch. 2.

37. J. F. Hammond, *The Village Labourer* (London, 1911), 225–239; C. R. Fay, *Life and Labour in the Nineteenth Century* (Cambridge, 1920), 89–108.

38. *Mark Lane Express,* May 4, 1835; *Labourers' Friend Magazine* (London), 1837, 107; Sussex Association for Improving the Condition of the Labouring Classes, *Quarterly Report* (Lindfield), no. 2 (1832), 5; no. 3 (1832), app., 1; S. Dutot, *De l'expatriation, considérée sous ses rapports économiques, politiques et moreaux* (Paris, 1840), 47.

39. "State of the Labouring Class in England — Emigration," *Quar. Jour. of Agr.* (Edinburgh), III (1831–1832), 551; Dorking Emigrants

330 BIBLIOGRAPHY AND NOTES

Who Went to Upper Canada in the Spring of 1832, *Letters* (Charles Barclay, ed., London, 1833); Select Committee on Agriculture, *Report*, 248.

40. *Quebec Mercury*, Jan. 23, 1834; [T. N. Sackett], *Emigration. A Letter to a Member of Parliament Containing a Statement of the Method Pursued by the Petworth Committee in Sending out Emigrants to Upper Canada in the Years 1832 and 1833* (2nd edn., Petworth, 1834), 7, 9–10; letter of F. Sackett, April 5, 1836, C. O. 384/41.

41. 4 and 5 Will. IV, ch. 76.

42. *Ibid.*, sec. lxii.

43. *Mark Lane Express*, March 9, Aug. 3, 17, 1835; April 11, July 25, Nov. 21, 1836; Feb. 6, 13, April 17, 1837.

44. Letter of J. P. Ray, Feb. 13, 1836, C. O. 384/41; *Mark Lane Express*, May 4, Aug. 24, 1835; Feb. 1, June 13, 1836; Nov. 14, 1842; *Struggle; Devoted to the Advocacy of Free Trade and the Repeal of the Corn Laws* (Preston), 1842, no. 5, 2.

45. Henry Ashworth, "Statistical Illustrations of the Past and Present State of Lancashire," Statistical Soc. of London, *Jour.*, V (1842), 255.

46. *Mark Lane Express*, Aug. 17, Oct. 5, 1835; May 23, July 25, Oct. 3, Nov. 14, 1836; Jan. 9, Feb. 6, March 27, April 3, 17, 24, Sept. 11, Oct. 9, 1837; Jan. 15, May 7, June 18, 25, Aug. 13, Dec. 24, 1838; May 20, Oct. 7, 1839; Jan. 6, 1840.

47. *Mark Lane Express*, Aug. 6, Oct. 8, 1838; Jan. 14, 1839; Jan. 6, 1840.

48. *New Statistical Account of Scotland* (Edinburgh, 1845), II, 78, 226; III, 15; IV, 211; VI, 70, 844; VIII, 83; XIV, 322.

49. *Mark Lane Express*, Dec. 1, 1834; May 23, 1836; July 16, 1838; June 3, 1839; *New Statistical Account of Scotland*, II, 78; XI, 463; XIII, 42.

50. *New Statistical Account of Scotland*, I, 549; II, 219, 255, 353; IV, 17, 60, 115, 539.

51. *Ibid.*, II, 34, 75, 226; III, 198; X, 339; XI, 241, 316; *British Farmer's Magazine* (London), n. s., I (1837), 293.

52. *New Statistical Account of Scotland*, III, 291.

53. *Ibid.*, VII, 98; X, 569, 1156; XIV, 197.

54. Letters of T. F. Elliot, July 29, Oct. 17, 1837, C. O. 384/41, 384/42; Alexander Macgregor, "On the Causes of the Destitution of Food in the Highlands and Islands of Scotland in the Years 1836 and 1837," *Quar. Jour. of Agr.*, IX (1838–1839), 159–199; same author, "On the Advantages of a Government Grant for Emigration from the Highlands and Islands of Scotland," *ibid.*, XI (1840–1841), 257–297.

55. P. White, *History of Clare and the Dalcassian Clans of Tipperary, Limerick, and Galway* (Dublin, 1893), 330.

56. George Shaw-Lefevre, *Peel and O'Connell* (London, 1887), 104; White, *History of Clare*, 334, 337.

57. R. H. Murray, *Ireland* (Boston, 1924), 141; White, *History of Clare*, 338.

58. 10 Geo. IV, ch. 8; Select Committee on Emigration from the United Kingdom, *Third Report* (*Parliamentary Papers*, 1826–1827, V), 268; *Annual Register for 1827*, 25; *for 1829*, 98.

59. A. C. Buchanan, *Emigration Practically Considered* (London, 1828), 64.

60. *Freeman's Journal*, Dec. 22, 1835; James Sedgwick, *A Letter to the Rate-Payers of Great Britain, on the Repeal of the Poor-Laws* (London, 1833), 146–147; "On Ireland," *Quar. Jour. of Agr.*, VIII (1837–1838), 127–153; Commissioners for Inquiring into the Condition of the Poorer Classes in Ireland, *First Report* (*Parliamentary Papers*, 1836, XXXIII), App. F, supp., 17, 22, 26, 203.

61. *Freeman's Journal*, April 10, 1834.

62. *Irish Farmer's and Gardener's Magazine* (Dublin), VI (1839), 23; "On Irish Landlords," *Quar. Jour. of Agr.*, IV (1833–1834), 394; "Canada and the Illinois," *ibid.*, VI (1835–1836), 130.

63. Select Committee on Orange Lodges, Associations or Societies in Ireland, *Report* (*Parliamentary Papers*, 1835, XV), 183.

64. Petition of James Rogers, Oct. 6, 1830, C. O. 384/23.

65. C. O. 384/16, 400.

66. Committee on Orange Lodges, *Report*, 182.

67. Commissioners for Inquiring into the Condition of the Poorer Classes in Ireland, *Third Report* (*Parliamentary Papers*, 1836, XXX), 9–10, 16.

68. *Ibid., First Report*, App. F, supp., 356.

69. Letter of A. C. Buchanan, April 24, 1828, C. O. 384/20, 421; Buchanan, *Emigration*, 36.

70. *Freeman's Journal*, June 10, 1830; April 19, 1832.

71. Commissioners for Inquiring into the Condition of the Poorer Classes, *First Report*, App. F, supp. 371.

72. Select Committee on Agriculture, *Report*, 366; Andrew Picken, *The Canadas, as They at Present Commend Themselves to the Enterprize of Emigrants, Colonists and Capitalists* (London, 1832), 160.

73. *Allgemeine Zeitung*, Sept. 7, 1836; [Friedrich Blaul], *Träume*

und Schäume vom Rhein (Speyer, n. d.), 149–150; A. A. III, R. I, Aus. gen. 2, Vol. VII, no. 4898.

74. *Freeman's Journal*, June 8, 1837.

75. *Irish Farmer's and Gardener's Magazine*, IV (1837), 28.

76. "Ordnance Memoir — County of Londonderry," *Quar. Jour. of Agr.*, VIII, 575.

77. *Missionsblatt* (Barmen), June 18, July 2, 1838.

78. Letters of Robert Manners, July 13, 1837, Jan. 11, 1838, F. O. 5/315, 5/324.

79. A. A. III, R. I, Aus. gen. 2, Vol. VIII, no. 2788; *Leipziger Allgemeine Zeitung*, June 27, 1838.

80. A. A. III, R. I, Aus. gen. 2, Vol. IX, no. 2306; letter of Charles Graebe, June 20, 1840, Consular Letters, Hesse-Cassel, I (1835–1850).

81. *Allgemeine Kirchen Zeitung* (Darmstadt), July 5, 1823; May 16, 1840.

82. *Gesellschafter, oder Blätter für Geist und Herz* (Berlin), Jan. 8, 1838; John McClintock and James Strong, *Cyclopædia of Biblical, Theological, and Ecclesiastical Literature* (N. Y., 1867–1881), IX, 1007–1008.

83. C. E. Vehse, *Die Stephanische Auswanderung nach Amerika* (Dresden, 1840), 3–4.

84. *Allgemeine Kirchen Zeitung*, June 24, 1843; *Leipziger Allgemeine Zeitung*, July 24, Oct. 6, 1838; *Allgemeine Zeitung*, July 29, 1838.

85. *Leipziger Allgemeine Zeitung*, July 24, 1838.

86. *Gesellschafter*, July 25, 1838; *Leipziger Allgemeine Zeitung*, July 14, 1838.

87. *Leipziger Allgemeine Zeitung*, Oct. 6, 1840.

88. *Allgemeine Kirchen Zeitung*, June 25, 1843.

89. *Leipziger Allgemeine Zeitung*, Nov. 25, Dec. 3, 1838.

90. *Kirchliche Mittheilungen aus und über Nord-Amerika* (Berlin), 1844, no. 7; *Leipziger Allgemeine Zeitung*, June 19, 1838.

91. *Leipziger Allgemeine Zeitung*, July 10, 1839; *Deutscher Anzeiger des Westens* (St. Louis), June 9, 1842. There is a full discussion of the Stephanist migration in J. F. Köstering, *Auswanderung der sächsischen Lutheraner im Jahre 1838* (St. Louis, 1867).

92. *Morgenblatt für gebildete Leser* (Stuttgart), Sept. 6, 1839; *Leipziger Allgemeine Zeitung*, July 25, 1839; *Gesellschafter*, Sept. 20, 1839.

93. *Allgemeine Zeitung*, Jan. 9, 1841.

94. *Leipziger Allgemeine Zeitung*, April 14, 1839.

95. *Allgemeine Kirchen Zeitung*, Oct. 28, 1824; June 15, 1830; June 7, 1836; Aug. 2, 1838; W. J. Mann, *Lutheranism in America* (Phila., 1857), 68–69.

96. *Allgemeine Zeitung*, Sept. 18, 1838; *Kölnische Zeitung*, June 24, 1838; *Leipziger Allgemeine Zeitung*, June 30, July 18, Aug. 27, 29, 1838.

97. *Leipziger Allgemeine Zeitung*, March 21, June 3, 1843.

98. Kate E. Levi, "Geographical Origin of German Immigration to Wisconsin," State Hist. Soc. of Wis., *Colls.*, XIV (1898), 341–393; *Allgemeine Zeitung*, July 6, 1841.

99. *Leipziger Allgemeine Zeitung*, March 29, Dec. 26, 1839; June 22, 1843.

100. Peter Beer, "Geschichte, Lehren, und Meinungen der Juden," *Quar. Rev.* (London), XXXVIII (1828), 117.

101. The condition of the Jews in Bavaria is described in Gotthard Deutsch, "Dr. Abraham Bettmann, a Pioneer Physician of Cincinnati," Am. Jewish Hist. Soc., *Publs.*, no. 23 (1915), 105–116.

102. *Israelitische Annalen* (Frankfurt-am-Main), Aug. 16, 1839.

103. Fallati, "Ein Beitrag aus Württemberg zu der Frage vom freien Verkehr mit Grund und Boden," *Zeitschrift für die gesammte Staatswissenschaft* (Tübingen), II (1845), 326–328.

104. *Israelitische Annalen*, Feb. 21, 1840.

105. *Allgemeine Zeitung des Judenthums* (Leipzig), April 2, 1839; *Israelitische Annalen*, July 5, 1839.

106. *Allgemeine Zeitung des Judenthums*, Jan. 9, 1841.

107. Professor Hansen intended to give a fuller treatment of the background of the Scandinavian and Dutch movements, of which excellent accounts may be found by the reader in T. C. Blegen, *Norwegian Migration to America, 1825–1860* (Northfield, 1931), G. M. Stephenson, *The Religious Aspects of Swedish Immigration* (Minneapolis, 1932), and Jacob Van der Zee, *The Hollanders of Iowa* (Iowa City, 1912). — A. M. S.

108. *Times* (London), July 29, 1843.

109. Commission of Inquiry for South Wales, *Minutes of Evidence* (*Parliamentary Papers*, 1844, XVI), 52, 75, 416; A. H. Dodd, "The Old Poor Law in North Wales," *Archaeologia Cambrensis* (London), LXXXI (1926), 122, 126.

110. Thomas Pryce, "History of the Parish of Llandysilio," *Colls. Hist. & Archaeol. Relating to Montgomeryshire* (London), XXXI (1900), 269–270.

111. *Times*, Oct. 3, 1843; Commission of Inquiry, *Minutes of Evidence*, 28, 162, 293; Pryce, "History of Llandysilio," 269–270.

112. D. R. Phillips, *The History of the Vale of Neuth* (Swansea, 1925), 212, 214; Royal Commission on Land in Wales and Monmouthshire, *Report (Parliamentary Papers*, 1896, XXXIV), 185.

113. Royal Commission on Land, *Report*, 312; Phillips, *History of Vale of Neuth*, 211, 214.

114. *Times*, July 21, Aug. 1, 1843; "Rebecca," *Quar. Rev.*, LXXIV (1844), 143; Royal Commission on Land, *Report*, 59.

115. Commission of Inquiry, *Minutes of Evidence*, 187–188; Royal Commission on Land, *Report*, 154.

116. *Times*, July 22, Aug. 1, 1843; "Rebecca," 127; R. D. G. Price, "Rebeccaism," *Nineteenth Century*, IX (1881), 691–694; Commission of Inquiry, *Minutes of Evidence*, 295.

117. George Borrow, *Wild Wales* (London, 1923), 93–94.

118. E. W. Jones, "The Early Welsh Settlers of Oneida Co., N. Y.," *Cambrian* (Utica), IX (1889), 39; "A Call for a Welsh Pioneer Meeting," *ibid.*, VIII (1888), 212.

119. H. E. Thomas, "The Welsh in the United States," *ibid.*, X (1890), 99.

120. A translation of this booklet, B. W. Chidlow, *The American* (2nd edn., Llanrwst, 1840), is to be found in Hist. and Philos. Soc. of Ohio, *Quar. Publ.*, VI (1900), no. 1.

121. *Liverpool Mercury*, Jan. 3, 31, 1840; Nov. 12, 1841; Jan. 7, April 8, 22, June 24, July 22, 1842; *Mark Lane Express*, July 4, Aug. 15, 1842.

122. *Liverpool Mercury*, March 4, 25, April 8, 22, May 13, 27, June 10, 1842; *Australasian Record and Indian Observer* (London), June 25, July 23, 1842.

123. *Liverpool Mercury*, Oct. 29, 1841; John Finch, *Statistics of Vauxhall Ward, Liverpool* (Liverpool, 1842), 22.

124. Henry Ashworth, "Statistics of the Present Depression of Trade at Bolton," Statistical Soc. of London, *Jour.*, V, 75; *Irish Friend* (Belfast), V (1842), 172; Finch, *Statistics*, 22–23.

125. *Mark Lane Express*, Dec. 12, 1842; May 15, 1843; *Liverpool Mercury*, Nov. 18, 25, Dec. 2, 1842; July 7, Dec. 29, 1843.

126. *Allgemeine Zeitung*, Feb. 5, 1843; *Leipziger Allgemeine Zeitung*, April 27, 1843; *Kölnische Zeitung*, Sept. 11, 1843; letter of Colonial Land and Emigration Commissioners, March 24, 1843, C. O. 384/74; Colonial Land and Emigration Commissioners, *General Report (Parliamentary Papers*, 1844, XXXI), 12.

CHAPTER VII. AMERICA BECOMES THE COMMON
MAN'S UTOPIA

1. C. O. 384/7, 869–870.

2. L'Amérique ou guide utile aux personnes qui veulent connaître ce pays et y faire un voyage heureux et avantageux (Belfast, n. d.), 15; Reisebericht der Familie Köpfli und Suppiger nach St. Louis am Mississippi und Grundung von New Switzerland im Staate Illinois (Sursee, 1833), 26.

3. An Emigrant, pseud., Hints and Observations on the Disadvantages of Emigration to British America (London, 1833), 6.

4. C. O. 384/15, 477; 384/9, 741.

5. Neckar Zeitung, April 4, 1827.

6. Carrick's Morning Post (Dublin), Aug. 4, 1818.

7. E. L. Brauns, Praktische Belehrungen und Rathschläge für Reisende und Auswanderer nach Amerika (Brunswick, 1829), 16; Thomas Dyke, Advice to Emigrants (London, 1832), 57; C. O. 384/12, 129.

8. E. L. Brauns, Ideen über die Auswanderung nach Amerika (Göttingen, 1827), 567.

9. Hannoverisches Magazin, June 21, 1845.

10. Blätter für literarische Unterhaltung (Leipzig), April 26, 1834; Brauns, Praktische Belehrungen, 266–267.

11. Didaskalia, oder Blätter für Geist, Gemüth und Publizität (Frankfurt-am-Main), Oct. 29, 1833.

12. Neckar Zeitung, Nov. 24, 1823; Allgemeine Kirchen Zeitung (Darmstadt), Oct. 20, 1833; Jan. 24, 1834; Thüringer Volksfreund (Jena), March 28, 1829; Deutsche Vierteljahrs Schrift (Stuttgart), 1839, no. 1, 239–251; A. A. III, R. I, Aus. gen. 2, Vol. VII, no. 9144 [Wohlgemeinter Rath der deutschen Gesellschaft von Maryland (Balt., 1834), 3–4].

13. Allgemeine Zeitung des Judenthums (Leipzig), I, 424, 453–454.

14. New Statistical Account of Scotland (Edinburgh, 1845), XIII, 37.

15. Ibid., XII, 710; XIII, 37.

16. Chambers's Information for the People (London, 1835); Struggle; Devoted to the Advocacy of Free Trade and the Repeal of the Corn Laws (Preston), 1842, no. 52, 4; British Farmer's Magazine (London), IX, 107.

17. Statistical and Social Inquiry Society of Ireland (Dublin), Journal, pt. xxvi, IV, 14; Nation (Dublin), Jan. 25, 1862.

18. Memorial of John Berford, Nov. 20, 1843, C. O. 384/75; *Australasian Record and Indian Observer* (London), Jan. 8, 1842; Statistical Society of Ireland, *Journal*, pt. xxi, III, 246.

19. *A True Picture of Emigration: or Fourteen Years in the Interior of North America* (London, 1848), 5; An Emigrant Farmer, *pseud.*, *The Emigrant to North America from Memoranda of a Settler in Canada* (Edinburgh, 1844), 1; *Liverpool Mercury*, May 10, 1844.

20. *Emigrant and Colonial Advocate* (London), Aug. 19, 1848; *British Farmer's Magazine*, n. s., III (1839), 171.

21. Emigrant Farmer, *Emigrant to North America*, 1.

22. Select Committee on Colonization from Ireland, *Report* (*Parliamentary Papers*, 1847, VI), 102.

23. Letter of Richard Keating, containing the first annual report of the Limerick Emigrants' Friend Society, C. O. 384/36.

24. [J. U. Buechler], *Land- und Seereisen eines St. Gallischen Kantonsbürgers nach Nordamerika und Westindien* (St. Gallen, 1820), 74.

25. *Deutscher Anzeiger des Westens* (St. Louis), Sept. 24, 1836; *Die alte und die neue Welt* (Phila.), Jan. 11, June 21, July 4, 19, 1834.

26. *Quebec Mercury*, Aug. 17, 1839; July 14, 1840; letter of William Brown, Jan. 15, 1842, C. O. 384/73; Settlers in Upper Canada, *Letters and Extracts of Letters* (London, 1834), 7.

27. S. H. Collins, *The Emigrant's Guide to and Description of the United States of America* (4th edn., Hull, 1830), 145; Sussex Emigrants, *Emigration: Letters* (Thomas Sockett, comp., Petworth, 1833), 44; Dorking Emigrants Who Went to Upper Canada in the Spring of 1832, *Letters* (Charles Barclay, ed., London, 1833), 15.

28. Dorking Emigrants, *Letters*, 27; Sussex Emigrants, *Letters*, 30; *Quebec Mercury*, Jan. 17, 1826.

29. *Irish Penny Journal* (Dublin), Dec. 5, 1840; *Deutscher Anzeiger des Westens*, March 16, 1846; *Morgenblatt für gebildete Stände* (Stuttgart), Nov. 15, 1833; Sussex Emigrants, *Letters*, 8.

30. *Morgenblatt für gebildete Stände*, Nov. 21, 1833; *Missionsblatt* (Barmen), July 2, 1838; Wilhelm Grisson, *Beiträge zur Charakteristik der Vereinigten Staaten von Nord-Amerika* (Hamburg, 1844), 2; A. A. III, R. I, Aus. gen. 2, Vol. IX, no. 2151.

31. *Quebec Mercury*, Dec. 22, 1840.

32. *Leipziger Allgemeine Zeitung*, April 21, 1840.

33. A. A. III, R. I, Aus. Eur. (Auswanderung ausser Europe) 11, Vol. I, no. 8883 (Münster, Oct. 24, 1845, "Ueber die Ursachen der zunehmenden Auswanderung nach Amerika").

34. Letters of Consul George Salkeld, May 7, 1833, J. Buchanan, Oct. 10, 1835, W. Gray, Oct. 15, 1835, and Robert Malley, July 6, 1835, F. O. 5/285, 5/302, 5/303, 5/304.

35. *Morgenblatt für gebildete Stände*, Sept. 25, 1832; *Allgemeine Zeitung* (Augsburg), March 11, 1836; G. P. Scrope, *Extracts of Letters* (London, 1831), 26; Commissioners for Inquiring into the Condition of the Poorer Classes in Ireland, *Third Report (Parliamentary Papers, 1836, XXX)*, 11.

36. *Allgemeine Zeitung*, Nov. 7, 1843; June 8, 1845; *Hannoverisches Magazin*, Sept. 5, 1832.

37. *Kölnische Zeitung*, Feb. 9, 1843; *Leipziger Allgemeine Zeitung*, May 24, June 22, 1839.

38. A. A. III, R. I, Aus. gen. 2, Vol. VII, no. 9252.

39. *Allgemeine Zeitung*, May 10, 1833.

40. Letter of Ernest Schwendler, March 31, 1833, Consular Letters (Department of State, Washington, D. C.), Frankfort-on-the-Main, I (1829–1851); *Allgemeine Zeitung*, March 31, 1830.

41. Letters of Ernest Schwendler, March 31, 1833, Sept. 30, 1834, Jan. 31, 1837, Consular Letters, Frankfort-on-the-Main, I; letters of F. J. Michelhausen, July 20, 1830, Aug. 31, 1831, Consular Letters, Bremen, II (1827–1834).

42. *Dublin Morning Post*, Oct. 9, 1828.

43. *The Emigrant's Guide* (Westport, 1832), 67.

44. Dorking Emigrants, *Letters*, 17.

45. *Allgemeine Zeitung*, April 28, 1831; May 16, 1832; *Kölnische Zeitung*, June 25, 1833; *Sligo Journal*, Feb. 3, 1829; *Galway Free Press*, April 21, 1832; A. A. III, R. I, Aus. gen. 2, Vol. VII, no. 4898.

46. D. Griffiths, *Two Years' Residence in the New Settlements of Ohio* (London, 1835), 82; *America and England Contrasted: or the Emigrant's Handbook and Guide* (2nd edn., London, n.d.), 40; Scrope, *Extracts*, 33.

47. *Farmer's Magazine* (Edinburgh), XX, 261.

48. *Allgemeine Zeitung*, May 15, 1832; *Leipziger Allgemeine Zeitung*, April 21, 1840; Brauns, *Praktische Belehrungen*, 286.

49. William Cattermole, *Emigration. The Advantages of Emigration to Canada* (London, 1831), 184–185; F. A. Evans, *The Emigrant's Directory* (London, 1833), 78.

50. John Knight, *Important Extracts from Original and Recent Letters Written by Englishmen in U. S. of America to Their Friends in England* (Manchester, 1818), ser. 2, 36; Scrope, *Extracts*, 15; Sussex Emigrants, *Letters*, 45.

51. *Sequel to the Counsel for Emigrants* (Aberdeen, 1834), 22; *Emigrant's Guide*, 102, 133; G. Bossert, *Das Wanderbüchlein nach Nordamerika* (Rotweil, 1842), 34.

52. *Emigrant's Guide*, 95.

53. Sussex Emigrants Gone Out from the South Side of the Hills to Upper Canada, *Letters* (Chichester, 1837), 8.

54. *America and England Contrasted*, 40.

55. *Freisinnige* (Nuremberg), March 4, 1832; *Neckar Zeitung*, Sept. 12, 1827; *Bibliothek der neuesten Weltkunde* (Aarau), VIII, 50; Dorking Emigrants, *Letters*, 32.

56. *The People* (Wortley), I, no. 7, 53.

57. *Gesellschafter, oder Blätter für Geist und Herz* (Berlin), Sept. 30, 1833; *Deutsche Tribüne* (Munich), Jan. 21, 1832; *Morgenblatt für gebildete Stände*, Jan. 19, 1828; Friedrich Lange, ed., *Briefe aus Amerika von neuester Zeit, besonders für Auswanderungslustige* (Ilmenau, 1834), 133–134; Evans, *Emigrant's Directory*, 117.

58. *Dublin Morning Post*, Jan. 11, 1830.

59. *Ibid.*, Jan. 1, 1829; *Allgemeine Zeitung*, March 3, 1833; letter of F. J. Michelhausen, Feb. 20, 1833, Consular Letters, Bremen.

60. *Freisinnige*, March 5, 1832.

61. *Allgemeine Zeitung*, Sept. 18, 1829; Feb. 6, 1830; *Neckar Zeitung*, Dec. 15, 1828; *Thüringer Volksfreund*, April 25, 1829.

62. *Freeman's Journal* (Dublin), Jan. 14, 1833.

63. *Allgemeine Zeitung*, March 4, 1833.

64. *Freeman's Journal*, April 4, 1833.

65. *Allgemeine Zeitung*, Nov. 23, 1833; Sept. 18, 1837; Aug. 30, 1838; *Blätter für literarische Unterhaltung*, May 29, 1837.

66. *Allgemeine Zeitung*, May 29, 1843; *Gesellschafter*, Sept. 28, 1833; *Hannoverisches Magazin*, April 23, 1834; K. E. Richter, *Stimmen aus Amerika* (Zwickau, 1833), 7.

67. Griffiths, *Two Years' Residence*, 80.

68. Peter Neilson, *Recollections of a Six Years' Residence in the United States of America* (Glasgow, 1830), 28.

69. *Gesellschafter*, Oct. 11, 1833; *Didaskalia*, Sept. 25, 1833; *Sequel to Counsel for Emigrants*, 25.

70. John West, *A Journal of a Mission to the Indians of the British Provinces* (London, 1827), 222.

71. *Allgemeine Kirchen Zeitung*, May 17, 1827.

72. *Ibid.*, April 4, May 4, Aug. 6, 1826; March 20, Aug. 5, 1827; June 22, 1845; *Missionsblatt*, March 7, 1836; Scrope, *Extracts*, 5; T. Val

Hecke, *Reise durch die Vereinigten Staaten von Nord-Amerika* (Berlin, 1820), 5; A. A. III, R. I, Aus. gen. 2, Vol. IX, no. 2151.

73. *Morgenblatt für gebildete Leser* (Stuttgart), Nov. 17, 1838; *Allgemeine Zeitung*, Jan. 6, 1834; *Briefe von Deutschen aus Nord-Amerika mit besonderer Beziehung auf die Giessner Auswanderer-Gesellschaft vom Jahre 1834* (Altenburg, 1836), viii, x; Friedrich Dellmann, *Briefe der nach Amerika ausgewanderten Familie Steines* (Wesel, 1835), 8.

74. Robert Mudie, *The Emigrant's Pocket Companion* (London, 1832), 28–29.

75. *Allgemeine Zeitung*, Jan. 6, 1834; Nov. 16, 1835; May 17, 1837; *Leipziger Allgemeine Zeitung*, June 19, 1846; A. A. III, R. I, Aus. gen. 2, Vol. VI, no. 7079 [*Rechts-Verhältnisse der Württembergischen Auswanderer* (Heilbronn, 1833), 7]; letter of James Bilby, Dec. 10, 1836, C. O. 384/40.

76. *Blätter für literarische Unterhaltung*, Nov. 9, 1833; W. T. Harris, *Remarks Made during a Tour through the United States of America, in the Years 1817, 1818, and 1819* (London, 1821), 91.

77. *Chambers's Information for the People*, 7–8.

78. *Kölnische Zeitung*, Dec. 6, 1840.

79. C. O. 384/14, 1474.

80. Friedrich Arends, *Schilderung des Mississippithales, oder des Westen der Vereinigten Staaten von Nordamerika* (Emden, 1838), 569; *Sequel to Counsel for Emigrants*, 49–50; *Lesefrüchte vom Felde der neuesten Literatur* (Hamburg), 1832, no. 3, 78–79; letter of Frederick List, Jan. 7, 1831, Consular Letters, Hamburg, III (1823–1832).

81. *Carrick's Morning Post*, Jan. 9, Feb. 27, 1818; *Journal du Havre*, May 4–5, 1828; *Neckar Zeitung*, April 16, 1828; Alexander Lips, *Statistik von Amerika* (Frankfurt-am-Main, 1828), 5.

82. *Allgemeine Zeitung*, Sept. 7, 1843; *Die freie Auswanderung als Mittel zur Abhülfe der Noth im Vaterlande* (Dresden, 1831), 11; *Janus. Jahrbücher deutscher Gesinnung, Bildung und That* (Berlin), 1847, 790; *Bibliothek der neuesten Weltkunde*, 1830, II, 213. The quotation is from *Blätter für das Armenwesen* (Stuttgart), July 22, 1848.

83. H. W. C. Eggerling, *Kurze Beschreibung der Vereinigten Staaten von Nord-Amerika* (Wiesbaden, 1832), 273; *Chambers's Information for the People*, no. 5, 34.

84. Letter of John Ayling, July 24, 1836, C. O. 384/44.

85. Dorking Emigrants, *Letters*, 20.

86. Mudie, *Emigrant's Pocket Companion*, 189–199.

87. *True Picture of Emigration*, 5.

88. C. P. Strickland, *The Backwoods of Canada* (London, 1836), 105; *Sequel to Counsel for Emigrants*, 23; *British Farmer's Magazine*, IX, 113.

89. *Reisebericht der Familie Köpfli und Suppiger*, 288.

90. *Allgemeine Zeitung*, Sept. 26, 1834; June 24, 1836; *Briefe von Deutschen aus Nord-Amerika*, 154–155.

91. *Allgemeine Zeitung*, Aug. 19, 1833; *Deutsche Vierteljahrs Schrift* (Stuttgart), 1839, no. 1, 48.

92. *Blätter für literarische Unterhaltung*, Oct. 29, 1835; May 29, 1837; *Die alte und die neue Welt*, Jan. 4, 1834, June 27, 1835; August Witte, *Kurze Schilderung der Vereinigten Staaten von Nord-Amerika* (Hanover, 1833), 111–112.

93. *Deutscher Anzeiger des Westens*, June 10, 1843; *Die alte und die neue Welt*, Jan. 1, April 29, June 17, July 8, 15, 22, Oct. 28, Nov. 4, 1837; Feb. 17, Aug. 18, Oct. 27, Nov. 3, 1838; June 8, Aug. 10, 17, Nov. 9, 16, 23, 30, 1839.

94. *Deutscher Anzeiger des Westens*, July 29, 1837; *Die alte und die neue Welt*, Jan. 9, 1836.

95. *Allgemeine Zeitung*, June 22, 1838; June 5, 1840; *Kölnische Zeitung*, May 9, 1845.

96. *Deutsche Vierteljahrs Schrift*, 1839, no. 1, 38.

97. *Allgemeine Zeitung*, Feb. 18, 1841; *Kölnische Zeitung*, June 26, 1844.

98. *Kölnische Zeitung*, March 17, 1837; *Missionsblatt*, Nov. 14, 1836; July 10, 1837; *Allgemeine Zeitung*, Dec. 1, 1844; *Gesellschafter*, July 22, 1842; *Didaskalia*, Aug. 23, 1837; *Die alte und die neue Welt*, July 30, 1836; Sept. 23, 1837; *Deutscher Anzeiger des Westens*, Nov. 30, 1847; *Hannoverisches Magazin*, July 19, 1843.

99. *Freeman's Journal*, Nov. 13, 1841; Feb. 26, Sept. 17, 1842; June 17, 1843.

100. *Liverpool Mercury*, June 10, 1842.

101. *Didaskalia*, March 9, 1833.

102. *Mark Lane Express* (London), May 1, 1837; F. R. Eylert, *Rückblicke auf Amerika, oder: Bekenntnisse eines ausgewanderten Poeten* (Brunswick, 1841), 50–51; Grisson, *Beiträge zur Charakteristik*, 3.

103. *Freeman's Journal*, April 5, 1834.

104. *Pastoral Blatt* (St. Louis), LI, 52.

105. *Allgemeine Zeitung*, Feb. 19, April 1, Oct. 6, 1832; May 14, Aug. 14, Nov. 7, 1833; *Kölnische Zeitung*, May 9, 1832; May 12, 1833; *Leipziger Allgemeine Zeitung*, Feb. 22, 1841.

106. *Leipziger Allgemeine Zeitung*, Nov. 10, 1845; letters of Charles Graebe, Sept. 24, Dec. 27, 1845, Consular Letters, Hesse-Cassel, I (1835–1850).

107. *Morgenblatt für gebildete Stände*, April 20, 1832; Eggerling, *Kurze Beschreibung der Vereinigten Staaten*, 16; *Die freie Auswanderung*, 24; *Chambers's Information for the People*, no. 12, 96.

108. *Emigration Gazette, and Colonial Settlers' Universal Guide* (London), July 30, Aug. 27, 1842; Patrick Matthew, *Emigration Fields* (Edinburgh, 1839), 7; *Lesefrüchte vom Felde der neuesten Literatur*, 1832, no. 3, 79.

109. J. F. Elliott, *An Essay Showing the Expediency of Emigration* (London, 1822), 8, 10; Scrope, *Extracts* (2nd edn., London, 1832), vi, viii; J. H. Haggenmacher, *Ueber die Auswanderungen nach Amerika* (Heilbronn, 1839), 9, 74; letter of E. Cusack, Jan. 21, 1835, C. O. 384/39.

110. Johannes Scherr, *Die Auswanderungsfrage vom religiös-socialistischen Standpunkt betrachtet* (Stuttgart, 1845), 57–58, 67, 69–70, 89, 100.

CHAPTER VIII. COMMERCE BRIDGES THE ATLANTIC

1. *Encyclopædia Britannica* (11th edn.), VI, 806, 809; William Scoresby, "Observations on the Deviation of the Compass," Franklin Institute of the State of Pennsylvania, *Jour.*, XII (1833), 41.

2. R. T. Gould, "The History of the Chronometer," *Geog. Jour.*, LVII (1921), 253–268; Cornelius Varley, "Method of Condensing Brass," Franklin Institute, *Jour.*, VI (1828), 211.

3. Parkinson and Frodsham, "Chronometers," *Am. Jour. of Arts and Sci.*, XXIX (1836), 302–303; "Trials of Chronometers at Greenwich, in 1831," Franklin Institute, *Jour.*, X (1832), 411–412; "Universal Time-keeping," *Scientific Am.*, CIX (1913), 450.

4. L. C. Cornford, *The Sea Carriers, 1825–1925. The Aberdeen Line* (n.p., 1925), 34–35; *La grande encyclopédie*, XXIV, 871; *Encyclopedia Americana* (new edn., Phila., 1840), XI, 367–368.

5. Augustin Fresnel, *Oeuvres complètes* (Paris, 1870), II, v, xvii; Alan Stevenson, *Account of the Skerryvore Lighthouse with Notes on the Illumination of Lighthouses* (Edinburgh, 1848), 195.

6. Fresnel, *Oeuvres*, III, xxiv.

7. Stevenson, *Skerryvore Lighthouse*, 241, 248, 286; F. Honoré, "Le centenaire de Fresnel," *L'Illustration*, CLXX (1927), 491; "Our Light-House System," *Am. Rev.: A Whig Jour.*, I (1845), 323.

8. 32 Cong., 1 sess., *Senate Exec. Doc.*, no. 28, 6.

9. "British Lighthouses," *North British Rev.*, XXXII (1860), 513. The act of Parliament referred to is 6 and 7 Will. IV, ch. 79.

10. 25 Cong., 2 sess., *Senate Rep.*, no. 428, 9; 27 Cong., 1 sess., *House Rep.*, no. 811, 1, 23.

11. F. R. Hassler, "Survey of the Coast of the United States," *North Am. Rev.* XLII (1836), 76–78, 81–82, 84, 86; Joseph Henry, "Eulogy on Professor Alexander Dallas Bache," Smithsonian Institution, *Ann. Rep. for 1870*, 100; A. D. Bache, "On the Progress of the Survey of the Coast of the United States," Am. Assoc. for Advancement of Sci., *Procs. for 1849*, 164–165.

12. "Hydrography," *Popular Sci. Monthly*, VIII (1875–1876), 520; *Encyclopædia Britannica*, XIX, 293.

13. "Life-Boats, Lightning Conductors, Lighthouses," *North British Rev.*, XXXI (1859), 498–500, 502–503.

14. M. A. DeW. Howe, *The Humane Society of the Commonwealth of Massachusetts* (Boston, 1918), ch. v; R. B. Forbes, *Personal Reminiscences* (Boston, 1882), 254.

15. Frederick Martin, *The History of Lloyd's and of Marine Insurance in Great Britain* (London, 1876), 161–162, 342, 346, 354.

16. *Allgemeine Zeitung* (Augsburg), March 28, 1828; *Morgenblatt für gebildete Stände* (Stuttgart), July 1, 1829; *Journal du Havre*, Jan. 24, 1815; R. G. Albion, *Square-Riggers on Schedule* (Princeton, 1938), chs. i–ii, iv, vii.

17. *Leipziger Allgemeine Zeitung*, Aug. 28, 1841.

18. Select Committee on Emigration from the United Kingdom, *Report (Parliamentary Papers*, 1826, IV), 175.

19. "Die Beförderung der deutschen Auswanderung über deutsche Häfen," *Deutsche Vierteljahrs Schrift* (Stuttgart), 1851, no. 3, 69, 332.

20. *Carrick's Morning Post* (Dublin), July 8, 1817; Feb. 27, June 14, 1819; Oct. 24, 1820.

21. *Quebec Mercury*, Feb. 20, 1830.

22. *Times* (London), May 14, 1816; *Quebec Mercury*, March 15, 1832; *Londonderry Sentinel*, April 23, 1831; *Freeman's Journal* (Dublin), April 26, 1830; A. C. Buchanan, *Emigration Practically Considered* (London, 1828), 84.

23. *Quebec Mercury*, July 17, 1830; Buchanan, *Emigration*, 84; John Finch, *Statistics of Vauxhall Ward, Liverpool* (Liverpool, 1842), 22–23.

24. *Quebec Mercury*, Dec. 11, 1824; May 18, 1830; Dec. 27, 1842.

25. A. C. Buchanan, His Majesty's Resident Agent for Superintendence of Settlers and Emigrants in the Canadas, Evidence before the

Committee on Roads and Internal Communications, Dec. 1828, Public Archives of Canada, M 173; Commissioners for Inquiring into the Condition of the Poorer Classes in Ireland, *First Report* (*Parliamentary Papers*, 1836, XXXIII), App. F, supp., 274.

26. Buchanan, Evidence, Jan. 1832.

27. *Quebec Mercury*, July 20, 1830.

28. *Ibid.*, Dec. 11, 1830.

29. Letter of J. Buchanan, Dec. 31, 1828, F. O. 5/242; *Official Information for Emigrants Arriving at New York and Who Are Desirous of Settling in the Canadas* (Montreal, 1834); Settlers in Upper Canada, *Letters and Extracts of Letters* (London, 1834), 7.

30. Letter of John Martin and Co., Feb. 25, 1842, C. O. 384/73; *Quebec Mercury*, March 15, 1831; *Dublin Morning Post*, April 14, 1830; Robert Mudie, *The Emigrant's Pocket Companion* (London, 1832), 201.

31. A Resident of St. John, *pseud.*, *The Advantages of Emigrating to the British Colonies of New Brunswick, Nova Scotia* (London, 1832), 48.

32. Report of D. MacIntosh, Dec. 1826, F. O. 5/229; letters of D. MacIntosh, Jan. 20, 1832, James Sherwood, Feb. 1, 1839, and T. C. Grattan, Jan. 1843, *ibid.*, 5/277, 5/335, 5/394; Buchanan, *Emigration*, 59.

33. Letters of James Sherwood, Sept. 28, 1839, and Robert Manners, Jan. 9, 1839, F. O. 5/252, 5/336; *The Emigrant's Guide; Containing Practical and Authentic Information and Copies of Original and Unpublished Letters from Emigrants to Their Friends in the Counties of Mayo, Galway, and Roscommon* (Westport, 1832), 96; William Byrne, W. A. Leahy and others, *History of the Catholic Church in the New England States* (Boston, 1899), I, 597; II, 551.

34. *Liverpool Mercury*, April 17, 1818; *Londonderry Sentinel*, April 23, 1831.

35. *Sligo Journal*, June 14, Nov. 15, 1833; Feb. 21, 28, 1834; *Newry Telegraph*, March 23, 1837; *Freeman's Journal*, April 9, 1834.

36. Emigration Commissioners, *Twenty-Fourth General Report* (*Parliamentary Papers*, 1864, XVI), 13.

37. Letter of T. C. Grattan, Jan. 1844, F. O. 5/411.

38. Select Committee on the Passengers' Act, *Report* (*Parliamentary Papers*, 1851, XIX), 75, 156.

39. S. H. Collins, *The Emigrant's Guide to and Description of the United States of America* (4th edn., Hull, 1830), 80.

40. Letter of J. Buchanan, June 14, 1834, F. O. 5/294.

41. Letters of N. W. Ferguson, Nov. 15, 1834, and Lieutenant Friend, April 20, 1836, C. O. 384/36, 384/41; *Freeman's Journal*, April 10, 1834.

42. Letter of T. F. Elliot, Oct. 17, 1837, C. O. 384/42.

43. *Liverpool Mercury*, April 19, 1844.

44. Letter of M. McDonald, C. O. 384/36; *New Statistical Account of Scotland* (Edinburgh, 1845), IV, 539; XIV, 152, 208.

45. *Allgemeine Zeitung*, Jan. 19, May 13, 1833.

46. Letter of Frederick List, Jan. 20, 1831, Consular Letters (Department of State, Washington, D. C.), Hamburg, III.

47. *Journal du Havre*, Jan. 11, 1828; May 29, 1829; July 26, 1830; *Allgemeine Zeitung*, June 23, 1825; letters of R. G. Beasley, Aug. 1, 1832, and Jan. 7, 1835, Consular Letters, Havre, II, V; *Reisebericht der Familie Köpfli und Suppiger nach St. Louis am Mississippi und Grundung von New Switzerland im Staate Illinois* (Sursee, 1833), 40.

48. Lena B. Seiler, "Die Pioniere von McHenry County," *Deutsch-Amerikanische Geschichtsblätter* (Chicago), I (1901), no. 2, 20; Heinrich Bornmann, "Geschichte der Deutschen Quincys," *ibid.*, II (1902), no. 4, 44; *Westland* (Heidelberg), I, no. 3, 261, 265, 276–277; *Journal du Havre*, April 30, 1830; *Morgenblatt für gebildete Stände*, Sept. 25, 1832; *Gazette de Lausanne*, Oct. 15, 1824.

49. *Morgenblatt für gebildete Stände*, April 14, 1832; Nov. 19, 1833; *Reise nach dem Staat Ohio in Nordamerika von Niklaus Jass, gewesenen Schullehrer in Oberthal, Kanton Bern* (Bern, 1833), 2–4.

50. *Morgenblatt für gebildete Stände*, Jan. 3, 1828; Gustav Löwig, *Die Freistaaten von Nord-Amerika* (Heidelberg, 1833), 62; *Reise nach dem Staat Ohio*, 3; Heinrich von Martels, *Briefe über die westlichen Theile der Vereinigten Staaten von Nordamerika* (Osnabrück, 1834), 10.

51. *Journal du Havre*, Sept. 3, 1831; April 2, 1832; *Kölnische Zeitung*, July 8, 1832; Nov. 17, 1837; *Morgenblatt für gebildete Stände*, Sept. 25, 1832; July 21, 29, 1837; *Missionsblatt* (Barmen), Jan. 29, 1838; T. B. Bettinger, *Guide des emigrants aux États-Unis* (Havre, 1834), 28; *Reisebericht der Familie Köpfli und Suppiger*, 51; A. A. III, R. I, Aus. gen. 2, Vol. VI, nos. 2367, 3982.

52. A. A. III, R. I, Aus. gen. 2, Vol. VI, no. 2290 (Berlin, March 20, 1833), and no. 3603 (supplement to *Allgemeine Zeitung*, 1833, no. 146); *ibid.*, Vol. VII, no. 8383 (*Frankfurter Reportorium für Handel und Finanz-Wesen*, 1836, no. 26), and no. 10355 (Paris, July 22, 1836); *ibid.*, Vol. VIII, no. 4434 (Paris, May 25, 1837).

53. A. A. III, R. I, Aus. gen. 2, Vol. VIII, no. 3249.

54. *Allgemeine Auswanderungs Zeitung* (Rudolstadt), Jan. 27, 1852.

55. *Kölnische Zeitung*, Sept. 17, 1832; "Bremen, der natüraliche Hafen von Bayern, Thuringen und Hessen," *Taschenbuch für die vaterlandische Geschichte*, n. s., XVII (1846), 158–166; Friedrich Rauers, "Der bremische Binnenverkehr in der Zeit des grossen Frachtfuhrwerks," *Deutsche Geographische Blätter* (Bremen), XXX (1907), 78–131; XXXI (1908), 37–92, 194–245; J. J. Oddy, *European Commerce* (London, 1807), II, 182.

56. Treaty with the Hanseatic Republics, W. M. Malloy, comp., *Treaties, Conventions, International Acts* (Wash., 1910), I, 901–905.

57. Letters of H. Wheaton, Sept. 24, 1841, and Joshua Dodge, Feb. 14, 1838, Diplomatic Correspondence (Department of State, Washington, D. C.), Prussia, 1839–1841; letter of Joshua Dodge, Dec. 19, 1835, Consular Letters, Bremen, III (1835–1841); report of Marcus Derkheim, Oct. 28, 1841, *ibid.*; report of Francis Grund, Dec. 24, 1841, *ibid.*; *Allgemeine Zeitung*, Feb. 1, 1837.

58. *Abendzeitung* (Dresden), May 16, 1827; F. A. Rüder, "Ueber die starke Zunahme des Handels von Bremen," *Nationalökonom* (Mannheim), III (1835), 40–46.

59. Letters of Charles Graebe, Aug. 25, 1835, April 2, 1849, Consular Letters, Hesse-Cassel, I (1835–1850).

60. *Gesellschafter, oder Blätter für Geist und Herz* (Berlin), Jan. 29, 1836.

61. Letters of H. Wheaton, Sept. 24, 1841, and Charles Graebe, Jan. 14, 1836, Consular Letters, Hesse-Cassel, I; report of Marcus Derkheim, June 2, 1840, Consular Letters, Bremen, III; *Allgemeine Zeitung*, Nov. 22, 1835; *Zollvereinsblatt* (Stuttgart), Feb. 27, 1843; "Deutschlands Handel mit Amerika," *Ausland* (Munich), March 27, 1828.

62. E. L. Brauns, *Praktische Belehrungen und Rathschläge für Reisende und Auswanderer nach Amerika* (Brunswick, 1829), 48–49.

63. *Leipziger Allgemeine Zeitung*, Aug. 26, 1846; *Allgemeine Zeitung*, July 26, 1839; letter of J. H. Adami to H. Wheaton, Jan. 10, 1843, Diplomatic Correspondence, Prussia, 1841–1846; report of Marcus Derkheim, March 13, 1841, Consular Letters, Bremen, III.

64. *Allgemeine Zeitung*, Jan. 19, May 13, 1833; letter of Frederick List, Jan. 7, 1831, Consular Letters, Hamburg, III (1823–1832).

65. *Allgemeine Zeitung*, June 25, 1832; March 1, Sept. 6, 1835; Sept. 4, 1839; *Kölnische Zeitung*, July 24, 1832; Aug. 3, 1834; Jan. 25, 1838; April 14, 1843; A. A. III, R. I, Aus. gen. 2, Vol. VII, no. 4943 ("Obrigkeitliche Verordnung").

66. Heinrich Meidenger, *Die deutschen Ströme* (Leipzig, 1853–1854), IV, 32; *Kölnische Zeitung*, May 20, 1832.

67. Rauers, "'Bremische Binnenverkehr," *Deutsche Geographische Blätter*, XXX, 85.

68. G. Bossert, *Das Wanderbüchlein nach Nordamerika* (Rotweil, 1842), 17.

69. Baltimore's importance is shown by the destination of outgoing ships in 1838. Forty-six ships, carrying 5276 passengers, sailed for Baltimore as compared with the following: 26 to New York, 1340 passengers; 17 to New Orleans, 2022 passengers; 6 to Philadelphia, 189 passengers; 3 to Charleston, 30 passengers; 3 to Boston, no passengers; 1 to Richmond, 77 passengers. Compiled from *Zollvereinsblatt*, Feb. 27, 1843; Dec. 2–9, 1844; *Leipziger Allgemeine Zeitung*, Jan. 16, 1839.

70. *Allgemeine Zeitung*, April 8, July 26, 1839; letter of Joshua Dodge, Dec. 19, 1835.

71. *Allgemeine Zeitung*, July 7, 1837.

72. *Ibid.*, May 31, 1839; June 3, 1841; *Kölnische Zeitung*, June 6, 1841.

73. Letter of H. Wheaton, Sept. 24, 1841, and report of John Cuthbert, July 28, 1837, Consular Letters, Hamburg, V (1837–1841).

74. A. A. III, R. I, Aus. gen. 2, Vol. VIII, no. 3264 (*Verordnung in Betreff der Verschiffung der über Hamburg nach andern welttheilen Auswanderden*, Feb. 27, 1837).

75. *Leipziger Allgemeine Zeitung*, Dec. 5, 1841; Brauns, *Praktische Belehrungen*, 11; A. A. III, R. I, Aus. gen. 2, Vol. VIII, no. 3249.

76. *Allgemeine Zeitung*, Nov. 20, 1838; *Leipziger Allgemeine Zeitung*, Dec. 5, 1841; Friedrich Lange, ed., *Briefe aus Amerika von neuester Zeit, besonders für Auswanderungslustige* (Ilmenau, 1834), 7.

77. *Leipziger Allgemeine Zeitung*, Jan. 9, 1841.

78. *Ibid.*, Feb. 1, 1838; March 27, 1840.

79. A. A. III, R. I, Aus. gen. 2, Vol. VIII, no. 3020, and no. 3249 (meeting on March 3, 1840).

80. A. A. III, R. I, Aus. gen. 2, Vol. VIII, no. 3249.

81. E. J. Clapp, *The Navigable Rhine* (Boston, 1911), 13–14, 22.

82. Hanns Heiman, *Die Neckarschiffer* (Heidelberg, 1907), I, 176, 179; Meidenger, *Deutschen Ströme*, II, 131–134.

83. *Allgemeine Zeitung*, July 9, 1825; Jan. 24, 1828; *Münchener Politische Zeitung*, May 9, 1835; *Leipziger Allgemeine Zeitung*, July 4, 1838; Emile Jacquemien, *Allemagne agricole, industrielle et politique* (Paris, 1842), 83.

84. M. E. Perrot, "Des chemins de fer belges," Commission Centrale de Statistique, *Bulletin*, II (1845), 3–6; *Moniteur belge; journal officiel*

(Brussels), June 4, 1849; *Deutsche Auswanderer* (Darmstadt), I (1847), 743; II (1848), 273.

85. Hermann Achenbach, *Tagebuch meiner Reise nach den Nordamerikanischen Freistaaten* (Düsseldorf, 1835), 14.

86. *Allgemeine Zeitung*, May 2, 1841.

87. *Carrick's Morning Post*, June 11, July 8, Dec. 17, 1817; March 5, 1818; *Dublin Morning Post*, March 2, 1830.

88. *Carrick's Morning Post*, June 10, 1819; *Sligo Observer*, April 15, 1830; *Sligo Journal*, Sept. 10, 1830; *Dublin Mercantile Advertiser*, March 11, 1833; *Galway Free Press*, March 24, 1832; March 28, 1835.

89. Committee on Passengers' Act, *Report*, 36, 267.

90. *Abendzeitung*, May 30, 1832; *Reise nach dem Staat Ohio*, 6.

91. *Leipziger Allgemeine Zeitung*, April 28, 1850; May 24, 1852.

92. *Morgenblatt für gebildete Leser* (Stuttgart), July 31, 1837; Bettinger, *Guide*, 31; *Reise nach dem Staat Ohio*, 6; A. A. III, R. I, Aus. gen. 2, Vol. VII, no. 10355 (Paris, July 22, 1836); *ibid.*, Vol. VIII, no. 4434 (Paris, May 25, 1837).

93. Report of F. J. Grund, Feb. 10, 1842, Consular Letters, Bremen, IV (1842–1850).

94. *Allgemeine Zeitung*, March 28, 1833; *Morgenblatt für gebildete Stände*, Nov. 19, 1833; *Abendzeitung*, May 30, 1832.

95. *Extracts from Original and Recent Letters* (Belper, 1819), 90–91.

96. Calvin Colton, *Manual for Emigrants to America* (London, 1832), 186; Commissioners for Emigration, *Report* (*Parliamentary Papers*, 1831–1832, XXXII), 9; Commissioner of Inquiry into the State of the North American Provinces, *Report* (*ibid.*), 24.

97. *Morgenblatt für gebildete Stände*, July 1, 1829; [Fernagus de Gelone], *Manuel-guide des voyageurs aux États-Unis* (Paris, 1818), 17; A. A. III, R. I, Aus. gen. 2, Vol. VI, no. 2086 (Wohlgemeinter Rath, 12).

98. *Morgenblatt für gebildete Stände*, Sept. 26, 1832; Brauns, *Praktische Belehrungen*, 5.

CHAPTER IX. HOPES AND FEARS OF THE THIRTY YEARS' PEACE

1. Gustav Sundbärg, *Den svenska och europeiska Folköknings- och Omflyttningsstatistiken i sina Hufvuddrag* (Stockholm, 1910), 11.

2. Antonio Llano, "Population and Wages," *Am. Jour. of Sociology*, V (1900), 669.

3. Hermann Dieterici, "Ueber die Vermehrung der Bevölkerung in Europe seit den Ende oder der Mitte des Siebenzehnten Jahrhunderts,"

Philologische und historische Abhandlungen der königlichen Akademie der Wissenschaften zu Berlin aus dem Jahre 1850, 84.

4. The decline in the infant birth rate is illustrated in "Aenderungen der Sterblichkeit von Jahre 1751 zu 1870," *Jahrbücher für National-ökonomie und Statistik* (Jena), XXII (1874), 141–144.

5. Thomas Newenham, *A View of the Natural, Political, and Commercial Circumstances of Ireland* (London, 1809), 201–202, 210; Isaac Butt, *Repeal of the Union* (Dublin, 1843), 38–39.

6. Thomas Newenham, *A Statistical and Historical Inquiry into the Progress and Magnitude of the Population of Ireland* (London, 1805), 181.

7. *Irish Farmer's Gazette*, Jan. 4, 1851.

8. *A View of the Agricultural State of Ireland* (Cork, 1816), 18, 40.

9. An Ulster Landlord, *pseud.*, *Notes Relative to the Condition of the Irish Peasantry* (London, 1831), 6; William Bennett, *Narrative of a Recent Journey of Six Weeks in Ireland* (London, 1847), 31–32.

10. *Leinster Express* (Maryborough), Feb. 27, 1847.

11. *Irish Farmer's Gazette*, Dec. 20, 1845.

12. *Ibid.*, May 27, 1848.

13. Report of P. Robinson, April 2, 1824, C. O. 384/12, 138–139.

14. *Dublin Morning Post*, Oct. 27, 1821.

15. *Irish Farmer's Register, and Journal of Practical Agriculture* (Dublin), April 1842, 33; R. S. McAdam, "On the Potato," *Quar. Jour. of Agr.* (Edinburgh), V (1834–1835), 343.

16. *The South of Ireland and Her Poor* (London, 1843), 125.

17. *Irish Farmer's Gazette*, Sept. 25, 1847; July 26, 1851; July 8, 1854.

18. Royal Agricultural Improvement Society of Ireland, *Agricultural and Industrial Journal*, I (1848–1849), 19.

19. *Dublin Penny Journal*, I (Aug. 19, 1832), 58.

20. *Leinster Express*, April 28, 1849; *Dublin Penny Journal*, I (June 21, 1832), 28; J. P. Kennedy, *Instruct; Employ; Don't Hang Them* (London, 1835), 8–9; William Sturch, *The Grievances of Ireland, Their Causes and Their Remedies* (London, 1826), 25; Select Committee of the House of Lords Appointed to Inquire into the State of Ireland in Respect of Crime, *Report* (*Parliamentary Papers*, 1839, XII), 1202.

21. W. N. Hancock, *The Tenant — Right of Ulster Considered Economically* (Dublin, 1845), 7, 11.

22. *Suggestions for the Improvement of Ireland* (London, 1824), 31; Sturch, *Grievances of Ireland*, 6; Commissioners for Inquiring

into the Condition of the Poorer Classes in Ireland, *First Report* (*Parliamentary Papers*, 1836, XXXIII), App. F, supp., 220.

23. Computed from figures presented in Commissioners of Inquiry into the State of the Law and Practice in Respect to the Occupation of Land in Ireland, *Evidence* (*Parliamentary Papers*, 1845, XXII), 274–275.

24. [John Wiggins], *Hints to Irish Landlords* (London, 1824), 13.

25. An Englishman, *pseud.*, *Some Effects of the Irish Poor Law* (London, 1849), 7; *Mark Lane Express* (London), Aug. 3, 1835; *Freeman's Journal* (Dublin), April 1, 1850; *Limerick Chronicle*, Feb. 10, 1841; *Irish Farmer's and Gardener's Magazine* (Dublin), II (1835), 10.

26. Bennett, *Narrative of a Recent Journey*, 7.

27. *Irish Farmer's and Gardener's Magazine*, II, 9; Select Committee on Poor Laws, *Seventh Report* (*Parliamentary Papers*, 1849, XV, pt. i), 38.

28. *Freeman's Journal*, Feb. 27, 1834; R. Wilmot-Horton, *The Causes and Remedies of Pauperism in the United Kingdom Considered* (London, 1829), 134; G. P. Scrope, *Some Notes of a Tour in England, Scotland, and Ireland* (London, 1849), 26.

29. *Mark Lane Express*, Sept. 29, 1834.

30. *Ibid.*, Jan. 16, 1837; J. G. V. Porter, *Ireland* (London, 1844), 19; Alexander Mundell, *The Necessary Operation of the Corn Laws* (2nd edn., London, 1831), 73.

31. *Carrick's Morning Post* (Dublin), Sept. 21, 1818; *Freeman's Journal*, June 11, 1833; *Irish Farmer's and Gardener's Magazine*, I (1833–1834), 557.

32. *Mark Lane Express*, March 6, Oct. 9, 1837; Feb. 17, 1840; May 12, 1851.

33. *Ibid.*, July 22, Nov. 4, 1844; *Irish Farmer's and Gardener's Magazine*, IV (1837), 11.

34. *Irish Farmer's Gazette*, Jan. 4, April 12, 1845; *Mark Lane Express*, Aug. 4, 1834; March 6, 1843; Sept. 9, 1844; *Irish Farmer's and Gardener's Magazine*, III (1836), 418; VIII (1841), 575; Mr. Stephens, "On the Agricultural State of Ireland," *Quar. Jour. of Agr.*, III (1831–1832), 764–765.

35. *Dublin Mercantile Advertiser*, April 23, 1832; *Irish Farmer's and Gardener's Magazine*, II, 136–137.

36. *Galway Patriot*, Aug. 15, 1838; Ulster Landlord, *Condition of Irish Peasantry*, 17.

37. *Dublin Morning Post*, June 3, 1830; *British Farmer's Magazine* (London), IV (1830), 61; V (1831), 432; George Strickland, *A Discourse on the Poor Laws of England and Scotland* (London, 1827), 83.

38. *Journal of Agriculture* (Edinburgh), n. s., I (1843–1845), 521.

39. *Irish Farmer's Gazette*, Dec. 13, 1851.

40. Statistical and Social Inquiry Society of Ireland (Dublin), *Journal*, I (1855), pt. i, 10; Commissioners of Inquiry into the State of Law and Practice in Respect to Occupation of Land in Ireland, *Report (Parliamentary Papers,* 1845, XIX–XXI), pt. i, 89; pt. ii, 164, 343; pt. iii, 3, 147.

41. *Irish Farmer's Gazette*, Sept. 6, 1845; Commissioners of Inquiry in Respect to Occupation of Land in Ireland, *Report,* pt. ii, 731; *The Catholic Emigration Society, Its Necessity, Objects and Advantages* (London, 1843), 10.

42. 5 and 6 Vict., chs. 47 and 49; *Mark Lane Express,* May 2, 1842; Jan. 2, Aug. 28, 1843; *Emigration Gazette, and Colonial Settlers' Universal Guide* (London), April 16, 30, 1842.

43. *Mark Lane Express,* Nov. 20, Dec. 18, 1843; Jan. 8, 1844; Jan. 6, 1845; *Irish Farmer's Gazette,* May 25, June 1, 8, 1844; Jan. 4, 1845.

44. *Dublin Morning Post,* June 1, 1822; *Freeman's Journal,* Feb. 27, 1834; *Limerick Chronicle,* May 19, 1841.

45. D. C. O'Connor, *Seventeen Years' Experience of Workhouse Life* (Dublin, 1861), 12.

46. F. List, "Die Ackerverfassung, die Zweigwirthschaft und die Auswanderung," *Gesammelte Schriften,* II, 163; *Land- und Forstwissenschaftliche Zeitschrift für Braunschweig, Hannover und die angrenzenden Länder* (Brunswick), III (1835), 359–360.

47. W. Hesse, *Rheinhessen in seiner Entwickelung von 1798 bis Ende 1834* (Mainz, 1835), 91; "Über den Zustand der Rheinlande," *Rheinische Blätter,* Jan. 11–12, 1817, 23–24, 27–28; L. Rau, *Studien über süddeutsche Landwirthschaft* (Speyer, 1852), 46.

48. *Blätter für das Armenwesen* (Stuttgart), March 25, 1848; *Amtlicher Bericht über die XVI Versammlung deutscher Land- und Forstwirthe* (Munich, 1854), 225.

49. Schüz, "Ueber das Verehelichungs- und Uebersiedelungsrecht mit besonderer Rücksicht auf Württemberg," *Zeitschrift für die gesammte Staatswissenschaft* (Tübingen), V (1848), 25–89.

50. *Allgemeine Zeitung* (Stuttgart), July 9, 1840; J. G. Elsner, *Die Politik der Landwirthschaft* (Stuttgart, 1835), 213–214.

51. K. W. Arnold, "Ueber die materielle Lage der arbeitenden Klassen in den Weinbaudistrikten," *Annalen der Landwirthschaft* (Berlin), XV (1850), 107–156, esp. 109; Rutenberg, "Der deutsche Weinbau namentlich im Jahre 1846 und der Weinhandel Deutschlands,"

Zeitschrift des Vereins für deutsche Statistik, I (1847), 168–186, 1007–1024; II (1848), 82–91, esp. 83–84.

52. K. Göriz, "Ueber die kulturfähigen Bodenfläche und ihrem Anbau bevorstehenden grösseren Veränderungen," *Zeitschrift für die gesammte Staatswissenschaft*, IV (1847), 122; *Verhandlungen der St. Gallisch-Appenzellischen gemeinnützigen Gesellschaft an der Hauptversammlung in Wattwill* (St. Gallen, 1852), 50.

53. *Gesellschafter, oder Blätter für Geist und Herz* (Berlin), Nov. 15, 1841.

54. *Gemeinnützige und Unterhaltende Rheinische Provinzial-Blätter*, IV (1833), 155.

55. Rau, *Studien über süddeutsche Landwirthschaft*, 93–94.

56. *Leipziger Allgemeine Zeitung*, June 14, 1852.

57. A. A. III, R. I, Aus. Eur. 11, Vol. I, no. 8883 (Münster, Oct. 24, 1845, "Ueber die Ursachen der zunehmenden Auswanderung nach Amerika").

58. "Irlands Verhältniss zu England," *Janus. Jahrbücher deutscher Gesinnung, Bildung und That* (Berlin), I (1846), 791; *Verhandlungen des Kurhessischen Landtages* (Kammer), 1831, supp. no. 1, 4.

59. Wilhelm von Baumer, *Betrachtungen über die Abnahme der Wälder, ihre Ursachen und Folgen* (Nördlingen, 1846), 53.

60. "Die Holznoth," *Deutsche Vierteljahrs Schrift* (Stuttgart), 1839, no. 1, 288; Baumer, *Betrachtungen über die Abnahme der Wälder*, 53.

61. *Agronomische Zeitung* (Leipzig), Feb. 12, 1847; *Allgemeine Zeitung*, March 26, 1845; Baumer, *Betrachtungen über die Abnahme der Wälder*, 19; "Die Holznoth," 283.

62. *Allgemeine Kirchen Zeitung* (Darmstadt), Aug. 19, 1843; August von Holzschuher, *Die materielle Noth der untern Volksklassen und ihre Ursachen* (Augsburg, 1850), 53; *Amtlicher Bericht über die XVII Versammlung deutscher Land- und Forstwirthe zu Cleve* (Bonn, 1856), 178–179.

63. *Blätter für das Armenwesen*, Jan. 19, 1856.

64. *Agronomische Zeitung*, Jan. 18, 1850; *Blätter für das Armenwesen*, Sept. 23, 1854; *Hannoverisches Magazin*, Dec. 11, 1844; *Didaskalia, oder Blätter für Geist, Gemüth und Publizität* (Frankfurt-am-Main), Oct. 14, 1837; "Blicke auf die materiellen Zustände in Württemberg," *Zeitschrift des Vereins für deutsche Statistik*, I, 1076–1091; II, 47–61, 112–124, 447–459.

65. *Hannoverisches Magazin*, Sept. 3, 1831.

66. *Allgemeine Zeitung*, Feb. 18, 1836; *Kölnische Zeitung*, April 8, 1847; *Amtlicher Bericht über die XVI Versammlung deutscher Land-*

und Forstwirthe zu Nürnberg (Munich, 1854), 70–72; Fallati, "Ein Beitrag aus Württemberg zu der Frage vom freien Verkehr mit Grund und Boden," *Zeitschrift für die gesammte Staatswissenschaft*, II (1845), 319–376.

67. G. Heusinger, "Ueber die Verwahrlosung des deutschen Bauernstandes," *Minerva*, II (1844), 60–103, esp. 90.

68. Otto Reinhard, "Die Grundentlastung in Württemberg," *Zeitschrift für die gesammte Staatswissenschaft*, XXXVI (1910), 1–6.

69. Otto Reinhard, "Die Zehntablösung in Württemberg," *ibid.*, LXIX (1913), 187–190; Adolf Kopp, *Zehentwesen und Zehentablösung in Baden* (Freiburg, 1899), 6, 14–15, 47–49, 69–71.

70. Gerhard Kraus, *Landwirthschaftliche Betriebsverhältnisse in Ostpreussen, 1815–1870* (Berlin, 1914), 9; "Die Stein-Hardenbergsche Bauernbefreiung und ihre sozialen Folgen," *Jahrbuch des Bodenreform* (Jena), XVIII (1922), 6–7, 9–10, 14–15.

71. Stichling, "Ueber die Wahl der Mittel zur Erleichterung der Grundpflichtigkeits-Ablösungen," *Zeitschrift für die gesammte Staatswissenschaft*, V, 3–5; Albert Judeich, *Die Grundentlastung in Deutschland* (Leipzig, 1863).

72. Reinhard, "Grundentlastung in Württemberg," 14, 23–24, 42.

73. Johannes Scherr, *Die Auswanderungsfrage vom religiös-socialistischen Standpunkt betrachtet* (Stuttgart, 1845), 85; "Bericht des Abgeordneten von Waitz, Namens des Ausschusses der ersten Ständekammer, über den Gesetzenwurf die Landes-Kreditkasse betreffend," *Verhandlungen des Kurhessischen Landtages* (Kammer), I (1852), supp. no. 2.

74. *Allgemeine Kirchen Zeitung*, Aug. 19, 1843; *Denkschrift für den Grossen Rath* (Zurich, 1848), 7; "Blicke auf die materiellen Zustände in Württemberg," *Zeitschrift des Vereins für deutsche Statistik*, I, 1076–1091; II, 47–61.

75. A. A. III, R. I, Aus. Eur. 11, Vol. I, no. 8883.

76. *Leipziger Allgemeine Zeitung*, Aug. 12, 1842; April 8, May 1, 1843; "Die Trockenheit des Jahrs 1842," *Württembergische Jahrbücher*, 1842, 199–230.

77. *Württembergische Jahrbücher*, 1843, 36.

78. *Ibid.*, 1844, 18, 41; Heinrich Weber, "Bamberger Weinbuch. Ein Beitrag zur Culturgeschichte," *Bestand und Wirken des historischen Vereins zu Bamberg*, XLVI (1883), 82.

79. "Histoire de la maladie des pommes de terre en 1845," *Journal d'agriculture pratique* (Paris), ser. 2, III (1845–1846), 231–240, 273–276, 403–410.

80. Pierre Clerget, "Peuplement de la Suisse," Société Royal Belge de Géographie (Brussels), *Bulletin*, XXX (1906), 73–97.

81. E. de Laveleye, "Economie rurale de la Suisse," *Revue des deux mondes* (Paris), April 15, 1863, 823–856; "Schweizerische Zustände," *Minerva*, I (1834), 471–517.

82. "The State and Tendency of Property in France," *British and Foreign Rev.* (London), III (1836), 375–500, esp. 388.

83. A. de Foville, *Le morcellement* (Paris, 1855), 65.

84. G. G. Richardson, *The Corn and Cattle Producing Districts of France* (London, 1878), 26.

85. J. F. Flaxland, "Quelques considérations sur le morcellement des terres en Alsace," *Revue l'Alsace*, XI (1860), 81–92.

86. J. J. M. Férand, *Histoire, géographie et statistique du département des Basses-Alpes* (Digne, 1861), 150, 153; P. Moisson, "Mouvement de la population du département des Hautes-Alpes au XIX° siècle," *Géographie* (Paris), XX (1909), 111–116.

87. Charles Weld, *The Pyrenees* (London, 1859), 154–157; Élisée Reclus, *The Earth and Its Inhabitants. Europe* (E. G. Ravenstein, ed., N. Y., 1885), II, 200, 232.

88. Benoit Bouché, *Les ouvriers agricoles en Belgique* (Brussels, 1913), 1, 7; Émile Vandervelde, *La propriété foncière en Belgique* (Paris, 1900), 265, 293; Her Majesty's Representatives Respecting the Tenure of Land in the Several Countries of Europe, *Reports* (*Parliamentary Papers*, 1870, LXVII), pt. i, 111.

89. Édouard Ducpétiaux, *Mémoire sur le paupérisme dans les Flandres* (Brussels, 1850), 64–66; Jan St. Lewinski, *L'évolution industrielle de la Belgique* (Brussels, 1911), 87.

90. Her Majesty's Representatives Respecting Tenure of Land, *Reports*, pt. i, 214; "High Farming as Illustrated in the History of the Netherlands," U. S. Dept. of Agr., *Ann. Rep. for 1866*, 535.

91. L. Stein, "Die Handels- und Zoll-Verhältnisse der Herzögthumern Schleswig und Holstein mit besonderer Berücksichtigung eines Anschlusses an den Zollverein," *Zeitschrift des Vereins für deutsche Statistik*, II, 163–169.

92. Paul Kollmann, *Die Heuerleute in Oldenburgischen Münsterland* (Jena, 1898), 2–34, 41–42; Johannes Tack, *Die Hollandsgänger in Hannover und Oldenburg* (Leipzig, 1902), 35, 103–105; Adolf Brasmann, "Das Heuerlingswesen im Fürstentem Osnabrück," *Mittheilungen des Vereins für Geschichte und Landeskunde von Osnabrück*, XLII (1919), 53–171.

93. "Mecklenburger Zustände," *Grenzboten* (Leipzig), 1857, pt. iv, 348–350.

94. Henri Sée, *Esquisse d'une histoire du régime agraire* (Paris, 1921), 148–150; "Les reformes et la dernière crise en Danemark," *Revue des deux mondes*, Nov. 15, 1853, 738–769; "The Development of Agriculture in Denmark," Royal Statistical Soc., *Jour.*, LXIX (1906), 374–411; Her Majesty's Representatives Respecting Tenure of Land, *Reports*, pt. i, 193, 200, 202.

95. "Laing's Tour in Sweden in 1838," *Edinburgh Rev.*, LXIX (1839), 349–365; "Laing's Residence in Norway," *ibid.*, LXV (1837), 39–69; Sée, *Esquisse d'une histoire du régime agraire*, 154; Her Majesty's Representatives Respecting Tenure of Land, *Reports*, pt. ii, 350, 353.

96. Simen Skappel, *Træk af det norske Agerbrugs Historie i Tidsrummet, 1660–1814* (Kristiania, 1904), 22–23; *Beretninger om den œconomiske Tilstand m. m. i. Norge* (Kristiania, 1836), 20, 344.

CHAPTER X. COLONIZATION NO REMEDY

1. *Allgemeine Zeitung* (Augsburg), July 27, 1840.

2. *Ibid.*, May 24, 1846.

3. *Morgenblatt für gebildete Leser* (Stuttgart), Aug. 20, 1841.

4. *Allgemeine Zeitung*, Feb. 21, 1844.

5. *Ibid.*, Dec. 1, 1844.

6. *Ibid.*, May 28, 1840; Sept. 27, 1842; Aug. 25, 1845.

7. *Journal du Havre*, May 29–31, 1831.

8. *Kölnische Zeitung*, Aug. 9, 1843; *Morgenblatt für gebildete Leser*, Jan. 13, 1847; "Die Auswanderung nach Australien, Afrika, Asien," *Weltpost* (Leipzig), II (1882), 93–94; letter of Edward Dalius to A. Dudley Mann, Sept. 11, 1847, Special Agents (Department of State, Washington, D. C.), German States, Hungary, 1846–1852.

9. A. A. III, R. I, Aus. gen. 2, Vol. IX, no. 2711 (*Antrag des Abgeordneten v. Werner, die Bildung eines Emigrations und Colonisations-Vereins betreffend, 7*); *Kölnische Zeitung*, Feb. 2, 1843.

10. *Allgemeine Zeitung*, March 3, 1842.

11. *Leipziger Allgemeine Zeitung*, Dec. 5, 1841.

12. *Allgemeine Zeitung*, Dec. 15, 1841; March 26, 1842; *Leipziger Allgemeine Zeitung*, March 7, 1842; Heinrich Sieveking, "Hamburger Kolonisationspläne, 1840–1842," *Preussische Jahrbücher* (Berlin), LXXXVI (1896), 149–170.

13. *Allgemeine Zeitung*, April 20, 1842.

14. *Ibid.*, Feb. 3, 1842; *Leipziger Allgemeine Zeitung*, Jan. 4–5, 1842.

15. *Allgemeine Zeitung*, March 12, 1842.

16. *Ibid.*, March 26, April 6, 1842.

17. *Ibid.*, Nov. 20, 1843; July 20, 1844; *Leipziger Allgemeine Zeitung*, May 8, 1846. The various views with regard to the Verein are summarized in G. G. Benjamin, *The Germans in Texas* (N. Y., 1910), 34–37; the commercial motive is stated in a letter written April 20, 1844, by Bourgeois d'Orvanne to the Texan Secretary of State, in G. P. Garrison, ed., *Diplomatic Correspondence of the Republic of Texas*, pt. iii (Am. Hist. Assoc., *Ann. Rep. for 1908*, II, pt. ii), 1561.

18. *Allgemeine Zeitung*, June 4, 1844; *Kölnische Zeitung*, June 13, 1844.

19. *Allgemeine Zeitung*, Sept. 7, 1843.

20. *Ibid.*, Feb. 1, Oct. 2, 15, 1844.

21. *Ibid.*, Oct. 27, 1844.

22. Benjamin, *Germans in Texas*, 38–39; Garrison, *Diplomatic Correspondence*, pt. iii, 1184.

23. Benjamin, *Germans in Texas*, 38–52; Alfred Zimmermann, *Geschichte der preussisch-deutschen Handelspolitik* (Oldenburg, 1892), IV, 312–316.

24. *Leipziger Allgemeine Zeitung*, Aug. 19, 1845.

25. A. A. III, R. I, Aus. Eur. 11, Vol. I, no. 1458.

26. *Allgemeine Zeitung*, July 18, 1846.

27. *Ibid.*, April 21, 1847; *Leipziger Allgemeine Zeitung*, May 8, 1846; *Deutsche Auswanderer* (Darmstadt), I (1847), 325; II (1848), 602.

28. *Kölnische Zeitung*, June 20, 1847; *Leipziger Allgemeine Zeitung*, July 3, Nov. 5, 1847; letter of Ernest Schwendler, Feb. 15, 1848, Consular Letters (Department of State, Washington, D. C.), Frankfort-on-the-Main, I (1829–1851). The best picture of Texan affairs is given in a series of letters, "Briefe aus Texas," printed in *Ausland* (Stuttgart), June 22–27, 1848; March 26–29, Sept. 1–4, 1849.

29. H. A. Graef, *Santo Thomas de Guatemala* (Aachen, 1847), 6; M. P. Brouez, *Une colonie belge dans l'Amérique Centrale* (Mons, 1846), 126.

30. A. A. III, R. I, Aus. gen. 2, Vol. X, no. 2275.

31. *Allgemeine Zeitung*, Aug. 29, 1843; *Kölnische Zeitung*, Aug. 25, 1843; Nov. 18, 1844.

32. *Leipziger Allgemeine Zeitung*, Oct. 8, 1845.

33. Graef, *Santo Thomas*, 5, 7–8, 10, 25, 62–63, 68, 71, 74, 83–84; Brouez, *Colonie belge*, 90, 124; R. Le Pelletier de Saint-Remy, *De quelques essais de colonisation européenne sous les tropiques* (Paris,

1849), 76; E. Blondeel van Cuelebrouck, *Colonie de Santo Tomas* (Brussels, 1846), 1, 3, 9, 15, 49, 88, 93, 146.

34. Baron Bunsen, *Memoir* (London, 1868), II, 112–113.

35. A. A. III, R. I, Aus. Eur. 11, Vol. I, no. 1458.

36. *Leipziger Allgemeine Zeitung*, Nov. 10, 24, 1845; *Allgemeine Zeitung*, Nov. 14, 1845.

37. *Allgemeine Zeitung*, April 11, 1846; *Leipziger Allgemeine Zeitung*, Dec. 27, 1845; Zimmermann, *Geschichte der preussisch-deutschen Handelspolitik*, 316–317.

38. *Leipziger Allgemeine Zeitung*, May 12, 21, Oct. 24, Dec. 6, 1846; Feb. 14, 1847; A. A. III, R. I, Aus. Eur. 11, Vol. III, no. 883 (clipping from the *Morning Post*, Jan. 22, 1847).

39. *Morgenblatt für gebildete Leser*, Feb. 27, 1846.

40. *Allgemeine Zeitung*, Feb. 21, 1845.

41. *Ibid.*, May 25, 1841.

42. Ludwig Sevin, "Die Entwicklung von Friedrich Lists kolonial- und weltpolitischen Ideen bis zum Plane einer englischen Allianz," *Jahrbuch für Gesetzgebung, Verwaltung und Volkswirtschaft im Deutschen Reich* (Leipzig), XXXIII (1909), pt. iv, 299–341; Gustav Höfken, "Erweiterung des deutschen Handels und Einflusses durch Gesellschaften, Verträge und Ansiedlung," *Deutsche Vierteljahrs Schrift* (Stuttgart), 1842, no. 2, 172–218.

43. *Allgemeine Zeitung*, Nov. 28, 1844; April 2, 1846; *Kölnische Zeitung*, Aug. 26, 1844.

44. *Kölnische Zeitung*, Dec. 31, 1845.

45. *Allgemeine Zeitung*, Dec. 1, 1844; Friedrich Hundeshagen, *Die deutsche Auswanderung als Nationalsache insbesondere die Auswanderung des Proletariats* (Frankfurt-am-Main, 1849), 17, 19.

46. A. A. III, R. I, Aus. Eur. 11, Vol. I, no. 1458, and no. 3835 (memoir from Beroldinger to Prussian minister, April 24, 1845); *Kölnische Zeitung*, June 26, Oct. 9, 1844; Hundeshagen, *Deutsche Auswanderung*, 17.

47. *Allgemeine Zeitung*, April 22, 1843.

48. *Ibid.*, April 17, 25, 1843.

49. *Ibid.*, April 22, 1843.

50. A. A. III, R. I, Aus. gen. 2, Vol. XI, no. 1030 (memorandum of Ernst Amüller to v. Werner, Aug. 30, 1843); *Leipziger Allgemeine Zeitung*, July 30, 1843; March 8, 1845.

51. Ernst Dubois, "L'industrie du tissage du lin dans les Flandres," *Les industries à domicile en Belgique*, II (1900), 18, 26–30.

52. *Exposé de la situation du royaume (Statistique générale de la Belgique*; Brussels, 1865), *1851–1860*, III, 141.

53. *Leipziger Allgemeine Zeitung*, Feb. 3, 1843; *Württembergische Jahrbücher*, 1854, no. 2, 29–30; *Hannoverisches Magazin*, May 19, 1847.

54. Franz Baur, *Ist die Klage über zunehmende Verarmung und Nahrungslosigkeit in Deutschland gegründet; welche Ursachen hat das Uebel, und welche Mittel bieten sich zur Abhülfe dar?* (Erfurt, 1838), 63–65; *Zollvereinsblatt* (Stuttgart), VI (1848), no. 38, 593; A. A. III, R. I, Aus. Eur. 11, Vol. I, no. 8883 ("Ueber die Ursachen der zunehmenden Auswanderung nach Amerika," Münster, Oct. 24, 1845); *Hannoverisches Magazin*, Nov. 11, 1844.

55. *Allgemeine Zeitung*, Dec. 11, 1841; Feb. 4, 1843; July 21, 1847; Alfred Zimmermann, *Blüthe und Verfall des Leinengewerbes in Schlesien* (Breslau, 1885), 338.

56. *Leipziger Allgemeine Zeitung*, June 22, 1843; Hundeshagen, *Deutsche Auswanderung*, 6.

57. *Allgemeine Zeitung*, Dec. 23, 1843; June 13, Oct. 21, 1845.

58. Zimmermann, *Blüthe und Verfall des Leinengewerbes*, 352–362.

59. *Leipziger Allgemeine Zeitung*, April 22, 1843; June 5, 1845.

60. *Ibid.*, May 25, 1845; *Allgemeine Zeitung*, Jan. 22, 1840.

CHAPTER XI. THE FLIGHT FROM HUNGER

1. *Irish Farmer's Gazette*, July 19, Sept. 13, Oct. 4, 1845.

2. *Ibid.*, Oct. 11, 25, 1845; Feb. 14, 1846; *Mark Lane Express* (London), Oct. 27, 1845.

3. *Irish Farmer's Gazette*, May 29, 1847; *Mark Lane Express*, Jan. 12, 1846.

4. *Journal of Agriculture* (Edinburgh), n. s., II (1845–1847), 309; *Mark Lane Express*, Nov. 3, 1845.

5. *Morgenblatt für gebildete Leser* (Stuttgart), Dec. 3, 1845; *Allgemeine Zeitung* (Augsburg), Sept. 19, 1845; *Landwirthschaftliche Zeitschrift* (Dresden), II (1846), 179.

6. *Limerick Chronicle*, Nov. 19, 1845; *Irish Farmer's Gazette*, Dec. 20, 1845.

7. 7 Will. IV and 1 Vict., ch. 21.

8. 9 and 10 Vict., ch. 1.

9. Select Committee of the House of Lords, *Report on Consolidated Annuities of Ireland (Parliamentary Papers*, 1852, VI), v–vi.

10. *Mark Lane Express*, April 20, 1846.

11. *Leinster Express* (Maryborough), April 25, 1846; *Scarcity in Ireland* (*Parliamentary Papers*, 1846, XXXVII), 293.

12. *Farmer's Gazette* (Dublin), Oct. 3, 1846.

13. *Ibid.*, Oct. 10, 1846; *Leinster Express*, May 9, 1846; *Dublin Mercantile Advertiser*, April 24, 1846.

14. *Allgemeine Zeitung*, Jan. 5, 1846.

15. *Mark Lane Express*, June 9, Sept. 29, Dec. 29, 1845.

16. *Allgemeine Zeitung*, May 22, 1846.

17. *Ibid.*, Jan. 4, 1847.

18. *Journal du Havre*, April 1, 1846.

19. *Farmer's Gazette*, June 20, Aug. 22, 1846; *Scarcity in Ireland*, 128, 211.

20. *Scarcity in Ireland*, 142.

21. *Irish Farmer's Gazette*, May 27, 1848.

22. *Correspondence Relating to the Measures Adopted for the Relief of the Distress in Ireland* (*Parliamentary Papers*, 1847, LI), 4.

23. *Ibid.*, 104; *Liverpool Mercury*, Nov. 20, 1846; Jan. 15, 1847.

24. *Farmer's Gazette*, Oct. 10, 1846.

25. *Allgemeine Zeitung*, Aug. 14, 1846.

26. *Morgenblatt für gebildete Leser*, Sept. 15, 1846; *Allgemeine Zeitung*, Aug. 29, 1846; Sept. 10, 1847; *Staats- und Gelehrte Zeitung des Hamburgischen unpartheyischen Correspondenten*, Feb. 3, 1847.

27. *Agronomische Zeitung* (Leipzig), Sept. 11, 1846; March 17, 1848.

28. *Ibid.*, Sept. 25, Dec. 18, 1846.

29. *Journal of Agriculture*, n. s., III (1847–1849), 291–292.

30. 9 and 10 Vict., ch. 22.

31. *Farmer's Gazette*, Nov. 21, 1846; *Liverpool Mercury*, Sept. 18, Oct. 2, 23, 1846; *Correspondence Relating to Relief of Distress in Ireland*, 464.

32. *Mark Lane Express*, Nov. 9, 1846; Jan. 4, 11, 1847; William Bennett, *Narrative of a Recent Journey of Six Weeks in Ireland* (London, 1847), 6, 122.

33. Committee of the House of Lords on Colonization from Ireland, *Report* (*Parliamentary Papers*, 1847, VI), 243; *World* (Dublin), June 12, 1847.

34. *Mark Lane Express*, Jan. 4, 11, Feb. 1, 8, 15, 22, 1847.

35. *Ibid.*, Dec. 6, 1847.

36. *Irish Farmer's Gazette*, Sept. 4, 1847.

37. *Mark Lane Express*, Feb. 1, 8, 15, 22, 1847; Royal Agricultural Improvement Society of Ireland, *Reports and Transactions for 1848 and 1849*, 222, 223 n.

38. *Mark Lane Express*, Feb. 1, 1847.

39. *Ibid.*, March 29, 1847.

40. *Liverpool Mercury*, Jan. 22, 1847; *Mark Lane Express*, March 15, 22, 1847.

41. J. K. Ingram, "Considerations on the State of Ireland," Statistical and Social Inquiry Soc. of Ireland (Dublin), *Jour.*, IV (1864), 15.

42. 9 and 10 Vict., ch. 107.

43. *Irish Ecclesiastical Journal* (Dublin), IV (1847), 141.

44. Committee of House of Lords, *Report on Consolidated Annuities*, vii, xi, xxv–xxvi; Bennett, *Narrative of a Recent Journey*, 9–10, 38.

45. *Freeman's Journal* (Dublin), April 15, 1847; letters of Lieutenant Hodder, Feb. 7, 1847, and T. F. Elliot, April 19, 1847, C. O. 384/80.

46. Letter of T. F. Elliot, April 22, 1847, C. O. 384/78; Committee on Settlement, and Poor Removal, *First Report* (*Parliamentary Papers*, 1847, XI), 59.

47. *Freeman's Journal*, April 24, 1847; *Liverpool Mercury*, March 19, 1847; letter of A. Dudley Mann, Sept. 13, 1847, Special Agents (Department of State, Washington, D. C.), German States, Hungary, 1846–1852.

48. *Freeman's Journal*, April 2, 1847; *Mark Lane Express*, March 15, 1847; letter of A. Dudley Mann, Sept. 13, 1847.

49. Bennett, *Narrative of a Recent Journey*, 5, 53.

50. *Irish Farmer's Gazette*, Aug. 7, 1847.

51. *Freeman's Journal*, April 19, 1847; *Agricultural Review* (Dublin), I (1858), 354.

52. Committee on Colonization from Ireland, *Report*, 537; *Emigrant and Colonial Gazette*, July 29, 1849.

53. Committee on Colonization from Ireland, *Report*, 249–250; letter of Charles Franks, Feb. 19, 1847, C. O. 384/74.

54. *Leinster Express*, March 6, June 19, July 3, 1847; *Mark Lane Express*, March 8, 1847.

55. *Freeman's Journal*, April 2, 26, 1847; letter of C. H. Wandesforde, Nov. 21, 1847, C. O. 384/75.

56. *Liverpool Mercury*, Jan. 1, 15, Nov. 30, 1847; *Leinster Express*, March 20, 1847; letter of Lieutenant Hodder, Feb. 4, 1847, C. O. 384/80.

57. *Liverpool Mercury*, Oct. 22, 1847.

58. *Mark Lane Express*, Jan. 25, March 15, Nov. 15, 1847.

59. Letter of Charles Nicholls, Oct. 14, 1847, Consular Dispatches (Department of State, Washington, D. C.), Amsterdam, IV (1844–1850).

60. Letters of George Bancroft, Feb. 3, March 29, 1847, Diplomatic Correspondence (Department of State, Washington, D. C.), England, LVII (1846–1847).

61. Letter of Charles Graebe, April 12, 1847, Consular Letters (Department of State, Washington, D. C.), Hesse-Cassel, I (1835–1850).

62. Report of Charles Nicholls, March 31, 1847, Consular Dispatches, Amsterdam, IV.

63. *Allgemeine Zeitung*, March 18, 1847; *Kölnische Zeitung*, Feb. 10, 1847; *Allgemeine Auswanderungs Zeitung* (Rudolstadt), Feb. 3, 1847.

64. *Kölnische Zeitung*, April 28, 1847.

65. A. A. III, R. I, Aus. Eur. 11, Vol. III, no. 1980 (letter from Belgian minister of foreign affairs, Feb. 23, 1847).

66. *Leipziger Allgemeine Zeitung*, April 1, 1847; *Morgenblatt für gebildete Leser*, Jan. 13, 1847; *Allgemeine Kirchen Zeitung* (Darmstadt), Nov. 23, 1847.

67. *Weser Zeitung* (Bremen), Sept. 16, 1847; *Leipziger Allgemeine Zeitung*, March 7, 1847; *Staats- und Gelehrte Zeitung des Hamburgischen unpartheyischen Correspondenten*, Jan. 29, 1847.

68. *U. S. Statutes at Large*, IX, 127–128.

69. *Ibid.*, 149.

70. *Leipziger Allgemeine Zeitung*, May 6, 19, 25, 1847.

71. A. A. III, R. I, Aus. Eur. 11, Vol. III, no. 3767 (*Weser Zeitung*, May 5, 1847); *Allgemeine Zeitung*, May 12, 1847; *Kölnische Zeitung*, May 10, 1847.

72. *Allgemeine Auswanderungs Zeitung*, May 11, June 7, 1847; *Allgemeine Zeitung*, May 19, 1847.

73. *Leipziger Allgemeine Zeitung*, June 2, 1847; *Allgemeine Auswanderungs Zeitung*, June 14, 1847; *Allgemeine Zeitung*, June 17, 1847; *Weser Zeitung*, Sept. 16, 1847; *Deutsche Auswanderer* (Darmstadt), II (1848), no. 30, 467.

74. *Allgemeine Zeitung*, May 23, 1847; *Kölnische Zeitung*, June 24, 1848; *Leipziger Allgemeine Zeitung*, June 22, 1847. The Treasury circular is published in *Hunt's Merchants' Magazine*, XVII (1847), 99.

75. Letter of A. Dudley Mann, Sept. 13, 1847.

76. Letters of C. Alexander Wood, Aug. 4, 1848, and F. W. C. Murdock, June 3, 1848, C. O. 384/81.

77. Letters of S. W. French, Dec. 28, 1847, and Lieutenant Friend, Dec. 28, 1847, C. O. 384/81.

78. Colonial Land and Emigration Commissioners, *Eighth General Report* (*Parliamentary Papers*, 1847–1848, XXVI), 15.

79. Letter of C. Alexander Wood, Aug. 4, 1848, C. O. 386/83; Colonial Land and Emigration Commissioners, *Report*, 15.

80. Colonial Land and Emigration Commissioners, *Report*, 15.

81. *The Emigrant's Manual. British America and United States of America* (Edinburgh, 1851), 35.

82. Letters of F. W. C. Murdock, Dec. 8, 1847, Jan. 18, 1848, C. O. 386/83.

83. *Laws of Massachusetts for 1837*, ch. 238.

84. *Massachusetts Senate Documents for 1847*, no. 109.

85. *Massachusetts Senate Documents for 1848*, no. 46.

86. *Ibid.*, nos. 14–15, 46; *Boston Courier*, Jan. 18, 20, 22, 25, 29, Feb. 8, 1848; *Laws of Massachusetts for 1848*, ch. 313.

87. Board of Aldermen of New York City, *Documents for 1837*, IV, nos. 10, 12.

88. Comptroller of the City of New York, *Report for 1845*, 32.

89. *Laws of New York for 1847*, ch. 195.

90. *Baltimore American*, April 24, May 5, 12, 15, 18, 27, 1847.

91. The mayor's message is printed in the *Baltimore American*, May 27, 1847. The ordinance which was passed on May 27, 1847, is published in the issue for June 14, 1847.

92. *Ibid.*, July 13, 20, 26, Oct. 23, 1847; May 31, June 17, 1848.

93. *Laws of Louisiana for 1842*, no. 158; *for 1843*, no. 81.

94. *Daily Picayune* (New Orleans), April 30, 1847.

95. *Ibid.*, June 8, Sept. 2, 1847.

96. Messages from the mayor in the *Daily Picayune*, May 5, 13, June 19, 24–25, 1847; reports of committees, May 19, June 24, 1847; report of the secretary of the charity hospital, June 30, 1847.

97. *Daily Picayune*, Sept. 5, Nov. 10, 1847; Jan. 19, March 3, 9, May 17, 23, 1848.

98. Smith *v.* Turner, Norris *v.* City of Boston, 48 U. S., 282.

99. *Laws of Louisiana for 1850*, no. 295; *Laws of Maryland for 1849–1850*, ch. 46; *Laws of Massachusetts for 1850*, ch. 105; *Laws of New York for 1849*, ch. 350.

100. *U. S. Statutes at Large*, IX, 220–223.

101. *Irish Ecclesiastical Journal*, IV (1847), 157.

102. *Mark Lane Express*, March 8, 1847; *World*, May 1, 1847.

103. *Mark Lane Express*, Oct. 4, 1847; *Irish Poor Law: Past, Present and Future* (London, 1849), 16.

104. *Morgenblatt für gebildete Leser*, June 14, 1847; *Allgemeine Zeitung*, Sept. 12, 1847; letter of Charles Graebe, Aug. 12, 1847, Consular Letters, Hesse-Cassel, I.

105. *Mark Lane Express*, Feb. 21, 1848.

CHAPTER XII. NEW FORCES AT WORK

1. *Morgenblatt für gebildete Leser* (Stuttgart), Nov. 24, 1849; "Die deutsche Handelspolitik in ihrem Wendepunkte," *Deutsche Vierteljahrs Schrift* (Stuttgart), 1847, no. 3, 166.

2. *Mark Lane Express* (London), Oct. 28, 1850; Jan. 31, 1853.

3. *Ibid.*, July 17, Sept. 9, Oct. 14, 1850.

4. *Ibid.*, Feb. 11, 18, Oct. 14, 1850.

5. *Ibid.*, Oct. 14, Dec. 9, 1850; March 27, 1854.

6. John Orr, *A Short History of British Agriculture* (London, 1922), 85; C. J. Hall, *A Short History of English Agriculture and Rural Life* (London, 1924), 132.

7. *Mark Lane Express*, Jan. 10, 1848; March 12, 1849; James Begg, *Pauperism and the Poor Laws* (2nd edn., Edinburgh, 1849), 10.

8. *Mark Lane Express*, Sept. 3, 1849.

9. *Ibid.*, Feb. 5, 12, 1847; Dec. 3, 1849.

10. *Sidney's Emigrant's Journal* (London), Oct. 5, 1848, 2; Dec. 7, 1848, 73; Feb. 1, 1849, 138–139, 181; *Emigrant and Colonial Gazette*, Nov. 18, 1848.

11. *Emigrant and Colonial Gazette*, Jan. 13, 1849; *Mark Lane Express*, Jan. 22, July 16, 1849.

12. G. P. Scrope, *Some Notes of a Tour in England, Scotland and Ireland* (London, 1849), 8, 10.

13. *Irish Farmer's Gazette*, March 2, 1850; Feb. 20, March 6, Oct. 9, 1852; *Papers Relating to Proceedings for the Relief of the Distress, and State of Unions and Workhouses, in Ireland* (Parliamentary Papers, 1849, XLVIII), 87.

14. *Irish Farmer's Gazette*, Jan. 6, 1849; May 21, 1853; *Leinster Express* (Maryborough), Jan. 27, 1849.

15. 10 and 11 Vict., ch. 31; W. N. Hancock, "The Difference between the English and Irish Poor Law," Statistical and Social Inquiry Soc. of Ireland (Dublin), *Jour.*, III (1862), pt. xxi, 221–222.

16. *Irish Poor Law: Past, Present and Future* (London, 1849), 11; G. P. Scrope, *The Irish Poor Law* (London, 1849), 8–9.

17. Commissioners for Administering the Laws for the Relief of the Poor in Ireland, *First Annual Report* (*Parliamentary Papers*, 1847–1848, XXXIII), 13.

18. Scrope, *Irish Poor Law*.

19. Select Committee of the House of Lords Appointed to Inquire into the Operation of the Irish Poor Law, *Report* (*Parliamentary Papers*, 1849, XVI), 498; *Papers Relating to Proceedings for Relief of Distress in Ireland*, 30.

20. Royal Agricultural Improvement Society of Ireland, *Reports and Transactions for 1848 and 1849*, 95; *Papers Relating to Proceedings for Relief of Distress in Ireland*, 20; Committee to Inquire into Irish Poor Law, *Report*, 104.

21. Scrope, *Some Notes of a Tour*, 18, 29.

22. *Ibid.*, 29.

23. *Leinster Express*, Feb. 19, Oct. 28, 1848; *Emigrant and Colonial Advocate* (London), Sept. 30, Nov. 18, 1848; June 16, 1849.

24. Letter of J. N. Granes, April 7, 1848, C. O. 384/81; letters of Lieutenant Friend, Jan. 31, 1849, and F. W. C. Murdock, March 30, 1489, *ibid.*, 384/83; letter of F. W. C. Murdock, Feb. 6, 1849, *ibid.*, 384/84; *Quebec Mercury*, Sept. 9, 1848.

25. *Irish Farmer's Gazette*, Feb. 6, 1848; *Leinster Express*, Aug. 26, 1848; *Papers Relating to Proceedings for Relief of Distress in Ireland*, 16.

26. *Mark Lane Express*, July 17, Aug. 21, Sept. 18, Oct. 9, 1848; Jan. 15, 1849.

27. *Freeman's Journal* (Dublin), May 2, 1849; *Emigrant and Colonial Gazette*, March 17, May 5, 1849.

28. *Freeman's Journal*, April 13, 1849; *Papers Relating to Proceedings for Relief of Distress in Ireland*, 111–112, 116, 119.

29. Committee to Inquire into Irish Poor Law, *Report*, 517.

30. *Mark Lane Express*, April 30, 1849; *Agricultural and Industrial Journal* (Dublin), I (1849), 364, 476, 481, 487; *Leinster Express*, Nov. 11, 1848.

31. 11 and 12 Vict., ch. 48.

32. *King's County Chronicle* (Parsonstown), Nov. 3, 1852; *Mark Lane Express*, Aug. 20, 1855; *Irish Farmer's Gazette*, Jan. 24, Feb. 7, 1852.

33. 12 and 13 Vict., ch. 29.

34. *Kölnische Zeitung*, March 3, 1852; letter of Ernest Schwendler, April 15, 1847, Consular Letters (Department of State, Washington,

364 BIBLIOGRAPHY AND NOTES

D. C.), Frankfort-on-the-Main, I (1829–1851); letter of Charles Graebe, Jan. 31, 1853, Consular Letters, Hesse-Cassel, II (1851–1857).

35. A. A. III, R. I, Aus. Eur. 11, Vol. VI, no. 316.

36. *Kölnische Zeitung*, Sept. 17, 1853.

37. *Leipziger Allgemeine Zeitung*, Aug. 16, Nov. 4, 16, 1849; *Neue Zürcher Zeitung*, Nov. 4, 1849; *Staats- und Gelehrte Zeitung des Hamburgischen unpartheyischen Correspondenten*, Nov. 3, 1849.

38. *Leipziger Allgemeine Zeitung*, Aug. 8, Sept. 9, Oct. 14, 1849.

39. *Ibid.*, June 1, July 30, Aug. 2, 4, 1849.

40. *Ibid.*, Aug. 22, 1849.

41. *Ibid.*, Sept. 15, 1849; Jan. 16, July 3, 1850.

42. *Kölnische Zeitung*, March 3, 1852; *Leipziger Allgemeine Zeitung*, July 26, 1851; June 25, 1852; *Ueber Auswanderung und innere Colonisation in besonderer Beziehung auf Preussen* (Berlin, 1848), 13; *Amtlicher Bericht über die XVI Versammlung deutscher Land- und Forstwirthe* (Munich, 1854), 283; E. Gaebler, *Deutsche Auswanderung und Kolonisation* (Berlin, 1850), 5.

43. Letter of Charles Nicholls, March 7, 1848, Consular Dispatches (Department of State, Washington, D. C.), Amsterdam, IV (1844–1850); letter of W. J. Staples, March 31, 1848, Consular Letters, Havre, V (1847–1850); *Neue Zürcher Zeitung*, Nov. 18, 1848.

44. Letter of Charles Graebe, June 19, 1848, Consular Letters, Hesse-Cassel, I (1835–1850); letters of W. H. Robertson, March 17, July 14, Aug. 21, 1848, Consular Letters, Bremen, IV (1842–1850); *Deutsche Auswanderer* (Darmstadt), II (1848), no. 35, 548.

45. Letter of W. H. Robertson, March 17, 1848; A. A. III, R. I, Aus. Eur. 11, Vol. VI, no. 19.

46. *Allgemeine Auswanderungs Zeitung* (Rudolstadt), no. 34 (April, 1849), 135; no. 39 (May, 1849), 155.

47. Letter of W. J. Staples, May 17, 1849, Consular Letters, Havre, V; *Agronomische Zeitung* (Leipzig), April 20, 1849; *Leipziger Allgemeine Zeitung*, Feb. 20, April 3, 1849; *Allgemeine Zeitung* (Augsburg), Sept. 2, 1849; *Staats- und Gelehrte Zeitung des Hamburgischen unpartheyischen Correspondenten*, Aug. 23, 1849.

48. The features common to the legislation of all the states are summarized in Albert Judeich, *Die Grundentlastung in Deutschland* (Leipzig, 1863), 4–7, 223, 230.

49. Letter of E. W. Ellsworth, Feb. 21, 1849, Legation Dispatches (Department of State, Washington, D. C.), Sweden, VII (1845–1849); letter of George Bancroft, Jan. 12, 1849, Diplomatic Correspondence (Department of State, Washington, D. C.), England, LIX (1848–1849);

Emigrant and Colonial Gazette, Jan. 13, 20, 1849; *Leipziger Allgemeine Zeitung*, Sept. 10, 1853.

50. *Emigrant and Colonial Gazette*, Jan. 20, 1849; *Leinster Express*, Jan. 20, April 14, 1849; *Mark Lane Express*, Feb. 26, 1849.

51. *U. S. Statutes at Large*, IX, 125; *Allgemeine Auswanderungs Zeitung*, Nov. 29, 1851.

52. *Emigrant and Colonial Gazette*, March 17, 1849; *Allgemeine Auswanderungs Zeitung*, Oct. 22, 1850; *Allgemeine Zeitung*, Feb. 26, 1854.

53. *Allgemeine Auswanderungs Zeitung*, Sept. 25, 1848; Sept. 14, 1849; March 26, Oct. 12, 1850; *Kirchliche Mittheilungen aus und über Nord-Amerika* (Berlin), 1850, no. 5, 33, and no. 11, 85.

54. *Allgemeine Auswanderungs Zeitung*, March 21, 1850; Jan. 4, 7, 9, March 1, Oct. 9, Dec. 23, 1851.

CHAPTER XIII. THE GREAT MIGRATION

1. *Statistical Review of Immigration, 1820–1910* (U. S. Immigration Commission, *Reports*, III; Wash., 1911), 416.

2. Emigration Commissioners, *Report* (*Parliamentary Papers*, 1864, XVI), 13, has a table of the emigration from Ireland over a period of years.

3. *King's County Chronicle* (Parsonstown), Oct. 26, 1853.

4. Letter of A. Lawrence, Dec. 2, 1851, Diplomatic Correspondence (Department of State, Washington, D. C.), England, LXIII (1851–1852).

5. *Mark Lane Express* (London), Jan. 19, 1852; March 28, May 23, Oct. 3, 1853; Sept. 4, 1854.

6. *Leinster Express* (Maryborough), Oct. 18, 25, 1851; *Mark Lane Express*, Feb. 19, 1849; letter of C. Alexander Wood, Oct. 16, 1849, C. O. 386/83; letter of A. Lawrence, March 7, 1851, Diplomatic Correspondence, England, LXII (1851).

7. *King's County Chronicle*, March 23, 1853; *Mark Lane Express*, March 28, 1853; letter of F. W. C. Murdock, May 17, 1849, C. O. 384/84; Colonial Land and Emigration Commissioners, *Ninth General Report* (*Parliamentary Papers*, 1849, XXII), 2.

8. *Conservative* (Drogheda), March 19, 1853; *Irish Farmer's Gazette*, April 5, 1851; Sept. 3, 1852; July 9, 1853; *Emigrant and Colonial Advocate* (London), Sept. 30, 1848; *Mark Lane Express*, Feb. 14, 1853.

9. Committee on Poor Removal, *Report* (*Parliamentary Papers*, 1854, XVII), 118.

10. *Agricultural and Industrial Journal* (Dublin), I (1849), 470; Committee on Poor Removal, *Report*, 182.

366   BIBLIOGRAPHY AND NOTES

11. *Irish Farmer's Gazette*, Aug. 23, Sept. 27, 1851; Sept. 17, 1853; Sept. 2, 23, 1854; *Leinster Express*, Aug. 28, 1852.

12. *Irish Farmer's Gazette*, March 31, 1849; Jan. 10, Sept. 3, 1852; May 21, 28, Oct. 15, 1853; April 22, 1854; *Mark Lane Express*, April 21, June 16, 1851; April 17, May 29, 1854.

13. *Mark Lane Express*, April 18, Aug. 8, 1853; *Freeman's Journal* (Dublin), May 1, 1851; J. H. Burton, *Emigration in Its Practical Application to Individuals and Communities* (Edinburgh, 1851), 13–14.

14. Letter of A. Lawrence, Dec. 2, 1851; Select Commission on Outrages, *Report (Parliamentary Papers, 1852, XIV)*, 203.

15. *Mark Lane Express*, May 23, July 18, 1853; *Irish Farmer's Gazette*, April 5, 1851.

16. *Mark Lane Express*, April 7, Sept. 8, 29, 1851; Jan. 5, 1852; Letter of A. Lawrence, March 7, 1851.

17. *Mark Lane Express*, May 24, 31, 1852; March 7, 14, 1853; *The Emigrant's Manual. British America and United States of America* (Edinburgh, 1851), 3.

18. *Allgemeine Auswanderungs Zeitung* (Rudolstadt), March 8, 1853; L. C. Cornford, *The Sea Carriers, 1825–1925. The Aberdeen Line* (n.p., 1925), 35, 38–39.

19. *Mark Lane Express*, Aug. 18, Oct. 6, 27, 1851; Jan. 5, April 5, May 17, Dec. 13, 1852; Jan. 24, April 11, May 30, Aug. 22, 29, 1853.

20. *Ibid.*, Jan. 2, 30, Feb. 20, May 8, Aug. 14, 28, Oct. 9, Dec. 4, 1854.

21. Letter of Charles Graebe, Aug. 5, 1850, Consular Letters (Department of State, Washington, D. C.), Hesse-Cassel, I (1835–1850); letter of Ralph King, Jan. 18, 1850, Consular Letters, Bremen, IV (1842–1850); letter of Ralph King, Jan. 14, 1851, *ibid.*, V (1851–1852).

22. *Wochenblatt für Land- und Forstwirthschaft* (Württemberg), 1849, supp. no. 22; 1850, supp. no. 17; 1852, supp. no. 18; 1853, supp. no. 20.

23. *Leipziger Allgemeine Zeitung*, Oct. 26, 1850; Sept. 8, 1851; March 6, 1852; *Allgemeine Auswanderungs Zeitung*, Nov. 6, 1851; F. Bassermann-Jordan, *Geschichte des Weinbaus* (Frankfurt-am-Main, 1907), III, 752.

24. *Blätter für das Armenwesen* (Stuttgart), June 24, 1854; *Mark Lane Express*, Sept. 19, 1853.

25. *Allgemeine Auswanderungs Zeitung*, Oct. 10, 1854.

26. *Allgemeine Zeitung für die deutschen Land- und Forstwirthe* (Berlin), XXXII (1855), 103; *Allgemeine Zeitung* (Augsburg), Feb. 26, July 7, 1852; Jan. 1, 1853.

27. *Blätter für das Armenwesen,* Aug. 7, 1852; Sept. 23, 1854; *Kölnische Zeitung,* May 17, 1853; *Verhandlungen der Kammer der Abgeordneten des bayerischen Landtages im Jahre 1855/56,* supp. III, no. 124, 466.

28. Letter of Charles Graebe, Jan. 21, 1854, Consular Letters, Hesse-Cassel, II (1851–1857); Heinrich Erzinger, *Die Auswanderung im Kanton Schaffhausen, ihre Ursachen und Gegenmittel* (Schaffhausen, 1853), 7; Adolph Lette, *Die Vertheilung des Grundeigenthums* (Berlin, 1858), 109–126.

29. *Aftonbladet* (Stockholm), May 19, 1852; *Kölnische Zeitung,* March 3, 1852; Eduard Pelz, *Die Stellung der Arbeiter bei der Landwirthschaft* (Breslau, 1847), 15–16.

30. *Kölnische Zeitung,* Oct. 10, 1852; April 9, 1853; *Allgemeine Zeitung,* Jan. 22, 1853; April 7, 1854.

31. Rasmus Sørensen, *Første Brev til mine Venner og Landsmænd i Danmark* (Copenhagen, 1853), 27.

32. *Kölnische Zeitung,* Feb. 23, 1853.

33. *Leipziger Allgemeine Zeitung,* Feb. 21, 1851; July 20, 1852; July 28, 1853; *Allgemeine Zeitung,* June 17, Aug. 1, 1853.

34. A. A. III, R. I, Aus. Eur. 11, Vol. IX, no. 13277 (*Fünfter Jahres Bericht der deutscher Gesellschaft von New-Orleans,* June 2, 1852).

35. *Allgemeine Auswanderungs Zeitung,* Jan. 18, 1853; *Leipziger Allgemeine Zeitung,* April 19, 1849; Sept. 14, 17, 1852; *Morgenblatt für gebildete Leser* (Stuttgart), May 30, 1851.

36. *Morgenblatt für gebildete Leser,* May 30, 1851.

37. *Leipziger Allgemeine Zeitung,* Jan. 23, 1853.

38. *Neue Zürcher Zeitung,* Dec. 27, 1849; *Abendzeitung* (Dresden), May 2, 1850; *Amtlicher Bericht über die XV Versammlung deutscher Land- und Forstwirthe* (Hanover, 1853), 78.

39. Some of the regulations are published in *Jahrbuch für Volkswirthschaft und Statistik* (Leipzig), 1855, 301–303.

40. *Leipziger Allgemeine Zeitung,* March 4, 1854; *Allgemeine Zeitung,* April 3, 1853; March 18, 1854; letter of Charles Graebe, April 16, 1853, Consular Letters, Hesse-Cassel, II.

41. A. A. III, R. I, Aus. Eur. 11, Vol. IX, no. 12654.

42. *Ibid.,* Vol. VI, no. 2846; *Leipziger Allgemeine Zeitung,* April 20, 1850.

43. The legislation regarding agents is summarized in *Moniteur belge; journal officiel* (Brussels), Nov. 15, 1853, 3814–3815.

44. *Leipziger Allgemeine Zeitung,* April 28, 1850; March 18, May 24,

June 23, 1852; *Bremer Handelsblatt*, Dec. 13, 1851; *Allgemeine Zeitung*, Jan. 16, 1852.

45. *Journal du Havre*, July 13, 1854; *Leipziger Allgemeine Zeitung*, April 28, 1850; *Allgemeine Auswanderungs Zeitung*, June 7, 1853; Feb. 14, April 15, 1854; Jan. 11, 1856; *Deutsche Auswanderer* (Darmstadt), II (1848), no. 2, 20.

46. Hermann Grüning, *Hamburgs neueste Zeit* (Hamburg, 1866), 349, 387; *Deutsche Auswanderer*, II, no. 18, 273.

47. A. A. III, R. I, Aus. Eur. 11, Vol. V, no. 2970 (from consul at Hamburg, Oct. 16, 1848); *ibid.*, Vol. VII, no. 8819 (Hamburg orders of June 3, 1850, and May 28, 1851); *Allgemeine Auswanderungs Zeitung*, Oct. 2, Nov. 20, 1848; March 30, 1852; March 30, 1854; *Leipziger Allgemeine Zeitung*, March 10, 15, 1853; *Morgenblatt für gebildete Leser*, July 3, 1853.

48. "Deutschlands Seeschiffahrt," *Deutsche Vierteljahrs Schrift* (Stuttgart), 1850, no. 1, 292; *Fliegende Blätter aus dem Rauhen Hause zu Horn* (Munich), IX (1852), 362; "Ein Auswandererschiff," *Gartenlaube* (Leipzig), 1854, 448–452; "Ein Besuch in Bremerhaven," *ibid.*, 1859, 228–238.

49. *Leipziger Allgemeine Zeitung*, Jan. 12, 1852; *Morgenblatt für gebildete Leser*, Sept. 18, 1853.

50. *Kölnische Zeitung*, Sept. 11, 1852; *Leipziger Allgemeine Zeitung*, April 16, 1852.

51. *Leipziger Allgemeine Zeitung*, Jan. 1, 1854; *Allgemeine Zeitung*, May 19, 1853; *Morgenblatt für gebildete Leser*, May 28, 1851.

52. *Blätter für das Armenwesen*, 1853, supp. no. 4; *Leipziger Allgemeine Zeitung*, May 24, 1852.

53. *Leipziger Allgemeine Zeitung*, May 24, 1852; *Bremer Handelsblatt*, May 1, 1852; *Allgemeine Auswanderungs Zeitung*, April 3, 1852.

54. *Allgemeine Zeitung*, March 13, 1852; *Leipziger Allgemeine Zeitung*, Sept. 6, 1851; March 17, 1852.

55. *Fædrelandet* (Copenhagen), Jan. 26, 1852; *Allgemeine Auswanderungs Zeitung*, April 24, Nov. 13, 15, 1851; March 20, 1852; Aug. 11, 1853; March 30, 1854; *Leipziger Allgemeine Zeitung*, June 3, Sept. 3, 1851; *Allgemeine Zeitung*, April 29, 1852.

56. J. S. Carr, "On Rural Economy Abroad," Royal Agricultural Soc. of England, *Jour.*, I (1840), 129–130; *Landwirthschaftliche Annalen des Mecklenburgischen patriotischen Vereins* (Rostock), I (1846), 75; II (1847), 118; Reinhold Nizze, *Volkswirthschaftliche Zustände in Mecklenburg* (Rostock, 1861), 18–20, 22–23, 34, 39–40; Richard Ehrenberg, "Die

Einlieger-Ländereien," *Archiv für exakte Wirtschaftsforschung* (Jena), V (1913), 586–590, 597, 599–600.

57. A. Soetbeer, "Ueber den Einfluss der neueren Reformen in der baltischen Handelsgesetzgebung auf Deutschland," *Jahrbuch für Volkswirthschaft und Statistik*, II (1854), 387–400.

58. *Leipziger Allgemeine Zeitung*, Jan. 17, 1854; *Allgemeine Auswanderungs Zeitung*, May 6, 1854; June 2, 1856; Dec. 21, 1860. The statistics for this emigration can be found in E. H. Dietzsch, *Die Bewegung der Mecklenburgischen Bevölkerung von 1850 bis 1910* (Schwerin, 1918), 23.

59. P. F. Schliemann, "Zur Mecklenburgischen Auswanderung nach Amerika," *Archiv für Landeskunde in den Grossherzogthümern Mecklenburg* (Schwerin), XIII (1863), 561–574.

60. Ehrenberg, "Die Einlieger-Ländereien," 641.

61. *Hamburgische Correspondent*, April 2, 1851; *Allgemeine Auswanderungs Zeitung*, April 15, Nov. 13, 15, 18, 1851.

62. *Blätter für das Armenwesen*, 1853, supp. no. 3; *Verhandlungen der St. Gallisch-Appenzellischen gemeinnützigen Gesellschaft an der Hauptversammlung in Heiden, Montags, den 2 September, 1850* (St. Gallen, 1850), 128.

63. Letters of George H. Goundie, March 27, 1846, May 28, 1849, Consular Letters, Basle, I (1830–1850).

64. *Journal du Havre*, March 6, 1853; *Morgenblatt für gebildete Leser*, Feb. 26, 1854.

65. *Neue Zürcher Zeitung*, Oct. 23, 1848.

66. C. C. Larsen, *Det danske landbrugs Historie* (2nd edn., Copenhagen, 1913), 50, 99; Harry Rainalls, "Report upon the Past and Present State of the Danish Monarchy; Its Products with Comparative Tables of Exports," Royal Agricultural Soc. of England, *Jour.*, XXI (1860), 315.

67. P. S. Vig, "Danske i Amerika, 1841–1850," *Danske i Amerika* (Minneapolis), I (1908), 202; J. P. Trap, *Kongeriget Danmark* (Copenhagen, 1898–1906), I, 34.

68. *Morgenstjernen. Et historisk-biografisk Maanedsskrift* (Salt Lake City), I (1882), 1–7.

69. *Ibid.*, 15.

70. *Fædrelandet*, Jan. 21, July 5, 1853; A. Listov, "Om Laeseriet, Separatismen, og Reformen og Statskirken i Sverrig," *Dansk Maanedskrift* (Copenhagen), VII (1858), 355–382.

71. *Aftonbladet*, March 17, April 6, 1852; June 4, 1853.

72. *Ibid.*, July 8–9, 1853; June 22, July 18, 29, Aug. 17, 1854.

73. *Fædrelandet*, Feb. 24, 1853.

74. *Ibid.*, May 4, 1854; June 20, 1855.

75. *Ibid.*, April 28, 1853.

76. S. Skappel, "Om Husmandsvæsenet i Norge, dets Oprindelse og Utvikling," *Skrifter utgit av Videnskabsselskabet i Kristiania*, 1922, 1–192; J. C. Lous, *Om Husmandsvæsenet* (Kristiania, 1851), 5, 9, 19–20, 33, 35–36; Ewald Bosse, *Norwegens Volkswirthschaft vom Ausgang der Hansaperiode bis zur Gegenwart* (Jena, 1916), II, 307, 309, 312, 315–316, 318–319.

77. Josef Buzek, "Das Auswanderungsproblem und die Regelung des Auswanderungswesens in Österreich," *Zeitschrift für Volkswirtschaft, Socialpolitik und Verwaltung* (Vienna), X (1901), 446, gives the statistics for Bohemian emigration in the 50's.

78. Letter of James M. White, Jan. 4, 1845, Consular Letters, Liverpool, X (1845–1850); *Allgemeine Zeitung*, Sept. 29, 1854; *Leipziger Allgemeine Zeitung*, Jan. 27, 1852.

79. Select Committee on Emigrant Ships, *First Report* and *Second Report* (Parliamentary Papers, 1854, XIII); 18 and 19 Vict., ch. 119.

80. For the various cases of enforcement, see *Hunt's Merchants' Magazine*, XXVI (1852), 394; *Boston Courier*, April 12, May 8, 24, 1848; May 29, July 1, 14, Aug. 2, 1851; *Daily Picayune* (New Orleans), June 22, Aug. 8, 1851.

81. 33 Cong., 1 sess., *Senate Rep.*, no. 386.

82. *U. S. Statutes at Large*, IX, 220–223.

83. *Mark Lane Express*, June 13, 1853.

84. *Allgemeine Auswanderungs Zeitung*, March 8, 1853; *Papers Relative to Emigration* (Parliamentary Papers, 1851, XL), 21.

85. *Allgemeine Zeitung*, Feb. 7, 1853; *Allgemeine Auswanderungs Zeitung*, April 15, 1854; Jan. 26, 1855.

86. *Allgemeine Auswanderungs Zeitung*, Dec. 5, 1854.

87. Hildegarde Rosenthal, *Die Auswanderung aus Sachsen im 19. Jahrhundert* (Stuttgart, 1931), 71–72.

88. *Allgemeine Auswanderungs Zeitung*, Feb. 13, 1851; June 12, 1857.

89. *Bremer Handelsblatt*, March 30, June 1, 1855; Robert Mohl, "Ueber Auswanderung," *Zeitschrift für die gesammte Staatswissenschaft* (Tübingen), IV (1847), 320–348.

90. *Leipziger Allgemeine Zeitung*, March 2, 1847.

91. *Belleviller Zeitung* (Belleville, Ill.), Oct. 4, 1849; *Deutscher Anzeiger des Westens* (St. Louis), March 18, April 29, June 25, 1848;

Dec. 7, 11, 1849; March 14, 23, Aug. 2, 1850; *Deutsche Auswanderer,* II, 22–23.

92. *Allgemeine Auswanderungs Zeitung,* April 11, 15, Dec. 23, 1854; *Allgemeine Zeitung,* March 23, 1854; Select Committee on Poor Removal, *Report (Parliamentary Papers,* 1854, XVII), 99–100.

93. *Mark Lane Express,* Sept. 11, 18, 1854; *Allgemeine Zeitung,* Oct. 14, 1854.

94. *Bremer Handelsblatt,* Jan. 12, 1855; *Allgemeine Auswanderungs Zeitung,* March 16, July 20, 1855; *Leipziger Allgemeine Zeitung,* March 21, 1855.

95. *Morgenblatt für gebildete Leser,* Feb. 11, 1855.

96. *Belleviller Zeitung,* May 8, July 3, 1855.

97. *Bremer Handelsblatt,* June 1, 1855; *Allgemeine Auswanderungs Zeitung,* Jan. 19, Dec. 28, 1855; Jan. 18, 1856; *Leipziger Allgemeine Zeitung,* April 27, 1855; C. Heusinger, *Die Auswanderung. Ein Mahnwort für Alle die es angeht* (Brunswick, 1855), 16.

98. Letter of F. W. C. Murdock, Feb. 7, 1857, C. O. 386/84; *Irish Farmer's Gazette,* Oct. 10, 1857.

99. *Blätter für das Armenwesen,* Nov. 14, 1857; Jan. 1, 1859; *Emigration Record and Colonial Journal* (London), Jan. 16, 1858; letter of Max Stettheimer, March 20, 1857, Consular Letters, Stuttgart, I (1842–1863).

INDEX

INDEX

Printed in the United States
89220LV00007B/92/A

9 781931 313292